European Yearbook of International Economic Law

EYIEL Monographs - Studies in European and International Economic Law

Volume 21

EYIEL Monographs is a subseries of the European Yearbook of International Economic Law (EYIEL). It contains scholarly works in the fields of European and international economic law, in particular WTO law, international investment law, international monetary law, law of regional economic integration, external trade law of the EU and EU internal market law. The series does not include edited volumes. EYIEL Monographs are peer-reviewed by the series editors and external reviewers.

More information about this subseries at http://www.springer.com/series/15744

Maximilian Eduard Oehl

Sustainable Commodity Use

Its Governance, Legal Framework, and Future
Regulatory Instruments

 Springer

Maximilian Eduard Oehl
Berlin, Germany

ISSN 2364-8392   ISSN 2364-8406   (electronic)
European Yearbook of International Economic Law
ISSN 2524-6658   ISSN 2524-6666   (electronic)
EYIEL Monographs - Studies in European and International Economic Law
ISBN 978-3-030-89495-5   ISBN 978-3-030-89496-2   (eBook)
https://doi.org/10.1007/978-3-030-89496-2

The pre-press stage and the publication were supported by the Swiss National Science Foundation (SNSF).

This Springer imprint is published by the registered company Springer Nature Switzerland AG.
The registered company address is: Gewerbestrasse 11, 6330 Cham, Switzerland

To Lausanne, Geneva, Berkeley,
Munich, Edling, Berlin,
and all the wonderful people
I met along the way

'I come from one of the richest countries on the planet. Yet the people of my country are among the poorest of the world. The troubling reality is that the abundance of our natural resources – gold, coltan, cobalt and other strategic minerals – is the root cause of war, extreme violence and abject poverty. We love nice cars, jewellery and gadgets. I have a smartphone myself. These items contain minerals found in our country. Often mined in inhuman conditions by young children, victims of intimidation and sexual violence. When you drive your electric car; when you use your smart phone or admire your jewellery, take a minute to reflect on the human cost of manufacturing these objects. As consumers, let us at least insist that these products are manufactured with respect for human dignity. Turning a blind eye to this tragedy is being complicit.'—Dr. Denis Mukwege, 2018 Nobel Peace Prize Laureate[1]

---

[1] Nobel Lecture given by 2018 Nobel Peace Prize Laureate Denis Mukwege, 10 December 2018, Oslo. The full speech is available at The Nobel Prize (2021) Denis Mukwege – Nobel lecture, https://www.nobelprize.org/prizes/peace/2018/mukwege/55721-denis-mukwege-nobel-lecture-2/ (last accessed 14 May 2021).

Contents

Abbreviations

AAPG	Addis Ababa Principles and Guidelines for the Sustainable Use of Biodiversity
AB	Appellate Body
ACHPR	African Commission on Human and Peoples' Rights
ACNR	ASEAN Agreement on the Conservation of Nature and Natural Resources
AfCHR	African Charter on Human and Peoples' Rights
AfCNR	African Convention on the Conservation of Nature and Natural Resources
AIPN	Association of International Petroleum Negotiators
AJIL	American Journal of International Law
AMDC	African Minerals Development Centre
AMV	Africa Mining Vision
AP	Additional Protocol
ASEAN	Association of Southeast Asian Nations
AU	African Union
BIT	Bilateral Investment Treaty
BMWi	Bundesministerium für Wirtschaft und Energie [German Federal Ministry for Economic Affairs and Energy]
CAC	Convention Against Corruption
CBD	Convention on Biological Diversity
CBDR	Common but differentiated responsibility
CDDC(s)	Commodity Dependent Developing Country(ies)
CEDAW	Convention on the Elimination of All Forms of Discrimination against Women
CETA	Comprehensive Economic and Trade Agreement
CFC	Common Fund for Commodities
CISDL	Centre for International Sustainable Development Law
CoE	Council of Europe
COP	Conference of the Parties

CPTPP	Comprehensive and Progressive Agreement for Trans-Pacific Partnership
CRAMRA	Convention on the Regulation of Antarctic Mineral Resource Activities
CSR	Corporate Social Responsibility
DD	Due diligence
DDA	Doha Development Agenda
DDG	Due diligence guidance
DMO	Domestic market obligation
DRC	Democratic Republic of the Congo
DT	Double Taxation
DTA	Double Taxation Agreement
EAER	[Swiss] Federal Department of Economic Affairs, Education and Research
EC	European Commission
ECLC	CoE Civil Law Convention on Corruption
ECT	Energy Charter Treaty
EEZ	Exclusive Economic Zone
EIA	Environmental Impact Assessment
EITI	Extractive Industries Transparency Initiative
EJIL	European Journal of International Law
EP	Equator Principles
ERC	Economic Rights Charter
EU	European Union
FAO	Food and Agriculture Organisation
FDF	[Swiss] Federal Department of Finance
FDFA	[Swiss] Federal Department of Foreign Affairs
FDI	Foreign Direct Investment
FET	Fair and Equitable Treatment
FPIC	Free, prior and informed consent
FRD	Friendly Relations Declaration
FTA	Free Trade Agreement
GATT	General Agreement on Tariffs and Trade
GCG	Global Commodity Governance
GSP	Generalised System of Preferences
GTC	Grains Trade Convention
HC	Havana Charter
HR	Human Rights
IAC	International armed conflict
IACtHR	Inter-American Court of Human Rights
IAEA	International Atomic Energy Agency
IAO	International Agreement on Olive Oil and Table Olives
IBA	International Bar Association
ICA(s)	International Commodity Agreement(s)

ICAC	International Cotton Advisory Committee
ICACRR	Rules and Regulations of ICAC
ICB	International Commodity Body
ICC	International Chamber of Commerce
ICCPR	International Covenant on Civil and Political Rights
ICERD	International Convention on the Elimination of All Forms of Racial Discrimination
ICESCR	International Covenant on Economic, Social and Cultural Rights
ICGLR	International Conference on the Great Lakes Region
ICJ	International Court of Justice
ICO	International Commodity Organisation
ICocA	International Cocoa Agreement
ICofA	International Coffee Agreement
ICofO	International Coffee Organisation
ICS	Investment Court System
ICSID	International Centre for Settlement of Investment Disputes
IEL	International Environmental Law
IFC	International Finance Corporation
IFCPS	IFC Performance Standards on Environmental and Social Sustainability
IGC	International Grains Council
IGF	Intergovernmental Forum on Mining, Minerals, Metals and Sustainable Development
IHL	International Humanitarian Law
IIL	International Investment Law
IISD	International Institute for Sustainable Development
ILA	International Law Association
ILC	International Law Commission
IMF	International Monetary Fund
IO	International Organisation
IOC	International Olive Council
IOGP	International Association of Oil and Gas Producers
IPIECA	International Petroleum Industry Environmental Conservation Association
IRMA	Initiative for Responsible Mining Assurance
ISA	International Sugar Agreement
ISDS	Investor-state dispute settlement
ISG	International Study Group
ISI	Import Substitution Industrialisation
ISO	International Organisation for Standardisation
ISugO	International Sugar Organisation
ITPGR	International Treaty on Plant Genetic Resources for Food and Agriculture
ITTA	International Tropical Timber Agreement

ITTO	International Tropical Timber Organisation
LDCs	Least Developed Countries
MFN	Most-favoured nation
MMDA	IBA Model Mine Development Agreement
MNE	Multinational Enterprise
NGO	Non-governmental organisation
NIAC	Non-international armed conflict
NIEO	New International Economic Order
NLBIT	Netherlands Model Bilateral Investment Treaty
NR	Natural Resources
NRC	Natural Resource Charter
NRGI	Natural Resource Governance Institute
NRL	Natural Resources Law
OECD	Organisation for Economic Co-operation and Development
OECDG	OECD Guidelines for Multinational Enterprises
PE	Permanent establishment
PPP	Polluter pays principle
PSNR	Permanent Sovereignty over Natural Resources
PTA	Preferential Trade Agreement
PWYP	Publish What You Pay
R2R	Responsibility to respect
RFD	Right to freely dispose over natural resources
RFI	Resources for Infrastructure
SADC	Southern African Development Community
SADCPF	SADC Protocol on Forestry
SADCPM	SADC Protocol on Mining
SD	Sustainable Development
SDG(s)	Sustainable Development Goal(s)
SDL	Sustainable Development Law
SLO	Social License to Operate
SOE	State-owned enterprise
TCL	Transnational Commodity Law
TEU	Treaty on European Union
TFEU	Treaty on the Functioning of the European Union
TNC	Transnational Corporation
TWAIL	Third World Approaches to International Law
UDHR	Universal Declaration of Human Rights
UN	United Nations
UNCLOS	United Nations Convention on the Law of the Sea
UNDP	United Nations Development Programme
UNEP	United Nations Environment Programme
UN GA	United Nations General Assembly
UN GC	UN Global Compact
UN GP	UN Guiding Principles for Business and Human Rights

UN HRC	Human Rights Committee
UN PRI	UN Principles for Responsible Investment
UN SC	United Nations Security Council
UN SG	United Nations Secretary General
US	United States
VCLT	Vienna Convention on the Law of the Treaties
VGGT	FAO Voluntary Guidelines on the Responsible Governance on Tenure of Land, Fisheries and Forests in the Context of National Food Security
VPSHR	Voluntary Principles on Security and Human Rights for the Extractive and Energy Sectors
WSSD	World Summit on Sustainable Development
WTO	World Trade Organisation

Chapter 1
Introduction

Human development would not have been possible without the materials, which nature provides. Mindful of their crucial role, historians have named entire eras after the minerals that were being sourced at that time—be it the Neolithic Age, Bronze Age, or the Iron Age.[1]

Today, we are living in a world of globalised markets. Close to no value creation would be possible without the use of natural resources, more precisely primary commodities.[2] The Sustainable Development (SD) agenda has become *the* universally accepted political agenda of our time.[3] In view of the important challenges for global resource management, which will be elucidated throughout the course of this book, the field of Global Commodity Governance (GCG) has emerged over the past two decades. It describes a new turn in human history: towards a coordinated, transnational approach to regulating the complexities of commodity activity.

Now more than ever, global commodity management is subject to a large variety of multi-stakeholder initiatives and standards, which exhibit a conscious consideration of the particularities of commodity industries and share one goal: making the commodity sector work for SD. However, one can easily get lost in the complex net of international agreements, principles, transnational standards and domestic regulation, which govern commodity activity.[4]

Therefore, the present book investigates the following question: *How effective is the current legal framework in ensuring a functional commodity sector?* For the

---

[1] Ruddiman et al. (2015), pp. 38–39.

[2] On exact definitions of these central terms, cf. Chap. 2 below.

[3] UN GA (2015) Resolution A/RES/70/1, 25 September 2015, Transforming our world: the 2030 Agenda for Sustainable Development. http://www.un.org/ga/search/view_doc.asp?symbol=A/RES/70/1&Lang=E (last accessed 14 May 2021); cf. instead of many Cordonier Segger and Weeramantry (2017). The core concept of SD 'can be defined as the consolidation of socio-economic development and environmental protection', Oehl (2019), p. 12; cf. Sects. 4.1 and 5.1 below.

[4] On the definition of *commodity activity*, cf. Sect. 3.2.2.1 below.

© The Author(s) 2022
M. E. Oehl, *Sustainable Commodity Use*, EYIEL Monographs - Studies in European and International Economic Law 21, https://doi.org/10.1007/978-3-030-89496-2_1

purpose of this investigation, the commodity sector will be characterised as *functional* where it exhibits a balance between the *five major interests* associated with commodity activity: economic gain; development; preservation; control; and participation. These interests as well as the *policy trade-offs* that arise in between them delineate the *commodity governance matrix*. In order to identify the legal framework applicable to commodity activities, we will conceptualise the field of Transnational Commodity Law (TCL).

As we shall learn, the principle of *sustainable use* not only constitutes one of the few *balancing norms*, which foster the effectiveness of TCL. Given the universal nature of the SD agenda, the specific normative quality of SD as a legal concept, and its status within a sizable series of international treaties, *sustainable use* can be defined as the *regulatory objective* of TCL. As our discussion will illustrate, it thus spearheads and coheres the legal framework applicable to commodity activities.

Certainly, one may critically ask whether the scope of this book, which covers commodities *per se*, is not too broad. An alternative approach would have been more specific, designed to portray the regulatory environment for specific commodity subsectors, such as agriculture or mining, or even singular commodities like cocoa or coal. The intention of this book, however, is to identify the commonalities of commodity governance in general—as well as its distinctiveness from related fields, such as natural resource or environmental governance.

Consequently, this treatise deliberately renounces a comprehensive display of the law regulating sustainable commodity use. Instead, it focuses on providing commodity governance and law with more definitional and conceptual clarity. This approach serves the purpose of intensifying the understanding of the normative patterns, regulatory challenges, and gaps associated with transnational commodity activity—which, in turn, shall inspire more targeted future research and lawmaking.

In order to provide the reader with an overview of the considerable *substance* of TCL, however, a corresponding *table* has been annexed to this work. The agreements, standards, and guidance documents referenced therein display the normative foundation on which the conceptualisations of GCG and TCL, as its legal framework, have been performed.

The investigation proceeds in six incremental steps:

First, it identifies, defines, and describes GCG as the transnational mode of governing commodity activities.

Second, it defines ensuring a functional commodity sector as the principal task of GCG.

Third, it defines a functional commodity sector by referring to the five major interests associated with commodity activity and the 'matrix' of policy trade-offs they create.

Fourth, in order to identify the current legal framework of GCG, it conceptualises Transnational Commodity Law (TCL).

Fifth, it assesses several normative patterns of TCL, which are instructive regarding its effectiveness.

Sixth, it provides suggestions on how the effectiveness of TCL in fostering a functional commodity sector may be improved.

These steps feature in the subsequent four chapters according to the following outline:

Chapter 2 describes the emergence of GCG as the governing mode of the commodity sector. It first defines the term 'commodity', portrays the political and economic circumstances of commodity activity, and determines what constitutes a functional commodity sector. Second, it exhibits the historical emergence of GCG and contours its balanced approach as a disruptive feature. Third, it addresses the role of the law for GCG, particularly in creating a 'balanced' commodity sector, and therefore establishes a basis for our discussions of the legal framework of GCG.

Chapter 3 is concerned with the conceptualisation of TCL as the legal framework of GCG. It first discusses the purpose of this undertaking. Second, it expounds some methodological underpinnings that have guided the conceptualisation. Third, it presents the organisational framework of TCL. Fourth and last, it displays sources and structure of the normative substance of TCL as well as its operation against the backdrop of the commodity governance matrix.

Chapter 4 expounds several patterns of TCL, which are instructive regarding its limited effectiveness in ensuring a functional commodity sector. It first demonstrates that the principle of Permanent Sovereignty over Natural Resources (PSNR) constitutes its central normative cornerstone. Subsequently, it highlights the fact that PSNR entails the central balancing norm of TCL—the sustainable use principle—and that, therefore, the effectiveness of TCL relates to the operationalisation of the latter. Moreover, it sets forth that TCL is largely 'indirect' in the sense that it does not reflect a conscious consideration of commodity interests and trade-offs—and that where it does, it is not balancing commodity interests comprehensively. In addition, it displays that 'direct' TCL is largely of 'soft' character or stems from private standards respectively. Furthermore, it portrays that the instruments of TCL are hardly integrated. Lastly, it unveils that the TCL framework is imbalanced in favour of economic objectives and exhibits several regulatory gaps.

To conclude this book, Chap. 5 provides suggestions on how to foster the effectiveness of TCL in ensuring a functional commodity sector. In this connection, it discusses the legal nature of SD and suggests defining *sustainable use* as the object and purpose of TCL. In addition, it advocates for using the technique of full integration in order to specify the normative contents of the sustainable use principle. Moreover, it analyses current International Commodity Agreements (ICAs) with a view to their quality as regulatory instruments *de lege ferenda* fostering the effectiveness of TCL. In doing so, it demonstrates how ICAs could serve to codify concrete 'balancing norms', which give more effective legal meaning to 'sustainable use'.

References

Literature and IO/NGO Publications

Cordonier Segger MC, Weeramantry JCG (2017) Introduction. In: Cordonier Segger MC, Weeramantry JCG (eds) Sustainable development principles in the decisions of international courts and tribunals 1992–2012. Routledge, New York, pp 1–24

Oehl M (2019) The role of sustainable development in natural resources law. In: Bungenberg M, Krajewski M, Tams C, Terhechte JP, Ziegler AR (eds) European yearbook of international economic law 2018. Springer, pp 3–38

Ruddiman WF, Ellis EC, Kaplan JO, Fuller DQ (2015) Defining the epoch we live in. Science 348(6230):38–39

UN GA (2015) Transforming our world: the 2030 agenda for sustainable development. Resolution A/RES/70/1, 25 September 2015. http://www.un.org/ga/search/view_doc.asp?symbol=A/RES/70/1&Lang=E

Chapter 2
The Emergence of Global Commodity Governance

Whereas the challenges of GCG are manifold, its principal task lies in ensuring a functional commodity sector (Sect. 2.1). The 'balanced' mode through which it pursues this objective constitutes a departure from historical approaches to regulating transnational commodity activity (Sect. 2.2). The remainder of this treatise will be concerned with the role of the law in fostering the effectiveness of GCG (Sect. 2.3).

2.1 The Task: Ensuring a Functional Commodity Sector

International legal scholarship to date has brought about little clarity regarding the scope of the term 'commodity'—a status that we shall first remedy (Sect. 2.1.1) before approaching the political and economic circumstances of commodity activity (Sect. 2.1.2), which need to be borne in mind when defining what constitutes a functional commodity sector (Sect. 2.1.3) as well as GCG (Sect. 2.1.4).

2.1.1 Defining the Term 'Commodity'

In international law dealing with the extraction and/or trade of resources, the term 'commodity' is quite widely applied. This is not last portrayed by the established term 'international *commodity* agreement',[1] which refers to i.a., agreements covering coffee, sugar, or tropical timber.[2]

---

[1]Cf. the numerous treatises on ICAs, e.g. Reynolds (1978); Law (1975); Khan (1982); Chimni (1987). My emphasis.

[2]Cf. Sect. 5.2 below.

© The Author(s) 2022
M. E. Oehl, *Sustainable Commodity Use*, EYIEL Monographs - Studies in European and International Economic Law 21, https://doi.org/10.1007/978-3-030-89496-2_2

Considering the enormous significance of international commodity trade,[3] it is remarkable that the definition of the term 'commodity' in much of academic literature either consists of the denomination of a series of commodities[4] or is simply presumed as clear;[5] in many cases, an abstract definition is not provided. Furthermore, in order to address a material that originates in the environment, one will mostly make use of the terms 'commodity', 'raw material' or 'natural resource', not uncommonly applying these notions synonymously.[6] Many publications establish their own definition of the term 'commodity' in order to define their objects of investigation. This phenomenon leads to an unclear definitional state of the word 'commodity'. In order to resolve this ambiguity, hereafter an abstract definition of the notion shall be developed.

2.1.1.1   General Meaning

Standard dictionaries generally define 'commodity' as a 'substance that can be traded, bought or sold'[7] or 'any article of commerce',[8] whilst some glossaries are more specific by requiring a certain origin of the material, e.g. 'a raw material or primary agricultural product that can be bought and sold'[9] or 'basic items or staple products, as of agriculture or mining'.[10] The latter definitions thus limit the term 'commodity' to agricultural and mining products. The Merriam Webster dictionary is providing the perhaps clearest definition. Accordingly, a 'commodity' is to be defined as 'an economic good' that exhibits one of the following qualities: (a) 'a product of agriculture or mining', (b) 'an article of commerce especially when delivered for shipment', (c) 'a mass-produced unspecialized product'.[11]

Against the backdrop of the objective of this book to specifically deal with legal and governance issues related to certain materials that are first removed from nature and later—typically—subjected to trade, such as coffee, coal, oil, rare earths or the

---

[3]In 2011, world commodity trade accounted for 33% of overall merchandise trade, UNCTAD (2013).

[4]Gale and Haward (2011), p. 1 for instance refrain from stating a definition and instead name a list of commodities, such as oil, iron, gold etc.

[5]Cf. e.g. Weiss (2009), paras. 6–25.

[6]Cf. e.g. OECD (2014), pp. 9–11.

[7]Cambridge dictionary (2021) Entry 'commodity', http://dictionary.cambridge.org/dictionary/british/commodity (last accessed 14 May 2021).

[8]Collins dictionary (2021) Entry 'commodity', http://www.collinsdictionary.com/dictionary/american/commodity (last accessed 14 May 2021).

[9]Oxford dictionary (2021) Entry 'commodity', http://www.oxforddictionaries.com/definition/english/commodity (last accessed 14 May 2021).

[10]Collins dictionary (2021) Entry 'commodity', http://www.collinsdictionary.com/dictionary/american/commodity (last accessed 14 May 2021).

[11]Merriam Webster dictionary (2021) Entry 'commodity', http://www.merriam-webster.com/dictionary/commodity (last accessed 14 May 2021).

like,[12] the term 'commodity' cannot be defined as simply referring to 'any article of commerce.' Otherwise GCG would be more or less synonymous to world trade governance.

For the purpose of this book, it would seem more adequate to for instance refer to commodities as 'raw materials or primary agricultural products that can be bought or sold' or 'products of agriculture or mining'. However, these descriptions lack the necessary precision in order to serve as a legal definition. The former, for example, requires another definition—the one of the term 'raw material'; the latter arbitrarily excludes items of forestry and fishery as well as mineral products.

Also, it would seem methodologically unsound to simply choose a definition provided by a standard dictionary and employ it as a legal definition, especially given their ambiguity. It appears natural to define a legal term according to the purpose it is intended to serve, thus teleologically.[13] Its definition, furthermore, should respect the historical development of the legal notion (Sect. 2.1.1.2) and their contemporary use (Sect. 2.1.1.3).

Yet, the displayed standard definitions cast the foundation of a practical legal definition by fairly marking the boundaries of the notion. Based on this foundation, we shall now further specify 'commodity' as a legal term.

2.1.1.2 Definition According to the Havana Charter

One of the first international law definitions of the term 'commodity' had been elaborated in the Article 56(1) of the 1948 Havana Charter (HC). Accordingly, a 'primary commodity' was defined as

> any product of farm, forest or fishery or any mineral, in its natural form or which has undergone such processing as is customarily required to prepare it for marketing in substantial volume in international trade.

According to Article 56(2) HC this definition is expanded to

> cover a group of commodities, of which one is a primary commodity as defined in paragraph 1 and the others are commodities, which are so closely related, as regards conditions of production or utilization, to the other commodities in the group, that it is appropriate to deal with them in a single agreement.

Just as some of the displayed definitions by general dictionaries, the Havana Charter, by applying the term '*primary* commodity', refers to the state of processing

---

[12] Cf. the definition of 'commodity activity', which is provided in Sect. 3.2.2.1 below. Where this study speaks of 'extraction', it—depending on the context—may at times also refer to the *removal* or rather *harvesting* of e.g. agricultural commodities, thus somewhat not being entirely in line with the general meaning of the term. On mining, cf. n 68 below.

[13] Similarly, for instance the WTO DSB (2004) *US–Softwood Lumber IV*, Report of the Appellate Body, 19 January 2004, para. 59, which states that 'the treaty interpreter should seek the meaning that gives effect, simultaneously, to all the terms of the treaty, as they are used in each authentic language.'

that a certain material has undergone. Only such materials that do not dispose of a degree of manufacturing, which goes beyond one that is necessary for international trade, are meant to fall within the scope of the notion.

Consequently, a tree trunk is as much a 'primary commodity' as wood parts that have been debarked and cut into pieces from the original trunk for shipment. To stick with this example, planks treated with a wood preservative in order to reach higher sales prices would presumably already constitute regular 'commodities', thus normal articles of merchandise just like even more processed goods such as wooden tables, chairs etc.

Distinguishing between 'primary commodities' as defined by Article 56(1) HC and other regular articles of commerce is a compelling approach. It allows narrowing down the term 'primary commodity' to such items that are, in their shape and degree of processing, still close to their natural origin; it thus excludes end products, which are the outcome of a more intense manufacturing process.[14]

Confining the term 'commodity' to these items appears to be indicated when one bears in mind what has been described as 'commodification'—the observation that today more items than ever are being classified as commodities.[15] Once categorised as such, these items are typically being perceived as economic goods and thus subjected to market forces. As a consequence, their availability is strongly regulated by prices—which potentially may exclude market participants that cannot afford them. This is particularly problematic, where actors are seeking to qualify such items that are indispensable for human survival—like water, or even air—as economic goods.[16]

Notably, Article 56(1) HC excludes both of these vital substances from the scope of the notion 'commodity'.[17] Against this backdrop as well as given that Article 56(1) HC describes the historic origins of coordinated commodity regulation on the global level, its approach in defining the term 'commodity' appears to be an apt starting point for our definition.

---

[14]This also resolves potential terminological issues particularly with regard to the German translation of 'commodity' as either 'Grund-' or 'Rohstoff', cf. Weiss (2009), paras. 2–4.

[15]Weiss (2009), paras. 2–4.; Bakker (2007), p. 442; Gunderson (2017).

[16]Bakker (2007), p. 432. Such endeavours have i.a. been criticised as the 'neoliberalisation of nature', yet more accurately consist of measures such as 'privatization, marketization, [...] commercialization, and corporatization...', p. 433. With regard to water, it corresponds with the debate whether there is a HR to water, pp. 436–440. Cf. moreover Riedel (2005), pp. 585–606; moving on and focusing particularly on the implementation of the HR to water Singh (2016).

[17]While it would go beyond the scope of this book to enter the debate on 'commodities versus commons' in more detail—extensively, however, Bakker (2007)—we shall bear in mind the great significance of classifying a certain item as one or the other. Regardless of this debate, as well as corresponding classifications of items and resource management approaches, what shall guide our further discussion, is the ultimate objective of utilising resources in a way that creates the greatest possible benefit for the global community. Balancing the diverging interests and community-based or market-oriented approaches on how this goal can be achieved, is one of the major challenges of GCG and its legal framework, TCL—both of which will be described in more detail throughout the subsequent chapters of this book.

Further, we need to reflect whether the expansion of the definition along the lines of Article 56(2) HC is conducive to the purposes of our investigation. The norm constitutes a *teleological extension* of Article 56(1) HC that aims to provide international actors with a comprehensive governance tool, which is not limited to covering only 'primary commodities', but also goods that are subject to like economic and political—or governance—circumstances.

This approach is also compelling. The aim of GCG is to address specific challenges that generally occur in connection with the trade of 'primary commodities'. If one can witness the same issues with regard to other, strongly related items, there is no evident reason, why the same governance strategies and tools should not be applied to these goods as well. By introducing the legal concept of 'appropriateness', Article 56(2) HC also delivers a parameter for determining whether or not there is a sufficient comparability of the governance challenges faced. Thus, the definition becomes more and more of a normative concept.

This normativity is also displayed in Article 56(3) HC,[18] which seeks to still further expand the scope of chapter VI of the Havana Charter. Accordingly, the provisions shall in 'exceptional circumstances' also apply to agreements that concern items that are not covered by the notion according to Article 56(1), (2) HC. This, however, leaves the definition pursuant to Article 56(1), (2) HC untouched. Article 56(3) HC uses the expression 'inter-governmental agreements regarding that commodity' and not the term usually employed in chapter 6 'inter-governmental commodity agreements', thus not expanding the definition of a commodity. Also, the applicability of the provisions was made dependent upon a decision of the ITO that recognises the conditions set forth in Article 62 HC.[19] Article 56(3) HC therefore concerns case-by-case applicability and does not affect the definition provided for in Article 56(1), (2) HC.

2.1.1.3   Use by WTO and UNCTAD

International publications on commodities often employ diverging notions to identify their object of reference. This leads to rather inconsistent usage of the term 'commodity' and its neighbouring notions 'raw material' and 'natural resource' respectively.

For instance, in its 2014 World Trade Report, the WTO defines 'commodities' as referring to both

---

[18] Article 56(3) HC reads as follows: 'If, in exceptional circumstances, the Organization finds that the conditions set forth in Article 62 exist in the case of a commodity which does not fall precisely under paragraphs 1 or 2 of this Article, the Organization may decide that the provisions of this Chapter, together with any other requirements it may establish, shall apply to inter-governmental agreements regarding that commodity.'

[19] The ITO, however, never came into being not least due to a lack of political support and consequently denial to ratify the Havana Charter by the US congress, cf. Stoll (2014), para. 2.

"soft commodities" (predominantly agriculture) and to (. . .) "hard commodities" (predominantly mining) and "energy commodities" (predominantly oil and gas). Mineral products (including metals) and energy products (coal, oil and natural gas) will fall under the designation of "natural resources". Agricultural products, in turn, will include traditional products, fresh fruit and vegetables, specialty products and processed products. . .[20]

Hence, in this report the WTO provides definitions by naming groups of commodities. In refraining from establishing abstract definitions of the applied terms, this approach is quite exemplary for the practice exhibited in many publications on commodity governance that either presume the existence of a universal definition without (re)stating it or merely describe commodities by referring to various food, mining etc. items. Neither approach is satisfactory from a legal perspective.

The inconsistencies of this approach are being acknowledged by WTO authors in the 2010 World Trade Report, which describes a 'commodity' as

a homogeneous product which can be exchanged among consumers and producers. The term "commodities" is often used in the relevant literature to refer to agricultural goods, but it also includes a number of other products that are classified as natural resources in this report. Examples are fuels, forestry products, minerals and metals.[21]

UNCTAD, in its 2012 Commodities and Development Report, defines 'commodity' as 'any homogenous good traded in bulk.'[22] This abstract definition is quite vast. It would include e.g. microchips, screws, golf balls etc.[23] Evidently, such a definition does not serve the purpose of addressing specific governance challenges that occur concerning materials, which are being extracted from nature. In the same report, however, UNCTAD presents a clear overview of what it perceives as commodities, whereas industrially processed goods are not mentioned.[24] Yet again, the term 'commodity' is thus primarily defined by stating a catalogue of items.

The fact that there is no established definition of the term 'commodity' at this point, again, demonstrates that the legal coverage of related economic activities and corresponding governance challenges has thus far been quite sparse. The following section is going to fill this gap by formulating an abstract, legal definition of the notion 'commodity'.

---

[20] WTO (2014) World Trade Report 2014, https://www.wto.org/english/res_e/booksp_e/world_trade_report14_e.pdf (last accessed 14 May 2021), p. 130.

[21] WTO (2010) World Trade Report 2010, https://www.wto.org/english/res_e/booksp_e/anrep_e/world_trade_report10_e.pdf (last accessed 14 May 2021), pp. 59–60; cf. Bürgi Bonanomi et al. (2015) The Commodity Sector and Related Governance Challenges from a Sustainable Development Perspective: The Example of Switzerland, WTI Bern Working Paper 7/2015, https://boris.unibe.ch/71327/1/WTI_CDE_IWE%20Working%20paper%20July%202015_The%20Commodity%20Sector%20and%20Related%20Gov....pdf (last accessed 14 May 2021), p. 2.

[22] UNCTAD (2012) Commodities and Development Report, April 2012, UNCTAD/SUC/2011/9, http://unctad.org/en/PublicationsLibrary/suc2011d9_en.pdf (last accessed 14 May 2021), p. x.

[23] Cf. Weiss (2009), para. 3.

[24] UNCTAD (2012), p. xi, table A; cf. Bürgi Bonanomi et al. (2015), p. 2.

2.1.1.4 Definition for the Purpose of This Book

In this book, we shall establish a definition of the term 'commodity' that is largely based on the one provided by Article 56(1), (2) HC.[25] This approach is advantageous in that it establishes a methodologically consistent scope, which is grounded on a historically established notion, for GCG and transnational commodity law respectively. Although the Havana Charter never came into effect, it nevertheless represents a multilaterally negotiated document that largely foreshadowed the world economic order after WWII and, moreover, served as one of the main documents of reference during the emergence of the WTO. The authoritative potential of chapter VI of the Havana Charter is illustrated in particular by the fact that, by means of ECOSOC Resolution 30 (IV), the world community in 1947 decided to establish the provisions set forth therein as guidelines for the conclusion of ICAs.[26]

Consequently, the following abstract definition of the term 'commodity' is proposed:

Any product of agriculture, forest, fishery or mining[27] and any mineral product in its natural (=raw) form and in such forms that are customarily required for its international trade, especially shipment, in substantial volumes.

This abstract definition is to be supplemented with a 'normative clause':

Any item that does not constitute a commodity according to the abstract definition of the term can nevertheless be considered a 'commodity' where appropriate ('normative commodity'). Appropriateness prevails in principle, where the relevant item is similar to a 'commodity' as regards conditions of exploitation or utilisation and subject to identical governance challenges.

This understanding of the term 'commodity' in the (modified) sense of a 'primary commodity' according to Article 56(1) HC clearly contours the field of GCG as the governance frame addressing the exploitation and trade of raw, as well as cultivated, materials and respective materials in a slightly processed state that is necessary for international trade. Hereby, GCG is sufficiently specified in its scope and differentiated from international trade governance.

In elaborating our abstract definition of 'commodity', the following changes introduced to the definition provided by Article 56(1) HC deserve further mention: First, products of 'mining' were explicitly included. The term is to be understood in

---

[25] Proceeding in the same vein, cf. e.g. Pelikahn (1990), p. 32, n 12 with numerous further references to other authors.

[26] ECOSOC (1947) Resolution 30 (IV) of 28 March 1947 recommended i.a that 'pending the establishment of the International Trade Organization, Members of the United Nations adopt as a general guide in inter-governmental consultation or action with respect to commodity problems the principles laid down in Chapter [VI] as a whole'; Weiss (2009), para. 15.

[27] To be understood in the widest sense of the word, thus also including the exploitation of mineral/ crude oil, natural gas and every other material that is being *extracted* from Earth. Water, which is especially being *pumped*, does not constitute a commodity, cf. Sect. 2.1.1.2 above as well as n 33 below.

its widest possible meaning and was introduced to also cover natural gas. Neither crude oil nor natural gas constitute minerals in a geological sense and thus generally do not fall within the scope of Article 56(1) HC.[28] Second, the notion 'natural' has been equated with the term 'raw', thus identifying 'raw materials' as a sub-category of 'commodities'.[29] Third, the definition was supplemented by the phrase 'especially shipment'. This refers to the practice of international trade that largely relies on shipping.[30] The addendum is supposed to establish an additional parameter for the assessment whether an item has been processed only for the purpose of its international trade or whether it already constitutes a more sophisticated product—thus no longer a 'commodity', but an ordinary commercial good.[31]

Thus, according to our definition, energy does not qualify as a 'commodity'. Rather, it is the product of either the combustion of a primary commodity (in most cases of a raw material like oil, coal etc.) or the harnessing of a natural resource (sun, water, wind etc.). Only the trade of energy commodities, not the one of electrical energy itself thus falls within the scope of this book.[32]

Concerning the definition of a 'normative commodity', the term is quite self-explanatory. This additional clause allows approaching governance challenges that do not concern 'commodities' in the actual sense of the term, but items that are highly comparable to them within the framework of and with the instruments provided by GCG.[33]

---

[28] On the geological definition of the term 'mineral', cf. Nickel (1995); on the distinction between the geological notion of what constitutes a mineral and the legal definition, cf. the judgment of the Pennsylvania Supreme Court (2014) in *Butler v. Charles Powers Estate*, discussed by Wilhelm (2014).

[29] Cf. Sect. 2.1.1.6 below.

[30] On the crucial role of shipping and corresponding effects of exercise of market power on trade and development Hummels et al. (2009).

[31] The qualifications of 'economic usefulness' and 'scarcity', on the other hand, were not introduced. These terms serve the purpose of excluding natural resources like seawater and air, WTO (2010), p. 46. However, the latter do not fall within the scope of the definition in any case. The qualification would thus have been redundant.

[32] Cf. the differentiation between energy and commodities in European Commission (2011), p. 6. Annex EM to Article 1(5) of the Energy Charter Treaty lists 'electrical energy' in line with a set of commodities. This list, however, is used to define the term 'energy materials and products', whereas 'electrical energy' is undoubtedly a product, thus the outcome of e.g. the combustion or other use of a commodity. Cf. Sect. 5.2.1.3 in more detail below.

[33] In accordance with Article 56(1) HC, however, *water* and *air* shall under no circumstances be considered to constitute 'commodities'. While the further realms of this debate lie beyond the scope of this treatise, it is the opinion of the author that both elements constitute public goods, which are indispensable for human life, belong to humankind overall and therefore should not be subjected to market forces. On the corresponding debate on a HR to water, cf. already Riedel (2005) as well as Singh (2016) above. Likewise excluding water from its scope, Article 1.9(1) CETA.

2.1.1.5 Types of Commodities

International literature frequently distinguishes between different types of commodities.

To begin with, a differentiation can especially be made according to the *origin* (agricultural, fishery, forestry, mining, mineral) or the *intended usage* (food, industrial, energy) of a commodity.

Further, the distinction according to the '*texture*' of a commodity, thus between 'soft' (livestock, grains, agricultural and industrial crops and fisheries) and 'hard' (petroleum products, metals and minerals) commodities, has become more and more popular.[34] This is most likely due to the fact that they are subject to at times substantially different production processes (farming or fishing on the one hand, mining or drilling on the other) and therefore may relate to diverging governance challenges.

UNCTAD employs yet another differentiation according to the intended use of a commodity, namely between *energy* (petroleum products, gas, coal, but also nuclear products and renewables) and *non-energy commodities* (metals, agricultural and fishery products).[35] A succinct overview of the different commodity categories mentioned is displayed in the 2012 UNCTAD Commodities and Development Report (Fig. 2.1).[36]

Yet another distinction that has a double meaning is the one between 'primary' and 'secondary' commodities. The differentiation can refer to either the degree of processing that the commodity has experienced, as in Article 56(1) HC, or to the usage of the commodity for original production ('primary') or recycling ('secondary'), an example for the latter especially being scrap.[37]

From an economic point of view, commodities constitute factors of production as well as goods in themselves.[38] Which of these perspectives one employs can have an effect on the governance strategies she proposes.[39]

---

[34] UNCTAD (2012), p. xi. Cf. Bürgi Bonanomi et al. (2015), p. 2.

[35] UNCTAD (2012), p. ix.

[36] UNCTAD (2012), p. ix. Cf. also the original work by Farooki and Kaplinsky (2012), Table 3.1; NB: the classification displayed in the chart of plutonium as a non-energy commodity appears to be incorrect since its contemporary main use is to produce electrical energy, cf. World Nuclear Association (2018) Plutonium, http://www.world-nuclear.org/info/Nuclear-Fuel-Cycle/Fuel-Recycling/Plutonium/ (last accessed 14 May 2021).

[37] The latter distinction is especially employed in European Commission (2008) as well as European Commission (2011).

[38] WTO (2010), p. 46.

[39] More detailed discussions of these matters of *natural resource economics* naturally lie beyond the scope of this book. It goes without saying that the economics behind GCG, which are being peripherally touched upon throughout our subsequent discussions, are a decisive factor when it comes to the challenge of developing a sustainable, equitable global commodity sector. On the origins of (exhaustible) NR economics Hotelling (1931); cf. also comprehensively Perman et al. (2011); expertly Radetzki and Warrell (2016).

Primary sector	Commodity categories	Sub categories	Examples of individual commodities
Hard commodities	Energy commodities	Petroleum products	Crude oil
			Gasoline
			Natural Gas
			Coal
			Renewables
			Nuclear
	Non-energy commodities	Industrial metals	Aluminium
			Copper
			Zinc, Lead
		Rare metals	Plutonium, cobalt
		Ferrous metals	Iron ore
		Precious metals	Gold, Silver
			Platinum and palladium
		Minerals	Diamonds
Soft commodities		Livestock	Cattle, Dairy products,
			Poultry, Pigs
		Grains	Wheat
			Maize, Rice
			Soybeans,
		Agricultural and industrial crops	Sugar
			Timber
			Cotton
			Roots and tubers
			Tea, coffee, cocoa
			Vegetable oils
		Fisheries	Prawns, Cod, Tuna

Fig. 2.1 Primary commodities classification by categories, UNCTAD (2012), p. ix. (Source: adapted from Farooki and Kaplinsky 2012)

A highly detailed classification of different commodities is provided by the 'multipurpose international product nomenclature' elaborated by the World Customs Organisation under the title Harmonised System (HS), which naturally also contains a comprehensive itemisation of commodities.[40] Also the EU's Combined Nomenclature is based on the HS.[41]

---

[40] World Customs Organisation (2019) Overview, http://www.wcoomd.org/en/topics/nomenclature/overview.aspx (last accessed 14 May 2021).

[41] The Combined Nomenclature is contained in Annex I to Council Regulation (EEC) No 2658/87 on the tariff and statistical nomenclature and on the Common Customs Tariff and can be accessed at http://eur-lex.europa.eu/legal-content/EN/TXT/PDF/?uri=OJ:L:2014:312:FULL&from=EN (last accessed 14 May 2021). Cf. further Schorkopf (2011), para. 8 with reflections on the nomenclature's sections applicable to commodities.

2.1.1.6 Neighbouring Terms

'*Raw material*' is generally defined as a 'basic material from which a product is made.'[42] More precisely, it is being described as 'material still in its natural or original state, before processing or manufacture.'[43] In the context of Article 56(1) HC, the notion 'raw material' delivers a sub-definition of the term 'primary commodity'.[44] It depicts materials in their 'natural form'. As soon as the materials undergo any form of processing, even as limited as e.g. the debarking and cutting of a tree trunk, they become 'primary commodities' but no longer constitute 'raw materials'. The term 'raw material' thus constitutes one of the elements of and complements the definition of Article 56(1) HC of 'primary commodity'.

'*Natural resources*' are commonly defined as 'materials or substances occurring in nature which can be exploited for economic gain.'[45] In more exact terms, Collins Dictionary speaks of 'an actual or potential form of wealth supplied by nature, as coal, oil, water power, arable land etc.'[46] Accordingly, the notion 'natural resource' also refers to such entities that can be used for economic gain, e.g. the generation of energy, but are at the same time *immovable* like rivers, forests or the sunlight.

The term thus only refers to the very sources of renewable energy and not to their methods of production or products. In this connection, solar panels do not constitute a 'natural resource' since they are a processed good and thus not supplied by nature. Solar energy collected through photovoltaic systems neither is a 'natural resource' since it does not occur in nature but is a result of the sun's radiant light and heat being harnessed as electrical energy by human technology. Only the sunlight or the sun itself is a 'natural resource'.

The notion is thus both wider and narrower than the term 'primary commodity' since on the one hand it also includes non-tradable, immovable entities and on the other excludes processed materials.[47] The term, consequently, is more strongly

---

[42] Oxford dictionaries (2021) Entry 'raw material', http://www.oxforddictionaries.com/definition/english/raw-material (last accessed 14 May 2021).

[43] Collins dictionary (2021) Entry 'raw material', http://www.collinsdictionary.com/dictionary/american/raw-material (last accessed 14 May 2021). An OECD paper titled Export Restrictions in Raw Materials Trade 'for the purpose of this publication' defines raw materials as 'the minerals and metals that are crucial for the capital and consumer goods industries around the world, and the agricultural commodities that supplement domestic food supplies in many countries and sustain the global food processing industry', cf. OECD (2014), p. 9, thus proceeding in a manner paradigmatic for the varying *ad hoc* definitions being employed in many international publications on commodity (-related) matters.

[44] Cf. already Sect. 2.1.1.4 above.

[45] Oxford dictionaries (2021) Entry 'natural resources', http://www.oxforddictionaries.com/definition/english/natural-resources (last accessed 14 May 2021).

[46] Collins dictionary (2021) Entry 'natural resource', http://www.collinsdictionary.com/dictionary/american/natural-resource (last accessed 14 May 2021).

[47] In the same vein also Clark et al. (2001), p. 3.

related to issues of environmental governance, whereas the term commodity exhibits a stronger economic connotation.[48]

Nevertheless, several authors use the term 'natural resources' particularly also in the context of trade.[49] For instance, WTO authors have defined the term as

> stocks of materials that exist in the natural environment that are both scarce and economically useful in production or consumption, either in their raw state or after a minimal amount of processing.[50]

'Natural resource' here is used almost synonymously to 'primary commodity', except for the qualifications of scarcity and economic usefulness. However, the authors exclude agricultural goods and foods from the scope of the definition, which are items covered by Article 56(1) HC. Fish and forestry products, to the contrary, are defined as 'natural resources'.[51]

Given that verbatim natural resources include immovable entities, it is to my mind more precise and thus preferable to employ the term 'commodity' whenever we seek to address challenges that arise from the removal of objects from nature, which are later being employed for economic purposes, particularly trade.[52]

2.1.2 Economic, Political and Technical Circumstances of Commodity Activity

Commodity activity constitutes the precondition for economic production—without a primary commodity, no goods can be produced.[53] Where exhaustible commodity deposits are concerned,[54] they frequently constitute important economic assets for the state that owns them.[55] Taken together, these factors raise important issues of

---

[48] See already Oehl (2019), p. 6, n 20.

[49] Cf. Schrijver (1997), pp. 14–15; Oehl (2019), p. 6, n 20.

[50] WTO (2010), p. 46. This is not surprising given that Article XX(g) GATT refers to 'natural resources', thus departing from the terminology introduced by Article 56(1) HC.

[51] The fact that the definition exhibits the mentioned inconsistencies yet again shows that it was mainly created in order to economically assess effects to items that are subject to like circumstances. The qualifications of scarcity and economic usefulness *here*, however, are compelling since they allow excluding such 'natural resources' that are not traded in markets, e.g. air and seawater, from the scope of the notion, WTO (2010), p. 46. On the definition of 'commodity' in the same report, cf. already Sect. 2.1.1.4 above.

[52] Oehl (2019), p. 6, n 20; cf. in more detail Sect. 5.1.1.3 below.

[53] On the so-called Commodity Value Chain, cf. Sect. 3.2.2.1 below.

[54] As has been pointed out, the notion of *sustainability* has to be different for exhaustible commodities compared to renewables since the balancing exercise regarding economic, social and environmental concerns may differ, Bellmann (2016); cf. also the distinction between non-renewable 'stock' and renewable 'flow' resources portrayed i.a. by Schrijver (1997), pp. 13–4.

[55] Calder (2014), p. 2. In the case of exhaustible commodities, 'a key opportunity cost of extracting today is the future extraction foregone', which can be particularly problematic, where the extraction

global economic equity between an economic *centre*, in which commodities are being turned into end products, and a commodity-exporting *periphery* that seeks to make use of its commodity export revenues for its own industrialisation, which naturally requires corresponding technology.[56]

From the perspective of CDDCs, commodity governance is a crucial development factor: Commodity export revenue for some of these countries may be the only opportunity to grow and industrialise their national economies.[57] Their needs appear to frequently clash with the paradigm of trade liberalisation, which is dominant in the global trade system still today. Whereas for instance the US developed their own economy relying i.a. on infant industry protection measures,[58] the paradigm of liberalised trade today substantially limits countries' policy space to implement such measures, including ones e.g. fostering so-called *Import Substitution Industrialisation*.[59] The same holds true for the 'structural adjustment' programs (SAPs) maintained by the World Bank.[60]

Furthermore, several factors, including high capital intensity, high sunk costs, long development and operating periods, need for imports of expertise and technology, volatile markets, and overall economic uncertainty and risks, particularly in the extractive industries, contribute to the significant dominance of large TNCs—most of them headquartered in the economic *centre*—in the commodity sector.[61]

---

and corresponding economic benefits cannot be turned into SD. On the various efforts UNCTAD is undertaking in order to tackle pervasive commodity dependence—a key challenge to the SD of the Global South, UNCTAD (2018), pp. 6–8.

[56] On his 'centre-periphery analytics', which 'open[] a window onto the structures of power and hierarchy in a larger system and onto the continuation of war in times of peace through the dynamics of domination and reciprocal influence among unequal actors in such a system[]', fundamentally Kennedy (2013), pp. 77–86. On the *Prebisch-Singer hypothesis*, for instance, cf. Sect. 2.2.3 below; Toye and Toye (2003), pp. 437–438; cf. also Arezki et al. (2013). Furthermore, the need for CDDCs to industrialise relates to the challenges of creating sufficient *linkages* between commodity operations and the respective host economy, such as capacity building, technology transfer, and other *local content* measures.

[57] Instead of many, Morris and Fessehaie (2014).

[58] Tickner (1990), pp. 69–70.

[59] Gale and Haward (2011), p. 5; cf. Hirschman (1968) with a comprehensive account of the origins of ISI and respective policies in Latin America.

[60] On '[t]he IMF's neo-classical emphasis on liberalization and macroeconomic stabilization' as well as the ensuing repercussions for borrowers, Schlemmer-Schulte (2014), paras. 4–5. It may be due not least to these liberalisation requirements that resource-endowed states, particularly in Sub-Saharan Africa are increasingly relying on so-called resources for investments (RFI) deals. On the latter, focusing on the DRC-Sicomines deal, Landry (2018).

[61] Calder (2014), pp. 2, 6, who points to the fact that 'risk is not unique to natural resources, but the magnitude and pervasiveness of natural resource risks are exceptional'; IMF (2012), p. 10; cf. also AU (2009), p. 8; on the challenge of regulating TNCs instructively Muchlinski (2007). Apart from private TNCs, also state-owned commodity enterprises have evolved as major players, notably in the oil and gas sector. The governance of SOEs can pose particular challenges, especially where these entities manage large flows of public revenue and/or assume multiple government functions (e.g. project financing, operation, oversight, accounting) at once, thus often conferring a

Correspondingly, much of commodity activity occurs transnationally, thus giving rise to additional governance challenges, such as benefit sharing[62] as well as information asymmetries between the commodity-endowed state and the foreign corporate.[63] Also, in view of the pervasive economic risks associated with commodity projects, maintaining a stable fiscal regime including reliable legal underpinnings may be of particular importance for attracting foreign investment.[64]

Apart from the great economic risks associated with commodity activity, it also entails significant environmental and social risks and can potentially cause i.a., air, water and land pollution, energy and water waste, land alteration and deforestation, public health risks, the disruption of existing ecosystems, the displacement of local communities and exploitative labour practices affecting vulnerable population segments such as children.[65] Moreover, where commodity extraction is taking place in areas that had hitherto been used for farming, hunting or fishing, commodity activities not only concern land rights, but also a variety of HR, including cultural rights of indigenous peoples in view of role the natural environment can play in their rites and beliefs.[66] Due to the high social sensitivity of commodity activities, commodity companies are said to require a *social license to operate*—in addition to the formal license issued by the state government—in order to carry out their desired projects.[67]

Many of the risks caused are particular to the type of commodity activity, such as mining, oil and gas exploitation, or agriculture.[68] The detrimental effects on the

---

disproportionately strong position onto the SOE within the government apparatus, which may jeopardise constitutional checks and balances and therefore make the entire governance system prone to corruption, cf. e.g. EITI (2019) Role of state-owned enterprises, https://eiti.org/role-of-stateowned-enterprises (last accessed 14 May 2021).

[62] IMF (2012), p. 10. From a government perspective, a non-standard, commodity-directed fiscal regime is generally advised in order adequately capture commodity profits and rents, cf. Calder (2014). In view of their large volumes, managing financial flows resulting from commodity activity and maintaining respective transparency are two equally important and intricate challenges of commodity governance. On EITI, PWYP, and other transparency standards, cf. Sect. 4.2.2.2.1.1 below.

[63] Especially Commodity-Dependent Developing Countries (CDDCs), on their definition cf. UNCTAD (2017), p. x, often do not dispose of the necessary funds to carry out exploration activities—which can be very capital-intensive, particularly in the mining sector—and correspondingly determine relevant geological data themselves. Instead, they need to rely on the information that commodity companies gather, which may put them at a disadvantage when negotiating the economic terms of the exploitation of a respective deposit, cf. AU (2009), pp. 15–17.

[64] On stabilisation clauses in the commodity sector, see instructively Hauert (2016); on investment protection in the commodity sector, cf. Sect. 4.3.1 below.

[65] Espa and Oehl (2018), p. 5; Bellmann (2016); Bürgi Bonanomi et al. (2015).

[66] Cf. Sects. 4.2.1.1 and 4.2.2.1.1 below.

[67] NRGI (2014), p. 11; cf. Moffat and Zhang (2014).

[68] Mining for instance can cause severe environmental repercussions. Since minerals are contained in a matrix, it typically requires the unearthing of huge volumes of rock. Once these have been brought to the surface, the ore is being separated from waste rock and treated i.a. with leaches such as alkaline cyanide solutions or sulphuric acid solutions in order to liberate the desired metal from

environment that are specifically caused by commodity exploitation can potentially affect all spaces of planet Earth, including mining in the Deep Sea as well as drilling activities in the Arctic. Again the risks associated with commodity activity may be similar to the risks associated with other economic activity, yet they are exceptional in their 'magnitude and pervasiveness'.[69] In fact these risks may at times be of such overwhelming nature that states fail to adequately manage them—a scenario, which has become known under the notion 'resource curse'.[70]

2.1.3   Defining a Functional Commodity Sector

These economic, political and technical realities in which commodity activity occurs need to be borne in mind when considering what constitutes a well-governed or 'functional' commodity sector. While there are naturally many ways to approach the definition of a complex term such as 'functional commodity sector', we shall characterise the latter by identifying its central *policy trade-offs*.

In order to identify these policy trade-offs, I first analysed the political objectives associated with commodity activity by studying a considerable volume of inter-,

---

the gangue, Spohr (2016), p. 48. The gangue material that is left behind is usually being deposited into tailings, which are often retained by dams or embankments consisting of waste rock. Due to the prior chemical treatment, gangue often exhibits residual concentrations of leaches. As a consequence, many tailings contain significant concentrations of these chemicals. Their seepage can lead to ground and surface water contamination as well as other environmental damage. Tailings dam failures can lead to a further proliferation of chemicals in the surrounding environment and, depending on the size of the tailings, destroy entire ecosystems, Spohr (2016), pp. 48–49; cf. the Fundao tailings dam-burst, which caused 19 casualties and polluted a nearby river in Brazil, BBC (2016) Samarco dam failure in Brazil 'caused by design flaws', 30 August 2016, http://www.bbc.com/news/business-37218145 (last accessed 14 May 2021), as well as the dam-burst in Brumadinho and Lewis (2019) Second Vale dam burst in Brazil likely to curb mining risk appetite. Reuters, 26 January 2019, https://www.reuters.com/article/us-vale-sa-disaster-risks/second-vale-dam-burst-in-brazil-likely-to-curb-mining-risk-appetite-idUSKCN1PK0N1 (last accessed 14 May 2021).

[69] Calder (2014), p. 6. While this claim by Calder is being made with regard to extractive industries, it is also fair to employ it with regard to other commodity sectors, including agriculture and fisheries. In all sectors, large-scale, intensive intrusions into the natural environment are not uncommon, as reflected in for example incidents of large-scale land grabbing and illegal, unreported, and unregulated (IUU) fishing, cf. e.g. Bürgi Bonanomi et al. (2015), pp. 46–47 as well as FAO (2016). On the endeavour of this treatise to identify, instead of focusing on individual commodities, commonalities of governance challenges related to commodities in general and its corresponding conceptualisation of TCL, cf. Chap. 2 below.

[70] On empirical evidence for the phenomenon that resource rich states often do not number among developed nations, Sachs and Warner (2001), p. 828; cf. Hauert (2016), p. 33. Cf. also NRGI (2015), p. 1. Comprehensively Frankel (2012); Bonnitcha (2016), p. 43; critically Desai and Jarvis (2012), p. 104. The decrease of productivity in other industrial sectors that commodity exports can bring about has been described as the related phenomenon of 'Dutch disease', cf. Davis (1995), likewise with a critical view on the 'resource curse thesis'.

supra-, and national strategic guidance documents; the regulatory objectives of various inter-, trans-, and national instruments applicable to commodity activity; as well as the central individual legal norms governing commodity activity on a transnational level. As a second step, I clustered the objectives expressed in these sources according to five major interests they are associated with—economic gain, development, preservation, control, and participation:

First, many, if not most, actors involved in commodity activity are pursuing the objective of *economic gain*. The commodity company, which may be involved in exploration, extraction and perhaps processing as well as shipping or trading activities, will typically be looking for profits. The host government, which disposes of natural resources, will generally attempt to capture sufficient resource rents through taxes or royalties. As commonly the case in the oil and gas sector, the host government may also pursue profit-oriented activities itself, usually through state-owned enterprises (SOEs). In addition, various actors along the commodity value chain may be seeking profits, be it suppliers, subcontractors or third-party service providers of any kind. The services and goods they offer may range from highly technical expertise and products, such as the refinement of precious minerals, to services fulfilling the basic needs of e.g., the personnel of the commodity company carrying out the removal process, such as grocers and food suppliers.[71]

A second interest, which occurs frequently in connection with commodity activity, is the one of *development*. For many countries, commodities constitute a major or even the only significant source of income. This is particularly the case for so-called CDDCs.[72] Frequently, the revenues generated through commodity activity will be the only substantial means available for those states to develop. As a consequence, the respective governments will typically seek to implement policies, which foster the development contribution of the commodity sector to the greatest possible extent. Their actions will oftentimes be monitored and potentially criticised by civil society groups, which likewise demand a 'fair share' in commodity export earnings for the respective host population. On the part of industrialised states, security of commodity supply constitutes a central element of continued development.

Both interests introduced so far frequently conflict with the third interest of *preservation*. Ideally host governments, and typically especially local populations and civil society groups will advocate for an adequate protection of the natural wealth of their country or municipality. This advocacy can be particularly vigorous where local populations, especially indigenous peoples, rely on a particular part of the natural environment for their livelihoods or identify with it culturally e.g., as 'ancestral land'. The preservation of nature is a challenge, which applies along the entire commodity value chain and involves diverse subject matters, such as the

---

[71]Cf. insofar the policy challenge of creating sufficient *linkages* between the commodity activity, particularly the removal activity, and the host economy—an issue, which depicts potential policy trade-offs between economic gain and development.

[72]Cf. definition provided by UNCTAD (2017), p. x.

protection of watercourses against waste materials from extraction works, adequate restoration of the natural environment after a removal process has ceased or limiting the emission of greenhouse gas during a refinement or shipping process.

A fourth interest, which is pursued mainly by government actors, is *controlling* the commodity activity in various respects. The respective authorities on national and subnational levels typically strive to maintain control over what resources are being extracted by whom and under what conditions. This interest can correlate with the one of economic gain but is still separate from it. Control may also relate to enforcing particular labour, anti-corruption or shipping standards, i.e. upholding the general rule of law in regard to commodity activity. Consequently, internal conflicts within the government or between government branches may occur, for instance over the award of exploration or extraction rights to a particular actor by the executive branch, which the judiciary may deem to be a violation of due process. In situations of armed conflict, maintaining the overall control over, and thus security of, commodity operations constitutes a central objective that adversarial actors may be striving for.

Fifthly and lastly, all of the interests outlined so far may conflict with the interest of *participation*. This interest typically concerns respective host state populations, in particular civil society organisations on national and local levels.[73] Given the often large-scale nature of commodity activities,[74] a removal process may bear on the daily lives and interests of many residents. As a consequence, their proponents frequently voice their demand to participate in decision-making processes at the various levels of government. They want to be involved in the decision, what resources are being exploited by what actor and under what conditions. Potentially, they may claim compensation for temporary or permanent loss of their livelihoods. The demand for participation may also relate to specific activities carried out by commodity companies, such as for instance ways to remedy detrimental side effects of extraction activities. Likewise, commodity companies may seek participation in governmental decision-making.

While each of these five interests can conflict with one another, and thus create various policy trade-offs, some evidently clash more severely than others. For instance, the quest for economic gain, no matter pursued by which actor, frequently creates trade-offs with the objective of preservation and potentially development. Likewise, it will often conflict with the concern for participation. Participation, in turn will typically influence the *degree* of control that an actor can exercise over a specific activity.

This list of interests creating commodity-specific policy trade-offs is not meant to be conclusive. Yet, it depicts an analytical framework, which helps to aptly

---

[73] Today, several civil society organisations/NGOs are active transnationally, thus demonstrating what can be termed the emergence of a 'transnational civil society'. Cf. generally on the challenge of sufficiently involving these transnational actors in the continuously intensifying global regulatory cooperation and related matters of democratic legitimacy, e.g. Buszewski et al. (2016). On globally active commodity initiatives and organisations, cf. Sect. 2.2.5 below.

[74] Cf. Calder (2014), p. 10; also, Sect. 2.1.2 above.

categorise the majority of trade-offs that typically occur in relation to commodity activity. Evidently, the remarks made above can only give a rough, exemplary idea of what kind of scenarios may be categorised as conflicts of the five diverging interests; and oftentimes, these scenarios will comprise several trade-offs, not just one. Still, one should generally be able to subsume large parts of the factual scenarios occurring in the commodity sector under the analytical framework presented above.

Moreover, it shall be noted here that *qualitative* statements about for instance the degree to which the global commodity sector is *factually* being governed in a functional manner lie beyond the scope of this book. What we can approximate, however, is an answer to our principal research question—how the current *legal framework* relates to the goal of ensuring a functional commodity sector. In that connection, what shall accompany us throughout the remainder of this book is the analytical parameter of *balance* between the five major interests associated with commodity activity.

Therefore, for the purposes of this book,

> the global commodity sector shall be deemed to be functional when and where it exhibits a balance between the five major interests associated with commodity activity.

2.1.4   Defining Global Commodity Governance (GCG)

It ought to appear relatively clear what the term 'global' refers to within the meaning of GCG. Generally, the word is defined as 'relating to the whole world' or 'world-wide'.[75] Speaking of GCG, it is this exact meaning that the term depicts: commodity governance is to be looked at from a global perspective, thus inspecting its world-wide structures and rules.[76] 'Governance' is generally defined as 'the exercise of political power to manage a nation's affair'[77] or 'the action, manner, or system of governing'.[78] More specifically, it is defined as 'the way that organizations or countries are managed at the highest level, and the systems for doing this'[79] or

---

[75] Oxford Dictionaries (2021) Entry 'global', http://www.oxforddictionaries.com/definition/english/global (last accessed 14 May 2021).

[76] Insofar, regional, national and local-level issues as a general rule will only feature in this book where, e.g. because of their pervasiveness, they are pertinent to governance on the global level.

[77] Dann (2013), p. 115 pointing to a respective entry in Webster's dictionary as well as to World Bank (1989), p. 60.

[78] Collins dictionary (2021) Entry 'governance', http://www.collinsdictionary.com/dictionary/english/governance (last accessed 14 May 2021).

[79] Cambridge dictionary (2021) Entry 'governance', http://dictionary.cambridge.org/dictionary/british/governance (last accessed 14 May 2021).

'the way that a city, company, etc., is controlled by the people who run it'.[80] It thus refers to the modality of the exercise of governing power.

Within the context of international law, it was the World Bank that originally developed the concept of 'governance', when it realised the deficient structures in many of the recipient countries of its programs.[81] No later than in the second half of the 1990s, the governance discourse was taken up by international scholars outside of the World Bank.[82] Over the course of the years, the notion of governance was elaborated towards a more normative concept, the one of *good* governance.[83] This development is best illustrated by the 2002 Monterrey consensus, which states i.a.:

> Good governance is essential for sustainable development. Sound economic policies, solid democratic institutions responsive to the needs of the people [. . .] are the basis for sustained economic growth, poverty eradication and employment creation.[84]

This book will address issues of *good* governance. However, its emphasis lies on the conceptualisation of the legal framework of GCG. For these purposes, it employs the rather descriptive notion of governance developed by the Brandt commission as

> the sum of the many ways individuals and institutions, public and private, manage their common affairs. It is a continuing process through which conflicting or diverse interests may be accommodated and co-operative action may be taken. It includes formal institutions and regimes empowered to enforce compliance, as well as informal arrangements that people and institutions either have agreed to or perceive to be in their interest.[85]

Apart from the normative concept of '*good* governance', also the concept of governance thus in itself bears a whole set of 'revolutionary' approaches that challenge the doctrine of state sovereignty and with it the 'classical' system of international law. According to Ladeur, it describes a flexible decision-making process, represents a heterarchical philosophy, and constitutes a product and symbol of transnationalism or transnational law.[86] It is emblematic of the increasing perme-ability of legal regimes and challenges the homogeneity and unity of the 'old system' of international law.[87] Furthermore, governance is more comprehensive than

---

[80]Merriam Webster dictionary (2021) Entry 'governance', http://www.merriam-webster.com/dictionary/governance (last accessed 14 May 2021).

[81]Dann (2013), p. 115, pointing to Killinger (2003), pp. 20–30. These programs in many cases were not or only little successful due to a lack of institutions and structures ('fragile statehood') that could provide the effective implementation of the policies demanded, Dann (2013), p. 85 with reference to Van de Walle (2001), p. 51, n 80. The concept of governance in this connection is, therefore, to be understood not in the sense of political reform but of 'technocratic consolidation' and thus aims at an amelioration of the functioning and the efficiency of the government apparatus, but does not necessarily involve democratic reform or other normative policy changes, Dann (2013), p. 116.

[82]Dann (2013), p. 116.

[83]Dann (2013), pp. 116–118.

[84]UN (2002) Report of the International Conference on Financing for Development, 'Monterrey Consensus', UN Doc. A/CONF.198/11, para. 11; cf. Dann (2013), p. 117.

[85]Commission on Global Governance (1995), p. 2; cf. Brown Weiss and Somarajah (2013), para 2.

[86]Ladeur (2010), i.a. at paras. 6, 14, 15, and 33.

[87]Ladeur (2010), paras. 20, 22.

'government' as it comprises the 'informal underpinnings of political decision-making that have always supplemented formal procedures'.[88] As such, it includes the actions, policies and contributions of other actors of society, such as NGOs etc.[89] Governance thus constitutes

> an open mode of co-ordination of both actors and rules, which presupposes a dynamic and experimental mode of decision-making with "entangled" hierarchies and the reciprocal interference of national and international regulatory structures.[90]

Bearing this in mind, we shall define GCG as follows:

> The sum of the ways that public and private institutions and individuals within the worldwide multi-level system manage commodity activities.

2.2 The Historical Emergence of GCG

Before illustrating the disruptive features of GCG (Sect. 2.2.5), we shall briefly revisit historical approaches to governing the global commodity sector, which were motivated primarily by economic objectives and are characterised by five phases: the 'Anglo-Dutch phase', the 'League phase' (both Sect. 2.2.1), the 'Havana phase' (Sect. 2.2.2), the 'NIEO-UNCTAD phase' (Sect. 2.2.3), and the 'phase of post-interventionism' (Sect. 2.2.4).[91]

2.2.1 Commodity Policy Before 1945: The 'Anglo-Dutch' and 'League' Phases

Global commodity policy before 1945 was dominated by the logics of colonialism.[92] The exploitation and trade of commodities in colonised states was regulated and controlled by the colonial powers or their associated private producing companies, such as the (British) East India Company and the Dutch East India Company.[93]

---

[88] Ladeur (2010), para 1.

[89] Cf. Menkel-Meadow (2011), p. 103.

[90] Ladeur (2010), para 35.

[91] Cf. Khan (1982), pp. 52–76; for a concise account see especially Weiss (2009), paras. 6–25. Hereinafter, the brief historical outline of global commodity policy shall be limited to aspects expedient to this monograph. For more detailed historical remarks, one may, as far as the first four historical phases of commodity policy are concerned, be referred to Khan (1982), pp. 52–80; Chimni (1987), pp. 16–32; and Pelikahn (1990), pp. 87–149.

[92] Cf. Gale and Haward (2011), p. 4; the authors—probably somewhat sarcastically—describe past Imperialism a then 'well-established form' of GCG, Gale and Haward (2011), p. 4.

[93] Khan (1982), pp. 52–53; Pelikahn (1990), p. 89; Weiss (2009), para. 7; cf. e.g. Prakash (1985), pp. 75–83, on the trade rivalry of the Dutch and the English in Bengal in the seventeenth century.

Therefore, regulatory approaches in that era employed the perspective of the colo-nizers—which then effectively were commodity *producers* reaping the benefits of their international sale. The international law regulating commodity activity was mainly shaped by ICAs seeking to stabilize prices.

In the *Anglo-Dutch phase* the two colonial superpowers and great trading nations United Kingdom and the Netherlands introduced a number of agreements, which concerned their principal trade goods, such as sugar, rubber, tin and tea.[94] They were concluded between producing states and/or their producing companies and thus constituted mere 'producer agreements', such as the International Sugar Agreement of 1864 and its succeeding treaties, the 1902 Sugar Convention and the 1937 Sugar Agreement; the 1931 Tin agreement; or the 1933 International Tea Agreement.[95] Furthermore, similar agreements on petroleum, lead, zinc, copper and wheat were concluded.[96] Consumers did not participate.[97] These agreements were different from ordinary producer cartels between private corporations to the extent that public authority was involved.[98] This government participation was aspired as a 'corollary' of economic regulation, and was i.a. supposed to render implementation of the agreements more effective.[99] All of these treaties were, mostly by the introduction of buffer stocks or quotas,[100] aimed at hindering an overproduction of the commod-ity concerned and thus at stabilising global market prices[101]—a vital economic interest for both the UK and the Netherlands.[102] The mechanisms put in place by these early ICAs were, however, only rudimentary and thus proved not to be too effective.[103]

The *League phase* brought substantial developments in international commodity policy. Although already founded in 1919, it was only under the influence of the Great Depression, which started in 1929 that the League of Nations became a central forum   for   'co-ordination   of   the   production   and   marketing   of   certain

---

[94] Khan (1982), p. 52.

[95] Weiss (2009), para. 7; Chimni (1987), pp. 17–19. The original texts of the agreements are provided in ILO (1943).

[96] Weiss (2009), para. 7; Chimni (1987), p. 17; ILO (1943).

[97] Weiss (2009), para 7; Chimni (1987), pp. 17–19.

[98] Khan (1982), p. 55.

[99] Khan (1982), p. 55.

[100] A buffer stock is 'a large supply of a commodity [. . .] that is bought and stored when extra is available, and sold when there is not enough, in order to control its price and quantity in the economy', Cambridge Dictionary (2021) Entry 'buffer stock', http://dictionary.cambridge.org/dictionary/business-english/buffer-stock (last accessed 14 May 2021); Weiss (2009), para. 7; Khan (1982), p. 52.

[101] Weiss (2009), para. 7.

[102] Khan (1982), pp. 52–54. The UK was especially dependent on commodity trade revenues given their debts owed to the USA, see Khan (1982), p. 53. As far as the Netherlands are concerned, tin production in the Dutch East Indies back then was state-owned, the trade revenues thus accruing directly to the national budget, see Khan (1982), p. 52.

[103] Weiss (2009), para. 7.

commodities'.[104] The most crucial changes for international commodity markets and their legal regulation were discussed and later formulated at the 1933 London World Monetary and Economic Conference.[105] In response to the great economic challenges of the 1930s, international commodity policy left the spheres of mere national interest considerations and for the first time evolved to a more global approach. Key to this new approach was the involvement not only of producers, but also of consumer states.[106] Furthermore, in order to build confidence in commodity schemes, the role of governments in these agreements was substantially increased, basically introducing the intergovernmental commodity agreement type that would later dominate the 1970s and 80s. During the conference, the League formulated nine pioneering principles for ICAs, advocated for the conclusion of such treaties and created a link between ICAs and its bureau.[107] Major developments that the League phase brought about include that ICAs were seen as a legitimate exception to the MFN clause and that they evolved to become 'dual-interest' rather than 'single-interest phenomena'.[108] Thus, the League phase cast important foundations for the objective of ICAs to come: creating a 'win-win' situation for producers and consumers alike.[109]

2.2.2 The Havana Phase

After a devastating WWII, the global community, under the guidance especially of the new Western superpower USA was seeking to restructure the world economy. The innovations this would bring to global commodity policy were already foreshadowed in the 1941 Atlantic Charter. Driven by the liberal idea of free markets, access to commodities worldwide should generally be open for all; producers should renounce protectionism.[110]

Although the Havana Charter was never ratified, the discussions in Cuba were nevertheless groundbreaking for the new world economic order, including global commodity trade.[111] This is not least due to the fact that the GATT was separated

---

[104] Khan (1982), p. 57 with reference to League of Nations (1933) Report of the conference, LoN Doc. C.435.M.220 (1933).

[105] Khan (1982), pp. 57–58.

[106] Cf. Chimni (1987), p. 19.

[107] Khan (1982), pp. 58–59 lists all nine principles, which touched upon what types of commodities should be regulated by ICAs (only significant ones), and moreover envisaged i.a. that also related and substituted products should be included; that the agreements should be fair to both consumers and producers, including the maintenance of fair and remunerative price levels; and that there should be no discrimination of third countries.

[108] Khan (1982), p. 66.

[109] Cf. Weiss (2009), para. 10.

[110] Weiss (2009), para. 11; Krappel (1975), p. 18.

[111] Cf. extensively Krappel (1975).

from the general negotiations on the establishment of an International Trade Organisation, concluded on 30 October 1947 and entered into force on 1 January 1948.

The GATT generally also applies to international commodity trade, however without specifically addressing commodities—apart from a few exceptions.[112] Article XX:h GATT constitutes one of these exceptions. Accordingly, a measure that meets the requirements of the 'chapeau' of Article XX GATT and is

> undertaken in pursuance of obligations under any intergovernmental commodity agreement which conforms to criteria submitted to the CONTRACTING PARTIES and not disapproved by them or which is itself so submitted and not so disapproved

shall not constitute an infringement of the GATT.

In Annex I to the GATT an addendum clarifies concerning Article XX:h GATT:

> The exception provided for in this sub-paragraph extends to any commodity agreement which conforms to the principles approved by the Economic and Social Council in its resolution 30 (IV) of 28 March 1947.

The principles put forward by ECOSOC Resolution 30 (IV) concerning commodity agreements are thus included in the GATT. This Resolution

> *[r]ecommends* that [...] Members of the United Nations adopt as a general guide in intergovernmental consultation or action with respect to commodity problems the principles laid down in Chapter [VI] as a whole – i.e. the chapter on intergovernmental commodity arrangements of the draft Charter appended to the Report of the First Session of the Preparatory Committee of the United Nations Conference on Trade and Employment....[113]

Accordingly, and pursuant especially to Article 62 HC, the introduction of market-interventionist ICAs is permitted only in a state of emergency. The GATT Contracting Parties, however, were at all times mandated to renegotiate general parameters for ICAs but refrained from doing so. Never has an ICA been presented to the GATT parties for approval—the criteria set forth by Articles 55 ff. HC have thus never been applied in connection with the GATT.[114]

Developing countries, however, began to raise the issue of price stability in global commodity trade.[115] Many former colonies were—and still are today—highly

---

[112] Relevant provisions of the GATT and their application to commodity activities will be discussed in Chap. 4 below.

[113] ECOSOC (1947) Resolution 30 (IV), 28 March 1947, reprinted in WTO (2019) GATT Doc. TRE/W/17 of 7 September 1993, annex, https://www.wto.org/gatt_docs/English/SULPDF/91720248.pdf (last accessed 14 May 2021), original emphasis; cf. Khan (1982), p. 67. The 'draft Charter' referred to by Resolution 30 (IV) represents the so-called 'London version' of the Havana Charter, which is in its relevant parts identical to the final version of the HC as concluded on 28 March 1948, Weiss (2009), para. 15 and n 23.

[114] Weiss (2009), para. 16.

[115] Further central issues and claims included '[c]ompensation for shortfalls in export proceeds', and 'long-run downward trends in the prices of primary commodities in relation to the prices of manufactured goods, or of declining or stagnating export proceeds from traditional exports of low income countries over long periods of time', Mikesell (1963), pp. 297–298; on the *Prebisch-Singer hypothesis* cf. shortly below.

dependent on commodity export revenues. The GATT reacted to the criticism from its developing country members by introducing a new part IV titled 'trade and development' to GATT, with its Article XXXVII:1:a obliging the contracting parties to facilitate market access to 'products currently or potentially of particular export interest to less-developed contracting parties.' Article XXXVIII:2:a GATT, moreover, sets the parameter that ICAs should benefit developing countries in helping them with global market access. In practical terms, however, also the introduction of its new part IV brought—apart from a few exceptions[116]—no big turn in GATT's passive attitude towards ICAs.[117]

2.2.3   The NIEO-UNCTAD Phase

Not least due to the GATT parties' passive stance regarding the called-for market stabilisation measures,[118] developing countries pushed for the creation of UNCTAD in 1964.[119] Not only the emergence of the NIEO movement[120] and the principle of *Permanent Sovereignty over Natural Resources* can be perceived as a backlash from former colonies against the free trade doctrine,[121] but also the creation of UNCTAD itself. As such, the *Prebisch-Singer hypothesis*, according to which 'commodity prices decline[] over time relative to industrial goods due to the interaction of supply and demand',[122] constituted one of the central philosophical pillars of the organisation's activities from the outset.[123] Consequently, UNCTAD became the central actor pursuing commodity price stabilisation measures, i.a. through ICAs.[124] The

---

[116] Weiss (2009), para. 18 refers to the milk product and the beef agreement respectively.

[117] Weiss (2009), para 18. Concerning today's role of the WTO as the organisation succeeding the GATT secretariat, Stoll (2014), para. 3; see also Sect. 4.3.2 below.

[118] Cf. also e.g. Mikesell (1963), p. 310 who advocated for the creation of 'a committee on commodity problems of low income countries', composed of representatives of i.a. IMF, IBRD, GATT and ECOSOC.

[119] Weiss (2009), para. 17; cf. UNCTAD (2021), history, http://unctad.org/en/Pages/About% 20UNCTAD/A-Brief-History-of-UNCTAD.aspx (last accessed 14 May 2021).

[120] Sacerdoti (2015); UN GA (1974), Resolution A/RES/S-6/3201, 1 May 1974, https://iow.eui.eu/ wp-content/uploads/sites/28/2018/01/Reading-1-GA-Res-3201.pdf (last accessed 14 May 2021).

[121] The origins and content of PSNR will be discussed in detail in Sect. 4.1 below.

[122] Gale and Haward (2011), p. 5. Consequently, 'poor countries [are] locked in a long-term 'secular' decline in their terms of trade' and therefore 'constantly [need to] produce a greater volume of commodities to secure the same volume of industrialised imports', Gale and Haward (2011), p. 5.

[123] Raúl Prebisch was UNCTAD's founding Secretary-General. In 1982, the Raúl Prebisch lectures were instituted by UNCTAD, depicting the continued thought leadership of the Argentine economist, https://unctad.org/en/pages/publications/Ra%C3%BAl-Prebisch-Lectures.aspx (last accessed 14 May 2021). On the legacy of Prebisch already during his lifetime, Hirschman (1968).

[124] The latter had already been recognised as workable price stabilisation instruments in a UN study in 1951, Weiss (2009), para. 19 with reference to UN (1951).

latter 'were considered an important part of the [...] [NIEO] in the 1960s and 1970s.'[125]

Paradigmatically, the 1974 'Economic Rights Charter' (ERC) according to its Article 5 particularly emphasises the right for states to form associations of primary commodity producers, i.a. in order to 'achieve stable financing for their development'.[126] Moreover, Article 6 ERC touches upon states' duty to develop international goods trade, i.a. by concluding multilateral commodity agreements and at the same time emphasises that all states 'share the responsibility to promote the regular flow and access of all commercial goods traded at stable, remunerative and equitable prices...' Article 14 ERC reflects the complex scenario at the time of a free trade doctrine, which was increasingly faced with price stabilisation measures. On the one hand, it emphasises a duty for states to 'co-operate in promoting a steady and increasing expansion and liberalization of world trade' while on the other hand mentioning 'measures designed to attain stable, equitable and remunerative prices for primary products'.

This normative backdrop quite tangibly describes the situation, in which developing countries—more precisely the 'Group of 77' or 'G77'[127]—mandated UNCTAD with the task of elaborating commodity control agreements.[128] The efforts to create more balanced world markets by means of ICAs that were supposed to stabilise profits for developing countries eventually paid off, when a breakthrough in the difficult negotiations between global North and global South finally led to the adoption of Resolution 93 and with it to the creation of the *Integrated Programme for Commodities* (IPC) at UNCTAD's fourth session in 1976.[129] The IPC's objective was mainly to ensure market stabilisation for a group of 18 'core commodities'. This objective was to be achieved for one through the comprehensive Common Fund for Commodities (CFC) and by the negotiation of single commodity agreements for the other.

The CFC provided two main 'accounts': buffer stocks on the one hand and loans for commodity-specific development projects on the other. The negotiations on the CFC, however, proved to be difficult and therefore lasted until March 1979. Due to many states' hesitation in ratifying the respective agreement, it was not before 19 June 1989 that the CFC entered into force.[130] By this point in time, developing countries had already considerably lost faith in the new Fund not least given that most Western states refused to provide an amount of 'directly contributed capital'

---

[125] Desta (2010), para. 22.

[126] UN GA (1974) Res. 3281 (XXIX), 12 December 1974, https://www.un.org/ga/search/view_doc.asp?symbol=a/res/3281(XXIX) (last accessed 14 May 2021).

[127] The G77 was created at the end of the first UNCTAD session in 1964, G77 (2019) About, http://www.g77.org/doc/ (last accessed 14 May 2021).

[128] Gale and Haward (2011), p. 6.

[129] Cf. Weiss (2009), paras. 19–21.

[130] Ohler (2013), para. 2.

that would allow the CFC to fulfil its mandate.[131] A further reason why the CFC never reached its potential was the lack of dynamics concerning the conclusion of single agreements, the IPC's second strand. Given i.a. a lack of interest to enter into binding commodity agreements on the part of industrialised nations, only few new ICAs had been negotiated since the beginning of the 1980s.[132] Yet it came even worse for those that favoured market-interventionist approaches to commodity policy: Due i.a. to falling market prices, several ICAs had to seize the operations of their buffer stocks.[133] The International Tin Council (ITC), for instance, collapsed financially in 1985.[134] This was due for one to tin producers increasingly leaving or refraining from joining the agreement, which resulted in a decrease in the ITC's market share from 71% in 1981 to 57% by 1985.[135] Furthermore, several states such as the UK developed techniques on how to circumvent the ITC's rules and quotas, further weakening the functioning of the scheme.[136]

Additionally—and this applied to almost all buffer stocks—problems originated from the invention of synthetic substitutes such as plastics and aluminium that lead to a further downswing in global market prices.[137] In order to balance out these developments, the stock manager bought more and more tin—hoping for an increase in tin prices, which would mark the moment to sell the merchandise. However, due to the increased availability of cheap substitutes and the overall increase of global tin production, prices simply would not rise sufficiently.[138] As a consequence, on 24 October 1985, the ITC declared 'that it could no longer meet its financial obligations.'[139] For similar reasons effectively all operating buffer stocks were eliminated by the end of the 1990s.[140] Given that it was especially due to low commodity prices, on their part caused by technological progress and the development of substitute materials, as well as comportment of ICA member states that was undermining the operation of buffer stock that the seizure of their operations

---

[131] Cf. Pelikahn (1990), pp. 659–661.

[132] Weiss (2009), para. 23.

[133] Weiss (2009), para 23.

[134] Hartwig (2011), para. 7; Chandrasekhar (1989), pp. 309, 315.

[135] Chandrasekhar (1989), p. 313.

[136] Chandrasekhar (1989), p. 313 pointing to Chimni (1987), p. 200.

[137] Chandrasekhar (1989), p. 314; Hartwig (2011), para. 6.

[138] Chandrasekhar (1989), p. 315.

[139] Chandrasekhar (1989), p. 315, n 44.

[140] The buffer stock of the *International Cocoa Organisation* was eliminated in 1990; its accumulated stock sold until 1998: the buffer stock for rubber was eliminated in 1999, Weiss (2009), para. 23 n 34. See also UNCTAD (2016), p. 2: 'However, historically, only three ICAs (on coffee, on cocoa, and on natural rubber) were reasonably successful over limited periods of time. In the first two cases, international prices were maintained at "an adequate level" through retention schemes, while in the third one, the buffer stock was in place. In October 1999, the International Agreement on Natural Rubber, the last remaining by that time ICA with price-regulating mechanism, terminated its activities.'

occurred, it would, however, be premature to argue that market interventionist approaches as such are 'out-dated'.[141]

From their collapse, one cannot infer that market-interventionist mechanisms would be obsolete. In fact, the continued need for CDDCs to stabilise market prices today demonstrates the contrary:[142] the debate on how to adequately control commodity trade is still essential. What the collapse of the buffer stocks between 1985 and the new millennium illustrated instead, was the advent or reoccurrence—and continued dominance today—of the doctrine of (neo)liberalism. The reinforcement of the free trade agenda during the respective eras of 'Thatcherism' in the UK and 'Reaganomics' in the US,[143] may well constitute the aggregate root cause for the failure of the commodity policies advocated for by UNCTAD.[144] Under the free trade doctrine, ICAs were seen as improper interference with market forces.[145] Paradigmatically, the world would soon witness the emergence of a new institutional powerhouse of global trade substantially representing the neoliberal economic order: the GATT Uruguay round, which was launched in 1986 eventually lead to the creation of the World Trade Organisation (WTO) in 1995.[146]

2.2.4 The Phase of 'Post-Interventionism': Shift Towards Cooperative Agreements

As a consequence of abandoning their market-interventionist mechanisms, numerous International Commodity Organisations (ICOs)—the IOs administering respective ICAs—lost their main field of activity. Instead of abolishing these organisations—which over time had gathered substantial commodity-specific expertise–, their respective member states largely decided to keep the ICOs as fora for the exchange of information between producers and consumers. Some ICOs additionally provide services to their members, such as commodity-specific research. The originally market-interventionist ICAs have thus largely been transformed into

---

[141] To the contrary Schorkopf (2011), para. 46.

[142] On the desirability of market-interventionist mechanisms, cf. Gilbert (1996). Moreover, raising commodity prices can at all times bring about a strengthened negotiation position for these countries and therefore greater respect for potential price stabilisation measures. In this respect remarkable is the regulatory attention that the commodity sector has experienced since supply shortages with regard to non-energy minerals impended in view of Chinese export restrictions, cf. also Sect. 5.2.1. 2.3.1 below.

[143] Margaret Thatcher was appointed as UK Prime Minister on 4 May 1979, US president Ronald Reagan was elected on the 4 November 1980. On 'Reaganomics' and their effect on developing countries, cf. i.a. Tickner (1990).

[144] Cf. in the same vein also Desta (2010), para. 27: '...none of these market-intervention devices survived the ideological shift that took place in the 1980s[]'; Gale and Haward (2011), p. 6.

[145] Gale and Haward (2011), p. 6.

[146] Stoll (2014), para. 3.

what might most aptly be described as cooperation agreements.[147] As such, they exhibit more or less exclusively soft obligations and have largely lost their legally binding dimension.[148]

It seems obvious that commodity policy-making has shifted largely to other fora and mechanisms, such as the EU-ACP agreements or the WTO.[149] With the 'ideological shift' in the 1980s and the ensuing emergence of the WTO, ICOs today have largely become minor, commodity-specific fora that appear to play a rather peripheral role in GCG.[150] At the beginning of the new millennium, the proponents of NIEO thus had to clearly concede defeat in the face of the vigorous reawakening and ensuing institutionalisation of neoliberalism. However, not least due to the history of its emergence, developing countries remained suspicious of the new free trade agenda and the WTO as its primary organ:

> ...not only had industrialised countries presented them with take-it-or-leave-it positions on agriculture and intellectual property rights but the promised benefits that were to flow from the agreement failed to materialise, perpetuating the organisation's legitimacy crisis.[151]

This scepticism on the part of developing countries as well as the continued insistence on trade liberalization by industrialized nations, i.a. while maintaining subsidies for their agricultural commodities, led to what is generally being referred to as the 'deadlock' of the Doha Round of negotiations, which was initiated in 2001.[152] Whereas 'obituary notices' for the DDA may have been a little premature,[153] the fate of the talks still remains unclear despite recent advancements with regard to the crucial issue of export subsidies for agricultural commodities.[154] Overall, it appears

---

[147] Weiss (2009), para 24; Desta (2010), para. 27.

[148] On the current state of ICAs, cf. in detail Sect. 5.2.1 below.

[149] Weiss (2009), para. 25. However, on the hesitant stance of the WTO cf. shortly below.

[150] The function of ICOs and ICAs in GCG today will be subject to a detailed discussion in Sect. 5.2.1; how ICAs could be 'revived' to play a more substantial role in regulating commodity activity will be discussed in Sect. 5.2.2 below.

[151] Gale and Haward (2011), p. 6.

[152] Given its emphasis on securing trade liberalisation benefits for developing countries, the Doha Round is also being termed Doha Development Agenda (DDA), Gale and Haward (2011), p. 6.

[153] Cf., however, Kleimann and Guinan (2011).

[154] WTO (2015) Ministerial Decision of 19 December 2015, 'Nairobi package', WT/MIN(15)/45, cf. https://www.wto.org/english/news_e/news15_e/mc10_19dec15_e.htm accessed 24 February 2019; cf. already WTO (2013) Bali Ministerial Declaration of 7 December 2013, https://www.wto.org/english/thewto_e/minist_e/mc9_e/balideclaration_e.htm; see also Strubenhoff H (2016) The WTO's decision to end agricultural export subsidies is good news for farmers and consumers. Brookings, 8 February 2016, https://www.brookings.edu/blog/future-development/2016/02/08/the-wtos-decision-to-end-agricultural-export-subsidies-is-good-news-for-farmers-and-consumers/.
However, as Bardoneschi R (2017) Accelerating the elimination of export subsidies in agriculture. ICTSD, 30 October 2017, https://www.ictsd.org/opinion/accelerating-the-elimination-of-export-subsidies-in-agriculture (all last accessed 14 May 2021) highlights, almost no effective concessions by member states have thus far been made. He also refers to the 'soft law' nature of the Nairobi decision and suggests that states should include the provisions of the Nairobi package also in their schedule of concessions.

nebulous still today whether and to what extent the WTO will in the future make use of its mandate to actively shape commodity governance.[155]

Reluctance from states to openly pursue commodity governance along the legalistic lines of the WTO system may be due to a general perception of commodities being of too great strategic importance.[156] It is not least against this backdrop that the emergence of GCG, which was driven i.a. by a variety of multi-stakeholder initiatives, can be perceived.

2.2.5 The Appearance of GCG

As the examination of historical approaches to regulating international commodity activity has demonstrated, prior regulation was driven and shaped largely by motives of raising the economic benefits for the actors involved. GCG constitutes a fundamental departure from these approaches. Its disruptive feature lies in perceiving commodity activity not exclusively as an economic issue, but as a comprehensive regulatory challenge, which requires the consideration of its social and ecological prerequisites as well as effects.

Already Principle 2 of the 1972 Stockholm Declaration recognised the need for natural resources to be safeguarded for future generations through 'careful management or planning'. Gro Harlem Brundtland, who led the efforts of the World Commission on Environment and Development, which had been instituted by the UN General Assembly and mandated with the task to rethink the interrelatedness of the environment and development, already in 1991 pointed to the importance of 'strengthening commodity markets' in favour of developing countries in order to boost their SD.[157] In the same publication, then-president of the World Bank, Barber Conable, 'ushers in the era of sustainable development' by pointing to the significance of the management of natural resources for that purpose.[158]

Based on these developments and not least in view of a lack of comprehensive commodity policies being pursued by global institutions, starting in the 1990s more and more initiatives emerged that were seeking to standardise the commodity sector.[159] These so-called 'new governance' arrangements included particularly certification schemes and other voluntary initiatives created by business associations as well as civil society organisations, and partly also involved IOs.[160] Examples of

---

[155] Weiss (2009), para. 18 sees the WTO following in the—passive—footsteps of the GATT in this respect.

[156] Cf. with regard to the oil and gas sector Desta (2003), p. 529.

[157] Brundtland (1991), p. 30.

[158] Conable (1991), p. 32.

[159] Gale and Haward (2011), p. 3.

[160] Gale and Haward (2011), p. 3; on the emergence of today's understanding of what constitutes global governance and its objectives in general Commission on Global Governance (1995).

these early initiatives include the Forest Stewardship Council founded in 1993, the Marine Stewardship Council founded in 1996,[161] the Kimberley Process established in 2000 or the EITI, which was launched at the World Summit on Sustainable Development (WSSD) in Johannesburg in 2002.[162]

This trend continues until today, with now numerous standards, certification schemes, and other initiatives in place worldwide that are each tackling the commodity sector specifically. One of its most prominent proponents is the Natural Resource Governance Institute, which together with partner institutions in academia as well as civil society advocates vigorously for greater attention to the regulatory necessities in the commodity sector. Paradigmatic for the comprehensive policy approach it postulates, is its signature publication, the Natural Resource Charter, which was first launched in 2010. The Charter sets forth twelve precepts on how the development potential of resource wealth can best be harnessed.[163]

Moreover, in the past decade, one could also witness an increased attention to commodity activities from states and supranational organisations. Given the continued antagonisms between consumers in the global North and producers in the global South, reflected in the deadlock of the WTO negotiations, several Western nations took action on developing new, comprehensive commodity policy programs when China started to introduce restrictions on its commodity exports in 2008.[164] For instance, in 2008 the European Commission launched its Raw Materials Initiative, which is largely based on the three pillars of ensuring access to raw materials; setting the right framework in order to foster sustainable commodity supply from European sources; and boosting overall resource efficiency, i.a. through recycling and therefore decreasing import dependence.[165] The German government introduced its new commodity strategy, which is likewise particularly concerned with supply security regarding non-energetic mineral commodities, in 2010.[166] An update was presented in January 2020.[167] In Switzerland, several government branches joined forces in 2013 in order to compile a comprehensive report on the manifold economic, social, ecological, as well as financial implications of commodity policy.[168]

In 2012, the United Nations adopted its Report *The Future We Want*, in which it recognises sustainable natural resource management i.a. as an 'overarching

---

[161] Cf. Gale and Haward (2011), who discuss the emergence of GCG in light of these two schemes.

[162] On these and many more standards and guidelines, cf. Chap. 4 as well as the extensive TCL outline in the annex.

[163] NRGI (2014), p. 4.

[164] Cf. the US request for consultations, G/L/888, WT/DS394/1 of 25 June 2009, which lists the respective measures in detail. On the entire topic expertly Espa (2015). For a succinct account of the arising WTO disputes, cf. Sect. 4.3.2 below.

[165] European Raw Materials Initiative, European Commission (2008, 2011, 2013, 2014).

[166] BMWi (2010).

[167] Cf. BMWi (2020) Rohstoffstrategie der Bundesregierung, https://www.bmwi.de/Redaktion/DE/Publikationen/Industrie/rohstoffstrategie-der-bundesregierung.pdf?__blob=publicationFile&v=4 (last accessed 14 May 2021).

[168] FDFA, FDF, EAER (2013).

objective' and 'essential requirement' for SD.[169] Following these statements the world community in its 2015 resolution titled *Transforming Our World: the 2030 Agenda for Sustainable Development* envisions

> [a] world in which consumption and production patterns and use of all natural resources – from air to land, from rivers, lakes and aquifers to oceans and seas – are sustainable.[170]

According to SDG 12.2, the international community has committed to 'achiev [ing] the sustainable management and efficient use of natural resources' by 2030. The special advisor to the UN Secretary-General on the SDGs, Jeffrey Sachs, has alluded to the management of the planetary boundaries that exist with regard to commodity activity, and therefore the overall management of the sector, as being at the 'heart' of SD.[171] The EU has now linked all of its efforts in the context of the Raw Materials Initiative to the SDGs.[172]

Therefore, to my mind GCG can best be perceived as a commodity-directed emanation of the global SD agenda. Thus, it aims to integrate social and ecological challenges associated with economic objectives. This correlates with its principal task of ensuring a functional commodity sector—a task, which requires GCG to balance the interests associated with commodity activity.

2.3 Role of the Law

From a legal perspective, this imposes the question what the law can contribute to mastering the challenge of achieving this balance and thus ensuring a functional commodity sector?

---

[169] UN GA (2012) Resolution A/RES/66/288, 27 July 2012, The future we want. http://www.un. org/ga/search/view_doc.asp?symbol=A/RES/66/288&Lang=E (last accessed 14 May 2021), para. 4.

[170] UN GA (2015) Resolution A/RES/70/1, 25 September 2015, Transforming our world: the 2030 Agenda for Sustainable Development. http://www.un.org/ga/search/view_doc.asp?symbol=A/RES/70/1&Lang=E (last accessed 14 May 2021), para. 9.

[171] Sachs (2015), p. 181.

[172] European Commission (2019), Policy and strategy for raw materials, https://ec.europa.eu/growth/sectors/raw-materials/policy-strategy_en (last accessed 14 May 2021); cf. likewise UNDP (2016), as well as the commission's contribution to implementing the SDGs regarding measures derived from the Raw Materials Initiative, European Commission (2019), https://ec.europa.eu/docsroom/documents/25401/attachments/1/translations/en/renditions/native (last accessed 14 May 2021). Measures include i.a. support for the FORAM project, which intends to set up 'an EU-based platform of international experts' that makes 'the current complex maze of existing raw material related initiatives more effective. As such, the FORAM project will be the largest collaborative effort for raw materials strategy cooperation on a global level so far', FORAM, project, http://www.foramproject.net/index.php/project/ (last accessed 14 May 2021).

2.3.1 Purpose of the Law

According to Jhering, it is the purpose, which is responsible for the creation of all law. Without purpose, there would be no law. He defines the ultimate purpose of law in its role to safeguard living conditions for human society.[173] As Green points out, many traditional thinkers formulate *constitutive aims* of the law—only if a norm pursues such aims, it can be qualified as law. He points to Thomas Aquinas who defined the overall purpose of law, as 'an ordinance of reason made for the common good'. More recent views define the purpose of law as 'guiding conduct', 'coordinating activity for the common good', 'doing justice' or 'licensing coercion'.[174]

Hart states that he deems 'it quite vain to seek any more specific purpose which law as such serves beyond providing guides to human conduct and standards of criticism of such conduct.'[175] He thus describes the *purpose* of the law by pointing to one of its major *functions*—the provision of guidelines for human behaviour. According to Lauterpacht,

> [t]he function of law is to regulate the conduct of persons, natural or juridical, by reference to rules whose formal – as distinguished from their historical – source of validity lies, in the last resort, in a command imposed from outside.[176]

It is by this *externalisation* through law of what is legitimate and what is wrongful that we typically seek to ensure greater discipline of the addressees in their respect for rules. We create law in order to regulate behaviour in the most effective way possible.[177]

2.3.2 Law as the Catalyst of a Functional Commodity Sector

As we have learned, in the context of commodity activity human behaviour can be said to be regulated in the most effective way possible, where the five interests associated with it are balanced. This status describes the task—or constitutive aim—of GCG to ensure a functional commodity sector. The law can be a catalyst in this quest if and when it contributes to the *balancing* of the various interests of the diverse stakeholders of GCG. Thus, in order to be *effective* towards ensuring a functional commodity sector, the law needs to address the specific policy trade-offs that arise from commodity activity.

---

[173]Cf. Penski (2004), p. 406 pointing to von Jhering (1904), p. V.

[174]Green (2012), p. xxxiv.

[175]Hart (2012), p. 249.

[176]Lauterpacht (2011), p. 3.

[177]Cf. Vos (2013), p. 7, pointing to Lauterpacht; cf. Lauterpacht (2011), p. 3. On the interrelation between consensus and the effectiveness of the law Allott (1981).

The law is effective in contributing to a reasonably managed and thus functional commodity sector, where it provides answers to questions such as: How much to extract? Where to extract? How to extract? How to process or trade? How to make a decision to extract? How much to trade? How much and what to tax? What resources to protect? What land rights to protect? Where it cannot provide these answers, for instance since the privilege of ultimately answering them falls within the political domain, it is effective where it provides guidelines on how these questions should be answered. The type of norms that is required for the law to be a catalyst of GCG and thus of a functional commodity sector are 'balancing norms', which guide the balancing decisions in view of the policy trade-offs that arise from the five major interests associated with commodity activity.

2.3.3 The Effectiveness of the Legal Framework of GCG

In order to understand the contribution of the current legal framework of GCG to the goal of ensuring a functional commodity sector, we first need to clarify its scope and content. This will be the subject of our conceptualisation of TCL in Chap. 3 below—which thus shall be in itself a first contribution to fostering the effectiveness of the current framework.[178]

In Chap. 4 we will analyse in more detail what can be said about the effectiveness of the current TCL framework overall. A word of caution in this respect shall be shared. While our analysis is based on a comprehensive appraisal of the regulatory instruments and standards applicable to commodity activity, a well-founded quality assessment of this vast body of law would require extensive analysis, e.g. based on the possibilities provided by computational text analysis.[179] The statements on the effectiveness of the TCL framework we provide in Chap. 4 below therefore do not claim to be absolute, but rather constitute an approximation to this complex question.

References

Literature and IO/NGO Publications

Allott A (1981) The effectiveness of law. Valparaiso Univ Law Rev 15(2):229–242
Arezki R, Hadri K, Loungani P, Rao Y (2013) Testing the Prebisch-Singer hypothesis since 1650: evidence from panel techniques that allow for multiple breaks. IMF Working Paper, WP/13/180,

---

[178] On the related work of the ILA Committee on the Role of International Law in Sustainable Natural Resources Management for Development, which the author had the honour of modestly contributing to, cf. the respective 2020 Final Report and Guidelines, ILA (2020).

[179] Fundamentally on this 'future of legal analysis', Livermore and Rockmore (2019).

15 August 2013. https://www.imf.org/~/media/Websites/IMF/imported-full-text-pdf/external/
pubs/ft/wp/2013/_wp13180.ashx
AU (2009) Africa mining vision. February 2009. http://www.africaminingvision.org/amv_
resources/AMV/Africa_Mining_Vision_English.pdf
Bakker K (2007) The 'commons' versus the 'commodity': alter-globalization, anti-privatization
and the human right to water in the global south. Antipode 39(3):430–455
Bellmann C (2016) Trade and investment frameworks in extractive industries: challenges and
options. E15 Expert Group on Trade and Investment in Extractive Industries, Policy Options
Paper, E15Initiative, International Centre for Trade and Sustainable Development (ICTSD) and
World Economic Forum, Geneva. http://e15initiative.org/wp-content/uploads/2015/09/E15_
ICTSD_Trade_Investment_Frameworks_Extractive_Industries_report_2015.pdf
BMWi (2010) Rohstoffstrategie der Bundesregierung: Sicherung einer nachhaltigen
Rohstoffversorgung Deutschlands mit nicht-energetischen mineralischen Rohstoffen. October
2010. http://www.rohstoffwissen.org/fileadmin/downloads/160720.rohstoffstrategie-der-
bundesregierung.pdf
Bonnitcha J (2016) Foreign investment, development and governance: what international invest-
ment law can learn from the empirical literature on investment. J Int Dispute Settlement (JIDS)
7(1):31–54
Brown Weiss E, Somarajah A (2013) Good governance. In: Wolfrum R (ed) Max Planck encyclopaedia of public international law. Oxford University Press, Oxford
Brundtland GH (1991) Our common future. In: Tolba KM, Biswas AK (eds) Earth and us:
population – resources – environment – development. Butterworth-Heinemann, Oxford
Bürgi Bonanomi E et al (2015) The commodity sector and related governance challenges from a
sustainable development perspective: the example of Switzerland. CDE WTI IWE Joint Working Paper No. 1, 14 July 2015. https://boris.unibe.ch/71327/1/WTI_CDE_IWE%20Working%
20paper%20July%202015_The%20Commodity%20Sector%20and%20Related%20Gov....pdf
Buszewski S, Martini S, Rathke H (2016) Freihandel vs. Demokratie: Grundsätze transnationaler
Legitimation: Partizipation, Reversibilität, Transparenz. Nomos, Baden-Baden
Calder J (2014) Administering fiscal regimes for extractive industries: a handbook. IMF. http://
eduart0.tripod.com/sitebuildercontent/sitebuilderfiles/AdministeringFiscalRegimesForEI.pdf
Chandrasekhar S (1989) Cartel in a can: the financial collapse of the International Tin Council.
Northwest J Int Law Bus 10(2):309–332
Chimni BS (1987) International commodity agreements. Croom Helm, London
Clark EA, Lesourd JB, Thiéblemont R (2001) International commodity trading: physical and
derivative markets. Wiley, Chichester
Commission on Global Governance (1995) Our global neighbourhood. Oxford University Press,
Oxford
Conable B (1991) Ushering in the era of sustainable development. In: Tolba KM, Biswas AK (eds)
Earth and us: population – resources – environment – development. Butterworth-Heinemann,
Oxford
Dann P (2013) The law of development cooperation: a comparative analysis of the World Bank, the
EU and Germany. Cambridge University Press, Cambridge
Davis GA (1995) Learning to love the Dutch disease: evidence from the mineral economies. World
Dev 23(10):1765–1779
Desai D, Jarvis M (2012) Governance and accountability in extractive industries: theory and
practice at the World Bank. J Energy Nat Resour Law (JERL) 30:101–128
Desta MG (2003) The organization of petroleum exporting countries, the World Trade Organiza-
tion, and regional trade agreements. J World Trade (JWT) 37(3):523–551
Desta MG (2010) Commodities, international regulation of production and trade. In: Wolfrum R
(ed) Max Planck encyclopaedia of public international law. Oxford University Press, Oxford
EITI (2019) The EITI Standard 2019. EITI International Secretariat, 15 October 2019. https://eiti.
org/sites/default/files/documents/eiti_standard_2019_en_a4_web.pdf

Espa I (2015) Export restrictions on critical minerals and metals. Cambridge University Press, Cambridge

Espa I, Oehl M (2018) Rules and practices of international law for the sustainable management of mineral commodities, including nickel, copper, bauxite and a special focus on rare earths. In: ILA Sydney conference report of the committee on the role of international law in sustainable natural resource management for development, second report of the committee, 2016–2018, pp 5–11. https://ila.vettoreweb.com/Storage/Download.aspx?DbStorageId=11926&StorageFileGuid=dc356ab0-e751-4f8b-a3c5-a41d362cb732

European Commission (2008) The raw materials initiative - meeting our critical needs for growth and jobs in Europe. Communication from the commission to the council and the European parliament. COM(2008) 699 final. https://eur-lex.europa.eu/LexUriServ/LexUriServ.do?uri=COM:2008:0699:FIN:en:PDF

European Commission (2011) Tackling the challenges in commodity markets and on raw materials: communication from the commission to the European parliament, the council, the European economic and social committee and the committee of the regions. COM(2011) 25 final. http://www.europarl.europa.eu/meetdocs/2009_2014/documents/com/com_com(2011)0025_/com_com(2011)0025_en.pdf

European Commission (2013) On the implementation of the Raw Materials Initiative. COM(2013) 442 final. https://eur-lex.europa.eu/LexUriServ/LexUriServ.do?uri=COM:2013:0442:FIN:EN:PDF

European Commission (2014) On the review of the list of critical raw materials for the EU and the implementation of the Raw Materials Initiative. COM(2014) 297 final. https://eur-lex.europa.eu/legal-content/EN/TXT/PDF/?uri=CELEX:52014DC0297&from=SK

FAO (2016) Illegal, unreported, and unregulated fishing. I6069E/1/09.16, Rome. http://www.fao.org/3/a-i6069e.pdf

Farooki M, Kaplinsky R (2012) The impact of China on global commodity prices: the global reshaping of the resource sector. Routledge, London

FDFA, FDF, EAER (2013) Background report: commodities. 27 March 2013. http://www.news.admin.ch/NSBSubscriber/message/attachments/30136.pdf

Frankel J (2012) The natural resource curse: a survey of diagnoses and some prescriptions. HKS Faculty Research, Working Paper Series RWP12-014. http://nrs.harvard.edu/urn-3:HUL.InstRepos:8694932

Gale F, Haward M (2011) Global commodity governance. Palgrave Macmillan, Basingstoke

Gilbert CL (1996) International commodity agreements: an obituary notice. World Dev 24(1):1–19

Green L (2012) Introduction. In: Hart HLA (ed) Concept of law, 3rd edn. Oxford University Press, Oxford

Gunderson R (2017) Commodification of nature. The international encyclopaedia of geography. Wiley, Hoboken

Hart HLA (2012) Concept of law, 3rd edn. Oxford University Press, Oxford

Hartwig M (2011) The International Tin Council. Max Planck encyclopaedia of public international law. Oxford University Press, Oxford

Hauert J (2016) Ergebnis- und prozessorientierte Stabilisierungsmechanismen und staatliches Regulierungsinteresse. Nomos, Baden-Baden

Hirschman AO (1968) The political economy of import-substituting industrialization in Latin America. Q J Econ LXXXII(1):1–32

Hotelling H (1931) The economics of exhaustible resources. J Polit Econ 39(2):137–175

Hummels D, Lugovskyy V, Skiba A (2009) The trade reducing effects of market power in international shipping. J Dev Econ 89:84–97

ILA (2020) Kyoto Conference, Committee on the Role of International Law in Sustainable Natural Resources Management for Development, Final Report, Guidelines. https://ila.vettoreweb.com/Storage/Download.aspx?DbStorageId=25358&StorageFileGuid=390b1c64-481d-44fa-8257-b93c78afd534

ILO (1943) Intergovernmental Commodity Control Agreements. Montréal

IMF (2012) Fiscal regimes for extractive industries: design and implementation. 15 August 2012. https://www.imf.org/external/np/pp/eng/2012/081512.pdf

Kennedy D (2013) Law and the political economy of the world. In: de Búrca G, Kilpatrick C, Scott J (eds) Critical legal perspectives on global governance: Liber Amicorum David M Trubek. Hart, Oxford

Khan KR (1982) The law and organisation of international commodity agreements. Martinus Nijhoff, The Hague

Killinger S (2003) The World Bank's non-political mandate. Heymann, Köln

Kleimann D, Guinan J (2011) The Doha Round: an obituary. European University Institute, Robert Schuman Centre for Advanced Studies, Global Governance Programme Policy Brief No. 1/2011. http://ssm.com/abstract=1881069

Krappel F (1975) Die Havanna-Charta und die Entwicklung des Weltrohstoffhandels. Duncker & Humblot, Berlin

Ladeur KH (2010) Governance, theory of. In: Wolfrum R (ed) Max Planck encyclopaedia of public international law. Oxford University Press, Oxford

Landry D (2018) The risks and rewards of resource-for-infrastructure deals: lessons from the Congo's Sicomines agreement. Resour Policy 58:165–174

Lauterpacht H (2011) The function of law in the international community. Oxford University Press, Oxford

Law AD (1975) International commodity agreements. Lexington Books, Lexington

Livermore MA, Rockmore DN (2019) Law as data: computation, text, and the future of legal analysis. SFI Press, Santa Fe

Menkel-Meadow C (2011) Why and how to study transnational law. UC Irvine Law Rev 1(1):97–129

Mikesell R (1963) Commodity agreements and aid to developing countries. Law Contemp Probl 28(2):294–312

Moffat K, Zhang A (2014) The paths to social licence to operate: an integrative model explaining community acceptance of mining. Resour Policy 39:61–70

Morris M, Fessehaie J (2014) The industrialisation challenge for Africa: towards a commodities based industrialisation path. J African Trade 1(1):25–36

Muchlinski PT (2007) Multinational enterprises and the law, 2nd edn. Blackwell Publishers, Oxford

Nickel EH (1995) The definition of a mineral. Can Mineral 33:689–690

NRGI (2014) Natural Resource Charter, 2nd edition. https://resourcegovernance.org/sites/default/files/documents/nrcj1193_natural_resource_charter_19.6.14.pdf

NRGI (2015) The resource curse: the political and economic challenges of natural resource wealth. NRGI reader, March 2015. https://resourcegovernance.org/sites/default/files/documents/nrgi_primer_nrc-decision-chain.pdf

OECD (2014) Export restrictions in raw materials trade: facts, fallacies and better practices. http://www.oecd.org/tad/benefitlib/export-restrictions-raw-materials-2014.pdf

Oehl M (2019) The role of sustainable development in natural resources law. In: Bungenberg M, Krajewski M, Tams C, Terhechte JP, Ziegler AR (eds) European yearbook of international economic law 2018. Springer, pp 3–38

Ohler C (2013) Common fund for commodities. In: Wolfrum R (ed) Max Planck encyclopaedia of public international law. Oxford University Press, Oxford

Pelikahn HM (1990) Internationale Rohstoffabkommen. Nomos, Baden-Baden

Penski U (2004) Der Zweck des Rechtes ist das Recht — Zur Teleologie und Selbstbezüglichkeit des Rechts. Arch Philos Law Soc Philos 90(3):406–418

Perman R et al (2011) Natural resource and environmental economics, 4th edn. Addison Wesley, Boston

Prakash O (1985) The Dutch East India Company and the economy of Bengal, 1630–1720. Princeton University Press, Princeton

Radetzki M, Warrell L (2016) A handbook of primary commodities in the global economy, 2nd edn. Cambridge University Press, Cambridge

Reynolds PD (1978) International commodity agreements and the common fund. Praeger, New York

Riedel E (2005) The human right to water. In: von Arnauld A, Matz-Lück N, Odendahl K (eds) Veröffentlichungen des Walther-Schücking-Instituts für Internationales Recht an der Universität Kiel, Festschrift Delbrück, Bd. 155. Duncker & Humblot, Berlin, pp 585–606

Sacerdoti G (2015) New International Economic Order (NIEO). In: Wolfrum R (ed) Max Planck encyclopaedia of public international law. Oxford University Press, Oxford

Sachs J (2015) The age of sustainable development. Columbia University Press

Sachs JD, Warner A (2001) Resource curse. Eur Econ Rev 45(4–6):827–838

Schlemmer-Schulte S (2014) International Monetary Fund, structural adjustment programme. In: Wolfrum R (ed) Max Planck encyclopaedia of public international law. Oxford University Press, Oxford

Schorkopf F (2011) Europäische Rohstoffverwaltung. In: Terhechte JP (ed) Verwaltungsrecht der Europäischen Union. Nomos, Baden-Baden, pp 811–835

Schrijver N (1997) Sovereignty over natural resources: balancing rights and duties. Cambridge University Press, Cambridge

Singh N (2016) The human right to water. Springer, Cham

Spohr M (2016) Human rights risk in mining: a baseline study. German Federal Institute for Geosciences and Natural Resources (BGR), Max-Planck-Foundation for International Peace and the Rule of Law (MPFPR). https://www.bmz.de/rue/includes/downloads/BGR_MPFPR__ 2016__Human_Rights_Risks_in_Mining.pdf

Stoll PT (2014) World Trade Organisation. In: Wolfrum R (ed) Max Planck encyclopaedia of public international law. Oxford University Press, Oxford

Tickner (1990) Reaganomics & the Third World: lessons from the founding fathers. Polity 23(1):53–76

Toye J, Toye R (2003) The origins and interpretation of the Prebisch-Singer thesis. Hist Polit Econ 35(3):437–467

UN (1951) Measures for international economic stability. Report by a group of experts appointed by the secretary-general, 27 November 1951, UN Doc. E/2156(ST/ECA/13), United Nations, New York. https://digitallibrary.un.org/record/816049/files/E_2156_ST_ECA_13-EN.pdf

UN (2002) Berlin II Guidelines for Mining and Sustainable Development. https://commdev.org/ userfiles/files/903_file_Berlin_II_Guidelines.pdf

UN GA (2015) Transforming our world: the 2030 agenda for sustainable development. Resolution A/RES/70/1, 25 September 2015. http://www.un.org/ga/search/view_doc.asp?symbol=A/RES/ 70/1&Lang=E

UNCTAD (2012) Commodities and development report (April 2012) UNCTAD/SUC/2011/9 x. http://unctad.org/en/PublicationsLibrary/suc2011d9_en.pdf

UNCTAD (2013) Facts and figures on commodities and commodities trade. UNCTAD/PRESS/IN/ 2013/002, 13 March 2013. https://unctad.org/en/pages/InformationNoteDetails.aspx? OriginalVersionID=38

UNCTAD (2016) A brief on international commodity bodies. Updated on 1 February 2016. https:// unctad.org/Sections/ditc_commb/docs/suc2016_InternationalCommsBodies_en.pdf

UNCTAD (2017) Commodities and Development Report. UNCTAD/SUC/2017/1. https://unctad. org/en/PublicationsLibrary/suc2017d1_en.pdf

UNCTAD (2018) Forging a path beyond borders: the global south. UNCTAD/OSG/2018/1, United Nations, New York. https://unctad.org/en/PublicationsLibrary/osg2018d1_en.pdf

UNDP (2016) Mapping mining to the Sustainable Development Goals: an atlas. White paper, July 2016. http://www.undp.org/content/dam/undp/library/Sustainable%20Development/Extrac tives/Mapping_Mining_SDGs_An_Atlas.pdf

Van de Walle N (2001) African economies and the politics of permanent crisis: 1979–1999. Cambridge University Press, Cambridge

von Jhering R (1904) Der Zweck im Recht. Zweiter Band. In: Helfer C (ed) Reprint of fourth edition of 1904, 1970. Georg Olms, Hildesheim

Vos JA (2013) The function of public international law. TMC Asser-Springer, The Hague
Weiss F (2009) Internationale Rohstoffmärkte. In: Tietje C (ed) Internationales Wirtschaftsrecht. De Gruyter, Berlin, pp 276–286
Wilhelm MT (2014) 'All' is not everything: the Pennsylvania Supreme Court's restriction of natural gas conveyances in *Butler v. Charles Powers Estate ex rel. Warren*. Villanova Law Rev 59: 375–407
World Bank (1989) Sub-Saharan Africa: from crisis to sustainable growth. Stock #11349, November 1989. http://documents.worldbank.org/curated/en/498241468742846138/pdf/multi0page.pdf
WTO (2010) World Trade Report 2010.https://www.wto.org/english/res_e/booksp_e/anrep_e/world_trade_report10_e.pdf
WTO (2014) World Trade Report 2014. WTO Publications 2014. https://www.wto.org/english/res_e/booksp_e/world_trade_report14_e.pdf

Cases

WTO DSB (2004) *United States – Final Countervailing Duty Determination with Respect to Certain Softwood Lumber from Canada* (*'Softwood Lumber IV'*), report of the Appellate Body, adopted 19 January 2004, WT/DS257/AB/R, https://www.wto.org/english/tratop_e/dispu_e/257abr_e.doc

Chapter 3
Conceptualising TCL

This chapter first shares additional thoughts on the purpose and legitimacy (Sect. 3.1) of our conceptualisation of TCL before presenting the organisational framework of TCL (Sect. 3.2) as well as the sources, structure, and application of its normative substance (Sect. 3.3).

3.1 The Purpose of TCL

As we have discussed above, we are conceptualising TCL as the field of law governing commodity activities in order to gain a better understanding of the applicable framework and to ultimately assess its effectiveness. This approach may raise questions regarding the legitimacy of our undertaking: Is it necessary to conceptualise a new field of law?

A look in the literature reveals that conceptualising fields of law is a comparatively 'free' discipline, meaning that there is little to no dogmatic guidance on why or how it should be performed. In fact, some nineteenth century scholars have argued that the search for the 'true scientific division of the legal field' is tantamount to attempting to find the philosopher's stone because just like this item steeped in legend—it does not exist.[1] Based on this observation, Mariner states that it 'appears that the division of legal principles into fields of law remains a function of the purpose for which division is useful.'[2] Thus, within the literature one can discern roughly four different—strongly interlinked—purposes for conceptualisations of new fields of law, namely *accessibility*, *coherence*, *effectiveness* and *political cause*.

---

[1] Mariner (2009), p. 80 quoting Bishop (1868), p. 221: 'Still, as a matter of practical convenience, we may divide off the legal field in various ways, as may best suit the particular purpose of the division, or our tastes.'

[2] Mariner (2009), p. 81 goes on to state: 'Or perhaps it's just a matter of taste'.

© The Author(s) 2022
M. E. Oehl, *Sustainable Commodity Use*, EYIEL Monographs - Studies in European and International Economic Law 21, https://doi.org/10.1007/978-3-030-89496-2_3

Sherwin sees the purpose of a classification scheme in its function to 'provide a vocabulary and grammar that can make law more *accessible* and understandable to those who must use and apply it...'[3] Mariner insofar highlights how frequent treatises were in nineteenth century US scholarship that arranged norms according to the subject matter they were applicable to e.g., the law of highways, of railways, and of telegraphs.[4] The fact that repeatedly in the past scholars have sought to conceptualise fields of law in such manner may well be understood as an indication of the usefulness of even these, conceptually speaking, rather simple approaches. Even in instances where such taxonomy may lack any apparent *doctrinal* value, it may still render the rules, which apply to the respective subject matter *clearer* and more comprehensible. One of the aims of conceptualising TCL is to display the current legal framework of GCG, including its deficits and regulatory gaps.[5] Thus, it aims to render the inter- and transnational norms regulating the commodity sector more *accessible* for academics, practitioners, government officials, and other stakeholders dealing with the regulation of commodity activities.

As Aagaard puts it, '[t]axonomy inevitably and inherently is a quest for *coherence*'.[6] In respect to a legal field, he defines 'coherence as the strength, simplicity, and predominance of the field's patterns'.[7] Ruger speaks of the 'dramatic potential for explanation and illumination', which coherence entails.[8] Given the 'unified, predictable and rational' account of the law that it promises,[9] it facilitates the study and application of the respective legal field,[10] thus contributing also to the purpose of accessibility discussed above. Yet, Ruger also questions the 'orthodox conception' of coherence, which he defines as consisting of

---

[3] Sherwin (2008), p. 119; emphasis added. Cf. Tai (2015), p. 123.

[4] Mariner (2009), p. 79.

[5] It shall be mentioned here that this endeavour is not entirely new. In fact, a group of German researchers in the 1970s launched a 10-year research project on 'International Commodity Law' (Internationales Rohstoffrecht), which was aimed at analysing the legal frameworks applicable to various commodity activity-related challenges, including investment and fiscal law regime. The project was led by the hypothesis 'daß die systematische und detaillierte Erforschung eines wichtigen Teilbereichs des Internationalen Wirtschaftsrechts gehaltvollere Aussagen über diesen zunehmend wichtigeren Rechtsbereich erlauben könnte als die bis dahin herrschende Diskussion über allgemeine Thesen und Gegenthesen zur "Neuen Weltwirtschafsordnung"[]', Mertens and Spindler (1989), p. 526; on the results of the research project overall, cf. Jaenicke et al. (1977–1986); likewise resulting from this research project and a corresponding conference volume, notably taking a *transnational* perspective Buxbaum (1988).

[6] Aagaard (2010), p. 229. Emphasis added.

[7] Aagaard (2010), p. 231.

[8] Ruger (2008), p. 96; cf. Aagaard (2010), p. 230.

[9] Saiman (2007), p. 511; cf. Aagaard (2010), p. 230.

[10] Aagaard (2010), p. 230 notes additionally that the 'archetypal common law fields', which constitute the central fields of study in the respective legal education 'are often characterized by strongly coherent, even essentialist, models'.

(1) a reductionist focus on internal logic; (2) a focus on essential legal form; (3) an emphasis on linear historical development; and (4) a high level of institutional specification and centralization.[11]

He emphasises that the dominant conception of coherence is itself the result of methodological choices that have been made by legal scholars in the past century. Therefore, he advocates for relativising the conventional account of coherence in favour of a more flexible understanding.[12] Moreover, the 'quest for coherence' may also cause disadvantages in view of the final taxonomy of the field. It can namely lead to oversimplification i.e., the creation of an 'appearance of coherence' where no coherence actually exists.[13] Furthermore, given that incoherence illustrates a lack of consensus among lawmakers, the attempt to create coherence through 'internal logic' may only cause the law-making institutions to push the coherence to other areas of law.[14] Finally, it may also discourage experimentation in law-making.[15]

The aim of coherence often corresponds to the purpose of *effectiveness*. According to Ruhl and Salzmann, the creation of a new field of law can 'ensure effectiveness by reorienting laws and policies in a more productive structure.'[16] Sherwin states that classifications can 'make[] it easier for lawyers to argue effectively about the normative aspects of law, for judges to explain their decisions, and for actors to coordinate their activities in response to law.'[17] In the event that specialised technical or deep knowledge arises, creating a new field of law, instead of 'forc[ing] an existing field to morph itself to absorb the topic whole', may further contribute to regulatory efficiency—and thus ultimately effectiveness.[18] Our conceptualisation of TCL seeks to inspire subsequent international scholarship as well as regulatory endeavours, which aim to elaborate the existing regulatory framework. It therefore is intended to ultimately foster the *effectiveness* of the law regulating the commodity sector. This holds true in regard to all transnational, domestic or any other norms, which together form the overall legal framework of particularly *trans*national commodity activities. In this connection, the standards that TCL comprises could later be integrated in e.g. domestic legal orders. Instead of 'forcing' established fields of international law to 'absorb the topic whole', TCL adverts to alternative regulatory options. The organisational framework we provide

---

[11]Ruger (2008), p. 629.

[12]Ruger (2008), p. 648 concludes that '[h]ealth law unquestionably falls short of many of the attributes of field coherence that comprise the conventional account, and in my view will continue to do so given the basic attributes of the field. But to say as much ought not to also implicate a normative judgment about the field's intelligibility or ultimate status within the legal academy.'

[13]Aagaard (2010), p. 233.

[14]Aagaard (2010), p. 235.

[15]Aagaard (2010), p. 235.

[16]Ruhl and Salzman (2013), p. 989.

[17]Sherwin (2008), p. 119; cf. Tai (2015), p. 123.

[18]Ruhl and Salzman (2013), p. 989.

may serve as a guide in logically arranging the norms of TCL, thus fostering its *coherence* and therefore further contributing to its effectiveness.

The call for redefining the canonically accepted fields of law in the interest of a greater degree of effectiveness, can also be witnessed in Meessen's work. In his view, instead of maintaining the traditional arrangement of norms according to, first, the level of sources (international, supranational, transnational, domestic law), and second to their legal tradition (e.g. HR or environmental law), we should more strongly emphasise the *factual social behaviour* that these norms are governing in our classifications of the law.[19] Meessen, referring to economic law, thus advocates for the conceptualisation of fields of law, which correspond to day-to-day issues in human interactions, such as franchise law or the law governing the closing times of businesses.[20] On an 'intermediary level', he proposes 'globalized market law', which ought to comprise trade liberalisation law, transnational capital and labour law, transnational investment and establishment law, as well as domestic competition, privatisation and deregulation laws.[21] He concludes that for fields of law to be more relevant—and thus effective—they need to be designed with sufficient, for one, *reference to the factual problem at hand* and,[22] for the other, *closeness to reality*.[23]

With Meessen, the taxonomer deems the conceptualisation of this field of law around the specific factual context, policy trade-offs, interests and legal doctrine of commodity activities as a legal taxonomy, which meets these requirements. The factual governance challenges that arise in the commodity sector occur in connection with a distinguishable social behaviour—commodity activity. Whereas these challenges involve various subject matters that are being addressed by separate branches of international law, such as Human Rights, international environmental law, world trade law and international investment law, none of these branches exhibit sufficient closeness to the factual context, interests and policy trade-offs of the commodity sector. Moreover, they are lacking the necessary coherence and consistency to effectively address policy trade-offs. Whereas the established fields of international

---

[19] Meessen (2001).

[20] Meessen (2001), pp. 44–45.

[21] Meessen (2001), pp. 43–44 also points to the fact that the need to be aware of the legal traditions and dogmatics underlying the norms, which we are reconceptualising, still persists; corresponding methodology in e.g., the interpretation of international agreements on the one hand and EU law on the other, needs to be respected. Restructuring legal fields therefore not only requires a rigorous research of the relevant legal sources but also needs to be mindful of the dogmatic origins of the respective rules. Meessen (2001), p. 47 in this connection alludes to the necessity of cultivating 'international and comparative legal theory'—a legal theory that is mindful of and therefore reconciles comparative, international, supranational, and transnational law and which needs to be 'prefixed' to newly arranged legal fields. Elaborating such legal theory constitutes a challenge for legal scholarship, which Meessen (2001), p. 47 describes as 'enormous'.

[22] Meessen (2001), p. 44: 'Recht muss daher so ausgelegt und angewandt werden, dass es seine Fähigkeit zur Regelung und Steuerung sozialen Verhaltens durch seinen inhaltlichen Problembezug unter Beweis stellt.'

[23] Meessen (2001), p. 47.

law may serve to adequately balance *some* of these trade-offs, they fail to do so with regard to others.[24] TCL is intended to fill this gap by emphasising the importance of introducing commodity-directed rules. Insofar, while the conceptualisation of TCL is primarily *descriptive* in nature in that it portrays direct as well as unintentional TCL,[25] the taxonomy presented here naturally also bears a *prescriptive* element.[26] As such, for the purposes of effectiveness, our conceptualisation of TCL will not be limited to a display of the current legal framework, but—again in the tradition of prescriptive legal taxonomies—provide suggestions for creating greater coherence of the law applicable to commodity activities.[27]

Finally, the conceptualisation of a new field of law can 'provide a forceful *political* statement' regarding the importance of the respective area.[28] Ruhl and Salzmann highlight how several social movements were accompanied or eventually resulted in the emergence of new fields of law, such as environmental law or LGBTIQ law, a current example being the one of disaster law.[29] Likewise, Tannenbaum emphasises the activist origins of animal law.[30] Understood in this way, the creation of a new field of law is meant to pave the way towards greater academic, practical and political attention to the particular topic at hand. In academia, apart from the intensified scholarly analysis of the issue it is supposed to generate, the conceptualisation is particularly also meant to have an *educational* effect—through the integration of respective courses in law school curricula, future generations of lawyers shall be trained to think of the field as an important, legitimate area of practice.[31]

Again, political reasons for the conceptualisation of a field of law often cross-fertilise other purposes, such as accessibility, effectiveness and coherence. It may be true that to some degree, every definition of a legal field bears political motives. Whereas they may typically be less dominant with regard to fields, which exhibit conventional doctrinal coherence, such as torts or contract law, the emergence of other fields is more clearly lead by political motives.[32] Yet, this does not imply that one can infer a lack of methodological legitimacy—or coherence—from a strong political motivation or vice versa. To the contrary, where the political will to regulate is particularly strong, it is more likely that lawmakers are going to establish a comprehensive, coherent legal framework.

---

[24] On direct and unintentional TCL as well as the regulatory gaps that remain, cf. Chap. 4 below.

[25] On this distinction, see Sect. 4.2 below.

[26] Cf. Aagaard (2010), p. 240.

[27] Cf. in detail Chap. 5 below.

[28] Ruhl and Salzman (2013), p. 988. Emphasis added.

[29] Ruhl and Salzman (2013), p. 988.

[30] Tannenbaum (2013), pp. 899–906.

[31] Ruhl and Salzman (2013), p. 988.

[32] Cf. however on the origins of e.g. the German Civil Code, which naturally need to be perceived also against the backdrop of conflicting political interests, Riegert (1970), pp. 54–58.

Beyond the examples already mentioned above, many other legal fields have been established in the past roughly half century for more or less political reasons.[33] In the 1960s, international investment law was developed out of a set of norms dealing with the so-called 'diplomatic protection' of the properties of nationals living and/or exercising business activities abroad.[34] Initially due to efforts by mainly Western governments, a net of bilateral investment treaties was created, which in turn emerged to a proper field of international law. Other examples on a rather domestic level, yet with relevance globally, include the law of internet technology or cyberlaw,[35] which seeks to increase scholarly, political and overall attention to the effects of IT on the law and vice versa;[36] as well as consumer protection law, which, given systemic information and economic asymmetries between consumers and producer companies seeks to implement specific protection mechanisms in favour of the former.[37]

A further example is the one of International Development Law (IDL).[38] The reasons for its creation were expressly 'politically committed'. IDL is supposed to challenge classical international law in order 'to work towards the reduction of inequalities and the realization of a new order.'[39] This new order would measure all norms and institutions of international law according to their contribution to the alleviation of poverty and underdevelopment.[40] As such, the 'particular merit' of IDL is said to relate to the introduction of 'the economic factor and level of development into the legal analysis and evaluation of the relations between States.'[41]

As a consequence, IDL seeks to shift the focus away from a purely 'formalistic' analysis of the norms in place and towards a perception, which appreciates the power

---

[33] On a potential 'law of globalization' Koh (2007), p. 572: 'While sometimes derided as the proverbial "Law of the Horse," one of the analytic challenges facing the law of globalization is asking whether there is "in fact a distinctive, emerging law of which topics like human rights and international business transaction are a part."'

[34] Cf. e.g. Vandevelde (2005), pp. 158–161; comprehensively Hobe (2015).

[35] Cf. already the famous debate on its nature as a 'law of the horse' spurred by the remarks by Easterbrook (1996).

[36] Cf. Lessig (1999), explicitly replying to Easterbrook (1996).

[37] Cf. Rösler (2007), pp. 497–501; on the origins of EU consumer protection law, cf. Weatherill (2013), pp. 5–15.

[38] It is, in fact, debated whether IDL constitutes a separate branch of IL. While some categorise it either as a sub-branch of public international law or international economic law, others speak of its 'singularity' given its distinct objective, Mahiou (2013), para. 8.

[39] Mahiou (2013), para. 9; cf. in this respect also the TWAIL movement e.g., the strong stance by Mutua and Anghie (2000). Both schools of thought can be perceived in context with the struggle for a NIEO, cf. Sect. 2.2.3 above.

[40] Mahiou (2013), para. 12.

[41] Mahiou (2013), para. 13. Furthermore, IDL also challenges international legal scholarship, which it deems to be 'only neutral in appearance' since the discussion and analysis of international norms would automatically entail a 'siding with the status quo' given that these rules have generally been elaborated primarily by the dominant centre and therefore imposed onto a dominated periphery, Mahiou (2013), para. 9.

imbalances between states with more and those with less influence on the design of international norms:

> The question of whether international law succeeds in creating a balance between the formal legal equality of all States and the de facto inequality of their relative power is fully addressed by international development law, which takes the equity factor into account while endeavouring to give content to an overall strategy of development.[42]

The taxonomer does not seek to obscure that the overall purpose of our updated conceptualisation of TCL is, in the tradition of i.a. IDL, and in view of the pivotal challenge of GCG to establish a functional commodity sector,[43] also *politically committed*. TCL shall translate the rapidly intensifying efforts in national, supranational, and global governance to subject commodity activities to a more vigorous regulatory framework into concrete implications for international legal doctrine.[44] Moreover, it intends to inspire academics as well as future generations of lawyers to consider TCL as an important area of research and practice.[45]

3.2   The Organisational Framework of Commodity Law

Now how do we move from identifying the purpose of our conceptualisation to actually organising the field of TCL? This relates to the question how fields of law emerge—and what our role, as taxonomers, is therein.

In the literature on the emergence of new fields of law, which notably largely stems from scholarship focusing on US and European domestic law, this process has been described as a 'narration'. Accordingly, three actors—legislators, courts and academia—are predominantly shaping the narrative on whether or not an area of legal inquiry is to be qualified as a proper *field* of law. This 'process of narration' is said to consist of three elements:

(a) The 'articulation of distinctive principles and themes',
(b) The expression of the emerging field of law as 'structurally coherent', and
(c) The understanding of the respective body of law as 'special and distinctive'.[46]

Mariner ascertains that '[l]egal fields arise and fade away, expand and contract according to the problems and possibilities of contemporary society and commerce.'[47] She observes that fields of law typically grow up 'according to quite different principles of organization, principles that are neither mutually exclusive

---

[42] Mahiou (2013), para. 15.

[43] Cf. Sect. 2.1 above.

[44] On these efforts, cf. Sect. 2.2.5 on the emergence of GCG above.

[45] Ruhl and Salzman (2013), p. 988.

[46] Hervey (2016), p. 357.

[47] Mariner (2009), p. 80.

nor internally consistent.'[48] In the end, she contends that there is 'no ultimate authority' competent to define what constitutes a field of law and what does not. Consequently, she argues, 'a field may be defined by its own practitioners for their purposes or tastes. The test of its validity lies in whether others accept it.'[49]

One remark shall be added to these observations. The emergence of fields of law differs in its degree of *coordination*. At times a new field of law is *deliberately* being created through an act or a series of acts of law. This scenario describes the *coordinated, planned* approach of conscious lawmakers that have identified the particular need to regulate specific behaviour not merely through a (few) norm(s), but through an entire rule system consisting of a series of interconnected norms. In the international law context, such is typically the case when the international community is adopting a novel international agreement, or series of agreements. One example for such a rather deliberate, coordinated creation of a field of law is WTO law.[50]

Another pathway for a field of law to emerge is a more *gradual* one. Under such a scenario, the three actors shaping the 'narrative' identified by Hervey interact in a *disorganised*, somewhat *incidental* manner. A court ruling may touch upon a not yet established 'field x', which in turn is being discussed in academic literature. Gradually, this trend may accrete and, in the end, elicit actions by national or supranational lawmakers. Despite still not fully conceptualised as such, more and more scholars and practitioners will reference the 'field x', eventually giving rise to the question, what *exactly* constitutes this legal field. What frequently follows are scholarly attempts to conceptualise the organisational framework of the respective field of law. It is this latter pathway, which can be observed (supra)nationally in the cases of e.g., environmental and (EU) health law. On the international level, one field, which emerged rather gradually is international investment law.[51]

Whenever we, as taxonomers, decide to create organisational frameworks of fields of law, we can choose between *descriptive/observational approaches* on the

---

[48]Mariner (2009), p. 81.

[49]Mariner (2009), p. 82.

[50]Of course, the distinction made here is ideal-typical. Generally speaking, the emergence of every field of law exhibits *coordinated* and *random* elements. Yet, despite the somewhat 'turbulent' origins of world trade law in the late 1940s, the GATT paved the way towards the creation of a field of world trade law, which is now clearly spelled out in the various WTO agreements (GATS, TRIPS, TRIMS, SPS, TBT agreements etc. in addition to the GATT). Naturally, WTO law, like any other field of law, constantly evolves based on the decisions of the WTO DSB as well as due to the large volumes of scholarship in the field. However, and this is the entire point I am making here, this evolution occurs based on a legal framework, which was deliberately, systematically established through the WTO agreements.

[51]Contrary to WTO law, international investment law evolved gradually through a net of bilateral investment treaties, cf. Brown (2015). By the time the dispute settlement mechanisms of these treaties produced more and more arbitral awards, the academic analysis of the field intensified, eventually giving rise to the discipline of international investment law. Despite the fact that attempts to negotiate multilateral investment agreement failed, IIL now appears to possess canonical status in international law.

one hand and more *normative approaches* on the other.[52] *Descriptive approaches* typically lead to conceptualisations of fields of law according to a specific subject matter they are addressing, such as the 'law of highways, the law of railways, the law of telegraphs, and the law of building associations . . .'[53] or the famous 'law of the horse'.[54] Many of those fields of law have evolved 'as a matter of historical accident or practical need'.[55] They stand for a taxonomy that 'does *not* attribute meaning to legal categories'.[56] Such classifications generally pursue the mere purpose of presenting the law in an orderly way, thus making it more comprehensible and as a consequence more accessible for legal practitioners and scholars alike.[57]

While some of these classifications depict fields of law that have long been established in legal doctrine and education, such as tort law,[58] merely descriptive conceptualisations of legal areas have been repeatedly ridiculed for their lack of coherence and normative value. Easterbrook established the term of the 'law of the horse' problem, which stands paradigmatically for a conceptualisation of the law, which appears to be devoid of any usefulness.[59] In his opinion, '"Law and . . ." courses should be limited to subjects that could illuminate the entire law', all other combinations are said to run the risk of 'multidisciplinary dilettantism' or the 'cross-sterilization of ideas'.[60]

More *normative approaches* to legal taxonomy pay greater attention to developing a proper methodology for the definition of a field of law 'beyond historical accident or subject matter'.[61] Under the *functional approach*, 'legal rules are classified according to the roles they perform within the legal system or society at large'[62] e.g., according to their functions as 'responses to wrongs' or as interpretation rules regarding private contracts.[63] The *formalist approach* emphasises the 'logical relations among categories of law' and is concerned rather with internal logic than social functions as a classification criterion.[64] However, as Sherwin highlights, no taxonomy can be purely formal in that it needs to rely on previously established categories of the law, which typically have evolved based on doctrinal

---

[52] Tai (2015), p. 118.

[53] Mariner (2009), p. 79; cf. also Tai (2015), p. 118.

[54] Easterbrook (1996).

[55] Mariner (2009), p. 79; cf. also Tai (2015), p. 118.

[56] Sherwin (2011), p. 237. My emphasis.

[57] Sherwin (2011), p. 237.

[58] Sherwin (2011), p. 237 submits that 'categories such as tort law are simply historical facts, taken at face value and displayed in an orderly way.'

[59] Easterbrook (1996), p. 207.

[60] Easterbrook (1996), p. 207.

[61] Tai (2015), p. 118. Easterbrook (1996), p. 207 insofar briefly speaks of 'unifying principles', which may justify the conceptualisation of a field of law.

[62] Sherwin (2009), p. 34.

[63] Sherwin (2009), p. 35.

[64] Sherwin (2009), p. 33.

traditions. Based on these categories the formal taxonomer aims to elaborate the most 'logically coherent classificatory scheme'.[65]

Despite these rough categorisations of the *approaches* to legal taxonomy, the literature on corresponding *methodology* until not long ago has been said to be 'notable for the absence of an epistemology or meta theory for positively defining the essential characteristics of a "field of law".'[66] As a consequence, nearly every somewhat logical arrangement of norms could potentially claim to depict a conceptualisation of a field of law. However, in the past decade, some scholars have attempted to fill this methodological gap by providing abstract reflections on the key elements of organisational frameworks of fields of law, particularly Aagaard.[67] In his 2010 article, he elaborates a comprehensive theoretical framework for the conceptualisation of fields of law.[68] Subsequently, the central elements of his approach will be outlined in brief. They have substantially guided the conceptualisation of TCL in this book.[69]

3.2.1 Definition of Commodity Law

As a first step in creating the organisational framework of a field of law, one needs to 'start with some understanding of what [one thinks] falls within the category of situations that comprise that field.'[70] Sherwin expounds that the first task of the taxonomer is to find a definition, which is 'sufficiently tailored and determinate to provide a comprehensible description of the instances that fall within [the organisational framework].'[71] Aagaard points out that the challenge is to define the field in a way that, for one, yields a coherent concept and, for the other, employs concepts, which assist us in analysing and understanding the field. As a

---

[65] Sherwin (2009), p. 33. Formalist approaches are normative in the sense that the taxonomer elaborates her logically coherent classification along legal rules as the 'characteristic features that should normatively configure fields of law', cf. Tai (2015), p. 119; however, the classification scheme *itself* is *not* normative, cf. Sherwin (2009), p. 34.

[66] Mariner (2009), p. 79; cf. also Tai (2015), p. 118.

[67] Aagaard (2010).

[68] Cf. the later works by Tannenbaum (2013), who employs a similar approach (yet without explicitly referring to Aagaard), as well as by Tai (2015), p. 121 who extensively relies on Aagaard's finding, describing his approach as 'appealing due to its express attempt at balance between descriptive and prescriptive considerations'. Cf. also the prior works Aagaard references by Sherwin (2008); Ruger (2008); and Mariner (2009).

[69] Apart from the methodology on how to conceptualise fields of law, Aagaard's findings on i.a. the 'explanatory power' of and coherence in legal fields will also inform further analyses regarding the normative force of the current legal framework of TCL in Chaps. 4 and 5 below.

[70] Aagaard (2010), p. 237.

[71] Sherwin (2008), p. 110; cf. Aagaard (2010), p. 237.

consequence, the taxonomer may have to revisit her initial definition once she has gained a more thorough understanding of the organisational framework of the field.[72]

Legal fields are frequently being defined around a substantive topic or specific subject matter.[73] As stated above, also a taxonomy, which merely distinguishes itself from other arrangements of the law through the factual context to which it applies may serve material purposes, such as rendering the law more accessible or increasing the scholarly and political attention to an important issue.[74] In order to conceptualise a field of law, which, in addition, displays coherence, one needs to identify features that are *legally relevant* and at the same time exhibit sufficient commonality as well as distinctiveness in comparison to other fields of law.[75]

Our conceptualisation of TCL will naturally first require a definition of the term *commodity*. Whereas there may typically be many ways to define such notion, our taxonomy insofar disposes of somewhat favourable starting conditions in that there already exists a definition of the term in the context of *international law*.[76] The decision to employ this historical notion of 'commodity', in essence contained in Article 56(1) HC, ensures doctrinal consistency with already existing norms and treatises addressing transnational commodity activities. Insofar, our conceptualisation of TCL is rather an *updated outline* of the transnational legal framework addressing GCG than the creation of an entirely novel field of law. It draws on the earlier undertakings aimed at an international regulation of commodity activities and seeks to carve out in more detail the specific requirements and circumstances of such an endeavour.[77] Put differently, and borrowing Aagaard's expression, we are 'interested in how the legal classification of [commodity] law illuminates the functioning of the' remainder of inter- and transnational law that commodity activities are already subjected to.[78]

This leads us to the task of defining *commodity law*. A useful definition needs to master the challenge of balancing over-inclusiveness and under-inclusiveness.[79] As the definition of the term commodity indicates, commodity law is supposed to cover a distinct, primarily economic activity, which relates to the depletion of natural

---

[72] Aagaard (2010), p. 237. Naturally obscured from the reader, the taxonomer may thus be 'going back and forth' between her definition and the elaboration of the organisational framework.

[73] Mariner (2009), p. 82; Tannenbaum (2013); Aagaard (2010), p. 237; Ruger (2008); Hervey (2016).

[74] Cf. Sect. 3.1 above.

[75] Aagaard (2010), pp. 242–244; Tannenbaum (2013), p. 906.

[76] Cf. the definition of the term based on Article 56(1) HC in Chap. 1 above: 'Any product of agriculture, forest, fishery or mining and any mineral product in its natural (=raw) form and in such forms that are customarily required for its international trade, especially shipment, in substantial volumes.'

[77] Cf. especially Jaenicke et al. (1977–1986); also, the summary i.a. by Weiss (2009) and Khan (1982); for a recent corresponding endeavour focusing on Germany, cf. Sanden et al. (2012).

[78] Aagaard (2010), p. 261.

[79] Aagaard (2010), p. 261.

resources for secondary purposes. Thus, it does not mean to comprise all laws, which are relevant with regard to commodities in any way. Rather, it purports to focus on this precise human activity, which will be spelled out in greater detail in the subsequent sections. For now, and for the purpose of the elaboration of its organisational framework, commodity law shall be defined as

all law that regulates commodity-related human activity and its impacts.

This definition is evidently still quite broad. It will be narrowed down further in the following section, which introduces the core conceptual characteristics of commodity law.

3.2.2 Core Conceptual Characteristics of Commodity Law

Aagaard conceptualises 'a legal field as the interaction among four underlying constitutive dimensions of the field: *factual context, policy trade-offs, values and interests*, and *legal doctrine*':[80]

> Every area of the law operates within a factual context, a set of factual characteristics shared in common by situations that arise within the field. These factual characteristics create certain policy trade-offs, which dictate the range of options available to lawmaking institutions such as courts, legislatures, executive branch agencies, and the public. The lawmaking institutions apply values and interests to choose among the available options dictated by the trade-offs. Legal doctrine – the law of the field – arises as the product of the lawmaking institutions' choices among available options – that is, the application of values and interests to policy trade-offs.[81]

Therefore, he claims that factual context should only be relevant for taxonomy where it either creates *policy trade-offs that matter to decision-making institutions* or *influences the values and interests* these institutions are basing their decisions on. Hence, when the taxonomer conceptualizes a field of law, she should draw on factual characteristics only where they give rise to policy trade-offs that, by restricting the available legal options, have an effect on legal doctrine.[82]

Legal scholarship exhibits examples for conceptualisations of fields of law based on each of the four dimensions.[83] However, only an imaginary 'perfect' model of a field of law would display cohesive patterns throughout all dimensions—thus, conceptualisations of fields of law can be based on only one or the combination of two or more dimensions.[84]

---

[80] Aagaard (2010), p. 238. Emphasis added.

[81] Aagaard (2010), p. 238. Internal footnotes omitted.

[82] Aagaard (2010), p. 239.

[83] Feinman (1989); Bell and Parchomovsky (2005); Gostin (2007); Williams (1991); cf. Aagaard (2010), p. 239.

[84] Aagaard (2010), p. 240.

Moreover, Aagaard defines two minimum requirements for conceptualisations of a field of law to depict a useful taxonomy. The first element is *commonality*, which refers to certain individual or aggregated features being common to the scenarios arising in the legal area. These commonalities can arise in any of the four constitutive dimensions of the field of law. One important requirement consists of the commonalities being *legally relevant* i.e., 'they must make a difference in how the law applies. [...] Otherwise, an area of law appears to be merely an amorphous amalgamation of portions of other, existing fields.'[85] Some proponents in the literature have questioned, whether a legal field must necessarily exhibit 'strict commonality'.[86] Instead, they deem it sufficient for a field of law to be cohered by 'a common pool of characteristics', which forms '"a complicated network of similarities overlapping and crisscrossing" that defines the concept.'[87]

The second minimum requirement for a field of law according to Aagaard is its *distinctiveness*—the 'idea that some features of a field are distinct to that field and not present in other fields.'[88] A distinct identity of the field legitimises its conceptualisation and isolated study. Consequently, the 'organizing feature' needs to be 'distinctive to the area', which can be due either to 'unique features of the field' or because of a 'unique interplay of otherwise nonunique features'.[89]

Ibrahim and Smith specify that

distinctiveness may manifest itself in the creation of a unique set of legal rules or legal practices, in the unique expression or interaction of more generally applicable legal rules, or in unique insights about law.[90]

While this statement suggests that distinctiveness needs to relate to legal doctrine, Aagaard claims that sufficient distinctiveness of fields of law can arise also from other characteristics, such as factual context.[91] Epstein contends that instead of looking at doctrinal content, it is more reasonable to look at *how* lawyers apply doctrinal principles given that these principles frequently operate in more than one traditional field of law.[92] Therefore, doctrine itself cannot constitute the only

---

[85] Aagaard (2010), p. 242. The talk is of the proverbial 'Law of the Horse': since the horse as a common element is 'legally irrelevant', the corresponding field of law is deemed to be a 'joke rather than a legitimate field of legal study because the various laws that govern activities related to horses have nothing legally important in common', ibid.

[86] Green (2004), pp. 28–29; Millon (1992), p. 18, n 54; Penner (1996), pp. 779–799; Solove (2002), p. 1096; cf. Aagaard (2010), p. 243.

[87] Aagaard (2010), p. 242 quoting Solove, pp. 1095–1098.

[88] Aagaard (2010), pp. 243–244; cf. also Tannenbaum (2013), p. 906.

[89] Aagaard (2010), p. 244 with reference to Ibrahim and Smith (2008), p. 85.

[90] Ibrahim and Smith (2008), p. 76; cf. Aagaard (2010), p. 244.

[91] Cf. Aagaard (2010), p. 275, who ascertains the distinctiveness of environmental law in view of its two characteristic elements of physical public resources and pervasive interrelatedness, which he defines as elements of factual context; cf. also Tannenbaum (2013), p. 907.

[92] Epstein (2007), pp. 560–563; cf. Tannenbaum (2013), p. 946, n 180.

determinant of the distinctiveness of a legal field.[93] In fact, the distinctive identity of various other legal fields has been confirmed due to characteristic features beyond doctrinal content.[94] Distinctiveness thus can arise from any constitutive dimension of a field of law. Besides, Aagaard highlights that distinctiveness shall not be confused with uniqueness. In his view, it is sufficient for a field of law, which merits unified consideration to be 'unified by sufficient similarity and distinctiveness— even if not perfect uniqueness. . .'[95]

Subsequently, two different constitutive dimensions of the organisational framework of commodity law will be analysed. For one, its core conceptual characteristics arise from the factual context in which commodity-related human activity occurs (Sect. 3.2.2.1). For the other, as we have seen commodity law exhibits policy trade-offs, which are distinct to its field (Sect. 3.2.2.2).

3.2.2.1 Factual

Two factual elements can in the simplest terms specify what constitutes 'commodity-related human activity', or in short 'commodity activity'. Such activity typically occurs in connection with, for one,

the *removal of an item from earth* and, for the other,

a *specific purpose that relates to the removed item*.

---

[93]Cf. Tannenbaum (2013), p. 946, n 180.

[94]Hamilton (1990), p. 503: 'One feature that separates agricultural law from such conceptual topics as property law, torts, or evidence is of special significance. As a sectoral analysis, agricultural law starts with the economic activity of agriculture and then confronts the unique legal issues associated with agriculture[]', cf. Tannenbaum (2013), p. 946, n 180. Very frank also Mariner (2009), p. 82: 'Defining a field by the subject matter around which legal principles are gathered has as credible a pedigree as any other approach.' In fact, also to me it appears to be an over-interpretation of the statement by Easterbrook (1996), p. 207 to perceive it as requiring a comprehensive search for a 'unifying principle' whenever one is to conceptualise a field of law, cf. however e.g., Hall (2002), p. 464 as quoted by Ruger (2008), pp. 630–631. In what appears to have been more of a side-remark in an oral speech that was later published, Judge Easterbrook merely stated that law school courses, which focus on specific subject matters, such as the 'law of the horse' may run the risk of missing 'unifying principles'—an objective certainly essential in teaching law school students. To interpret his remarks as requiring doctrinal distinctiveness of a new field of law, however, to my mind puts those out of context and moreover misconceives his speech as a methodological foundational work, which it clearly is not. Besides, I concur with Mariner (2009), p. 82: 'Complaints that "law and . . ." fields are necessarily illegitimate overstate the case.' Given the purpose that even subject matter-oriented classifications of legal fields can serve, cf. only e.g. sports law, the entire argument relating to the 'law of the horse' may in fact constitute a *pseudo* problem created by proponents seeking to *conserve* a certain methodological arrangement of norms that they have become acquainted with over the years. However, such comprehensible positions should not discourage efforts to conceptualise new fields of law, whenever there are compelling reasons to do so.

[95]Aagaard (2010), p. 245.

This evidently requires a few explanations. We shall begin with the first element of commodity activity, the *removal of an item from earth*. Human beings are using natural resources in various ways. Watercourses may be used for navigation purposes or in order to generate electricity, forests can serve as recreational areas; the sunlight and wind can likewise serve as sources of renewable energies. All these uses of natural resources are, however, distinct from commodity activity. None of them necessitates the removal of anything from the natural environment or, simply speaking, earth.[96] Consequently, commodity law can be classified as a distinct sub-branch of natural resources law (NRL).[97]

Both terms *removal* and *item* have deliberately been chosen for their broadness. While significant portions of these removal activities may aptly be characterised as 'extraction'—in particular in mining—the usage of this latter notion would generally exclude especially food commodities that are rather being 'harvested', 'farmed' or 'fished' as well as forestry products, which are usually being 'logged'.[98] The respective *item* becomes a 'commodity' *at the latest* once it has been removed from the natural environment, depending on the kind of item. The seeds of a cocoa plant, for instance, according to our definition of 'commodity' may already be considered as such, when the plant is still rooted in the ground on a plantation. Except for the harvesting process, the seeds have already acquired their natural or raw form, which suffices for them to constitute a commodity. A precious metal, to the contrary, will typically still be contained in an ore, which in turn is still incident to gangue material and waste rock. It becomes a commodity once it has been separated (extracted) from the natural environment in a way, which allows for its differentiated identification as a raw and/or tradable item. However, since

---

[96] Minor 'removals', such as the ones that may occur for instance when a river is being used for navigation and some water may spill on a respective ship's deck, which in turn may evaporate over time, shall for our purposes be ignored. We are thus focusing on the *intentional* removal of something from earth. The term 'earth' is being used in order to underline that also cultivated (food) commodities as well as livestock are being included. The notion 'natural environment', 'nature' or 'natural wealth' could suggest an exclusion of all items, which have been cultivated by humankind.

[97] Cf. already the definition provided by Oehl (2019), p. 6, as well as the additional reflections in n 20. On the undertakings in Germany aimed at elaborating a national resource protection law regime, cf. Sanden et al. (2012), Herrmann et al. (2012); Domke (2013); as well as Umweltbundesamt, https://www.umweltbundesamt.de/themen/abfall-ressourcen/oekonomische-rechtliche-aspekte-der/ressourcenschutzrecht (last accessed 14 May 2021). This resource protection law is intended to reduce the economic costs of resource use, as well as Germany's dependency on commodity exporting countries. In addition, it shall reduce negative environmental effects of resource use, Herrmann et al. (2012), p. 524. While it thus significantly converges with TCL, it is closer to NRL given that it defines resources as 'biotic and abiotic raw materials ['Rohstoffe'] (biomass and minerals) as well as water, air and surface ['Fläche']' (my translation), Herrmann et al. (2012), p. 524 referring to the definition by Schütz and Bringezu (2008), pp. 45–46.

[98] As I have already stated in Chap. 2 above, nothing in this book is meant to relativize the *specific* governance challenges of individual types of commodities, hard or soft, mineral or food. However, this conceptualisation deliberately seeks to emphasise the commonalities between *all commodities* and their related governance challenges.

commodity law, as will become clear subsequently, covers a broad range of activities also before and after the 'removal' has taken place, this distinction is rather less relevant.

Everything that is being removed from earth can potentially be considered a commodity—provided, it meets the second factual element of *a specific purpose that relates to the removed item*.[99] The specific purpose, which relates to the *removed item*, distinguishes commodity activity from other human activity, which involves the removal of natural resources, such as construction projects, particularly large infrastructure projects. When it comes to such projects, the removed matter, however, is typically not of (primary) interest for the actors concerned. It rather constitutes an impediment to the operations, which focus on the implementation of an aim that is unrelated to the removed item.

The *specific purpose* of commodity activity related to the removed item will naturally lie in using it for economic gain, i.e. selling or trading it, including various intermediary steps, such as processing and shipment. Therefore, one could also define an *economic purpose* related to the removed item as a core conceptual characteristic of commodity law. However, the *kind* of purpose that one pursues in relation to an item removed from earth does not at all alter the activity itself—which would remain the same also in the unlikely event that one should extract or harvest commodities with the end goal in mind to later donate them. In order to keep the organisational framework of commodity law as simple and abstract as possible, it shall therefore be defined regardless of an economic purpose that the 'remover' may be pursuing with regard to the removed item.[100]

These remarks already shed more light as to what can be understood as 'commodity activity'. Nevertheless, some further clarifications are necessary regarding the scope of activities, which occur *in connection with* the removal and still qualify as commodity activity. Naturally, the removal process itself, whether it involves harvesting, logging, fishing, or extraction constitutes a commodity activity. However, the commodity sector exhibits a whole range of different activities, which all relate to this removal process. These activities have most vividly been portrayed along the so-called *Commodity Value Chain*.[101] For our purposes, we shall use the commodity value chain to elucidate the range of activities, which occur in connection with the removal of an item from earth for a specific purpose that relates to this item. For instance, with regard to extractive industries, one can distinguish between the exploration, extraction, processing, storage and shipping, sale and trading as well as the post-extraction phases.[102] For other industries, the commodity value chain

---

[99] Naturally, this claim is only valid within the scope of our definition of the term 'commodity' established in Chap. 2 above, which notably excludes air and water.

[100] On the 'commodification of nature', cf. Sect. 2.1.1.2 above.

[101] It is typically being used as an analytical tool i.a., to illustrate the distribution of returns of a specific product at the different stages of its life cycle as well as to clarify related business and governance challenges, Midgley (2016); Kaplinsky (2000).

[102] Cf. NRGI (2018).

will be designed differently, notably using different terminology for the terms 'exploration', 'extraction' and potentially 'processing', and usually extending from producer to end-consumer.[103]

On a more abstract level, commodity activities can be said to range from pre-removal activities, which include exploration, but also cultivation, plantation and related undertakings, such as the clearance of a specific area in preparation of a 'removal' activity, to the ultimate post-removal activity of selling and/or trading the respective commodity. The intermediary steps are, of course speaking on a very abstract level, similar regardless of the type of commodity and involve processing, storage and shipping, sale and trading. Once a removal activity has been abandoned permanently, additional post-removal activities are required, such as a proper closing of the removal site (e.g. mine closure) including a restoration of the natural environment that may have been affected by the removal activities.

The manufacture of secondary or end products from commodities does *not* constitute commodity activity. While of course the removal activity is a necessary precondition for such manufacture to be possible, it does not shape these processes to the same extent as those activities, which occur in closer connection to it. Commodity activity constitutes a preliminary stage within the global value chain, which is followed by the ensuing, yet separate stage of manufacture.[104] Also, typically the governance challenges and policy trade-offs, which occur in connection with removal-related activities, are distinct from the ones to ensure a well-governed manufacture process.[105]

3.2.2.2   Policy Trade-Offs

The specific commodity policy trade-offs, which have been already elaborated above, constitute further commonalities of commodity law, which at the same time illustrate its distinctiveness from other fields. The existence of one or several of the policy trade-offs described above can thus be characterised as an additional common feature of commodity law. These policy trade-offs 'limit legal choice' in that the elaboration of the law regulating commodity activities should be guided by an awareness of their existence.[106] They thus 'reflect the analytical and instrumental

---

[103]Cf. IFAD (2014), p. 2; on the cocoa value chain cf. for instance UNCTAD (2016); on the commodity value chain of apples Midgley (2016).

[104]Cf. on the analytical significance of this differentiation Daviron and Gibbon (2002), pp. 141–143; cf. also Grilli and Yang (1988).

[105]On the policy trade-offs in the commodity sector, cf. the subsequent Sect. 3.2.2.2 as well as Sect. 2.1.3 above. This is further underlined by the established differentiation between the primary sector, which largely coincides with the commodity sector, on the one hand, and the secondary, manufacturing, sector on the other, cf. Alfaro and Charlton (2007), p. 2; cf. also the distinction employed by UNCTAD (2018), p. 8 between the primary, manufacturing, and services sector.

[106]Cf. Aagaard (2010), p. 239; Sect. 3.2.2 above.

aims' of the conceptualisation of TCL;[107] they 'make a difference in how the law applies'—or rather, in the many incidents where they are covered by indirect TCL,[108] *should* apply.[109]

This is furthermore underlined by the fact that many states have adopted specific regulatory and fiscal frameworks for the commodity sector, which are 'distinctly different' from the ones that apply to other industries.[110] States as the legislators of international law have thus repeatedly expressed their perception of commodity law as a distinct subject matter, which is i.a. reflected in chapter VI of the Havana Charter, several GATT provisions,[111] the various ICAs, which have been introduced and/or are still in existence today, as well as the Integrated Programme for Commodities (IPC), the Common Fund for Commodities (CFC), International Commodity Organisations (ICOs) and other commodity-directed governance programs of UNCTAD.[112] All of these examples thus support the contention that commodity activity as well as its associated policy trade-offs from the perspective of legal taxonomy constitute *legally relevant commonalities*, which should be governed by what one conceptualises as a distinct field of law.

Regarding its distinctiveness from other fields, the set of trade-offs discussed above may generally also be relevant in relation to other economic activities, such as large-scale infrastructure projects. However, the respective interests would be relevant to a different degree, i.e. their ratio to one another would differ. For instance, commodities are typically being considered as a form of 'national wealth'. Consequently, the demand for participation and adequate development effects of commodity activity will often be comparatively greater than in the case of infrastructure construction. Likewise, the great significance that commodity exports can have for the national economy of an individual state is typically not mirrored in a comparable significance of an infrastructure project.[113] There is thus a commodity-specific layout of these policy trade-offs. Since the threshold here is *distinctiveness* and not *uniqueness*,[114] the fact that other layouts, such as the construction-specific layout, of these trade-offs may be somewhat similar does not rebut the claim regarding the distinctiveness of commodity law also in this respect.

---

[107] Cf. Feinman (1989), p. 680.

[108] On the distinction between direct and indirect TCL, cf. Sect. 4.2 below.

[109] Cf. Aagaard (2010), p. 242; Sect. 3.2.2 above.

[110] Cf. UN (2002) Berlin II Guidelines, https://commdev.org/userfiles/files/903_file_Berlin_II_Guidelines.pdf (last accessed 14 May 2021), p. 8.

[111] Cf. Sects. 4.2.2.1.4.2 and 4.3.2 below as well as the TCL outline in the annex.

[112] Cf. Sect. 5.2.1 below.

[113] Cf. again Calder (2014), p. 10, according to whom 'risk is not unique to natural resources, but the magnitude and pervasiveness of natural resource risks are exceptional'.

[114] Aagaard (2010), p. 245; cf. above.

3.3 The Norms of TCL

After having delineated the organisational framework of commodity law, this section briefly outlines how the normative substance of TCL operates within the organisational framework we have presented above. The purpose of this exercise is to expound the transnational rules that are governing commodity activities. This approach corresponds with the overall aim of this book to first provide a conceptualised account of the transnational law regulating commodity activities and to then, as a second step, suggest specific instruments for reinforcing this existing regulatory framework. Rather than delivering a comprehensive account of *all* the norms governing commodity activities, the overview provided below therefore seeks to display the central *types* of norms as well as corresponding factual scenarios they apply to.[115]

As mentioned repeatedly, TCL is a *transnational* legal framework. This property relates to the concept of GCG.[116] First and foremost, its transnational nature constitutes an analytical category from which the normative framework applicable to commodity activity is being assessed.[117] Instead of exclusively focusing on rules of *inter-national* law—an approach that would relate to the classical concept of govern*ment*[118]—our conceptualisation will be based on international rules, and additionally comprise private standards and select domestic norms that exhibit a transnational scope.[119] This approach appears particularly natural in light of the transnational nature of commodity activity, especially whenever extracted materials are being traded, as well as given the pivotal role of TNCs and multi-stakeholder standard-setting institutions therein.[120]

---

[115] For a more comprehensive account, see the TCL outline in the annex, our discussions in Chap. 4 below as well as the work by Rüttinger and Scholl (2017). Their 'governance map', Rüttinger and Scholl (2017), p. 21, has decisively informed our subsequent examination.

[116] Cf. Sect. 2.1.4 above.

[117] Menkel-Meadow (2011), pp. 106–107; as many have ascertained, the classical model of *inter-national* law based on the sovereign nation state as the sole authoritative lawmaker 'fails to describe our world as we know it', Szablowski (2007), p. 5; Twining (2000), p. 51.

[118] Menkel-Meadow (2011), p. 103.

[119] Transnational law has been introduced prominently by Jessup (1956); it depicts a shift away from the conventional legal framework of international law and represents 'an expanded understanding of law in light of globalisation', Szablowski (2007), p. 6; cf. his n 18 for an account of literature exhibiting this expanded understanding. Szablowski (2007), p. 4 defines transnational law as referring to 'legal regimes which operate across national borders or which regulate actions or events that transcend national borders.' This book follows this definition. On the theoretical challenges and underpinnings of transnational perceptions of the law, cf. Szablowski (2007). Given this expanded, flexible understanding of what constitutes the law regulating transnational activity, it is not convincing to squeeze corresponding norms into the boxes of classical international law, see already Oehl (2019), p. 22. Instead, the concept, which we used to define as international law may sooner or later well be replaced with the one of transnational law. With a different approach, however, Ong (2010).

[120] Cf. in more detail Sect. 4.2.2.2 below.

3.3.1 Sources of TCL

The diverse legal sources that this conceptualisation is based on can be categorised as follows:

The *first category*, the *classical inter-national framework* can roughly be divided into international agreements, principles of international law, UN soft law, and standards issued or adopted by other international organisations, such as OECD or International Finance Corporation (IFC).

The *second category* consists of either industry, corporate, or civil society *standards*, which typically are elaborated through multi-stakeholder or broad industry or civil society processes. Frequently, these processes are either initiated or facilitated by international organisations.

A *third category* of sources used in the conceptualisation of TCL is the *domestic legal framework*. It includes the constitutional framework as well as domestic legislation and regulation, particularly in the fields of labour, environment, public accountability, taxation, fiscal terms, customs, non-discrimination, transparency, privacy, anti-corruption and licensing. This book, however, makes reference exclusively to those sources of domestic law, which exhibit transnational effects, and are of particular importance in the commodity sector.[121]

A *fourth category* is composed of *transnational contract law* insofar as it provides for rules, which proliferate beyond the application of contractual terms *inter partes*. This category plays a comparatively smaller role in our conceptualisation of TCL. Given that most rules, which can be abstracted as common, potentially customary elements from transnational contract law will typically already feature in at least the domestic legal order as a general principle of law, their analysis would presumably bring about only few new insights. This observation, however, does not in any way diminish the potentially great normative force that transnational contracts may exhibit, particularly in the commodity sector.[122]

All four types of sources are naturally subject to *judicial application and interpretation*, as well as to *scholarly analysis*—as a consequence, relevant inter-, transnational and domestic case law as well as international legal scholarship constitute *additional sources*, which informed our conceptualisation of TCL.

This categorisation of the sources of TCL, of course, can only be ideal-typical. For instance, the lines between soft law and civil society standards may often be blurred given the diverging roles that international organisations tend to play in multi-stakeholder processes as either mere *facilitators* or *owners*. In the latter case, the process of elaborating a new standard is typically followed by its formal adoption through the respective governing bodies of the international organisation in question.

---

[121] Apart from the fact that an analysis of more than these prominent transnational laws would go beyond the scope of this book, such an enterprise would rather fall under the category of comparative commodity law, which has witnessed relatively greater attention by legal scholarship in the past, cf. Bastida et al. (2005).

[122] Cf. Cotula (2010).

In the former case, the outcome may be a civil society or industry standard. While the differentiation between UN soft law as well as international organisation (IO) standards on the one hand and corporate as well as civil society standards on the other based on whether or not they have been formally adopted according to the internal procedures of the respective IO is of course logical from a formalist point of view, it makes a compelling case for perceiving the legal framework as a 'transnational whole', and thus abandoning the classical boxes of international law as spelled out in Article 38 ICJ statute.[123]

3.3.2   Structure of TCL

It would go beyond the realms of this treatise to portray the entire substance of TCL including its normative content. However, our subsequent analysis of normative patterns of TCL draws on a comprehensive study of the applicable instruments and standards. Consequently, Chap. 4 will discuss a variety of concrete normative content of the substance of TCL; a brief overview of its structure shall be provided here. In addition, an overview of the relevant instruments and provisions, which form the substance of TCL, can be found in the annex below.

While there are numerous possibilities to logically arrange the diverse sources outlined above and therefore expound the architecture of TCL they are revealing, Dederer in my opinion has provided the most clear, convincing structure.[124] The subsequent portrayal of TCL follows a version of his 'limited sovereignty' structure, which has been significantly modified and extended. However, as notably Schrijver has emphasised, instead of limiting it, norms of international law often rather tend to *qualify* the principle of PSNR in the sense of detailing how the sovereignty of states needs to be exercised.[125] Thus we shall employ the perspective of '*qualified sovereignty*' for the remainder of our investigation.

According to this outline, first of all, international law declares the nation state— or more precisely its respective population—as being principally competent to regulate the use of natural resources. This holds generally true with regard to those resources that are located on its territory or under its sovereign command. However, one can discern a certain tension with more recent concepts of international law, which emphasise the fact that commodities may be a 'common concern' of all of humankind. The corresponding principles of permanent sovereignty over natural resources and common concern will be subject to our analysis in Sect. 4.1 below.

Secondly, even where the nation state or its population respectively disposes of sovereignty over its commodity reserves, several fields of transnational, especially

---

[123] See already Oehl (2019), p. 22.

[124] Dederer (2012), pp. 37–56.

[125] On this question, see Sect. 4.1 in more detail below.

inter-national law *qualify* this sovereignty.[126] According to their subject matter, one can distinguish eight categories of these, largely *self-imposed*, qualifications: Human Rights; environmental protection; liberalised trade; shared resources; good governance; fiscal framework; financial regulation; and armed conflict. Several of these qualifications of a state's sovereignty over commodity resources will feature in our analysis in Chap. 4 below. For an overview see also the TCL outline contained in the annex.

Thirdly, sovereignty over resources typically comprises the competence to transfer commodity-related rights onto third parties, particularly from the private sector. The transfer of these rights is usually being performed through specific agreements between the state party and the transferee. The transfer process, as well as the arising obligations for transferees, is governed by various inter- and transnational standards, most of which qualify as either *soft law* or *private industry standards*. Once a state has transferred rights onto a third party, its sovereignty is further qualified by various obligations to protect these rights under international investment law.[127] The norms and standards regulating the transfer of commodity rights are illustrated in the TCL outline in the annex and will also inform our subsequent analysis in Chap. 4.

Besides, all qualifications of a state's sovereignty are typically being accompanied by 'secondary qualifications', which provide for procedures to regulate externalities or dispute settlement respectively. Corresponding mechanisms can also arise from private industry standards or investor-state agreements.

3.3.3 TCL in the Commodity Governance Matrix

While we have just learned about the abstract structure of TCL, we shall now examine how its norm subsets apply within the commodity governance matrix. As we have seen, commodity activities occur in a matrix of largely five interests and corresponding trade-offs, which arise between the different stakeholders: economic gain, development, preservation, control, and participation.[128] In this section we will

---

[126] On the remaining challenges to clarify the interrelation of inter- and transnational law Cotterrell (2012). Transnational law can qualify PSNR i.a. through 'bottom-up lawmaking', cf. Levit (2008), or wherever respective standards are being used as benchmarks in e.g. international or domestic legislation or jurisprudence. On the role of ICAs *de lege ferenda* in this respect see Sect. 5.2.2 below.

[127] This structure does not mean to obscure that, of course, international investment agreements can also entail a state's duty to admit foreign investments. However, since the focus will generally lie on protecting investments that have already been made, questions related to international investment law will typically be discussed in context with respective rights that have already been transferred onto third parties.

[128] Cf. Sect. 2.1.3 above.

give a brief account of which one of these five interests a selection of the various norm subsets of TCL are seeking to foster primarily.[129]

Naturally, all norms are serving multiple purposes. For instance, every norm will *ultimately* serve the purpose of *controlling* a commodity activity, i.e. upholding the rule of law. Moreover, as I have argued elsewhere, one can maintain that every legal norm ultimately is intended to foster the development of society.[130] Here, however, we shall *roughly* categorise the norm subsets of TCL according to their *primary* regulatory objective. The goal here is thus less to paint a dogmatic picture, which is entirely consistent, but rather to sketch an overview that exposes normative conflict lines between various norm subsets of TCL. For that purpose, we shall employ those understandings of the terms, which we have already developed in Chap. 2 above.

When it comes to reaping the *economic* benefits of commodity activities, the rules that come to mind first and foremost are the ones featuring in the applicable fiscal regime. Through these rules, the respective host government ensures that it receives financial benefits from the respective commodity business, i.a. through taxes and royalties. Not least in order to attract foreign investment in the commodity sector, the investment protection rules in place guarantee foreign investors certain safeguards against regulatory or other activities by the host state. Once the host government has decided to transfer—e.g. exploration or exploitation—rights onto private third parties, their right to property as well as potentially their 'legitimate expectations' are being protected under these rules.[131] Particularly so-called stabilisation clauses that are seeking to prevent unexpected changes in the regulatory environment, especially with regard to the fiscal regime, can serve to safeguard the economic expectations of the investor.[132] As a result, what may conflict here are the economic interests of investors on the one hand and host states on the other. Such conflicts arise for instance, when host states are of the view that they do not sufficiently benefit from commodity activities e.g., through so-called resource rents. Consequently, the host state may introduce changes in the fiscal regime for instance regarding the taxation of commodity corporations. This, in turn, may cause investors to seek compensation due to a frustration of their economic expectations.

Further provisions that primarily seek to promote the economic benefits from commodity activities are the ones liberalising international trade, particularly Articles I, II, III and XI:1 GATT.[133] By removing obstacles, such as duties and quantitative restrictions, in cross-border trade these rules are intended to facilitate trade and thus promote economic growth. Yet again, issues may arise with regard to the policy space that is left to states, which are for instance aiming to promote infant

---

[129]For a more comprehensive overview of how TCL operates within the commodity matrix, see the outline in the annex.

[130]Oehl (2019), pp. 25–28; cf. Sect. 5.1.1.2.2.2 below.

[131]On the diverging interpretations of the FET standard with regard to the protection of investors' 'legitimate expectations', see Sect. 4.3.1 below.

[132]Comprehensively Hauert (2016).

[133]Cf. Sect. 4.3.2 below.

industries or price stability in their commodity markets. Such measures may be interpreted by the WTO DSB as trade distortions, and therefore held to be unlawful under WTO discipline. In essence, this conflict demonstrates diverging perceptions of what economic policies bring about the most beneficial results. While consumer states typically favour liberalising commodity trade, as well as trade in manufactures, to the greatest extent possible, producer states, especially Commodity Dependent Developing Countries (CDDCs), may seek to pursue import substitution industrialisation measures and therefore put in place safeguards for emerging domestic industries.[134] Furthermore, also the norms covering the use of shared resources are seeking to foster the economic benefits of both—or all—parties concerned through cooperation and equitable utilisation. Joint development agreements are likewise serving this purpose.

In order to promote the *development* benefits of commodity activities, again particularly the fiscal rules that are applicable in the respective host state ensure the capture of an adequate share of resource rents. In an ideal state, these financial resources are being used in the most effective way for the society's development.[135] Further development benefits can be sought i.a. through local content provisions or other rules seeking to promote economic linkages between commodity activity and the host state's economy. Such clauses are often included in or annexed to investment contracts, concession or production-sharing agreements. However, applicable Bilateral Investment Treaties (BITs) as well as the Trade-Related Aspects of Intellectual Property Rights (TRIPS) and Trade-Related Investment Measures (TRIMS) agreements may significantly limit states' policy space when it comes to introducing such measures.

At the same time, WTO disciplines also contain a few provisions allowing for development policies, such as infant-industry promotion according to Article XVIII GATT or the special provisions for Commodity Dependent Developing Countries e.g. contained in Article XXXVI:4 GATT. However, these provisions are of limited effectiveness.[136] Moreover, while Part IV of the GATT—the chapter on trade and development—seeks to foster economic and social advancement, it does not refer to environmental protection in that connection, therefore leaving out the third pillar of

---

[134]The perceptions may differ not only between consumer and producer states, but also depending on what economic philosophy the respective country is being governed upon. More market-oriented governments will typically favour trade liberalisation, whereas governments operating from a more state-centric perspective will prefer maintaining control over trade. Not least the fact that this debate has not settled, yet still WTO discipline clearly takes sides in favour of the 'liberalisation doctrine' led to the 'deadlock' of the world trade regime, see already Sect. 2.2.4 above. Instead of assuming that with liberalisation, one has reached the 'end of history' as regards global economic policy, only revisiting these discussions appears to be the promising approach to remedying this stalemate.

[135]Unfortunately, however, especially many CDDCs witness challenges of corruption and mismanagement of resource revenues, in the most severe cases described as 'resource curse', cf. Sect. 2.1.3 above. To what degree these challenges persist will generally depend on the degree of *control* a state is able to exercise regarding commodity activities, see below.

[136]In more detail, cf. Sect. 4.2.2.1.4.2 below.

SD.[137] The Enabling Clause and the Generalised System of Preferences (GSP) open further possibilities to promote special treatment for developing countries. However, trade and development provisions—as opposed to the liberalisation provisions of the GATT—are said to be 'declaratory rather than obligatory', and therefore appear to be of little 'bite' when it comes to creating a trade environment that is cognisant of the imperatives of the developing world.[138] One major obstacle in that connection consists of ever rising SPS standards in the developed world, which effectively bar many products from developing countries from entering their markets.[139]

A state's competence to decide in what way and to what extent it develops its commodity deposits is further qualified by the internal dimension of the right to freely dispose over natural resources. Particularly where commodity activities have effects on the right to subsistence of local populations or indigenous peoples, such exploitation may be unlawful. Moreover, the right to development calls for the 'fair distribution of [the] benefits of development.'[140] Also standards addressing corporate behaviour, such as the OECD Guidelines for Multinational Enterprises (OECDG), are seeking to increase the SD benefits of business operations.

The objective of *preservation* is particularly being pursued by the various norms aimed at environmental protection, such as the precautionary principle as well as the principle of preventive action. Furthermore, the natural environment may also be protected under indigenous peoples' rights, especially where their cultural identities are deeply influenced by or comprise lands, territories, waters, or the like. Again, the right to freely dispose over natural resources (RFD) may require states to refrain from conducting or authorising commodity activities where those threaten the means of subsistence of local populations—and therefore effectively operate as a safeguard for the territories or waters concerned. With regard to shared resources, particularly the principle of equitable utilisation requires states to control, prevent, reduce, or eliminate any adverse environmental effects that may originate from shared resource use.[141] The more sophisticated joint development agreements are, the more likely they may be to also foster environmental protection.[142] In scenarios of armed conflict, several rules of international humanitarian law (IHL) are protecting commodity deposits from being harmed or unlawfully exploited.

The objective of *controlling* commodity activities is a subsidiary category to the objectives of economic gain, development and preservation described above. It relates to the general interest especially of host governments to maintain

---

[137] See, however, principle 10 of the 1972 Stockholm Declaration, which reconciles the objectives of price stability, adequate resource rents as well as environmental management.

[138] Lee (2011), p. 114; cf. Sect. 4.2.2.1.4.2 below.

[139] Desta and Hirsch (2012), p. 159.

[140] Marong (2010), para. 2; cf. Sect. 4.2.1.1 below.

[141] Moreover, the principle of sustainable use has been said to dispose of 'particular normative precision' as a rule of customary international law with regard to shared and common natural resources, ILA (2012), p. 36, statement #3.

[142] Cf. Sect. 4.2.2.1.4.1 below.

administrative power and the rule of law respectively over what commodity operations are being carried out where, when, by whom, and how. Governments in this respect particularly make use of licenses, concessions, and other public-private contracts that detail the obligations which private actors need to observe when conducting commodity activity. Ideally, and as is frequently the case, these contracts intertwine with a broader legal framework that comprises international labour rights, provides for land tenure rights, and other pertinent HR. For the objective of upholding the rule of law, especially with regard to compensation for wrongs suffered, the right to remedy, according to Articles 8 UDHR, 2(3) ICCPR, 6 CERD, and 2 (c) CEDAW bears particular significance.

Moreover, the objective of control is being fostered by the various good governance standards, such as the anti-corruption provisions as e.g. set forth in the UN Convention Against Corruption (CAC), the Berlin II Guidelines for Mining and Sustainable Development or the AMV. Transparency initiatives like the Extractive Industries Transparency Initiative (EITI) often constitute the first step towards regulating various aspects of commodity activity in a targeted manner. Under the UN Guiding Principles for Business and Human Rights (UN GP) framework, states are obliged to protect against HR violations by third parties, including corporations—and thus to especially regulate or legislate accordingly.[143]

Fifth and last, several norms of TCL are seeking to ensure the *participation* of various stakeholders in decision-making processes related to commodity activity. The right of the freedom of expression, the right to access to information and particularly the right to free, prior and informed consent (FPIC) are serving this purpose. Article 1(2) ICESCR obliges states to administer public resources in a transparent manner. Through the freedom of assembly as well as association, particularly private citizens, workers and civil society organisations have the right to actively voice their opinion regarding commodity policy. Again, also the internal dimension of the RFD may be relevant in this respect.

FPIC particularly requires states to obtain consent from indigenous and local populations prior to authorising or conducting a commodity operation. This duty evidently may conflict with the economic interests of host governments and investors. Where it has been violated, again the right to remedy plays a key role in addressing matters of compensation and reparation. In this respect, UN GP #22 sets forth that corporations should provide legitimate remediation processes for HR violations they have caused or contributed to. Similarly, the OECD Guidelines for Multinational Enterprises require states to maintain National Contact Points, which i.a. serve to address enquiries resulting from conflicts over the implementation of the guidelines, e.g. between Multinational Enterprises and civil society. The latter's ability to publicly advocate their interests has not least been fostered significantly by

---

[143] Naturally, also the trade, investment, or environmental protection norms touched upon above, serve the ultimate purpose of *controlling* commodity activity. This objective here constitutes a subsidiary analytical category, which comprises norms fostering primary objectives *other than* the ones of economic gain, development and preservation. On the UN GP framework, cf. Sect. 4.2.2.2. 2.1 below.

the resource transparency movement leading to the publication of commodity activity documentation.

References

Literature and IO/NGO Publications

Aagaard TS (2010) Environmental law as a legal field: an inquiry into legal taxonomy. Cornell Law Rev 95:221–282

Alfaro L, Charlton A (2007) Growth and the quality of foreign direct investment: is all FDI equal? Working paper, May 2007. https://www.hbs.edu/faculty/Publication%20Files/Growth%20and %20the%20Quality%20of%20Foreign%20Direct%20Investment-%20Is%20all%20FDI% 20Equal_8de61b6b-1bb6-491c-a750-9f32d251a4ce.pdf

Bastida E, Wälde TW, Warden-Fernández J (2005) International and comparative mineral law and policy: trends and prospects. Kluwer Law International, The Hague

Bell A, Parchomovsky G (2005) A theory of property. Cornell Law Rev 90(3):531–615

Bishop JP (1868) The first book of the law: explaining the nature, sources, books, and practical applications of legal science, and methods of study and practice. Little, Brown, & Co., Boston

Brown C (2015) The evolution of the regime of international investment agreements: history, economics and politics. In: Bungenberg M, Griebel J, Hobe S, Reinisch A (eds) International investment law: a handbook. Beck/Hart/Nomos, pp 153–185

Buxbaum R (1988) International mining projects as a research paradigm of transnational economic law. In: Jaenicke G et al (eds) International mining investment: legal and economic perspectives. Kluwer, Deventer

Calder J (2014) Administering fiscal regimes for extractive industries: a handbook. IMF. http://eduart0.tripod.com/sitebuildercontent/sitebuilderfiles/AdministeringFiscalRegimesForEI.pdf

Cotterrell R (2012) What is transnational law? Law Soc Inq 37(2):500–524

Cotula L (2010) Investment contracts and sustainable development: how to make contracts for fairer and more sustainable natural resource investments. Natural Resource Issues No. 20. IIED, London. http://pubs.iied.org/pdfs/17507IIED.pdf

Daviron B, Gibbon P (2002) Global commodity chains and African export agriculture. J Agrarian Change 2(2):137–161

Dederer HG (2012) Rohstoffausbeutung, -bewirtschaftung und -verteilung aus Sicht des allgemeinen Völkerrechts. In: Ehlers D, Herrmann C, Wolffgang HM, Schröder UJ (eds) Rechtsfragen des internationalen Rohstoffhandels. Deutscher Fachverlag GmbH, Fachmedien Recht und Wirtschaft, Frankfurt am Main, pp 37–56

Desta MG, Hirsch M (2012) African countries in the world trading system: international trade, domestic institutions and the role of international law. Int Comp Law Q 61:127–170

Domke F (2013) Ressourcenschutzrecht. Positionspapier, Dezember 2013. https://www.umweltbundesamt.de/sites/default/files/medien/378/publikationen/ressourcenschutzrecht_07.01.2014.pdf

Easterbrook FH (1996) Cyberspace and the law of the horse. University of Chicago Legal Forum 207. https://chicagounbound.uchicago.edu/cgi/viewcontent.cgi?referer=&httpsredir=1& article=2147&context=journal_articles

Epstein RA (2007) The erosion of individual autonomy in medical decisionmaking: of the FDA and IRBs. Georgetown Law J 96:559–582

Feinman JM (1989) The jurisprudence of classification. Stanf Law Rev 41:661–717

Gostin LO (2007) A theory and definition of public health law. J Health Care Law Policy 10:1–12

Green SP (2004) The concept of white collar crime in law and legal theory. Buffalo Crim Law Rev 8:1–34

Grilli ER, Yang MC (1988) Primary commodity prices, manufactured goods prices, and the terms of trade of developing countries: what the long run shows. World Bank Econ Rev 2(1):1–47. https://doi.org/10.1093/wber/2.1.1

Hall MA (2002) Law, medicine and trust. Stanf Law Rev 55(2):463–527

Hamilton ND (1990) The study of agricultural law in the United States: education, organization and practice. Arkansas Law Rev 43:503–522

Hauert J (2016) Ergebnis- und prozessorientierte Stabilisierungsmechanismen und staatliches Regulierungsinteresse. Nomos, Baden-Baden

Herrmann F, Sanden J, Schomerus T, Schulze F (2012) Ressourcenschutzrecht – Ziele, Herausforderungen und Regelungsvorschläge. Zeitschrift für Umweltrecht (ZUR) 10:523–531. https://www.zur.nomos.de/fileadmin/zur/doc/Aufsatz_ZUR_12_10.pdf

Hervey TK (2016) Telling stories about European Union health law: the emergence of a new field of law. Comp Eur Polit 15(3):352–369

Hobe S (2015) The development of the law of aliens and the emergence of general principles of protection under public international law. In: Bungenberg M, Griebel J, Hobe S, Reinisch A (eds) International investment law: a handbook. Beck-Hart-Nomos, pp 6–22

Ibrahim DM, Smith DG (2008) Entrepreneurs on horseback: reflections on the organization of law. Arizona Law Rev 50:71–89

IFAD (2014) Commodity value chain development projects. October 2014. https://www.ifad.org/documents/38714170/40311826/Commodity+value+chain+development+projects.pdf/504a1102-7bc7-47e8-a46c-003333fe9335

ILA (2012) Sofia Conference, Committee on International Law on Sustainable Development, Final Report. https://ila.vettoreweb.com/Storage/Download.aspx?DbStorageId=1177&StorageFileGuid=7dcf2ffb-6010-48cf-ad92-32453d8ee2b9

Jessup P (1956) Transnational law. Yale University Press

Kaplinsky R (2000) Globalisation and unequalisation: what can be learned from value chain analysis? J Dev Stud 37(2):117–146

Khan KR (1982) The law and organisation of international commodity agreements. Martinus Nijhoff, The Hague

Koh HH (2007) Is there a 'new' new haven school of international law? Yale J Int Law 32:558–573

Lee YS (2011) World trade organization and developing countries. In: Lee YS, Horlick G, Choi WM, Broude T (eds) Law and development perspective on international trade law. Cambridge University Press, Cambridge, pp 105–129

Lessig L (1999) The law of the horse: what cyberlaw might teach. Harv Law Rev 113:501–546

Levit JK (2008) Bottom-up lawmaking: the private origins of transnational law. Indiana J Glob Leg Stud 15(1):49–74

Mahiou A (2013) Development, international law of. In: Wolfrum R (ed) Max Planck encyclopaedia of public international law. Oxford University Press, Oxford

Mariner WK (2009) Toward an architecture of health law. Am J Law Med 35:67–87

Marong A (2010) Development, right to, international protection. In: Wolfrum R (ed) Max Planck encyclopaedia of public international law. Oxford University Press, Oxford

Meessen KM (2001) Zu einer Neuaufteilung des Fächerkanons: Wirtschaftsrecht im Zeichen internationaler und vergleichender Rechtstheorie. Zeitschrift für vergleichende Rechtswissenschaft (ZVglRWiss) 100:41–47

Menkel-Meadow C (2011) Why and how to study transnational law. UC Irvine Law Rev 1(1):97–129

Mertens HJ, Spindler G (1989) Internationales Rohstoffrecht – Bericht über ein DFG-Forschungsprojekt 1974–1986. Rabels Zeitschrift für ausländisches und internationales Privatrecht (RabelsZ) 53:526–550

Midgley SJE (2016) Commodity value chain analysis for apples. WWF-SA, South Africa. http://awsassets.wwf.org.za/downloads/wwf_pfu_commodity_report___apples__lowres_.pdf

Millon D (1992) Objectivity and democracy. NYU Law Rev 67(1):1–66

Mutua M, Anghie A (2000) What is TWAIL? Proceedings of the Annual Meeting (American Society of International Law), vol 94, 5–8 April 2000, pp 31–40

NRGI (2018) The Natural Resource Charter decision chain: converting resources into development. NRGI Primer, February 2018. https://resourcegovernance.org/sites/default/files/documents/nrgi_primer_nrc-decision-chain.pdf

Oehl M (2019) The role of sustainable development in natural resources law. In: Bungenberg M, Krajewski M, Tams C, Terhechte JP, Ziegler AR (eds) European yearbook of international economic law 2018. Springer, pp 3–38

Ong DM (2010) From 'international' to 'transnational' environmental law? A legal assessment of the contribution of the 'Equator Principles' to international environmental Law. Nordic J Int Law 79(1):35–74

Penner JE (1996) The 'bundle of rights' picture of property. UCLA Law Rev 43(3):711–820

Riegert RA (1970) West German Civil Code, its origin and its contract provisions. Tulane Law Rev 45:48–99

Rösler H (2007) Auslegungsgrundsätze des Europäischen Verbraucherprivatrechts in Theorie und Praxis. Rabels Zeitschrift für ausländisches und internationales Privatrecht (RabelsZ) 71(3):495–526

Ruger TW (2008) Health law's coherence anxiety. Georgetown Law J 96:625–648

Ruhl JB, Salzman J (2013) Climate change meets the law of the horse. Duke Law J 62:975–1027

Rüttinger L, Scholl C (2017) Verantwortungsvolle Rohstoffgewinnung? Herausforderungen, Perspektiven, Lösungsansätze. Zusammenfassung der Ergebnisse des Forschungsvorhabens Ansätze zur Reduzierung von Umweltbelastung und negativen sozialen Auswirkungen bei der Gewinnung von Metallrohstoffen (UmSoRess). Umweltbundesamt, Texte 66/2017, https://www.umweltbundesamt.de/sites/default/files/medien/1410/publikationen/2017-08-18_texte_66-2017_umsoress_zusamm.pdf

Saiman C (2007) Restating restitution: a case of contemporary common law conceptualism. Villanova Law Rev 52(3):487–531

Sanden K, Schomerus T, Schulze F (2012) Entwicklung eines Regelungskonzepts für ein Ressourcenschutzrecht des Bundes: Forschungsbericht 3709181521. Erich Schmidt, Berlin

Schütz H, Bringezu S (2008) Ressourcenverbrauch von Deutschland – aktuelle Kennzahlen und Begriffsbestimmungen. Dessau-Roßlau, Februar 2008. https://www.umweltbundesamt.de/sites/default/files/medien/publikation/long/3426.pdf

Sherwin E (2008) Legal positivism and the taxonomy of private law. In: Rickett C, Grantham R (eds) Structure and justification in private law: essays for Peter Birks. pp 103–26

Sherwin E (2009) Legal taxonomy. Leg Theory 15:25–54

Sherwin E (2011) Interpreting tort law. Florida State Univ Law Rev 39:227–242

Solove DJ (2002) Conceptualizing privacy. Calif Law Rev 90(4):1087–1155

Szablowski D (2007) Transnational law and local struggles: mining, communities and the World Bank. Hart, Oxford

Tai S (2015) Food systems law from farm to fork and beyond. Seton Hall Law Rev 45:109–171

Tannenbaum J (2013) What is animal law? Cleveland State Law Rev 61:891–955

Twining W (2000) Globalisation and legal theory. Cambridge University Press, Cambridge

UN (2002) Berlin II Guidelines for Mining and Sustainable Development. https://commdev.org/userfiles/files/903_file_Berlin_II_Guidelines.pdf

UNCTAD (2016) Agricultural commodity value chains: the effects of market concentration on farmers and producing countries – the case of cocoa. 14 October 2016. https://unctad.org/meetings/en/SessionalDocuments/tdb63d2_en.pdf

UNCTAD (2018) World investment report 2018: investment and new industrial policies. UN, Geneva. https://unctad.org/en/PublicationsLibrary/wir2018_en.pdf

Vandevelde KJ (2005) A brief history of international investment agreements. UC Davis J Int Law
     Policy 12:157–194
Weatherill S (2013) EU consumer law and policy. Edward Elgar, Cheltenham
Weiss F (2009) Internationale Rohstoffmärkte. In: Tietje C (ed) Internationales Wirtschaftsrecht.
     De Gruyter, Berlin, pp 276–286
Williams RA (1991) Columbus's legacy: law as an instrument of racial discrimination against
     indigenous peoples' rights of self-determination. Arizona J Int Comp Law 8(2):51–75

Chapter 4
The Effectiveness of TCL

The challenge for TCL lies in balancing the five interests associated with commodity activity—*control, participation, preservation, development,* and *economic gain.* Whereas our account of the application of TCL within the commodity governance matrix above has demonstrated which of these objectives the individual norm subsets are seeking to foster *primarily*, the subsequent assessment will focus on the balancing quality of TCL. Where it strikes a balance, it can be deemed to be effective in ensuring a functional commodity sector.

4.1 The Principle of PSNR as Normative Corner Stone

As the structure of TCL reveals, the principle of permanent sovereignty over natural resources (PSNR) plays a pivotal role therein. In fact, the development of PSNR itself mirrors the evolution of international regulatory approaches towards GCG.

The PSNR principle evolved mainly as a product of discussions among member states within the UN system, particularly in the UN General Assembly (UN GA), ECOSOC, Human Rights Committee (HRC) and UNCTAD,[1] before being incorporated and eventually codified in international treaty law.[2] First referred to in UN

---

[1] Schrijver (2008), para. 5. The principle's legal underpinnings already feature in the UN Charter. Article 1(2) UNC provides for the right of self-determination of peoples; the sovereign equality principle is stipulated in Article 2(1) UNC. Moreover, PSNR relates to two main concerns of the UN as outlined in the preamble of the UN Charter: the economic development of developing countries (para. 4) and the self-determination of colonial peoples (para. 2). As such, PSNR also bears on Article 55 UNC, which calls for economic and social progress, development, respect for HR and fundamental freedoms 'based on respect for the principle of equal rights and self-determination of peoples'; cf. Schrijver (2008), para. 3.

[2] Cf. Schrijver (2008), para. 3.

© The Author(s) 2022
M. E. Oehl, *Sustainable Commodity Use*, EYIEL Monographs - Studies in European and International Economic Law 21, https://doi.org/10.1007/978-3-030-89496-2_4

GA Resolution 523 and UN GA Resolution 626 respectively,[3] the principle, from the very outset, developed in the context of *decolonisation*.[4] In the process of newly formed independent governments taking control over their territories from former colonisers, the 'new nations' were seeking international legal guarantees, which would ensure them and their peoples sovereign rights over their national resource wealth.[5] The initial objective behind PSNR thus mainly related to gaining and maintaining control over national commodity deposits, which had formerly been controlled by colonial rulers—not least in order to prevent Western Transnational Corporations (TNCs) from gaining undue influence over extraction decisions and activities.[6]

In addition, from the outset, PSNR emerged in the context of *development*,[7] which is particularly reflected in the 'landmark' Declaration on PSNR, UN GA Resolution 1803.[8] Accordingly, PSNR 'must be exercised in the interest of [...] national development and of the well-being of the people of the State concerned'.[9]

Notably UNCTAD and also the UN GA later fortified this link between resource exploitation and development in the context of PSNR. The two bodies increasingly used the principle to advocate for heightened attention to the development needs and entitlements of the developing world with the ultimate goal of achieving a redistribution of wealth more favourable to the 'Global South'.[10] These desires culminated in the formulation by the G77 of a New International Economic Order (NIEO).[11] In the relevant Resolution 3201 of 1974, states are being accorded '[f]ull permanent

---

[3]UN GA (1952) Resolution 523 (VI), 12 January 1952, https://documents-dds-ny.un.org/doc/RESOLUTION/GEN/NR0/067/78/IMG/NR006778.pdf?OpenElement, preamble, para. 1; UN GA (1952) Resolution 626 (VII), 21 December 1952, https://documents-dds-ny.un.org/doc/RESOLUTION/GEN/NR0/079/69/IMG/NR007969.pdf?OpenElement (both last accessed 14 May 2021), para. 1.

[4]Schrijver (2008), para. 7.

[5]Schrijver (2008), para. 7.

[6]Cf. Schrijver (2008), paras. 1, 7.

[7]Cf. already UN GA (1952) Resolution 523 (VI), 12 January 1952, preamble, para. 1, according to which 'the under-developed countries [...] must utilize [their] resources in order to be in a better position to further the realization of their plans of economic development in accordance with their national interests and to further the expansion of the world economy'.

[8]UN GA (1962) Resolution 1803 (XVII), 14 December 1962, http://www.un.org/ga/search/view_doc.asp?symbol=A/RES/1803(XVII) (last accessed 14 May 2021); cf. Schrijver (2008), para. 9.

[9]UN GA (1962) Resolution 1803 (XVII), 14 December 1962, para. 1.

[10]Reflected in, e.g., UNCTAD (1964) Final Act and Report, 15 June 1964, UN Doc. E/CONF.46/141, Vol. I, https://unctad.org/en/Docs/econf46d141vol1_en.pdf, p. 10, general principle three and UN GA (1966) Resolution 2158 (XXI) of 25 November 1966, https://documents-dds-ny.un.org/doc/RESOLUTION/GEN/NR0/004/61/IMG/NR000461.pdf?OpenElement (both last accessed 14 May 2021). For instance, Resolution 2158, preamble, para. 5 demands that the 'exploitation and marketing [of NR] should be aimed at securing the highest possible rate of growth of the developing countries'. Cf. Schrijver (2008), para. 11.

[11]Cf. Sect. 2.2.3 above; cf. Schrijver (2008), para. 12.

sovereignty [...] over [their] natural resources and all economic activities.'[12] PSNR is said to entail the respective state's effective control over its natural resources as well as its right to nationalise and/or transfer any property or entitlements related to them to its nationals.[13]

The objectives of the developing world were further spelled out in the Economic Rights Charter (ERC; UN GA Resolution 3281).[14] Again, a major emphasis was put on PSNR, according to Article 2(1) ERC.[15] Moreover, the regulation of activities performed by transnational corporations was emphasised, according to Article 2(2) (b) ERC.[16] In fact, the Charter demonstrates a strong focus on national law and regulatory powers of the nation state respectively—Schrijver thus describes the period as one of *resource confrontationism*.[17]

This stance, however, in turn gave way to a more *cooperative approach*, notably in the context of *environmental protection*.[18] Especially the Stockholm (1972) and Rio (1992) Declarations called for international cooperation for the sake of protecting the planet and ultimately SD.[19] Principle 21 Stockholm, which has been repeated in Principle 2 of the Rio Declaration, places PSNR in the context of environmental protection, notably as provided for in the applicable national legislation as well as the obligation not to cause transboundary harm.[20] Most importantly, it postulates that PSNR shall only be exercised 'in accordance with the [UN Charter] and the principles of international law', thus implicitly referring to i.a. the principles of diligence, due care, good-neighbourliness, and state responsibility (regarding transboundary harm).[21] This cooperative dimension of PSNR is also reflected in the UNCLOS, where it is not limited to environmental protection. According to its Article 56(1)(a) UNCLOS, in the EEZ the coastal state has

> sovereign rights for the purpose of exploring and exploiting, conserving and managing the natural resources [...] of the waters superjacent to the seabed and of the seabed and its subsoil...

According to Article 74(3) UNCLOS, states with opposite or adjacent coasts 'in a spirit of understanding and cooperation, shall make every effort' to assure smooth

---

[12] UN GA (1974) Resolution 3201 (S-VI), 1 May 1974, https://digitallibrary.un.org/record/218450/files/A_RES_3201%28S-VI%29-EN.pdf, para. 4(e) (last accessed 14 May 2021).

[13] Ibid.; cf. Schrijver (2008), para. 12.

[14] UN GA (1974) Resolution 3281 (XXIX), 12 December 1974, http://www.un.org/ga/search/view_doc.asp?symbol=a/res/3281(XXIX) (last accessed 14 May 2021); cf. Schrijver (2008), para. 13.

[15] Ibid.; cf. Schrijver (2008), para. 13.

[16] Cf. Schrijver (2008), para. 13.

[17] Schrijver (2008), para. 13. Emphasis added.

[18] Schrijver (2008), para. 14.

[19] Schrijver (2008), para. 14.

[20] Cf. Schrijver (2008), para. 14.

[21] Schrijver (2008), para. 14.

delimitation of their EEZs between them, and consequently also trouble-free assignment of their respective PSNR.[22]

Despite the widespread scepticism within classical legal scholarship towards norms that have evolved through UN bodies as described above, PSNR by now, besides the UNCLOS, is also incorporated or reflected in various other international agreements, including the Human Rights Covenants.[23] Correspondingly, it has been proclaimed to be of customary character by the arbitral tribunal in the *Texaco v. Libya* case as well as most prominently by the ICJ in the *Armed Activities* case;[24] also the legal doctrine nowadays accepts its customary character.[25]

Accordingly, states—as well as their respective people—are generally competent to control and exploit the commodities located on their territory, which includes the territorial sea according to Article 2 UNCLOS. However, over time the principle of PSNR has increasingly become associated with not only *entitlements* of the respective state, but also *duties*. In the following we shall add clarity to its normative evolution from a *competence allocation* norm (Sect. 4.1.1) to a comprehensive principle aimed at fostering SD by envisaging *rights* (Sect. 4.1.2) as well as *duties*, especially the sustainable use principle (Sect. 4.1.3), thus decisively underpinning GCG.

4.1.1   Competence Norm

The somewhat 'traditional' function of the principle of PSNR lies in its quality as an allocation norm, which confers sovereignty over natural resources onto respective legal subjects. What is less obvious, however, is what legal subject it entitles.

The perhaps most prominent provision expressing PSNR can be found in common Article 1(2) of the HR Covenants. Accordingly,

> [a]ll peoples may, for their own ends, freely dispose of their natural wealth and resources without prejudice to any obligations arising out of international economic co-operation, based upon the principle of mutual benefit, and international law.

---

[22] On the 'the significance of maritime delimitation for the orderly conduct of maritime activities', cf. recent case law as summarised by Ioannides (2019).

[23] On common Article 1(2) HR Covenants cf. Sect. 4.1.1 shortly below; cf. moreover Schrijver (2015), pp. 24–25, who in addition points to Article 21 AfCHR; various ICAs (cf. extensively Sect. 5.2.1 below); Article 18 ECT; preamble and Article 15 CBD; preamble of the UNFCCC; as well as Article 1 of the ICGLR Protocol Against the Illicit Exploitation of Natural Resources of 30 November 2006.

[24] Texaco arbitral tribunal (1977) *Texaco v. Libya*, Award of 19 January 1977, para. 87; ICJ (2005) *Armed Activities on the Territory of the Congo*, Judgment of 19 December 2005, para. 244; cf. Schrijver (2008), para. 23; cf. Hobe (2015), pp. 10–12.

[25] Schrijver (2008), para. 23, who also contends that PSNR is not a peremptory norm (ius cogens) but has acquired a 'firm status within IL'; Dederer (2012), p. 39; Weiss and Scherzer (2015), pp. 45, 54.

The legal subject entitled here thus are *the people*.[26] Yet, as Schrijver has repeatedly emphasised,[27] PSNR exhibits two distinct *normative roots*: the principle of self-determination of *peoples* and the principle of sovereign equality of *states*.[28]

In the context of *decolonisation*, PSNR was thus intended to benefit both subjects: peoples that were seeking to free themselves from foreign rule; as well as newly formed states that were striving for economic independence from the industrialised economic 'centre',[29] i.a. their former colonisers.[30] This is illustrated i.a. in the 1962 Declaration on PSNR, which underlines that

> the right of *peoples and nations* to permanent sovereignty over their natural wealth and resources must be exercised in the interest of their national development and of the wellbeing of the people of the State concerned.[31]

Whereas states' PSNR, in light of the rather speedily emergence of the 'new nations', dominated respective debates for much of the 1960s and 1970s, PSNR as an aspect of the self-determination of peoples has increasingly witnessed attention particularly with regard to indigenous peoples in the past two decades.[32] As Dederer highlights, this illustrates that also peoples *within* a state—that do not constitute the state's people, i.e. the 'nation'—can be the bearers of PSNR.[33] As a consequence, the exercise of PSNR and territorial sovereignty do not necessarily converge.[34]

4.1.2   Rights Associated with PSNR

Next, naturally the question arises what rights PSNR entails. Sovereignty has been defined in the context of international law i.a. as 'ultimate power' or 'supreme authority'—that is 'alternatively or cumulatively'.[35] The following rights, as listed in Article 2 UNC and the Friendly Relations Declaration, are typically being associated with sovereignty:

---

[26] On the debate whether peoples constitute subjects of international law, see the overview provided by Walter (2007), paras. 8–9, 12; fundamentally, arguing for a new *jus gentium* as the international law for *humankind*, Cançado Trindade (2010).

[27] I.a. Schrijver (1997); Schrijver (2008); Schrijver (2015).

[28] Schrijver (2015), pp. 16–17.

[29] On centre–periphery, cf. Sect. 2.1.2 above.

[30] Schrijver (2015), pp. 16–17.

[31] UN GA (1962) Resolution 1803 (XVII), 14 December 1962, para. 1. Emphasis added. Cf. Schrijver (2015), p. 17.

[32] Schrijver (2015), pp. 22–23.

[33] Dederer (2012), p. 40, n 15.

[34] Dederer (2012), p. 40, n 15. Extensively with the hypothesis that states have transferred sovereign rights over NR onto non-state actors, Pereira and Gough (2013).

[35] Besson (2011), para. 114.

[P]lenary territorial and personal jurisdiction within one's territorial boundaries; the presumption of legality of one's sovereign acts; constitutional and organizational autonomy including self-determination; and the protection of one's domaine réservé.[36]

With regard to PSNR, Schrijver specifies the rights that have become associated with it since its inception in the decolonisation era. He first refers to a number of '*basic rights*', which include the 'rights to possess, use, freely dispose of, explore, exploit, market, manage, and conserve the natural resources.'[37] A second category he introduces, comprises '*related rights*', which are

the rights to regulate foreign investment, including the right to tax foreign investment and under certain specific circumstances and meeting international law requirements the right to take foreign property.[38]

The third and last category that Schrijver alludes to, consists of rights that he describes as '*controversial*'.[39] It includes the right to demand 'a share in the management of local subsidiaries of multinational companies, or to withdraw from unequal treaties or to revise unilaterally terms of agreed arrangements';[40] as well as 'the right to determine unilaterally the amount of compensation, and to settle international investment disputes solely upon the basis of national law.'[41]

4.1.3 The Sustainable Use Principle

Perhaps the most significant development in the dynamic emergence of the principle of PSNR relates to its quality as a norm conferring not only rights, but also *duties* upon its respective bearer.[42] As we have seen above, already UN GA Resolution 1803 required states and/or peoples entitled to PSNR to exercise their sovereignty 'in the interest of their national development and of the wellbeing of the people of the State concerned.'[43] In connection with the emergence of international environmental law, these duties were supplemented with an obligation to avoid harm to the environment.[44]

An early provision on sustainable use can be found in Article 2 of the 1958 Convention on Fishing and Conservation of the Living Resources of the High Seas, according to which enabling 'the optimum sustainable yield' is defined as the

---

[36] Besson (2011), para. 118.

[37] Schrijver (2015), p. 26. Emphasis added.

[38] Schrijver (2015), p. 26. Emphasis added.

[39] Schrijver (2015), p. 26. Emphasis added.

[40] Schrijver (2015), p. 26.

[41] Schrijver (2015), p. 26.

[42] Cf. e.g. Schrijver (2015), p. 27.

[43] Schrijver (2015), p. 27 contends that this obligation 'can be viewed as a good governance requirement *avant la lettre*.' Original emphasis.

[44] Cf. introduction to Sect. 4.1 above.

objective of resource conservation.[45] Article 2 of the Convention on Biological Diversity defines sustainable use as

> the use of components of biological diversity in a way and at a rate that does not lead to the long-term decline of biological diversity, thereby maintaining its potential to meet the needs and aspirations of present and future generations.

It has generally been said to put states

> under a duty to manage natural resources, including natural resources within their own territory or jurisdiction, in a rational, sustainable and safe way so as to contribute to the development of their peoples, with particular regard for the rights of indigenous peoples, and to the conservation and sustainable use of natural resources and the protection of the environment, including ecosystems. States must take into account the needs of future generations in determining the rate of use of natural resources. All relevant actors (including States, industrial concerns and other components of civil society) are under a duty to avoid wasteful use of natural resources and promote waste minimization policies.[46]

While the exact obligation it entails will typically differ depending on the concrete subject matter to which it applies, the principle has become more and more widely accepted, particularly with regard to

> established treaty regimes on such matters as fisheries, marine living resources and specific ecosystems (eg wetlands), [...] cooperative arrangements concerning transboundary and shared natural resources, especially watercourses, and [...] the increasingly specific guidance on [...] the rights of indigenous peoples and their management of local natural resources.[47]

Moreover, the principle is now also rooted in target 12.2 of the SDGs ('sustainable management and efficient use of natural resources').[48] It has been identified as a rule of customary international law, at a minimum with regard to common or shared resources.[49] As such, it substantially qualifies the respective legal subject's PSNR.[50]

In fact, this very principle gives further pivotal indications regarding the effectiveness of TCL. That is, the sustainable use principle constitutes a *balancing*

---

[45] Schrijver (2008), para. 16. On its historical evolution, cf. also Sect. 4.1 above. The sustainable use principle later developed to become part of the principle of SD, as contained in the 'Brundtland report' of 1987 and principle 2 of the 1992 Rio Declaration, cf. Beyerlin (2013), para. 21 as well as Sect. 5.1 below.

[46] ILA (2002), para. 1.2.; cf. also ILA (2012), p. 14.

[47] ILA (2012), p. 14. Cf. particularly with regard to fisheries also Article 2 1995 Straddling Stocks Agreement as well as the 1995 FAO Code of Conduct for Responsible Fisheries.

[48] Cf. Schrijver (2008), para. 16. On the functioning of SD as the regulatory objective of TCL, cf. Sect. 5.1 below.

[49] Cf. ILA (2012), Annex, p. 36, Sofia Guiding Statement #3; Oehl (2019), p. 35 with further references.

[50] According to Beyerlin (2013), para. 20, the sustainable use principle embodies the ideas of *distributive justice* as well as of *international solidarity* in a common struggle to preserve the planetary ecosystem.

norm.[51] Sustainable use reconciles all five commodity interests of control (1), participation (2), development (3), preservation (4), and economic gain (5) in that it obliges states

> to manage natural resources in a rational [1;5], sustainable and safe [4] way so as to contribute to the development [3;5] of their peoples [2], with particular regard for the rights of indigenous peoples [2;3], and to the conservation and sustainable use of natural resources and the protection of the environment, including ecosystems [4]. States must take into account the needs of future generations in determining the rate of use of natural resources [2;3;4;5].[52]

4.1.4 TCL Is Effective Where It Fosters Sustainable Use

This observation allows the following conclusions: The sustainable use principle exhibits the *normative contents* needed in order to achieve a functional commodity sector. Thus, the TCL framework would be effective where it concretises what sustainable use requires. This would involve providing balancing norms, which further detail how the commodity interests need to be balanced in respective commodity scenarios, e.g. depending on the subsector, actors, or individual commodity concerned.

4.2 The Contribution of TCL to a 'Balanced' Commodity Sector

To what extent the current TCL framework lives up to these requirements shall be investigated in the subsequent section. For that purpose, we are going to discuss several normative patterns, which TCL exhibits, including its largely 'indirect' nature (4.2.1) as well as the limited effectiveness of incidents of 'direct' TCL (4.2.2), which is i.a. caused by a lack of integration and 'hard' legal obligations respectively.

---

[51] Another approach, which however does not appear to have acquired the status of a legal concept, yet appears to cover all commodity interests, is the shared value perspective. It aims to reconcile market potential and societal development and is reflected i.a. in the UN GC's SDG Natural Resource industry matrix as well as the OECD Framework for Extractive Projects titled Collaborative Strategies for In-Country Shared Value Creation, which through its five-step framework i.a. addresses long-term strategies for the generation of shared value from commodity extraction.

[52] ILA (2002), para. 1.2. Reference numbers added.

4.2.1   TCL Is Largely Indirect

In analysing the substance of TCL, one can differentiate between *direct* TCL, on the one hand, and *indirect* TCL, on the other.[53] Direct TCL can be described as those norms of inter- and transnational law, which 'reflect a conscious consideration of' commodity activities and their implications for diverging stakeholder interests and corresponding policy trade-offs.[54] Thus, direct, or *intentional*, TCL demonstrates commonalities of TCL relating to *legal doctrine*, which are distinct from other fields of law.[55] Indirect TCL consists of rules that are *unintentionally* regulating commodity activities, and thus without exhibiting a conscious consideration for their particularities.

The 'indirect' nature of a norm of TCL may not be perceived as an indication of its (in)effectiveness *per se*. Instead, also rules formulated for a different purpose, such as investment protection, naturally contribute to the regulatory picture. However, in most instances, those rules, which have been introduced for objectives that are distinct from the overall objective of good commodity governance or fostering the SD of the commodity sector, are not suited to specifically address the policy trade-offs that typically result from commodity activities.

As we shall see by way of example, the 'indirect' norm subsets of TCL addressing Human Rights (Sect. 4.2.1.1), environmental protection (Sect. 4.2.1.2), the fiscal framework applicable to commodity operations (Sect. 4.2.1.3), scenarios of armed conflict (Sect. 4.2.1.4) as well as anti-corruption (Sect. 4.2.1.5) build 'regulatory circles' around individual interests. Yet, they largely do not provide answers to questions that relate to the legitimacy of the decision to extract. Apart from demanding conformity with the regime protecting or fostering the individual legal good they have been designed for, they do not spell out guidelines on how commodity policy trade-offs could be remedied. As a consequence, these answers, beyond the qualification of a state's sovereignty for the purposes of the individual regime, are left unregulated and thus widely subject to the discretion of the respective state.

---

[53] See insofar the references to 'commodity-directed' norms throughout this book.

[54] Cf. Aagaard's differentiation between 'laws that reflect a conscious consideration of the environment' and 'laws enacted without any conscious consideration of the environment', Aagaard (2010), p. 262.

[55] Again, the norms portrayed subsequently contribute to the *distinctive* identity of TCL; yet, their applicability is in many instances not *unique* to TCL. Instead, they may also feature in i.a., the broader, superordinate field of natural resources law or in legal fields, which have evolved around specific subject matters, such as the law of international watercourses or world trade law, cf. Sects. 3.1 and 3.2 above.

4.2.1.1 Human Rights

International Human Rights (HR) are widely applicable to commodity activities.[56] In fact, the pervasiveness of HR-related scenarios is thus great that international HR law has been deemed to sufficiently regulate distribution conflicts in the commodity sector.[57] Indirect HR, which are particularly pertinent in a commodity context, are the right to life, labour rights, land rights, rights to basic needs, the right to a clean environment, rights of indigenous peoples, rights in situations of violence, the right to remedy, and the right to development.[58]

The *right to life* is rooted in Article 6(1) ICCPR.[59] In connection with commodity activities, loss of life can naturally occur under circumstances such as the handling of toxic substances,[60] underground mining, or mudslides.[61]

Many HR violations in the commodity sector are occurring in a *labour context*.[62] For example, the displacement of fishers, farmers or artisanal miners, e.g. due to the implementation of an industrial commodity operation, may constitute a violation of the right to work provided for in Article 6(1) ICESCR.[63] Another labour right that is of great significance in the commodity sector is the *prohibition of forced or compulsory labour*, which is primarily being regulated by ILO Convention 29 ('Forced Labour Convention'). With regard to commodity activities, forced labour occurs most frequently in the mining or agricultural sector.[64] Sadly, it often appears in combination with *child labour*, particularly in small-scale mining contexts, where it is considered the 'worst form of child labour'.[65] Children are generally protected against child labour, according to Article 32 of the Convention on the Rights of the Child (CRC). Moreover, also Article 10(3) ICESCR seeks to protect children from

---

[56] Cf. only the long list of cases brought before US-American courts based on the Alien Tort Claim Act provided by Dederer (2012), p. 45, n 47. Cf. also for the oil and gas sector, European Commission (2011).

[57] Krajewski (2016).

[58] Cf. Spohr (2016).

[59] Cf. Spohr (2016), p. 61.

[60] For example, mercury poising in small-scale mining can pose a particular threat to children, cf. Bürgi Bonanomi et al. (2015), p. 29.

[61] Extensively on the risk of tailings dam failures including several case studies, Spohr (2016), pp. 59–61.

[62] Bürgi Bonanomi et al. (2015), p. 29.

[63] Spohr (2016), pp. 88–89.

[64] Bürgi Bonanomi et al. (2015), p. 29.

[65] Bürgi Bonanomi et al. (2015), p. 29. In 2013, more than one million children were said to be working in artisanal or small-scale mining operations in Africa, Latin America and Asia, Diallo et al. (2013), p. vii; cf. Spohr (2016), p. 104; the latter describes the following reality: 'Children start washing gold from 3 years on; from 6 years on they can be seen breaking rocks with hammers or washing ore; at the age of 9 they can be observed underground, and at 12 boys are working underground in many countries and do the same work as adults (see e.g. Bolivia, Cerro Rico / Potosi)', Spohr (2016), p. 105 with reference to M. Hansson (2006), p. 2; cf. also various case studies collected by Spohr (2016), pp. 106–109.

economic and social exploitation. Insofar as child labour causes detrimental effects to the health of a child, Article 12(2)(a) ICESCR and the obligation it entails with regard to fulfilling the preconditions for a healthy development of the child may be relevant.[66] The prohibition and elimination of the worst forms of child labour also features in the SDGs as target 8.7.

Further specific protection to *vulnerable groups in labour contexts* typically applies to women, indigenous peoples, migrants as well as disabled and older people. Ending the discrimination of women is enshrined in SDG target 8.5. In the commodity sector, women are still said to frequently 'hold little power, [be] ill-informed, and earn less than men'—a situation, which creates major obstacles in the pursuit of sustainability.[67]

Further HR violations in the commodity sector can occur with regard to *land tenure*, which is defined as 'the relationship, whether legally or customarily defined, among people, as individuals or groups, with respect to land.'[68] In a commodity context, land rights are typically concerned whenever a certain local or indigenous population needs to be relocated in connection with the creation of e.g. a plantation or mining site.[69] The granting of respective licenses by the state can constitute a breach of land tenure rights, whenever the acting authorities do not sufficiently respect existing land titles, including ones of customary nature. However, even forced evictions and resettlements can theoretically be justified under specific circumstances.[70] Such generally requires, i.a., 'appropriate resettlement' to areas, which provide adequate housing as well as access to water, food and work.[71]

Tenure rights are particularly recognised under international law with regard to indigenous peoples, such as by Articles 11, 12 ILO Convention 107 (Protection and Integration of Indigenous and other Tribal and Semi-Tribal Populations in Independent Countries), the preamble to the 1992 Convention on Biological Diversity as well as Articles 13 (general provision) and 14 (informal tenure rights) ILO convention 169. Article 15(1) ILO Convention 169 insofar constitutes an exception to the 'indirect' nature of HR, as it sets out that '[t]he rights of the peoples concerned to the *natural resources* pertaining to their lands shall be specially safeguarded. These rights include the right of these peoples to participate in the use, management and conservation of these resources.'[72]

---

[66]Cf. Spohr (2016), p. 111. It also constitutes a violation of the childrens' rights to education pursuant to Articles 13, 28 CRC, cf. Spohr (2016), p. 110.

[67]Hinton et al. (2003); cf. Bürgi Bonanomi et al. (2015), p. 29.

[68]FAO (2002), para. 3.1.

[69]On the scenario of area clearing, cf. Spohr (2016), pp. 34–36, including various case studies.

[70]Spohr (2016), p. 34; cf. also the case study of the village of Horno in Germany, as an example for a justified forced eviction, Spohr (2016), p. 35; in such scenarios, the right to privacy according to Article 17 ICCPR may be relevant, cf. Spohr (2016), pp. 136–137.

[71]Spohr (2016), p. 34; cf. in this respect also our discussion of the RFD in Sect. 4.2.2.1.1 below.

[72]Emphasis added. Generally, indigenous people are entitled to also profit from e.g. mineral resources, which are located on their 'lands'. The term is thus to be understood in broad terms, so as to comprise 'the whole territory they use, including forests, rivers, mountains, coastal sea, the

Given the great meaning that the natural environment can bear upon the *cultural identities* of indigenous peoples, issues relating to tenure have repeatedly been treated by the Human Rights Committee as a matter of Article 27 ICCPR.[73] Also Article 13(1) ILO convention 169 expressly provides that 'governments shall respect the special importance for the cultures and spiritual values of the peoples concerned of their relationship with the lands or territories, [...] which they occupy or otherwise use...'

Rights to basic needs can be concerned also where commodity activities negatively impact the environment, such as contaminations of groundwater or soil, water depletion, air pollution, devastation of the environment due to tailings dam failures or mudslides, acid mine drainage etc.[74] The right to an adequate standard of living, which includes the right to water, food and adequate housing is provided for in Article 11(1) ICESCR;[75] Article 12(1) ICESCR protects the physical and mental health. The latter provisions are frequently also employed in the context of environmental quality.[76] Thus, Article 12(1) ICESCR has been raised also regarding issues such as adequate supply of safe and potable water, basic sanitation, prevention and reduction of exposure to harmful substances 'or other detrimental environmental conditions that directly or indirectly impact upon human health.'[77]

---

surface, and the sub-surface', Spohr (2016), p. 45 with reference to ILO (2009), p. 91. Cf. also Dederer (2012), p. 48, n 66 who raises the question what resources the rights of indigenous peoples comprise. On this question moreover IACtHR (2001) *Mayagna (Sumo) Awas Tingni Community v. Nicaragua*, IACtHR Series C no. 79, judgment of 31 August 2001. The IACtHR qualified *logging concessions* as the cause of potentially long-term, irreversible damage to the natural environment, which the petitioners depended on economically—and therefore a violation of Article 21 ACHR, paras. 153–155; Boyle (2009), para. 22; see also para. 149 of the court ruling: 'Given the characteristics of the instant case, some specifications are required on the concept of property in indigenous communities. Among indigenous peoples there is a communitarian tradition regarding a communal form of collective property of the land, in the sense that ownership of the land is not centred on an individual but rather on the group and its community. Indigenous groups, by the fact of their very existence, have the right to live freely in their own territory; the close ties of indigenous people with the land must be recognised and understood as the fundamental basis of their cultures, their spiritual life, their integrity, and their economic survival. For indigenous communities, relations to the land are not merely a matter of possession and production but a material and spiritual element which they must fully enjoy, even to preserve their cultural legacy and transmit it to future generations.'

[73] Strydom (2013), para. 6 with reference to i.a. UN HRC (1990) *Ominayak, Chief of the Lubicon Lake Band v. Canada*; UN HRC (1994) *Länsman v. Finland*; cf. also Spohr (2016), p. 46: 'Some aspects of these rights protected under that article may consist in a way of life that is closely associated with territory and use of its resources, which is particularly true of members of indigenous communities.'; UN HRC (1994), paras. 3.2, 7; cf. also the *Awas Tingni* case mentioned above.

[74] Cf. Spohr (2016), pp. 49–54, 62.

[75] On the right to water UN CESCR (2003) 'General Comment No 15: The Right to Water (Arts 11 and 12)', 20 January 2003, https://www.refworld.org/docid/4538838d11.html (last accessed 14 May 2021); cf. Boyle (2009), para. 14.

[76] Boyle (2009), para. 14.

[77] UN CESCR (2000), para. 15; cf. Boyle (2009), para. 13.

Moreover, Articles 11(1) and 12(1) ICESCR respectively have repeatedly been interpreted so as to include a *right to access to basic energy* given that access to energy will typically be a precondition to the fulfilment of many socioeconomic HR.[78] SDG 7 aims 'to ensure access to affordable, reliable, sustainable and modern energy for all'. In a commodity context, this right can be relevant with regard to the sourcing of energy commodities, which needs to be conducted in the most sustainable way possible. Also, commencing commodity activities, particularly in the extractive industries, can create opportunities to at the same time e.g. electrify adjacent local communities.[79] Furthermore, it may have implications for the 'energy mix'—of renewable and non-renewable sources—that a government chooses and thus for the types of commodities that the state is deciding to grant exploitation rights for.[80]

Given the great impact commodity activities can have on local populations, *participatory rights* are crucial to ensure their interests are being adequately represented in corresponding governmental decisions.[81] Three components of public participation law are typically being distinguished: access to information, public participation in decision-making, and access to justice.[82] While the law of public participation has primarily evolved in the context of international environmental law, and is most notably enshrined in principle 10 Rio Declaration as well as the Aarhus Convention,[83] it is also partly rooted in international HR law. The *right to information* is based on Article 19 ICCPR as a part of the freedom to expression as well as Article 25(b) ICCPR, which entails the right to participate in public affairs.[84] Article 19(2) ICCPR provides for the *right to access to information*, thus 'the freedom to seek, receive and impart information and ideas of all kinds', which encompasses public interest information as well as information that is relevant for potential violations of individual rights.[85] Moreover, Article 1(2) ICESCR comprises the continued obligation of a state to ensure transparency when it regulates or administers public resources.[86]

Failure to adequately respect participatory—or other—HR can result in particularly infamous HR violations, which exhibit a rather *indirect* connection to commodity activities. The talk is of *situations of violence*, such as armed conflict or

---

[78] Bradbrook and Gardam (2006), p. 409; cf. also Ottinger (2014).

[79] On these *linkages*, cf. already Sect. 2.1.2 above.

[80] While typical non-renewable energy commodities include oil, gas and coal, also the so-called *renewable energies* require specific commodities, such as bauxite (for aluminium) or Rare Earths (e.g. for permanent magnets in wind turbines). Cf. comprehensively on the various uses of minerals in new technologies Espa and Oehl (2018).

[81] Cf. Sect. 2.1.3 above, which identifies 'participation' as one of the fundamental interests associated with commodity activity.

[82] Pring and Noé (2002), p. 28.

[83] Cf. extensively, Pring and Noé (2002), pp. 28–50; cf. also Sect. 4.2.1.2 below.

[84] Ebbesson (2009b), para. 30; Ebbesson (2009a), para. 26; Spohr (2016), p. 32.

[85] Spohr (2016), p. 32.

[86] Spohr (2016), p. 32.

violent clashes over distribution of benefits, tenure rights, or cultural impact.[87] Both resource dependence and abundance, particularly of precious minerals, have been found to conduce violence, armed conflict and, at times, civil war.[88] The state's obligation to refrain from encroachments on HR here relates to its own duty to respect HR as well as to protect everyone under its jurisdiction against HR violations, e.g. committed by security forces employed by private commodity companies.[89] Relevant rights that may be harmed in situations of violence include Articles 6 (right to life), 7 (freedom from torture or cruel, inhuman or degrading treatment or punishment), 9(1) (right to security of the person), and 21 (freedom of assembly) ICCPR as well as the prohibition of torture contained in Articles 1(1), 2(1) Convention Against Torture.[90]

Furthermore, the right to remedy, which is set out in Article 8 UDHR, Article 2 (3) ICCPR as well as Article 6 CERD and Article 2(c) CEDAW, ensures adequate enforcement of states' HR obligations. It is composed of the two duties to provide access to justice as well as to take substantive measures to prevent or redress rights violations.[91]

An HR that is relevant for GCG rather from a 'big picture' perspective, which has not yet been legally codified as such, is the right to development as defined in Article 1 of the Declaration on the Right to Development.[92] Given the great economic significance of the commodity sector for many developing countries, particularly CDDCs, the right to development oftentimes features in policy debates on terms of trade, technology transfer, or detrimental effects of commodity activities on development.[93]

4.2.1.2 Environmental Protection Norms

Commodity activities can have major impacts on the natural environment. For instance, the conversion of primary forests into plantations may have problematic effects for soil fertility, biodiversity, water quality and availability as well as the existence of organic carbon stocks.[94] Timber logging may have similar effects and,

---

[87]Cf. Spohr (2016), pp. 117–130.

[88]Bürgi Bonanomi et al. (2015), pp. 27–28; Spohr (2016), p. 125.

[89]Cf. Bürgi Bonanomi et al. (2015), p. 28.

[90]Cf. Spohr (2016), pp. 130–133. In extreme cases, even a violation of Articles 2, 3 UN Genocide Convention may become relevant.

[91]Shelton (2006), para. 2; the former includes the duty to provide access to relevant information concerning violations and reparation mechanisms, UN GA (2005) Basic Principles and Guidelines on the Right to a Remedy, Resolution 60/147, 16 December 2005, para. 11; cf. Spohr (2016), p. 57.

[92]On the historical underpinnings of the right to development and its relationship to the NIEO, Marong (2010), paras. 4–5.

[93]Cf. Marks (2004), p. 141.

[94]Bürgi Bonanomi et al. (2015), p. 33.

by reducing carbon stocks, may accelerate climate change.[95] The mining of commodities frequently causes water pollution or contamination, for instance from mine tailings, which result from copper, iron, coal, or gold production.[96] Moreover, surface contaminants may be spread by water and wind, which can lead to increased concentration of metal sediments that can damage aquifers and other water ecosystems.[97] A particular environmental problem, which occurs in connection with gold extraction, is the contamination of soils and waters with mercury.[98] Surface mining of commodities such as copper, iron, coal and gold particularly causes air pollution, with coal extraction exhibiting detrimental effects on biodiversity regeneration.[99] As Bürgi Bonanomi and others point out, particularly on the African continent, mining appears to elicit extensive deforestation of rainforests.[100]

These environmental effects need to be taken into account whenever a government considers extracting commodities. They are being addressed by today's international environmental protection regime, which began to emerge in the 1970s. Notably the 1972 Stockholm Declaration represents the first document addressing environmental protection, which witnessed quasi-universal support from the international community.[101] From the beginning, safeguarding natural resources for present and future generations constituted one of the central objectives of the environmental protection regime.[102]

However, international environmental law as an established branch of international law, including its somewhat coherent doctrine and substance,[103] only in some incidents reflects a conscious consideration of the particularities of commodity activity. It is characterised by a set of *central rules and principles*,[104] which have been concretised in the context of specific protection regimes provided for in various international legal instruments,[105] which are undeniably again quite close to

---

[95] Cf. Bürgi Bonanomi et al. (2015), p. 34; on the negative impacts of cocoa and coffee intensification on biodiversity likewise Bürgi Bonanomi et al. (2015), pp. 33–34 with further evidence.

[96] Bürgi Bonanomi et al. (2015), p. 36.

[97] Bürgi Bonanomi et al. (2015), p. 36.

[98] Cf. Espa and Oehl (2018). On the guidance provided by the Minamata Convention in this respect, cf. Sect. 5.2.1.2.3.1 below.

[99] Bürgi Bonanomi et al. (2015), pp. 36–37.

[100] Bürgi Bonanomi et al. (2015), p. 37.

[101] Beyerlin and Grote Stoutenberg (2013), para. 9. Prior to Stockholm, environmental protection efforts were mainly led by FAO, UNESCO and ECOSOC, yet the UN's competence to do so had still been disputed, cf. Beyerlin and Grote Stoutenberg (2013), para. 7.

[102] Cf. Principles 2, 3 and 5 Stockholm Declaration.

[103] Cf. Beyerlin and Grote Stoutenberg (2013), para. 3.

[104] Most of these central principles have been elaborated in legal language in either the Stockholm or Rio Declaration; cf. Barral (2012), p. 379.

[105] Cf. e.g. Sands and Peel (2018), pp. 101–106 on the emergence of international environmental agreements.

commodity activities, such as the ones regulating the protection of the atmosphere,[106] air,[107] freshwater,[108] wetlands,[109] oceans, seas and marine living resources,[110] flora and fauna,[111] forests and soils,[112] biological diversity,[113] and the Polar regions.[114] Further regimes address climate change[115] as well as wastes and hazardous substances.[116] Yet, most rules and principles do not reflect a conscious consideration of commodity policy trade-offs.

---

[106] Especially 1985 Vienna Convention for the Protection of the Ozone Layer; Montreal Protocol on Substances that Deplete the Ozone Layer; cf. Beyerlin and Grote Stoutenberg (2013), para. 33.

[107] Especially Convention on Long-Range Transboundary Air Pollution; as well as the ASEAN Agreement on Transboundary Haze Pollution; cf. Beyerlin and Grote Stoutenberg (2013), para. 32.

[108] Especially UN Convention on the Law of the Non-Navigational Uses of International Watercourses; cf. Beyerlin and Grote Stoutenberg (2013), paras. 64–65.

[109] Especially Convention on Wetlands of International Importance Especially as Waterfowl Habitat (Ramsar Convention); Revised African Convention on the Conservation of Nature and Natural Resources (Maputo Convention), cf. also Sect. 5.2.1.2.3.3 below; cf. Beyerlin and Grote Stoutenberg (2013), paras. 42–3.

[110] Especially 1995 Fish Stocks Agreement (global scope), as well as several fisheries agreements with a regional scope; UNCLOS; International Convention for the Prevention of Pollution from Ships; International Convention on Oil Pollution Preparedness, Response and Cooperation; 1996 Protocol to the Convention on the Prevention of Marine Pollution by Dumping of Wastes and Other Matter. For an account of further regional marine environmental protection conventions, cf. Baker and Share (2013). On all of the above, cf. Beyerlin and Grote Stoutenberg (2013), paras. 52–62.

[111] Convention on International Trade in Endangered Species of Wild Fauna and Flora (CITES), Convention on the Conservation of Migratory Species of Wild Animals (CMS).

[112] As Beyerlin and Grote Stoutenberg (2013), para. 49 contend, '[a] comprehensive system of forest protection is still missing in [IEL].' On the International Tropical Timber Agreement—and other ICAs—cf. especially Sect. 5.2.1.2 below. In the climate change context, Beyerlin and Grote Stoutenberg (2013), para. 50 are pointing to REDD+, cf. UNFCCC (2019), REDD+, web platform, https://redd.unfccc.int/ (last accessed 14 May 2021). With regard to soil protection, note the 1998 Protocol on the Implementation of the Alpine Convention of 1991 in the Field of Soil Conservation, as well as the UN Desertification Convention; cf. Beyerlin and Grote Stoutenberg (2013), para. 51.

[113] Convention on Biological Diversity; Bonn Guidelines; Nagoya Protocol; cf. in more detail Sect. 5.2.1.2.3.3 below. Moreover, cf. also the Aichi Biodiversity Targets; the Cartagena Protocol; as well as the FAO International Treaty on Plant Genetic Resources for Food and Agriculture; cf. Beyerlin and Grote Stoutenberg (2013), paras. 45–48.

[114] On CRAMRA, cf. Sect. 5.2.1.2.3.2 below.

[115] Cf. especially the UNFCCC; Kyoto Protocol; as well as the Paris Agreement; cf. Beyerlin and Grote Stoutenberg (2013), paras. 35–40.

[116] Especially 1989 Basel Convention; 1991 Bamako Convention; the 2001 Stockholm Convention on Persistent Organic Pollutants, which i.a. regulates several pesticides that have been used in the production of agricultural commodities, such as Chlordane, Dieldrin, DDT, or Endosulfans, cf. UNEP (2019) All POPs listed in the Stockholm convention, http://www.pops.int/TheConvention/ThePOPs/AllPOPs/tabid/2509/Default.aspx (last accessed 14 May 2021); as well as the Minamata Convention, which applies to mercury-containing waste, cf. its Article 5(1). Cf. also the overview of relevant instruments on international waste managements provided by Sands and Peel (2018), pp. 619–626; as well as Beyerlin and Grote Stoutenberg (2013), paras. 69–77.

The *obligation not to cause transboundary harm*, in short 'no harm' rule, had first been pronounced by the arbitral tribunal in the *Trail Smelter* case in 1941. It features in Principle 21 of the Stockholm Declaration and has been recognised as a rule of customary international law by the ICJ in its advisory opinion on the *Legality of the Threat or Use of Nuclear Weapons*.[117] In the commodity context, the no harm rule can be particularly significant with regard to dispersion of contaminants resulting from commodity activities via air or water to areas under the sovereignty of another nation state or constituting the common concern of humankind.[118]

According to Principle 15 Rio Declaration, states shall apply the *precautionary approach* in order to protect the environment.[119] In scenarios, in which the precautionary principle applies, states are obliged to take adequate measures to prevent the respective potential harm; however, the choice of *what kind* of measures exactly they are taking, remains their own.[120] The precautionary approach also applies to the sustainable utilisation of natural resources.[121] It is said to belong to the category of emerging customary international law, with some authors arguing that this status has already been consolidated.[122]

The *duty to carry out Environmental Impact Assessments* (EIAs), contained in Principle 17 Rio Declaration, relates to the concept of precaution.[123] It is further specified by the Convention on Environmental Impact Assessment in a Transboundary Context ('Espoo Convention'), particularly its Article 2(3). The provision is somewhat directly applicable to commodity activities given that appendix I, which it refers to, lists several commodity scenarios, such as crude oil

---

[117]ICJ (1996) *Legality of the Threat or Use of Nuclear Weapons*, Advisory Opinion, para. 29; Beyerlin and Grote Stoutenberg (2013), para. 23.

[118]Despite its categorisation, here, as 'indirect' TCL, the 'no harm' rule has also been put in context with the sustainable use principle, see ILA (2002), para. 1.1.

[119]Cf. also ILA (2002), principle #4.

[120]Beyerlin and Grote Stoutenberg (2013), para. 25 with reference to ITLOS (2011) Advisory opinion, 1 February 2011, paras. 131–132; cf. also Chen (2016).

[121]ILA (2002), para. 4.2.

[122]Beyerlin and Grote Stoutenberg (2013), para. 25; Sands and Peel (2018), p. 240 see 'reluctance to embrace a clear view' regarding the principle's customary status, which 'is no doubt informed by doubts and differences as to what the practical consequences of the precautionary principle or approach will be in a particular field or in a specific case.'

[123]Cf. ILA (2002), para. 4.2.c. The EIA obligation has been confirmed as customary international law by the ICJ (2010a) *Pulp Mills on the River Uruguay*, Judgment of 20 April 2010, paras. 204–205. Accordingly, it 'may now be considered a requirement under general international law to undertake an environmental impact assessment where there is a risk that the proposed industrial activity may have a significant adverse impact in a transboundary context, in particular, on a shared resource'; however, general international law does not specify how exactly an EIA needs to be carried out: 'it is for each State to determine in its domestic legislation or in the authorization process for the project, the specific content of the environmental impact assessment required in each case, having regard to the nature and magnitude of the proposed development and its likely adverse impact on the environment as well as to the need to exercise due diligence in conducting such an assessment[]'; cf. also ITLOS (2011), para. 145; on both cf. Beyerlin and Grote Stoutenberg (2013), para. 24.

refineries, major installations for the initial smelting of cast iron and steel and for the production of nonferrous metals, installations for the extraction of asbestos, large-diameter pipelines for the transport of oil, gas or chemicals, major quarries, mining, on-site extraction and processing of metal ores or coal or deforestation of large areas. This provision thus displays the particular significance in the context of commodity activities of the obligation to carry out an EIA.[124]

Further guidance on how to conduct environmental—but also cultural and social—impact assessments is provided by the Akwé: Kon Voluntary Guidelines for the Conduct of Cultural, Environmental and Social Impact Assessment, which have been adopted by the Conference of the Parties of the CBD in May 2000.

Moreover, the principle of preventive action constitutes a key element of international environmental law (IEL). While it is frequently referred to in the context of *precaution*, the principle of prevention needs to be differentiated from the former.[125] While the precautionary approach is relevant, whenever the risks of environmental damage are *uncertain*, the prevention principle applies for risks, which are certain.[126] Given that many commodity activities entail risks, which are certain, the principle of prevention needs to be observed during the planning and implementation of such activities whenever a transboundary context is concerned. The arbitral tribunal in the proceedings between the Philippines and China regarding the South China Sea held China's obligation to prevent damage to the marine environment, as rooted in Articles 192 and 194 UNCLOS, to be breached given that it had not prevented i.a., the harvesting of endangered sea turtles.[127]

Furthermore, the *polluter pays principle* (PPP) as enshrined in Principle 16 Rio Declaration numbers among the central elements of IEL. The same holds true for the *principle of common but differentiated responsibility* (CBDR), which may at times conflict with the PPP. The CBDR principle is closely linked to the concepts of SD as

---

[124] Note, however, that the Espoo Convention has been ratified in the framework of UNECE by 45 countries, thus mainly European states as well as the US and Canada, cf. UN treaty collection (2019) Espoo convention, https://treaties.un.org/Pages/ViewDetails.aspx?src=TREATY&mtdsg_no=XXVII-4&chapter=27&clang=_en (last accessed 14 May 2021). Yet, 'like the Water Convention, the Espoo and Aarhus Conventions both envision the broadening of their geographical scope by enabling the accession of States not members of the UNECE. While this is already possible under the Aarhus Convention ([Article] 19 (3)), the respective amendment to the Espoo Convention of 2001 has yet to enter into force[]', Beyerlin and Grote Stoutenberg (2013), para. 84.

[125] Cançado Trindade (2015), pp. 422–423, who points to the fact that given the 'overlap' of both principles they are frequently used interchangeably; cf. however on ongoing debates regarding the exact scope and status of principles of international environmental law even within the ICJ the separate opinions by judges Owada, Donoghue, Dugard, and Cançado Trindade to the ICJ (2015) *Certain Activities Carried out by Nicaragua* case as succinctly summarised by Yotova (2016), pp. 445–448. Dugard, in his Separate Opinion, speaks of '[t]he duty of due diligence [being] the standard of conduct required to implement the principle of prevention[]', ICJ (2015b), para. 7.

[126] Cançado Trindade (2015), p. 422; cf. ICJ (2010b) *Pulp Mills on the River Uruguay*, Separate Opinion Judge Cançado Trindade, para. 62; cf. moreover Viñuales (2012).

[127] PCA (2016) *The South China Sea Arbitration*, Award of 12 July 2016, para. 964.

well as intra-generational equity.[128] In a commodity context, CBDR can play a role particularly when it comes to the protection of shared resources.[129]

The CBDR principle also relates to the last principle of IEL, which shall be touched upon here: *the duty to cooperate*.[130] As already stated above, it is likewise expressly contained in Principle 7 Rio Declaration.[131] It moreover features in a series of international environmental agreements, including the UNFCCC as well as Articles 11.3 and 12 of the Paris Agreement.[132] Regarding commodity activities, the duty to cooperate is again of particular relevance when it comes to administering shared resources or also remedying transboundary harm. Apart from the duty to cooperate with one another, IEL also calls for *public participation*.[133] Besides the participation of a broad range of actors based on multi-stakeholder approaches on the global level, principle 10 of the Rio Declaration explicitly emphasises the obligation for states to provide appropriate access to environmental information also on the national level.[134] In addition, effective access to justice shall be provided. With regard to Europe, these obligations are further spelled out in the 1998 UNECE Convention on Access to Information, Public Participation in Decision-Making and Access to Justice in Environmental Matters ('Aarhus Convention').

4.2.1.3   Fiscal Framework

The degree to which a commodity-endowed state benefits from extraction depends substantially on its fiscal law framework. This relates not only to its interest of *economic gain*, but also the one of *development*—as an objective ideally shared between state and population. International instruments and standards provide some guidance on how to design the fiscal conditions under which commodity operations

---

[128] Hey (2011), para. 5 defines the CBDR principle as 'a means of translating the concept of intra-generational equity to the inter-State level, and the South-North context in particular, with a view to attaining sustainable development.'

[129] Oehl (2019), p. 34.

[130] Cf. Hey (2011), para. 5; ILA (2002) para. 3.1.

[131] Accordingly, '[s]tates shall co-operate in a spirit of global partnership to conserve, protect and restore the health and integrity of the Earth's ecosystem[]', cf. Wolfrum (2010), para. 28.

[132] Cf. Wolfrum (2010), paras. 29–30 moreover pointing i.a. to Article 1 of the 1993 North American Agreement on Environmental Co-operation as well as the 1985 Vienna Convention for the Protection of the Ozone Layer (cf. e.g. Article 2(2)(a)). Cf. also ITLOS (2001) *MOX Plant*, Order of 3 December 2011, para. 26, according to which the UK 'breached its obligations under Articles 123 and 197 of UNCLOS in relation to the authorisation of the MOX plant, and has failed to cooperate with Ireland in the protection of the marine environment of the Irish Sea inter alia by refusing to share information with Ireland and/or refusing to carry out a proper environmental assessment of the impacts on the marine environment of the MOX plant and associated activities and/or proceeding to authorise the operation of the MOX plant whilst proceedings relating to the settlement of a dispute on access to information were still pending[.]'

[133] Beyerlin and Grote Stoutenberg (2013), para. 82.

[134] Beyerlin and Grote Stoutenberg (2013), para. 82.

are taking place, such as double taxation agreements (DTAs). The general challenge for the host state of commodity activity consists of finding the right balance between capturing sufficient resource rents while maintaining an attractive business and investment environment.[135] Again, most guidance provided in international standards and instruments does not consciously consider commodity policy trade-offs.

The Model United Nations Double Taxation Convention between Developed and Developing Nations (UNDTC) and the OECD Model Tax Convention (OECDMTC) on Income and on Capital constitute two central instruments of transnational fiscal law.[136] Both conventions are primarily concerned with preventing double taxation (DT).[137] They have found wide acceptance today, with many states having effectively translated particularly the OECDMTC into their national tax laws.[138] In addition, both conventions have inspired the conclusion of more than 3000 bilateral DTAs.[139]

In the context of commodity operations, both conventions are relevant particularly with regard to corporate income taxation. According to Article 7 of the OECDMTC, corporate profits shall generally only be taxable in the state of corporate residency.[140] However, where the company maintains business through a so-called *permanent establishment* (PE) in another contracting state, the profits that are attributable to the PE may be taxed in that state—the state of source. Article 5 (1) OECDMTC generally defines a PE as 'a fixed place of business through which the business of an enterprise is wholly or partly carried on.' According to Article 5(2) (f) OECDMTC, the term PE includes especially 'a mine, an oil or gas well, a quarry or any other place of extraction of natural resources.' The UNDTC contains identical provisions. Consequently, the host state to a multinational commodity enterprise, which is headquartered elsewhere, may generally tax those profits of the corporation that have been generated through a commodity extraction site on its territory. However, Article 5(2)(f) OECDMTC is only indicative of the existence of a PE. As the commentary to the UNDTC with regard to the identical provision contained in the latter states, 'it does not provide that [a PE] necessarily does exist.'[141]

Despite this explicit reference to commodity activity in Article 5(2) (f) OECDMTC, some authors have highlighted that the PE clauses provided by

---

[135] Cf. UN (2017a), pp. 3–4.

[136] See also the US Model Income Tax Convention, available at US Treasury, https://www.treasury. gov/resource-center/tax-policy/treaties/Documents/Treaty-US%20Model-2016.pdf (last accessed 14 May 2021).

[137] Margalioth (2011b)—comparing it to the OECDMTC—describes the UNDTC as being 'bent in favour of developing countries, imposing fewer restrictions on the tax jurisdiction of the source country', para. 88.

[138] Margalioth (2011b), para. 5.

[139] Margalioth (2011a), para. 6.

[140] On the corresponding formal and substantive tests that states are typically carrying out in order to determine corporate residency, Margalioth (2011b), paras. 18–28.

[141] UN (2017b), p. 153; Almeida and Toledano (2018), p. 16.

the model conventions do not sufficiently cover the specificities of extractive industries.[142] Apart from the physical presence of the corporation, DTAs typically require business operations to be carried out for a certain period of time and to be of a particular character, especially not to be merely auxiliary activities.[143] In this respect, what can cause difficulties for source states is the intricate net of contracts, joint ventures, subcontractors, and consortia frequently surrounding commodity operations—particularly given that they may each be considered separately for tax purposes.[144] Especially operations carried out by subcontractors may be structured in a way so as to avoid the thresholds regarding time and type of activity under the applicable DTA.[145] As a result, the state concerned may be unable to tax the commodity activity.[146] In order to counter such trends and therefore increase the tax revenue of the respective source states, Almeida and Toledano i.a. propose a specific PE clause for resource-rich countries.[147]

Apart from the issue of what constitutes a PE—i.e. under what conditions the state in which the commodity activity occurs may levy a respective source tax –, both model conventions also set forth rules on *how* profits, which are attributable to a PE, shall be calculated. According to Article 7(2) OECDMTC, profits attributable to a PE

> . . .are the profits it might be expected to make, in particular in its dealings with other parts of the enterprise, if it were a separate and independent enterprise engaged in the same or similar activities under the same or similar conditions . . .

This provision, which is contained with similar wording also in Article 7 (2) UNDTC, is being generally referred to as the *arm's length principle*.[148] The main objective of this principle is to prevent the practice of so-called *transfer pricing*, which has been deemed to be 'one of the most important issues' in international taxation.[149] The arm's length principle counters this practice by allowing tax administrations to adjust the prices of intra-group transactions to

---

[142] Almeida and Toledano (2018), p. 1; cf. especially the corresponding 'Proposed Guidance on Permanent Establishment in the Extractive Industries' presented by the Committee of Experts on International Cooperation in Tax Matters, UN Doc. E/C.18/2016/CRP.22, https://www.un.org/esa/ffd/wp-content/uploads/2016/12/13STM_CRP22_Extractives_PEs.pdf (last accessed 14 May 2021) that the authors have built their deliberations on.

[143] Almeida and Toledano (2018), p. 13.

[144] Almeida and Toledano (2018), p. 13.

[145] Almeida and Toledano (2018), p. 14. The OECDMTC is less favourable for source states in this respect, for instance requiring a minimum period of 12 months for a construction activity to qualify as a PE according to its Article 5(3), whereas the UNDTC sets a respective threshold of only 6 months according to its Article 5(3)(a).

[146] Cf. Almeida and Toledano (2018), p. 14.

[147] Almeida and Toledano (2018), pp. 41–44.

[148] These provisions apply to intra-group transactions between different *branches* of the same corporation. Article 9(1) OECDMTC and Article 9(1) UNDTC constitute the respective provisions for *subsidiaries* or *associated enterprises*; Margalioth (2011b), para. 69.

[149] Tian (2018), p. 36.

usual market prices. Corresponding methods to approximate the 'arm's length price' are the Comparable Uncontrolled Price Method, the Cost Plus Method, the Resale Price Method, the Transactional Net Margin Method, as well as the Profit Split Method.[150] Not least given that a large share of commodity transactions is being conducted by TNCs,[151] transfer pricing constitutes a major issue also in our sector under investigation.[152]

Fiscal transparency and exchange of information between tax authorities are playing a key role in financial regulation. When it comes to cross-border collaboration of tax administrations and respective exchange of information, particularly the OECD Model Agreement on Exchange of Information on Tax Matters is providing important guidance. Pivotal international standards are so-called exchange of information requests (EOIR) as well as the automatic exchange of financial account information (AEOI), which feature in Articles 5 and 6 of the authoritative Convention on Mutual Administrative Assistance in Tax Matters respectively.[153]

4.2.1.4 Armed Conflict

Commodity activities in scenarios of armed conflict are particularly sensitive. Resource dependencies have proven to correlate with an increased risk of armed conflict.[154] Commodity deposits can i.a. play key roles in (attempted) coups d'état, the financing of warlordism, secession movements, mass rebellions, and foreign interventions in armed conflicts.[155] Generally speaking, one can distinguish between three core issues that are associated with armed conflicts, which occur in connection with natural resources: 'resource supply conflicts', 'conflict resources', and 'community-level resource conflicts'.[156] However, most of the applicable rules still constitute indirect TCL.

First and foremost international humanitarian law (IHL) qualifies a state's sovereignty in armed conflict.[157] With regard to the protection of commodities, one can roughly distinguish three 'indirect' legal avenues, which serve this very purpose and shall be considered subsequently: commodities can be protected as *civilian objects*,

---

[150]For a more detailed account of these methods, see Margalioth (2011b), paras. 71–78. On the so-called 'sixth method', Grondona (2018).

[151]Cf. e.g. UNCTAD (2016), p. 8.

[152]Cf. also Carbonnier and Zweynert de Cadena (2015), paras. 2–5.

[153]Cf. OECD (2017a), p. 2.

[154]Le Billion (2005), p. 13.

[155]Le Billion (2005), pp. 37–43.

[156]Le Billion et al. (2016), p. 2. Mostly original emphasis.

[157]With an elaborate account, Dam-de Jong (2010), pp. 37–52. However, also norms of international criminal law, particularly of the Rome Statute, will feature in the subsequent section wherever they are relevant for our discussion of commodity-related issues arising in armed conflict.

via *environmental protection* provisions, and through the *prohibition to destroy or seize property*, which includes the prohibition to pillage.

According to Article 52(1) of Additional Protocol I (AP-I),[158] *civilian objects* shall not be the object of attack or reprisals. They are being defined as all objects, which are not subject to military objectives, according to Article 52(1) AP-I. Article 52(2) AP-I specifies these objects to ones, which i.a. 'make an effective contribution to military action' and 'offer[] a definite military advantage.'[159] While the threshold of 'military advantage' set here does not seem to be very hard to overcome,[160] Article 54(2) AP-I provides specific protection for objects that are 'indispensable to the survival of the civilian population', including i.a. foodstuffs, crops, and livestock.

According to Article 54(2) AP-I, such objects may not be attacked, destroyed, removed, or rendered useless, thus not be damaged in any way.[161] The same obligation exists with regard to NIACs, according to Article 14 of Additional Protocol II (AP-II).[162] As Dam-de Jong points out, the list of indispensable objects provided by Articles 54(2) AP-I and 14 (AP-II) is not meant to be exhaustive, but rather may also include forests, lakes and rivers, and even mineral oil.[163]

Commodities may also fall under the general protection, which is being accorded to the *environment*.[164] Articles 35(3) and 55 AP-I set forth a prohibition to cause widespread, long-term, and severe damage to the environment. They entail a precautionary approach and may thus serve to prevent environmental damage resulting from the exploitation of commodity deposits, i.a. through impact assessments.[165] This basic protection of the overall environment however only applies during international armed conflict.[166] However, again the threshold of these protection

---

[158] The Protocol Additional to the Geneva Conventions of 12 August 1949, and Relating to the Protection of Victims of International Armed Conflicts (AP-I), of 8 June 1977, available at ICRC, https://www.icrc.org/en/doc/assets/files/other/icrc_002_0321.pdf (last accessed 14 May 2021).

[159] Dam-de Jong (2010), p. 37.

[160] Dam-de Jong (2010), pp. 37–38.

[161] According to Article 54(3) AP-I, this obligation does not apply in cases where the objects in question are used exclusively for the sustenance of the adverse party's military forces or in direct support of military action.

[162] Dam-de Jong (2010), p. 38. Protocol Additional to the Geneva Conventions of 12 August 1949, and Relating to the Protection of Victims of Non-International Armed Conflicts (AP-II), of 8 June 1977, available at https://treaties.un.org/doc/publication/unts/volume%201125/volume-1125-i-17513-english.pdf (last accessed 14 May 2021).

[163] Dam-de Jong (2010), p. 39. While according to Article 54(2) AP-I, the damage done to indispensable objects needs to be carried out 'for the specific purpose of denying them for their sustenance value to the civilian population', this provision is generally not understood as requiring a specific corresponding intent. It may thus 'be interpreted broadly so as to encompass all instances in which parties to an armed conflict deprive the population of objects indispensable to their survival, regardless of the motive', Dam-de Jong (2010), p. 40.

[164] Dam-de Jong (2010), p. 40.

[165] Dam-de Jong (2010), p. 42.

[166] Dam-de Jong (2010), p. 41.

provisions is set at a very high level, which as a consequence grants wide margins of discretion to states performing military operations.[167] Incidental damage resulting from commodity exploitation or plundering alone arguably does not suffice to constitute a violation of Articles 35(3), 55 AP-I since the damage generally must last several decades.[168]

In terms of soft law instruments, principle 24 Rio Declaration recognises that '[w]arfare is inherently destructive of sustainable development.' As a consequence, states are held to 'respect international law providing protection for the environment in times of armed conflict and cooperate in its further development, as necessary.'

The UN General Assembly Resolution on the Protection of the Environment in Times of Armed Conflict i.a., '[u]rges States to take all measures to ensure compliance with the existing international law applicable to the protection of the environment in times of armed conflict.'[169] The fact that depletion of natural resources can cause the liability of the acting state, is being demonstrated by UN SC Resolution 687, which

> reaffirms that Iraq [. . .] is liable under international law for any direct loss, damage – including environmental damage and the depletion of natural resources – or injury to foreign Governments, nationals and corporations as a result of its unlawful invasion and occupation of Kuwait.[170]

Within the realms of classical IHL, finally also the so-called 'Martens clause' has been said to provide environmental protection.[171] The clause was first incorporated in the 1899 Hague Convention (II) With Respect to the Laws and Customs of War on Land, and also features in the 1949 Geneva Conventions and the two 1977 additional protocols thereto.[172]

Moreover, the environment is also protected under international criminal law. According to Article 8(2)(b)(iv) Rome Statute, knowingly launching an attack that

---

[167] Dam-de Jong (2010), pp. 42–43.

[168] Dam-de Jong (2010), p. 43, who also highlights that '[t]he understandings that states have adopted concerning certain provisions of the ENMOD Convention have defined "widespread" as "encompassing an area on the scale of several hundred square kilometers" and "severe" to involve "serious or significant disruption or harm to human life, natural and economic resources or other assets', pointing to UN GA (1976) Report of the Conference of the Committee on Disarmament, volume I, 31st Session, Supplement no. 27, Doc. A/31/27, http://www.un.org/ga/search/view_doc.asp?symbol=A/31/27[VOL.I](SUPP) (last accessed 14 May 2021), at 91–92; cf. also Vöneky and Wolfrum (2016), para. 36.

[169] UN GA (1992) Resolution 47/37 of 25 November 1992, http://www.un.org/documents/ga/res/47/a47r037.htm (last accessed 14 May 2021), para. 1. On the resolution cf. ICJ (1996) *Legality of the Threat or Use of Nuclear Weapons*, Advisory Opinion, 8 July 1996, para. 32; cf. Vöneky and Wolfrum (2016), para. 1.

[170] UN SC (1991) Resolution 687 of 3 April 1991, https://unispal.un.org/DPA/DPR/unispal.nsf/0/FAB11BBFEA7E0B6585256C3F0065AEAE (last accessed 10 February 2019), para. 16; Vöneky and Wolfrum (2016), para. 49, who, however, contend that '[f]rom a realistic point of view, such a decision will not easily be taken again.'

[171] Vöneky and Wolfrum (2016), para. 48.

[172] Ticehurst (1997), pp. 125–126.

brings about 'damage to civilian objects or widespread, long-term and severe damage to the natural environment' that is disproportionate 'to the concrete and direct overall military advantage anticipated' constitutes a war crime.[173]

Apart from these rules, natural resources are also protected by the *prohibition to destroy or seize property*.[174] According to Article 23(g) of the 1907 Hague Regulations, it is 'forbidden [t]o destroy or seize the enemy's property, unless such destruction or seizure be imperatively demanded by the necessities of war[.]' According to Article 53 of Geneva Convention IV Relative to the Protection of Civilian Persons in Time of War, in times of occupation any destruction of private or public property is prohibited, unless it is absolutely necessary for military operations.[175] In addition, Article 28 Hague Regulations prohibits pillaging a village or town, 'even when taken by assault'; Article 33(2) Geneva Convention IV prohibits pillage altogether.[176] Pillage is likewise illegal in times of occupation according to Article 47 of the Hague Regulations, as well as in a NIAC, according to Article 4(2) (g) AP-II.[177]

Again, the unnecessary destruction or seizure of property, according to Articles 8 (2)(b)(xiii) and 8(2)(e)(xii) Rome Statute,[178] as well as 'pillaging a town or place, even when taken by assault', according to Articles 8(2)(b)(xvi) and 8(2)(e)(v) Rome Statute constitute a war crime in both IACs and NIACs.[179] Furthermore, Article 147 Geneva Convention IV defines the 'extensive destruction and appropriation of property, not justified by military necessity and carried out unlawfully and wantonly' as a grave breach under the Convention; such act constitutes a war crime according to Article 8(2)(a)(iv) Rome Statute.[180] The term 'property' within the relevant IHL conventions was always meant to include the natural environment, and thus with it the commodities, which form part of it.[181]

4.2.1.5 Anti-corruption

Despite the fact that corruption still constitutes a major impediment to harnessing the full potential of the commodity sector,[182] most of the rules addressing issues of

---

[173] Vöneky and Wolfrum (2016), paras. 1, 44.

[174] Dam-de Jong (2010), p. 44.

[175] Cf. Dam-de Jong (2010), p. 44.

[176] Dam-de Jong (2010), p. 48.

[177] Dam-de Jong (2010), p. 48.

[178] Dam-de Jong (2010), p. 46.

[179] Dam-de Jong (2010), p. 48, n 90.

[180] Dam-de Jong (2010), p. 48, n 90.

[181] Dam-de Jong (2010), p. 44.

[182] Extensively, including a typology of corruption risks OECD (2016b). With respect to e.g. the livestock sector in the Horn of Africa, cf. Desta and Hirsch (2012), pp. 131, 133. On the types of both demand- and supply-side corruption in the mining sector, Marshall (2001). On corruption in

corruption are 'indirect'. Corruption constitutes the 'abuse of public or private office for personal gain.'[183]

Corrupt practices may occur at every stage of the commodity value chain and are particularly proliferate when it comes to the award of mineral rights as well as the regulation of commodity operations.[184] Frequently, corruption in the commodity sector occurs due to wide discretionary powers and inadequate governance mechanisms, which result from the high politicisation of the sector and lead to clientelism and favouritism.[185] It may also be caused by gaps in the anti-corruption legal and judicial system.[186] Large-scale corruption has been observed particularly also in the 'procurement of goods and services, commodity trading, revenue management through natural resource funds, and public spending.'[187] Local actors as well as transnational corporations may 'act indistinctly as instigators or beneficiaries of the corruptive behaviour.'[188] State-owned enterprises (SOEs) seem to be particularly prone to corruption when it comes to awarding of rights, procurement, trading, and social expenditures.[189] This risk arises in particular, where SOEs function as both administrators and regulators of the commodity sector.[190] Typical offences include

> bribery of foreign officials, embezzlement, misappropriation and diversion of public funds, abuse of office, trading in influence, favouritism and extortion, bribery of domestic officials and facilitation payments.[191]

Bribery, trading in influence and collusion are used for instance in order to manipulate a state's decision to extract. These corrupt practices may lead to environmental law or HR being ignored in favour of allowing commodity extraction. They may occur within administrative, e.g. licensing procedures, on national as well as local levels or be applied to influence policies and legislation in the corporate interest or interests of the private elite. Oftentimes, the practices involve high-level

---

commodity trading Chêne (2016), who describes the commodity trading sector as 'notoriously opaque and poorly regulated, with low levels of transparency and accountability', p. 4. Cf. also Article 62(1) CAC, which recognises the negative effects of corruption on SD.

[183] OECD (2016b), p. 13 referring to OECD (2008).

[184] OECD (2016b), p. 9.

[185] OECD (2016b), p. 18.

[186] OECD (2016b), pp. 18–19.

[187] OECD (2016b), p. 9.

[188] Cf. also OECD (2016b), p. 10: 'At the local level, corruption may be favoured by a culture of clientelism and patronage as well as informal structured networks of local public officials, civil servants, community leaders and local business elite. It may also result from a hasty decentralisation process carried out without proper assessment of the capacity of the local economy and of the human, technical and administrative capabilities of subnational authorities to absorb new responsibilities and large inflows of resource revenues.'

[189] OECD (2016b), p. 9.

[190] OECD (2016b), p. 19.

[191] OECD (2016b), p. 9. Specific issues in commodity *trading* include trade mispricing, money laundering and 'bad deals', cf. Chêne (2016), pp. 5–7.

public officials, such as parliamentarians or ministers.[192] What contributes significantly to such corruption, is a lack of information and resources on the part of the host state of the commodity activity, which is thus unable to adequately assess its own resource wealth.[193] As a consequence, states often rely on research reports, which have been elaborated and paid for by extractive companies.[194]

Furthermore, specific risks occur with regard to social and environmental impact assessments, which are often subject to a highly politicised approval process and lack adequate participation of local communities. Also, 'ambiguous, outdated or unenforced legislation on the protection of socio-environmental rights' may increase the risk of corruption during the decision to extract, particularly where 'unclear and opaque land tenure systems', e.g. based on local customs, exist.[195]

After somewhat ignoring corruption-related issues until the 1970s, the international community in the past three decades has adopted several legal instruments dealing specifically with corruption. Typically, international anti-corruption agreements contain provisions regarding the scope of offences they are applicable to, preventive measures, law enforcement issues, international cooperation, and implementation mechanisms.[196] None of them, however, are directly aimed at tackling corruption in the commodity sector.

The arguably most prominent, almost universally ratified international agreement is the 2003 UN Convention Against Corruption (CAC).[197] The CAC in its preamble explicitly recognises that corruption constitutes 'no longer a local matter but a transnational phenomenon that affects all societies and economies, making international cooperation to prevent and control it essential'. According to Article 5 (1) CAC,

> [e]ach State Party shall, in accordance with the fundamental principles of its legal system, develop and implement or maintain effective, coordinated anti-corruption policies that promote the participation of society and reflect the principles of the rule of law, proper management of public affairs and public property, integrity, transparency and accountability.

---

[192] OECD (2016b), p. 32.

[193] OECD (2016b), p. 33 reports from countries, in which the competent department is making hydrocarbon reserve calculations manually and documents them in an Excel sheet. On these 'information asymmetries', cf. already Sect. 2.1.2 above.

[194] OECD (2016b), p. 33.

[195] OECD (2016b), p. 34. This finding further underlines the benefit of TCL as a transnational framework promoting corresponding standards for the protection of socio-environmental rights.

[196] Abbott (2009), paras. 23–29.

[197] UN GA (2003) Resolution 58/4 of 31 October 2003, https://www.unodc.org/documents/brussels/UN_Convention_Against_Corruption.pdf (last accessed 14 May 2021). The CAC is said to complement the 2000 United Nations Convention against Transnational Organized Crime, Annan K, Foreword to the UN CAC, https://www.unodc.org/documents/brussels/UN_Convention_Against_Corruption.pdf, p. iii. Transnational Organized Crime, UN GA (2000) Resolution 55/25 of 15 November 2000, https://www.unodc.org/documents/middleeastandnorthafrica/organised-crime/UNITED_NATIONS_CONVENTION_AGAINST_TRANSNATIONAL_ORGANIZED_CRIME_AND_THE_PROTOCOLS_THERETO.pdf (last accessed 14 May 2021).

Article 5(2) CAC mandates states to take *preventive* measures for this purpose, while Article 5(3) CAC postulates that states 'shall endeavour' to evaluate the adequacy of their legal instruments and administrative measures on a regular basis. According to Article 5(4) CAC states are held to collaborate with one another as well as international organisations in their fight against corruption. Article 6 CAC requires states to establish and maintain independent anti-corruption bodies, which ensure the implementation of policies pursuant to Article 5 CAC. According to Article 7(1)(a) CAC civil servants as well as non-elected public officials shall be recruited, hired and promoted 'based on principles of efficiency, transparency and objective criteria such as merit, equity and aptitude.' Furthermore, states shall provide them with adequate remuneration and equitable pay and offer training programmes, which promote awareness of the risks of corruption, according to Article 7(1) (c) and (d) CAC respectively. Article 8(3) CAC specifically refers to the International Code of Conduct for Public Officials, which may provide guidance for the elaboration of further national standards.

According to Article 9(1) CAC states shall 'establish appropriate systems of procurement, based on transparency, competition and objective criteria' in order to effectively prevent corruption. These systems shall address, i.a., the public distribution of information, conditions for participation in a tender, 'objective and predetermined criteria for public procurement decisions', an effective mechanism of domestic review, as well as measures addressing the behaviour of personnel, such as screening procedures and trainings. Article 12 CAC addresses prevention of corruption with regard to the private sector and i.a. sets forth that states 'shall provide effective, proportionate and dissuasive civil, administrative or criminal penalties' for violations of accounting and auditing standards. Article 12(2) CAC suggests specific measures, which states may take to achieve these ends, including the promotion of cooperation between law enforcement authorities and private actors, business standards and codes of conduct, transparency between private entities particularly regarding the 'identity of legal and natural persons involved in the establishment and management of corporate entities', the prevention of misuse of procedural rules with regard to subsidies and licences, as well as of conflicts of interest, i.a. by restricting the professional activities of former public officials, and ensuring sufficient auditing of private entities.[198]

According to Article 13 CAC, states shall 'promote the active participation of individuals and groups outside the public sector', particularly of NGOs and local communities, i.a. by ensuring effective access to information by the public, as well as '[r]especting, promoting and protecting the freedom to seek, receive, publish and disseminate information concerning corruption.' Article 14 sets forth specific measures to prevent money laundering.[199] Bribery of national and foreign public

---

[198] These measures naturally go hand in hand with the standards and guidelines designed for corporations, some of them specifically for the commodity sector, which will be discussed in more detail in Sect. 4.2.2.2 below.

[199] For more specific guidance on how to tackle the issue of money laundering, cf. FATF (2012–2018).

officials, embezzlement, trading in influence, and other abuses shall all be established as criminal offences, according to Articles 15–25 CAC. Article 26 CAC postulates that the liability of legal persons for the participation in these offences be established. According to Article 40 CAC bank secrecy laws must not hinder criminal investigations into potential corruption offences. Articles 43–50 CAC set forth several forms of international cooperation in order to tackle the increasingly transnational phenomenon of corruption, including extraditions, transfer of sentenced persons, mutual legal assistance, law enforcement cooperation and joint investigations.

Further regulatory instruments in the fight against corruption include the International Code of Conduct for Public Officials, the Convention on Combating Bribery of Foreign Public Officials in International Business Transactions,[200] as well as, on the regional level, respective anti-corruption Conventions in the Americas, Africa as well as Europe.[201]

The CoE Civil Law Convention on Corruption (ECLC) has been described as an 'innovative' instrument in the fight against corruption in that it,[202] according to its Article 1, mandates every state party to

> provide in its internal law for effective remedies for persons who have suffered damage as a result of acts of corruption, to enable them to defend their rights and interests, including the possibility of obtaining compensation for damage.

Article 3(1) ECLC further spells out that states shall adopt legislation, which grants all persons that have suffered damage from corruption 'the right to initiate an action in order to obtain full compensation for such damage.' According to Article 4(1) ECLC domestic legislation shall generally entitle victims of corruption to compensation if certain criteria are fulfilled. Article 5 ECLC requires states to establish respective procedures also in cases, in which the damage resulted from acts of corruption committed by public officials, thus directed against the state itself. Article 13 ECLC mandates states to 'co-operate effectively in matters relating to civil proceedings in cases of corruption'.

---

[200] Preceding recommendations: Recommendation of the Council on Bribery in International Business Transactions, 27 May 1994, https://www.oecd.org/daf/anti-bribery/anti-briberyconvention/1952622.pdf; Recommendation of the Council on the Tax Deductibility of Bribes to Foreign Public Officials, 11 April 1996, http://www.oecd.org/officialdocuments/publicdisplaydocumentpdf/?doclanguage=en&cote=c(96)27/final; Revised Recommendation of the Council on Combating Bribery in International Business Transactions, 23 May 1997, http://www.oecd.org/officialdocuments/publicdisplaydocumentpdf/?cote=C(97)123/FINAL&docLanguage=En (all last accessed 14 May 2021); Abbott (2009), para. 7.

[201] 1996 Inter-American Convention against Corruption; 2003 African Union Convention on Preventing and Combating Corruption; CoE Criminal Law Convention on Corruption; CoE Civil Law Convention on Corruption; 1997 Convention on the Fight against Corruption Involving Officials of the European Communities or Officials of Member States.

[202] Abbott (2009), para. 12.

4.2.1.6   Interim Conclusion

As our brief examination has indicated, indirect TCL generally does not provide guidelines on how potential conflicts between e.g., social development and environmental protection imperatives should be remedied. Thus, the current 'hard law' framework largely falls short of effectively tackling the *factual problem at hand*—which in the case of commodity activities typically lies in the value decision, which is to be translated into law, what commodity-related interest should prevail. This is the result of a legal framework, which gives effect to several, yet isolated individual interests instead of creating a coherent regulatory picture.[203]

With Meessen,[204] one therefore can contend that the current framework is not sufficiently *close to reality*. It is remote from the factual reality that the relevant human activity lies in handling commodities—which only *secondarily* may or may not constitute a corrupt practice, harm the environment or violate Human Rights. The latter categories are more abstract, theoretical legal 'boxes', which appear to serve the principal purpose of dogmatically clustering legal norms. The 'isolation' of the subsets of indirect TCL, which they bring about, however i.a. does not live up to the fact 'that the commodity sector's social and environmental impacts are inextricably intertwined.'[205] As a consequence, indirect TCL is little effective in creating the equilibrium necessary for a functional commodity sector.

4.2.2   The Limited Effectiveness of Incidents of Direct TCL

While not all of TCL qualifies as 'indirect', those incidents, which exhibit a conscious consideration of commodity policy trade-offs, are limited in their effectiveness due to various normative patterns. First, current examples of 'hard', direct TCL are not designed to comprehensively balance commodity interests (Sect. 4.2.2.1). Second, most of direct TCL constitutes *soft law* and/or is of private normative nature (Sect. 4.2.2.2). Third, whereas large parts of TCL spell out rather abstract rules and guidelines, those incidents of direct TCL, which exhibit a sufficient degree of *specificity*, largely address private actors (Sect. 4.2.2.3).

---

[203] On the purpose of fields of law, cf. Sect. 2.3 as well as Chap. 3 above.

[204] Meessen (2001), cf. Sect. 3.1.

[205] Bürgi Bonanomi et al. (2015), p. 47. 'Key areas of concern can be clustered as: (1) air, soil, and water pollution, natural hazards and related harmful effects on natural habitats, biodiversity, and the climate; (2) noise and visual impacts on landscapes; (3) destruction of sites of cultural, recreational, and social value; and (4) impairment of public health, safety, and the livelihoods of local (indigenous) communities', Bürgi Bonanomi et al. (2015), p. 47.

4.2.2.1   Hard, Direct TCL Does Not Balance Commodity Interests Comprehensively

Where rules have been created with a conscious consideration of commodity-related scenarios, they are typically not comprehensively addressing corresponding policy trade-offs. The respective rules generally foster individual commodity interests and at a maximum seek to strike a balance between two of them—economic gain and development (Sect. 4.2.2.1.1); economic gain and participation (Sect. 4.2.2.1.2); economic gain and environmental protection (Sect. 4.2.2.1.3); or between the economic interests of states (Sect. 4.2.2.1.4) respectively. Whereas integrating respective norm sets with one another may bring about legal rules that are more comprehensively balancing commodity interests, the current degree of integration in the TCL framework falls short of achieving this aim (Sect. 4.2.2.1.5).

4.2.2.1.1   Norms Balancing Economic Gain and Development

The *right to freely dispose over natural resources* (RFD) as provided for in common Articles 1(2) of the ICCPR and the ICESCR, seeks to strike a balance between the state's interest in exploiting natural resources, which will mostly consist of its endeavour to reap economic benefits, and development objectives, which local communities carry. It has been operationalized mainly in two contexts: regarding the RFD of indigenous peoples over their lands and territories and in situations where a people's *right to subsistence* is threatened.[206] With regard to the latter, common Article 1(2) Human Rights Covenants has been interpreted so as to oblige states

> to take measures to ensure that its own people are not in any case deprived of its own means of subsistence, including food [and water] [...] and to investigate any situation where such deprivation is alleged to be occurring.[207]

Article 21(2) AfCHR applies specifically to commodity scenarios and sets out that, '[i]n case of spoliation, the dispossessed people shall have the right to the lawful recovery of its property as well as to an adequate compensation.' Article 15(2) ILO

---

[206] Gilbert (2013), pp. 326–333; on the right to subsistence also UN CESCR (2003), para. 7: 'Taking note of the duty in [article 1(2) ICESCR], which provides that a people may not "be deprived of its means of subsistence", States parties should ensure that there is adequate access to water for subsistence farming and for securing the livelihoods of indigenous peoples'; cf. Gilbert (2013), p. 332.

[207] Alston (1984), pp. 39–40; cf. Gilbert (2013), p. 330. Cf. also ACHPR (2001) The Social and Economic Rights Action Center and the Center for Economic and Social Rights v. Nigeria (*Ogoniland* case), 155/96, decision of 27 October 2001, http://www.achpr.org/files/sessions/30th/comunications/155.96/achpr30_155_96_eng.pdf (last accessed 14 May 2021), para. 52, which ascertained a violation of the RFD enshrined in Article 21 AfCHR. On the notion of 'food sovereignty', which beyond universal access demands democratic control over food, cf. Shattuck and Holt-Giménez (2010), pp. 431–434.

Convention 169 obliges states to pay fair compensation to indigenous peoples for damages resulting from commodity activities. For cases, in which relocations cannot be prevented, Article 16(5) ILO Convention 169 equally requires the full compensation for any loss or injury. Article 8(2)(b) UNDRIP obliges states to provide effective mechanisms for prevention and redress of '[a]ny action which has the aim or effect of dispossessing [indigenous people] of their lands, territories or resources'. Article 40 UNDRIP lays down a general right 'to effective remedies for all infringements of their individual and collective rights.'[208]

In the context of armed conflict, the PSNR principle seeks to balance the occupant's interest of economic gain with the respective people's interest of development.[209] It has been repeatedly emphasised with regard *restitution rights* of the respective states and peoples under occupation. UN GA Resolution 3336 (XXIX)

> reaffirms the right [...] to the restitution of and full compensation for the exploitation, depletion and loss of, and damages to, the natural and all other resources and wealth of [occupied] States, territories and peoples[.][210]

Likewise, according to Resolution 62/181, the UN GA

> [r]ecognizes the right [...] to claim restitution as a result of any exploitation, damage, loss or depletion, or endangerment of [...] natural resources resulting from illegal measures taken by [...] the occupying Power...[211]

This claim has been repeated constantly since in the ensuing UN GA resolutions,[212] with the most recent one *explicitly* reaffirming

---

[208] It has been argued that the right to remedy constitutes customary international law, cf. Shelton (2006), para. 24.

[209] Cf. Schrijver (2008), para. 21.

[210] UN GA (1974) Resolution 3336 (XXIX) of 17 December 1974, https://unispal.un.org/DPA/DPR/unispal.nsf/0/610F6BBB6C6BDC9D852568CB006E71A5 (last accessed 14 May 2021), para. 3; Schrijver (2008), para. 21.

[211] UN GA (2007) Resolution 62/181 of 19 December 2007, https://unispal.un.org/DPA/DPR/unispal.nsf/0/1BFD3798C7567B4F852573FE005B8494 (last accessed 14 May 2021), para. 3; Schrijver (2008), para. 21.

[212] UN GA (2016) Resolution 71/247 of 21 December 2016; UN GA (2015) Resolution 70/225 of 22 December 2015; UN GA (2014) Resolution 69/241 of 19 December 2014; UN GA (2013) Resolution 68/235 of 20 December 2013; UN GA (2012) Resolution 67/229 of 21 December 2012; UN GA (2011) Resolution 66/225 of 22 December 2011; UN GA (2010) Resolution 65/179 of 20 December 2010; UN GA (2009) Resolution 64/185 of 21 December 2009; UN GA Resolution 63/201 of 19 December 2008, http://www.un.org/en/ga/search/view_doc.asp?symbol=A/RES/63/201 (last accessed 14 May 2021), which already explicitly '[r]eaffirms the inalienable rights of the Palestinian people and the population of the occupied Syrian Golan over their natural resources, including land and water', para. 1. Cf. also UN GA (1983) Report of the Secretary-General on the Implications, under International Law, of the United Nations Resolutions on Permanent Sovereignty over Natural Resources, on the Occupied Palestinian and Other Arab Territories and on the Obligations of Israel Concerning Its Conduct in These Territories, UN Doc. A/38/265, 21 June 1983, https://unispal.un.org/DPA/DPR/unispal.nsf/0/6D55C7F840E6DA06052567C9004B75DE (last accessed 14 May 2021); Dam-de Jong (2010), p. 30.

the inalienable rights of the Palestinian people and of the population of the occupied Syrian Golan over their natural resources, including land, water and energy resources.[213]

Generally, under international humanitarian law, the occupying state acts as administrator of immovable public property, according to Article 55 Hague Regulations.[214] The provision moreover establishes that the occupant must administer natural resources in accordance with the rules of usufruct[215]—it thus constitutes a 'direct' normative element. At the same time, the occupant notably is required to 'safeguard the capital of these properties.'[216] As Schrijver notes, this raises the question, what constitutes a violation of this obligation—particularly with regard to *non*-renewable resources.[217] Thus, every extraction of non-renewable commodities could be classified as a form of reducing their capital.[218] However, others contend that only 'wanton dissipation or destruction or abusive exploitation of public resources' constitutes a violation of Article 55 Hague Regulations.[219]

4.2.2.1.2   Norms Balancing Economic Gain and Participation

The *right to free, prior and informed consent* (FPIC) addresses the participation of *indigenous peoples* in particular.[220] The general right is rooted in Article 6 ILO Convention 169. Articles 15(2) and 16(2) ILO Convention 169 deal specifically with FPIC in scenarios of commodity activities, and corresponding relocations respectively. Moreover, Article 19 UNDRIP borrows the wording of the general FPIC right in Article 6 ILO Convention 169; Article 32 UNDRIP draws on Article 15(2) ILO Convention 169 and sets out that

> States shall consult and cooperate in good faith with the indigenous peoples concerned through their own representative institutions in order to obtain their free and informed

---

[213] UN GA (2017) Resolution 72/240, 20 December 2017, http://www.un.org/en/ga/search/view_doc.asp?symbol=A/RES/72/240 (last accessed 14 May 2021), para. 1.

[214] Dam-de Jong (2010), p. 50.

[215] Dam-de Jong (2010), pp. 50–51.

[216] Dam-de Jong (2010), p. 51.

[217] Schrijver (2008), para. 20.

[218] Schrijver (2008), para. 20.

[219] Schrijver (2008), para. 20.

[220] '*Free* implies that there is no coercion, intimidation or manipulation. *Prior* implies that consent is to be sought sufficiently in advance of any authorization or commencement of activities and respect is shown to time requirements of indigenous consultation/consensus processes. *Informed* implies that information is provided that covers a range of aspects, including the nature, size, pace, reversibility and scope of any proposed project or activity; the purpose of the project as well as its duration; locality and areas affected; a preliminary assessment of the likely economic, social, cultural and environmental impact, including potential risks; personnel likely to be involved in the execution of the project; and procedures the project may entail. This process may include the option of withholding consent. Consultation and participation are crucial components of a consent process[]', UN OHCHR (2013), p. 2; cf. also Spohr (2016), p. 23.

consent prior to the approval of any project affecting their lands or territories and other resources, particularly in connection with the development, utilization or exploitation of mineral, water or other resources.[221]

While ILO Convention 169 has thus far only been ratified by 22 countries and the UNDRIP constitutes a *soft law* instrument,[222] FPIC rights have also been recognised in the jurisprudence of human rights bodies, i.a. based on Article 27 ICCPR, Articles 1(2) and 15(1) ICESCR respectively as well as Article 5(d)(v), (e)(vi) ICERD.[223] Thus, FPIC does not (yet) possess the status of 'hard' law, yet it certainly creates a 'strong political obligation' at least for those 144 states, which voted in favour of the UNDRIP.[224] This perception corresponds to the general observation that there is a 'clear trend [...] toward increased public participation in laws and practice', particularly with regard to commodity activities.[225] Here, FPIC is frequently concerned throughout the entire life cycle of commodity operations and should generally be sought already during the pre-removal/exploration phase.[226]

Besides, the right to economic self-determination has been interpreted by the CESCR to require states to seek free and informed consent of the people concerned prior to concluding contracts with foreign mining companies.[227] A right to participate in development decisions, which concern respective local communities, has also been seen as enshrined in Article 24 AfCHR.[228]

4.2.2.1.3   Norms Balancing Economic Gain and Environmental Protection

Article 4(2) Convention on the Regulation of Antarctic Mineral Resource Activities (CRAMRA) aims to ensure that mineral resource activities are conducted in a

---

[221] FPIC is further referred to in Articles 10, 11(2), 28(1) and 29(2) UNDRIP.

[222] ILO (2019) Normlex, Ratifications of C169—Indigenous and Tribal Peoples Convention, 1989 (No. 169), http://www.ilo.org/dyn/normlex/en/f?p=1000:11300:0::NO:11300: P11300_INSTRUMENT_ID:312314 (last accessed 14 May 2021).

[223] Cf. Spohr (2016), pp. 28–29; Pring and Noé (2002), pp. 62–63.

[224] Spohr (2016), p. 30.

[225] Pring and Noé (2002), p. 76. The authors further expect that many of the *soft law* provisions related to public participation will gradually 'harden' to become legally binding law, Pring and Noé (2002), p. 72.

[226] Spohr (2016), pp. 22–23; as Articles 15(2), 16(2) ILO Convention as well as Article 32 UNDRIP illustrate, FPIC is of great significance in the commodity sector and especially concerned whenever removal activities necessitate a modification of nature, which provides for the livelihood of local or indigenous populations. Cf. also Bürgi Bonanomi et al. (2015), p. 29.

[227] Spohr (2016), p. 32.

[228] ACHPR (2001) *The Social and Economic Rights Action Center and the Center for Economic and Social Rights v. Nigeria* (*Ogoniland* case), 155/96, decision of 27 October 2001, http://www. achpr.org/files/sessions/30th/comunications/155.96/achpr30_155_96_eng.pdf; cf. also ECtHR (2005) *Taşkin and others v. Turkey*, application no. 46117/99, judgment of 30 March 2005, https://hudoc.echr.coe.int/webservices/content/pdf/001-67401?TID=soudeazyxk (both last accessed 14 May 2021); cf. Ebbesson (2009b), para. 30.

manner that does not significantly harm the environment—thus giving effect to the general no harm rule with regard to the Antarctic.[229] The CRAMRA, however, lacking the required number of ratifications never entered into force.[230]

Moreover, environmental norms dealing with mineral commodities in particular can be found in the special regimes regulating international wastes and recycling, such as the Basel Convention or the Minamata Convention on Mercury. The latter aims to reduce releases, usage and emissions of mercury, which is particularly used in gold production.[231] Also the International Maritime Organisation (IMO) Guidelines and Standards for the Removal of Offshore Installations and Structures on the Continental Shelf and in the Exclusive Economic Zone emphasise the objective of preventing and controlling marine pollution.[232]

4.2.2.1.4   Norms Balancing Economic Interests of States

Lastly, we shall discuss two additional normative patterns, which limit the balancing effect of direct TCL addressing states. As the example of the norms covering shared resource use illustrate, where hard, direct TCL 'bites', it will frequently concern an inter-state balance rather than being aimed at equilibrium within the commodity governance matrix (Sect. 4.2.2.1.4.1). Moreover, the commodity-directed norms within the liberalised trade regime despite their 'hard' law nature are rather 'declaratory' than legally binding (Sect. 4.2.2.1.4.2).

4.2.2.1.4.1   *Aiming at Inter-State Balance: Shared Resources*

Commodity deposits can stretch across national boundaries and thus fall under the sovereignty of more than one state.[233] For such scenarios, a distinct set of rules has evolved over time, mostly originating from bi- and at times plurilateral treaty law.[234] While some regimes are covering specific resources, such as water, migratory species, transboundary ecosystems or oil and gas deposits,[235] some general rules and principles are applicable to the exploitation of shared resources in general. Whereas the terminology in use here refers to 'resources'—and not 'commodities', the respective rules can still be deemed to constitute 'direct' TCL in the sense that they reflect a conscious consideration of the particularities of commodity exploitation.[236]

---

[229]Cf. Espa and Oehl (2018), p. 8.

[230]Cf. Espa and Oehl (2018), p. 8.

[231]Espa and Oehl (2018), pp. 8–9.

[232]IMO (1989) Resolution A.672(16), 19 October 1989, IMO. http://www.imo.org/blast/mainframe.asp?topic_id=1026 (last accessed 14 May 2021).

[233]Cf. del Castillo-Laborde (2010), para. 5.

[234]On transboundary agreements, cf. Rummel-Bulska (2008).

[235]Cf. del Castillo-Laborde (2010), para. 6.

[236]On the overlap between TCL and NRL, see already Sect. 3.2.2.1 above.

Shared resources law is aimed at balancing the interests of the respective states involved in the exploitation of the shared deposit. Two general rules, which are at the heart of this field of law, are the *duty to co-operate* on the one hand and the *principle of equitable utilisation* on the other.

The former is provided for in Article 3 of the Charter of Economic Rights and Duties of States. The *cooperation* of states when it comes to making use of a shared resource constitutes a major prerequisite towards achieving this aim.[237] The *principle of equitable utilisation* of shared resources has evolved from the general rule of equity and encompasses equitable principles such as good faith and good neighbourliness.[238] Although like the term cooperation, the principle of equitable utilisation has so far not yet been defined uniformly by international law, it can be identified as obliging states to manage shared resources equitably 'in order to balance the different demands of States'.[239] In addition, the result produced by this process must be equitable in itself.[240] Equitable utilisation is thus 'both the target and the process of its implementation' and rather a result to be achieved in view of the specific circumstances of the case at hand than an abstract rule.[241]

With regard to those shared resources that are located in or under the sea, the UNCLOS provides specific rules.[242] When it comes to living resources, particularly fisheries, Articles 61–64 UNCLOS set forth the principle of optimum utilisation as well as the duty to cooperate for this end. The latter applies according to Article 61(2) UNCLOS to measures meant to prevent the risk of over-exploitation in a coastal state's Exclusive Economic Zone (EEZ), which shall be taken in cooperation with international organisations 'as appropriate'. Article 64(1) UNCLOS mandates coastal states to cooperate with states whose nationals fish the highly migratory species contained in Annex I either directly or through IOs in order to ensure conservation and promote 'the objective optimum utilization'. Further UNCLOS

---

[237] Shelton (2008), p. 1.

[238] del Castillo-Laborde (2010), para. 10.

[239] del Castillo-Laborde (2010), para. 25.

[240] del Castillo-Laborde (2010), para. 25.

[241] del Castillo-Laborde (2010), para. 29. On the wide range of circumstances that may have to be taken into account, cf. e.g. Article 5(1) of the ILC Draft Articles on the Law of Transboundary Aquifers: 'Utilization of a transboundary aquifer or aquifer system in an equitable and reasonable manner within the meaning of draft article 4 requires taking into account all relevant factors, including: (a) the population dependent on the aquifer or aquifer system in each aquifer State; (b) the social, economic and other needs, present and future, of the aquifer States concerned; (c) the natural characteristics of the aquifer or aquifer system; (d) the contribution to the formation and recharge of the aquifer or aquifer system; (e) the existing and potential utilization of the aquifer or aquifer system; (f) the actual and potential effects of the utilization of the aquifer or aquifer system in one aquifer State on other aquifer States concerned; (g) the availability of alternatives to a particular existing and planned utilization of the aquifer or aquifer system; (h) the development, protection and conservation of the aquifer or aquifer system and the costs of measures to be taken to that effect; (i) the role of the aquifer or aquifer system in the related ecosystem.'

[242] Ong (2011), para. 1 indicates that most joint development agreements concern 'overlapping sea-bed claims'; only few agreements have been concluded regarding resources located on land.

provisions touching upon shared resources address the specific scenarios of enclosed or semi-enclosed seas (Article 123 UNCLOS) and resource deposits in the Area, which stretch across national boundaries (Article 142 UNCLOS).

Whereas the general rules applicable to shared resource use do not extend to shared management, 'but rather end[] at the threshold of co-operation for the implementation of equitable utilization',[243] more intensified forms of cooperation are generally implemented through bilateral instruments.[244]

One area in which such joint management systems are quite prevalent is the joint development of hydrocarbon fields.[245] In this connection, the general principles of cooperation and equitable utilisation establish the framework for individual state parties to seek a negotiated solution on a (mostly) bilateral basis.[246] Ong insofar differentiates between *three models* of intergovernmental joint development agreements:[247] 'Model I' agreements provide for the exploitation right of one state as well as a corresponding duty to transfer an agreed upon share of the revenues to the other state; 'Model II' agreements arrange the establishment of a legal framework for a system of joint ventures; and 'Model III' agreements require the creation of a common agency that grants licences for exploitation and creates regulatory norms.[248]

More recent 'model III'-type agreements exhibit a 'clear trend' of including environmental protection provisions.[249] According to Article 10(a) of the 2001 Timor Sea Arrangement, East Timor and Australia were obliged to cooperate in order to 'prevent and minimise pollution and other environmental harm.'[250] The most recent successor of this agreement, the 2018 Australia–Timor Leste Maritime Boundary Treaty,[251] requires parties, through a 'designated authority' to 'regulate the [Greater Sunrise] Special Regime Area according to Good Oilfield Practice', according to Article 6(2)(b) of Annex B, which includes 'environmental protection'

---

[243] del Castillo-Laborde (2010), para. 15.

[244] This intensified form of collaboration may also take the form of 'establishing commissions for the exchange of information, programmes for joint research, [or] common environmental standards', cf. del Castillo-Laborde (2010), para. 15 pointing to Articles 14 and 18 WCED Final Report. 'In sum, equitable utilization of shared resources is the process of implementing uses with an equitable approach in order to avoid harm to and to reach consensus with interested States', del Castillo-Laborde (2010), para. 15.

[245] Ong (2011), paras. 4–5.

[246] Cf. del Castillo-Laborde (2010), para. 15.

[247] Ong (2011), paras. 6–15; Ong (1999), pp. 788–792. The focus here lies on intergovernmental agreements.

[248] Ong (1999), pp. 788–792; Ong (2011), paras. 7–15.

[249] Ong (2003), p. 140; also, Ong (2011), para. 17.

[250] Ong (2003), p. 132.

[251] Treaty Between Australia and the Democratic Republic of Timor-Leste Establishing Their Maritime Boundaries in the Timor Sea, signed on 6 March 2018, available at https://dfat.gov.au/geo/timor-leste/Documents/treaty-maritime-arrangements-australia-timor-leste.pdf (last accessed 14 May 2021).

and 'calls for the adoption of methods and processes that minimise the impact of the Petroleum operations on the environment'. These clauses put the shared economic endeavour of the exploiting states in context with a joint objective of protecting the environment. Therefore, they are balancing two commodity interests, yet without providing any more concrete guidance on how to achieve this balance.

4.2.2.1.4.2   Commodity Trade and Development: Hard, Yet 'Declaratory' Provisions

The rules of Part IV of the GATT addressing the particularities of commodity trade are intended to balance the economic interests of developing states on the one hand and developed states on the other. As such, they are seeking to strike a balance also between development interests on both sides and to reconcile them with the liberalised trade regime.

The provisions rooted in Articles XXXVI-XXXVIII GATT have been included in the GATT only subsequently by amendment.[252] Article XXXVI:4 GATT pursues the overall aim of fostering the economic development of those less-developed contracting parties that continue to depend 'on the exportation of a limited range of primary products.' It basically lays out a roadmap with three causal conditions, which need to be fulfilled in order for commodity-dependent states to attain this goal: *access* to world markets for commodities; stabilized, improved conditions in world commodity markets, including '*stable*, equitable and remunerative *prices*'; as well as '*steady growth of the real export earnings* of these countries'.[253] However, measures designed to stabilise world commodity markets, shall be taken 'wherever appropriate'. Historically, ICAs were designed to pursue these exact objectives, with Article XX:h GATT granting justification for their implementation. Yet, as will be discussed in more detail below,[254] ICAs have been largely abandoned, and consequently Article XXXVI:4 GATT has been said to have become 'a dead letter' following the 'ideological shift' in the late 1980s.[255]

Article XXXVI:5 GATT further highlights that *diversification* of the economies of less-developed contracting parties—and thus 'avoidance of an excessive dependence on the export of primary products'—will facilitate the 'rapid expansion' of their economies. As a consequence, it recognises the 'need for increased access in the largest possible measure to markets under favourable conditions for processed and manufactured products currently or potentially of particular export interest to

---

[252] Stoll (2014), para. 83.

[253] Emphases added.

[254] Cf. Sect. 5.2.1 below.

[255] Desta (2010), paras. 23 and 30 respectively. The 'ideological shift' he refers to presumably relates to the liberalisation doctrine ensuing as a consequence of so-called *Reaganomics*, cf. already Chap. 2 above.

less-developed contracting parties.'[256] While Article XXXVI:7 GATT calls for collaboration between the contracting parties, intergovernmental bodies and relevant UN organisations in order to foster the development benefits of international trade, Article XXXVI:8 GATT clarifies that

> developed contracting parties *do not expect reciprocity* for commitments made by them in trade negotiations to reduce or remove tariffs and other barriers to the trade of less-developed contracting parties.[257]

Article XXXVII GATT spells out concrete commitments for developed countries in the context of trade and development, which include efforts in reducing and eliminating trade barriers to products, which are particularly important to developing country members; refraining from introducing customs duties or non-tariff barriers on such products; or maintaining 'trade margins at equitable levels'. Article XXXVIII GATT provides for joint action and collaboration between the contracting parties within the GATT framework as well as in other fora. Article XXXVIII:2:a GATT corresponds to the objective set forth in Article XXXVI:4 GATT and calls for corresponding international arrangements, which stabilise market conditions.

The trade and development provisions of the GATT have been criticized as being 'declaratory rather than obligatory' given the lack of effective sanctions.[258] Article XXXVII:1 GATT explicitly frees developed countries from their commitments if and where 'compelling reasons' make it impossible for them to implement the provisions of Article XXXVII GATT. These compelling reasons may—contrary to the general rule contained in Article 27 VCLT according to which a party may not invoke the provisions of its internal law as justification for its failure to perform a treaty—include domestic legal reasons.[259] Consequently, states seeking to justify deviation from their obligations under Part IV of the GATT may simply legislate against them.[260]

As such, the trade and development provisions of the GATT illustrate what holds true for much of hard law directly addressing commodity activity: It is of little binding effect for states and thus of little significance when it comes to the balancing of the interests associated with commodity activity.

---

[256] See note ad Article XXXVIII:5 GATT in the annex to the GATT: 'A diversification programme would generally include the intensification of activities for the processing of primary products and the development of manufacturing industries, taking into account the situation of the particular contracting party and the world outlook for production and consumption of different commodities.'

[257] Emphasis added. See also note ad Article XXXVIII:8 GATT in the annex to the GATT: 'It is understood that the phrase "do not expect reciprocity" means, in accordance with the objectives set forth in this Article, that the less-developed contracting parties should not be expected, in the course of trade negotiations, to make contributions which are inconsistent with their individual development, financial and trade needs, taking into consideration past trade developments.'

[258] Lee (2011), p. 114.

[259] Lee (2011), p. 114.

[260] Lee (2011), p. 114.

4.2.2.1.5   Integration Between Norm Subsets of TCL

As the sustainable use principle reflects, integration can create balancing norms, which cover more than two commodity interests.

Integration can also be observed between different norm subsets, which have brought about incidents of direct TCL. For instance, as far as commodity-related violations result from environmental causes, the UN Human Rights Committee (HRC) has held that duties of states under international environmental law inform the contents of Article 6(1) ICCPR and *vice versa*.[261] Thus, in these scenarios the implementation of the right to life will depend on the actions that states are taking with regard to the protection of the environment, such as protecting it against harm or pollution as well as ensuring sustainable use of natural resources or carrying out EIAs.[262] In order to fulfil their obligation of implementing the right of life, states should therefore act in conformity with applicable international environmental law.[263] In *Portillo Caceres v. Paraguay* a state violating its duty to protect the environment has been said to also be in violation of its duty to protect citizens against human rights violations.[264]

This form of integration thus combines two protection mechanisms: international environmental law (IEL) and Human Rights (HR) respectively are being used as benchmarks to assess whether or not a rule of IEL or international HR has been breached. From the perspective of the commodity matrix, the interests of environmental protection and of development are being combined into one clearer, perhaps more effective protection mechanism. Therefore, one can argue that it will contain objectives of economic gain and control more vigorously. What it does not achieve, however, is to provide more concrete guidelines how all five commodity interests should be brought into a state of equilibrium.

A further prominent example of integration is provided by the WTO Appellate Body's interpretation in *US–Shrimp* of the notion 'natural resources' in Article XX (g) GATT in light of IEL, particularly SD.[265] Taking this observation several steps further, this form of integration can be interpreted as an attempt to essentially limit the reach of trade liberalisation measures to the boundaries of IEL. By ways of oversimplification, one could argue that where they interfere with environmental protection, they should be held to be unlawful. However, despite the integration of the fields of IEL and world trade law, we are again left without guidelines how we should balance *all* interests associated with commodity activity.

It seems natural that these guidelines could only be brought about by a norm set— or legal field—which is being created in order to integrate norms fostering all

---

[261] UN HRC (2018), para. 62.

[262] UN HRC (2018), para. 62.

[263] UN HRC (2018), para. 62.

[264] UN HRC (2019) *Portillo Caceres vs. Paraguay*, decision of 25 July 2019, as discussed by Reeh (2019).

[265] WTO DSB (1998) *US – Shrimps*, Report of the Appellate Body, 12 October 1998, para. 129.

commodity interests. The *level of integration* that the legal order currently exhibits is insufficient to achieve this aim.

4.2.2.2   Direct TCL Is Largely of 'Soft' or Private Nature

Another pattern, which can be discerned within the body of TCL is that commodity-directed rules, i.e. direct TCL tends to be either of soft law character, thus primarily addressing states (Sect. 4.2.2.2.1); or to consist of standards that apply to private actors (Sect. 4.2.2.2.2).

4.2.2.2.1   Incidents of Soft, Direct TCL

Examples of soft, direct TCL are provided within the norm subsets covering good governance (Sect. 4.2.2.2.1.1) as well as the fiscal framework applicable to commodity activities (Sect. 4.2.2.2.1.2).

4.2.2.2.1.1   Good Governance

Good governance here is understood as a classificatory category, which comprises those rules that are primarily aiming to ensure smooth functioning of governance systems, thus especially rules addressing accountability, transparency and public participation.[266]

Increasing *transparency* is particularly important in a sector, which historically has often remained in great secrecy and still today is frequently being described as 'opaque'.[267] Against the backdrop of this lack of information, which has long been available on the commodity sector, its actors, financial flows and governance mechanisms, several international organisations, instruments and initiatives have evolved over the past decade, which seek to increase transparency, i.e. 'the flow of relevant, timely and reliable economic, financial, social, institutional and political information, which is accessible to all relevant stakeholders.'[268]

Presumably the most prominent international effort in this respect with regard to oil, gas and mineral resources is the Extractive Industries Transparency Initiative (EITI). Being of the view 'that a public understanding of government revenues and expenditure over time could help public debate and inform choice of appropriate and

---

[266]Despite the established interconnection of good governance and HR based approaches, this section insofar primarily focuses on norms, which do *not* originate from HR law—for those, cf. Sects. 4.2.1.1 and 4.2.2.1 above. On the degree to which corresponding good governance duties, such as transparency and accountability can be seen as already being incorporated in the PSNR principle, cf. Sect. 4.1 above.

[267]NRGI (2016), p. 1.

[268]Mooslechner et al. (2004), p. 217, referring to Kaufmann (2002); cf. also Vishwanath and Kaufmann (1999), p. 3.

realistic options for sustainable development', the multi-stakeholder participants of the founding 2003 Lancaster House conference 'underline[d] the importance of transparency by governments and companies in the extractive industries and the need to enhance public financial management and accountability.'[269] According to EITI principle 6, the 'achievement of greater transparency must be set in the context of respect for contracts and laws.'[270]

In Article 2(1) of its Articles of Association (AoA), EITI describes itself as

> an international multi-stakeholder initiative with participation of representatives from governments and their agencies; oil, gas and mining companies; asset management companies and pension funds [. . .] [;] and local civil society groups and international non-governmental organisations.[271]

As of this writing, 51 countries were implementing the 2019 EITI standard.[272] In order to be recognised as 'implementing country', so-called 'candidate countries' need to demonstrate that they meet the eight EITI requirements, which i.a. include effective oversight by a *national multi-stakeholder group*, disclosure of the legal and institutional framework applicable to commodity activities as well as *compiling and reconciling company payments and government revenues*. In this way, missing payments and corresponding corruption can be detected, as has been the case for instance with regard to Nigeria's national oil company in 2012.[273] Therefore, states are obliged to comprehensively disclose their taxes and revenues, including production entitlements, profits taxes, royalties, dividends, bonuses and licensing fees, their sale of potential shares of production or other revenues collected in kind, eventual infrastructure provisions and barter arrangements, particularly resource-for-infrastructure (RFI) programmes,[274] transportation revenues, transactions related to SOEs, and subnational payments.[275] The data provided must be sufficiently disaggregated, timely, and of adequate quality.[276]

Despite its considerable success in attracting implementing countries over the past decade,[277] EITI has also been criticised for various shortcomings. One point of criticism relates to the EITI's focus on transparency. While the latter may have improved in many implementing countries, this is not the case with regard to

---

[269] Principles #4 and #5, EITI (2019), p. 6.

[270] EITI (2019), p. 6.

[271] EITI (2019) EITI Articles of Association, https://eiti.org/document/eiti-articles-of-association (last accessed 14 May 2021).

[272] EITI (2019) Countries, https://eiti.org/countries (last accessed 14 May 2021).

[273] Lehmann (2015), p. 9.

[274] On these 'deals' extensively Landry (2018), who focuses on the DRC-Sicomines deal; on the definition, cf. also CCSI (2019) Resource for Infrastructure Deals, http://ccsi.columbia.edu/work/projects/resource-for-infrastructure-deals/ (last accessed 14 May 2021).

[275] EITI (2019), pp. 22–5.

[276] EITI (2019), pp. 25–6.

[277] Scanteam (2011), pp. 1–2.

accountability of relevant actors. As the EITI's official evaluators concluded in 2011,

> [t]here are thus few indications that EITI programmes are so far having impact on dimensions such as governance, corruption, poverty reduction or other objectives stated in EITI's Articles of Association.[278]

However, as the EITI's chairman Frederik Reinfeldt, points out, the initiative should not be misunderstood 'as the one-stop-shop for reversing the resource curse.' Instead, he argues that EITI 'must be mainstreamed and combined with other tools to ensure that natural resources are more prudently managed and better deployed towards both economic growth and sustainable human development.'[279]

Further transparency initiatives that are explicitly directed at the commodity sector, include the Publish What You Pay (PWYP) coalition, which consists of over 800 members worldwide, some of them NGOs that were created particularly for the purpose of addressing commodity governance issues, such as Global Witness or Revenue Watch, others long standing NGOs that increasingly devote resources to commodity governance-related programmes, such as Oxfam or Transparency International.[280] The Natural Resource Governance Institute (NRGI) seeks to foster 'the governance of natural resources to promote sustainable and inclusive development',[281] by providing 'policy advice, advocacy, and capacity development'—all based on '[o]riginal data, analysis, and applied research'.[282] The Africa Mining Vision, an intergovernmental effort, which emerged within the framework of the United Nations Economic Commission for Africa (ECA) and the African Union (AU) respectively, seeks to foster i.a. contract transparency, accession to transparency initiatives, such as EITI, as well as transparency in the overall 'management of revenue paid to various governmental authorities', which it recognises as 'an important part of the mineral policy agenda.'[283] Other players and initiatives e.g. include the Open Government Partnership, programmes launched within the framework of the G7 and G20, the World Bank, or the IMF.[284]

---

[278] Scanteam (2011), p. 3; cf. Lehmann (2015), p. 9.

[279] EITI (2018), p. 2. Reinfeldt is quoting the Nigerian Vice-President Yemi Osinbajo here.

[280] NRGI (2015), p. 1; PWYP closely collaborates with the EITI and coordinates the nominations of civil society representatives on the EITI Board, EITI (2017) Civil society seeks representatives for the EITI International Board, https://eiti.org/news/civil-society-seeks-representatives-for-eiti-international-board-0 (last accessed 14 May 2021).

[281] NRGI (2015–2019), p. 1.

[282] NRGI (2015–2019), p. 5; the NRGI publishes i.a. the annual Resource Governance Index as well as the Natural Resource Charter—'a set of principles for governments and societies on how to best harness the opportunities created by extractive resources for development', NRGI (2014), cf. already Chap. 2 above.

[283] AU (2009), pp. 18, 19, 38. The Africa Mining Vision will subsequently be discussed in more detail.

[284] Open Government Partnership (2019) About OGP, https://www.opengovpartnership.org/about/about-ogp (last accessed 14 May 2021); cf. moreover the G7 Alliance on Resource Efficiency, BMU (2019) Resource efficiency in the G7, https://www.bmu.de/en/topics/economy-products-

Some incidents of soft, direct TCL are covering commodity activities in a particularly *comprehensive* manner. For instance, the FAO Voluntary Guidelines on the Responsible Governance on Tenure of Land, Fisheries and Forests in the Context of National Food Security (VGGT) provide specific guidance on how to improve the governance of tenure.[285] Their general principles require states to

> [r]ecognize and respect all legitimate tenure right holders and their rights [. . .,] [s]afeguard legitimate tenure rights against threats and infringements [. . .,] [p]romote and facilitate the enjoyment of legitimate tenure rights [. . .,] [p]rovide access to justice to deal with infringements of legitimate tenure rights [. . ., and] [p]revent tenure disputes, violent conflicts and corruption.[286]

The VGGT moreover set forth ten principles, which shall guide the implementation of the guidelines: human dignity, non-discrimination, equity and justice, gender equality, holistic and sustainable approach, consultation and participation, rule of law, transparency, accountability, and continuous improvement.[287]

Specifically addressing governance challenges that occur in the context of *mining*, the 2002 Berlin Guidelines II for Mining and Sustainable Development are 'intended to provide general guidance for sound and sustainable management' of mining(-related) activities.[288] Based on their 1991 predecessors, the Berlin Guidelines stipulate 15 'Fundamental Principles for the Mining Sector'.[289]

Accordingly, states and mining corporations shall i.a. recognise environmental management, including impact assessments, as a 'high priority'; equally recognise 'the importance of socio-economic impact assessments and social planning'; '[e]stablish environmental accountability [. . .] at the highest levels of management and

---

resources-tourism/resource-efficiency/resource-efficiency-in-the-g-7/, or the G7 CONNEX programme, CONNEX history, http://connex-unit.org/connex-history/; the G20 Anti-Corruption Action Plan, which i.a. addresses beneficial ownership transparency, available https://www.mofa.go.jp/files/000185882.pdf; the commitments by the World Bank Group in the fight against corruption, i.a. its Stolen Asset Recovery (StAR) initiative, World Bank (2016) Statement, http://www.worldbank.org/en/topic/governance/brief/update-on-world-bank-group-commitments-following-the-uk-anti-corruption-summit-may-2016 as well as the IMF's Fiscal Transparency Code, IMF (2019) Fiscal transparency, https://www.imf.org/external/np/fad/trans/, which includes one pillar on resource revenue management. A 'Handbook on Fiscal Transparency relating to natural resources', is scheduled to be published in October 2019 and supposed to integrate the IMF (2007) Guide on Resource Revenue Transparency, https://www.imf.org/en/Publications/Policy-Papers/Issues/2016/12/31/Revised-Guide-on-Resource-Revenue-Transparency-PP4176 (all last accessed 14 May 2021). These initiatives illustrate the reality of continuously proliferating concepts of GCG, cf. Sect. 2.2.5 above.

[285] FAO (2012), para. 1.1.

[286] FAO (2012), para. 3.1. According to para. 3.2 non-state actors, particularly businesses, are held to observe their 'responsibility to respect human rights and legitimate land tenure rights', which appears to allude to the UN GP on Business and HR that will be discussed in more detail in Sect. 4.2.2.2.2 below.

[287] FAO (2012), para. 3B. On guidance regarding the conduct of social and cultural impact assessments, cf. Secretariat of the CBD (2004) Akwé: Kon guidelines.

[288] UN (2002), p. 2.

[289] UN (2002), p. 4.

policy-making'; ensure participation of affected communities, including full partic-ipation of women and other marginalised groups; '[a]dopt risk analysis and risk management in the regulation, 'design, operation and decommissioning of mining activities'; avoid environmental regulation, which may have the effect to unneces-sarily restrict trade and investment; '[r]ecognize the linkages between ecology, socio-cultural conditions and human health and safety, the local community and the natural environment'; '[e]valuate and adopt [. . .] economic and administrative instruments', which 'encourage the reduction of pollutant emissions and the intro-duction of innovative technology'; as well as '[e]ncourage long-term mining invest-ment [through] environmental standard with stable and predictable environmental criteria and procedures'.[290]

Moreover, the Berlin II Guidelines provide suggestions for the design of domestic legal frameworks, which apply to mining activities and thus seek to support gov-ernments in their task 'to provide a well-designed legislative framework for the mining industry that includes all aspects of the environment, both physical and social.'[291] In terms of instruments for the implementation of mining-related rules, the guidelines advocate for a 'mixture of regulatory instruments', which, apart from prescriptive systems, may also include 'performance targets', 'economic instru-ments', 'negotiated or voluntary agreements', or 'environmental management systems'.[292]

The Intergovernmental Forum on Mining, Minerals, Metals and Sustainable Development (IGF) is a voluntary initiative of over 60 states that are 'committed to leveraging mining for [SD]'.[293] Its Mining Policy Framework (MPF) provides comprehensive policy guidance that, if 'progressively implemented, will allow mining to make its maximum contribution to the sustainable development of devel-oping countries.'[294] The MPF provides guidance on how to implement a legal and policy environment conducive to sustainable mining; how to optimise financial as well as socio-economic benefits arising from mining; how to sustainably manage the natural resource base; how to manage post-mining transition; and how to foster the SD benefits of artisanal and small-scale mining (ASM).[295]

---

[290] All of the above as summarised at UN (2002), p. 4.

[291] UN (2002), p. 7. Accordingly, respective domestic legal frameworks typically consist of specific mining legislation, environmental legislation and other legislation, which may include diverse sets of rules, such as land law, conservation law, forest law, water resources law, air quality law, hazardous substances law, or radioactive substances law, UN (2002), pp. 8–10. On comparative commodity law, cf. Bastida et al. (2005).

[292] UN (2002), p. 11.

[293] IGF (2019) About, https://www.igfmining.org/about/ (last accessed 14 May 2021). The IISD currently serves as the IGF secretariat, cf. ibid.

[294] IGF (2013), p. 6.

[295] IGF (2013), pp. 6–16. The IGF is supported also by UNCTAD and as such somewhat reconciles comparable commodity-specific fora, such as the International Lead and Zinc Study Group (ILZSG), the International Nickel Study Group (INSG), or the International Copper Study Group

Pursuing a regional approach, the Africa Mining Vision (AMV) provides comprehensive guidance on how to harness Africa's resource endowments as a 'key' to the continent's development.[296] It identifies 'the formulation and implementation of workable [resource-based] industrialisation strategies' as *the* central issue.[297] Looking at the respective success stories from Nordic countries, the AMV recognises that, instead of relying on 'foreign inputs', 'proactive and deliberate actions from key stakeholders, particularly governments' are an important prerequisite for achieving this aim.[298] With its ambition 'to transform mineral sectors in an inclusive, sustainable way', the AMV correlates with 'other Pan-African development initiatives, such as the AU Agenda 2063.'[299] It is based on *seven tenets*[300] and six *major intervention areas*.[301]

Recalling the example of the Lagos Plan of Action, which is said to have remained 'part of the rhetoric of official declarations, dissociated from real policy', the 2011 International Study Group Report on Africa's Mineral Regimes called for concrete instruments for the implementation of the AMV.[302] Against this backdrop, the AU's 2011 Draft Action Plan for Implementing the AMV grouped respective measures and activities into *nine 'clusters'*: mining revenues and mineral rents management; geological and mining information systems; building human and institutional capacities; artisanal and small-scale mining; mineral sector governance; research and development; environmental and social issues; linkages and diversification; mobilising mining and infrastructure investment.[303] In December 2013, the AU established the African Minerals Development Centre (AMDC), which has the mandate 'to provide strategic operational support for the [AMV] and i.a. to elaborate so-called 'Country Mining Visions'.[304]

(ICSG). On these and other so-called International Commodity Bodies (ICBs), as well as their classification according to the CFC agreement, cf. Sect. 5.2.1 below.

[296] AU (2009), p. 2; on the regional policy initiatives the AMV has been inspired by, cf. the list at Oxfam (2017), p. 8.

[297] The AMV explicitly recognises that '[r]esource-based development and industrialization strategies are not a new mantra', but had already been envisaged in various strategic plans, such as the Lagos Plan of Action, the SADC Mineral Sector Programme, the Mining Chapter of the New Partnership for Africa's Development (NEPAD) as well as the Africa Mining Partnership', AU (2009), p. 3.

[298] AU (2009), p. 3.

[299] Oxfam (2017), p. 8; within the AU Agenda 2063, formulating 'a commodities strategy', i.e. '[e] nabling African countries add value, extract higher rents from their commodities, integrate into the Global Value chains, and promote vertical and horizontal diversification anchored in value addition and local content development', constitutes one of the 'flagship programmes', AU (2015), p. 17.

[300] UN ECA (2017), pp. 1–2.

[301] Oxfam (2017), p. 8.

[302] UN ECA (2011), p. 154.

[303] AU (2011), p. 9.

[304] UN ECA (2019) About AMDC, https://www.uneca.org/pages/about-amdc (last accessed 14 May 2021); AMDC (2014), p. 8.

4.2.2.2.1.2   Fiscal Framework

Within the guidance regarding the fiscal framework for commodity activities, examples of soft, direct TCL include the UN Handbook on Extractive Industries Taxation, which is providing guidance on how extractive industry activities should be taxed.[305] The handbook provides elaborate commodity-directed guidance on tax treaty issues; permanent establishment issues; transfer pricing issues; tax treatment of decommissioning; the overall government's fiscal take; tax aspects of negotiating and renegotiating contracts; and value added tax.

Furthermore, the Base Erosion and Profit Shifting (BEPS) process under action 10 has brought about specific guidance on the analysis of transfer pricing in 'cross-border commodity transactions between associated enterprises' (commodity transactions). Particularly relevant to commodity transactions is also the new guidance on applying the arm's length principle, which was developed under action 9, as well as the new standards for transfer pricing documentation, which have been developed as part of action 13.[306] The joint IGF-OECD Program on Tax Base Erosion and Profit Shifting in the Mining Sector is providing further commodity specific guidance i.a. on issues such as the undervaluation of mineral exports, indirect transfer of mining assets, and a practice called metals streaming.[307]

Besides, the IMF has developed a draft Natural Resources Fiscal Transparency Code (NRFTC),[308] which builds on its general Fiscal Transparency Code.[309] It requires states to establish a comprehensive legal framework and fiscal regime and to maintain 'open and transparent procedures for granting rights for resource extraction, and clear rules governing resource revenue collection and verification.'[310]

---

[305] In the case of inconsistencies between the handbook and the UNDTC, the latter explicitly prevails, UN (2017a), pp. iv–v.

[306] OECD (2015), pp. 51–52.

[307] IGF (2017), p. 2. 'Metals streaming involves mining companies selling a certain percentage of their production at a fixed cost to a financier in return for funds for partial or complete mine development and construction. Since the amount of financing provided is linked to the discounted mineral price, companies have strong incentives to agree to lower fixed prices to increase the up-front finance available. Streaming reduces the tax base of resource-producing countries, where royalties and income tax use sales revenue as part of calculations. There is virtually no guidance on these arrangements in the mining tax literature', IGF (2017), p. 8.

[308] IMF (2016) Release of the IMF's Natural Resource Fiscal Transparency Code, May 2016, http://www.imf.org/external/np/exr/consult/2016/ftc/ (last accessed 14 May 2021).

[309] Cf. IMF (2019), which 'integrates into the Fiscal Transparency Code (FTC) a new fourth pillar (Pillar IV) on natural resource revenue management', p. 1. The FTC is available at IMF, https://blog-pfm.imf.org/files/ft-code.pdf (last accessed 14 May 2021).

[310] IMF (2016), p. 5.

4.2.2.2.2 Incidents of Private, Direct TCL

Incidents of private, direct TCL concern corporate responsibility (Sect. 4.2.2.2.2.2). These rules need to be understood in the context of the general international standards applicable to corporations (Sect. 4.2.2.2.2.1).

4.2.2.2.2.1 General System of Corporate Responsibility

The general system of corporate responsibility naturally largely qualifies as indirect TCL. The UN Guiding Principles for Business and Human Rights (UN GP) currently constitute one of its pivotal instruments.[311] Principles #11–15 specify businesses' *responsibility to respect* (R2R).[312] According to UN GP #11, business enterprises should not infringe HR themselves and address HR violations 'with which they are involved'.[313] R2R requires businesses first to '[a]void causing or contributing to adverse [HR] impacts through their own activities, and address such impacts when they occur';[314] secondly, they need to '[s]eek to prevent or mitigate adverse [HR] impacts that are directly linked to their operations, products or services by their business relationships.'[315] This obligation applies also where they did not contribute to those impacts.

The UN GP also touch upon *remediation* and set forth that corporations should provide legitimate remediation processes wherever 'they have caused or contributed to' HR violations, according to UN GP #22.[316] Such shall be done ideally through 'operational-level grievance mechanisms', according to UN GP #29.[317] These mechanisms should be legitimate, accessible, predictable, equitable, transparent, rights-compatible, '[a] source of continuous learning', and '[b]ased on engagement and dialogue', according to UN GP #31.[318]

Apart from the fact that commodity corporations often operate in conflict-affected areas,[319] what makes them particularly prone to be concerned with negative HR impacts, is the complexity of their supply chains, respective local content

---

[311] Cf. Lindsay et al. (2013), p. 65; Sanders (2014), p. 2.

[312] UN (2011), pp. 13–16.

[313] UN (2011), p. 13.

[314] UN (2011), p. 14.

[315] UN (2011), p. 14.

[316] UN (2011), p. 24.

[317] UN (2011), p. 31.

[318] UN (2011), pp. 33–34.

[319] Cf. already above, Business and Human Rights Resource Centre (2010) The UN Protect, Respect and Remedy Framework for Business and Human Rights, https://www.business-humanrights.org/sites/default/files/reports-and-materials/Ruggie-protect-respect-remedy-framework.pdf (last accessed 14 May 2021), p. 1; Lindsay et al. (2013), p. 5. In such scenarios, the OECD Risk Awareness Tool for Multinational Enterprises in Weak Governance Zones provides additional guidance, cf. TCL outline in the annex.

requirements and thus the need to enter numerous contractual relations with third parties.[320] Where local capacities are underdeveloped, businesses aiming to uphold HR standards may even be required to proactively implement educational and other capacity-building measures.[321] The framework of the UN GP suggests that these challenges can best be met by the concept of *leverage*.[322] The latter in this context is being defined as the 'ability to effect change in the wrongful practices of an entity that causes a harm.'[323] In general, wherever a corporation is able to control the outcome of an activity potentially infringing upon HR, 'it should seek to prevent or mitigate [this] impact.'[324] Wherever it does not dispose of direct control, the company 'should seek to use leverage to secure outcomes which avoid or mitigate any adverse human rights impacts.'[325] One way to create leverage would be to 'secure significant and substantive commitments from a counterparty with respect to human rights', which, however, again may require the corporation to provide support to the contractual partner in order for it to meet its HR commitments, e.g. through capacity-building.[326]

Apart from using leverage in their contractual relations in order to ensure HR compliance within their supply chain, commodity companies may also 'be on the receiving end of leverage from external sources.'[327] Especially the IFC Performance Standards on Environmental and Social Sustainability (IFCPS)—as well as the banks abiding by the so-called Equator principles –, are said to be 'a key driver for improvements in the performance of [commodity companies] in relation to [environmental and social] issues.'[328]

The IFC Performance Standards on Environmental and Social Sustainability (IFCPS)

> are directed towards clients, providing guidance on how to identify risks and impacts, and are designed to help avoid, mitigate, and manage risks and impacts as a way of doing business in a sustainable way, including stakeholder engagement and disclosure obligations of the client in relation to project-level activities.[329]

Wherever IFC provides direct investments, it requires its clients to implement the eight individual standards that make up the IFCPS in order to foster the development benefits of the respective operation.[330]

The Equator principles (EP) are

---

[320]Lindsay et al. (2013), p. 42.

[321]Lindsay et al. (2013), p. 45.

[322]Lindsay et al. (2013), p. 43.

[323]UN (2011), p. 21; Lindsay et al. (2013), p. 43.

[324]Lindsay et al. (2013), p. 42; UN (2011), p. 14.

[325]Lindsay et al. (2013), p. 43.

[326]Lindsay et al. (2013), p. 44.

[327]Lindsay et al. (2013), p. 46.

[328]Lindsay et al. (2013), p. 46.

[329]IFC (2012), p. i.

[330]IFC (2012), p. i.

a risk management framework, adopted by financial institutions, for determining, assessing and managing environmental and social risk in projects and is primarily intended to provide a minimum standard for due diligence and monitoring to support responsible risk decision-making.[331]

The general idea is that the 94 so-called Equator Principles Financial Institutions (EPFIs) financing or advising business operations are responsible to ensure that these operations are being conducted in a socially responsible way and in a manner, which respects 'sound environmental management practices'.[332]

Another prominent 'indirect' standard, which addresses issues of corporate governance, are the OECD Guidelines for Multinational Enterprises (OECDG).[333] The OECDG are said to be 'recommendations addressed by governments to multi-national enterprises', which

aim to ensure that the operations of these enterprises are in harmony with government policies, to strengthen the basis of mutual confidence between enterprises and the societies in which they operate, to help improve the foreign investment climate and to enhance the contribution to sustainable development made by multinational enterprises.[334]

The OECDG generally provide voluntary good practice standards, which are consistent with international standards and typically also domestic laws.[335] According to their *general policies*, enterprises should i.a. contribute to SD; respect Human Rights (HR); 'encourage local capacity building' and 'human capital formation'; refrain from accepting exemptions, which are not provided for in the applicable regulatory framework; 'uphold good corporate governance principles'; '[a]void causing or contributing to adverse impacts', as well as seek to prevent impacts 'directly linked to their operations, products or services'; encourage business partners and suppliers 'to apply principles of responsible business conduct'; engage with local stakeholders; and abstain from 'improper involvement' in local politics.[336] The *HR* chapter of the OECDG draws upon the UN GP and largely reflects the core responsibilities of enterprises contained therein.[337] Regarding the objective of *environmental protection*, the OECDG draw largely on the principles and objectives provided for by the Rio Declaration, as well as the Aarhus Convention and such standards as the ISO Standard on Environmental Management Systems.[338]

In addition to these substantive responsibilities, the OECDG also provide specific implementation procedures, most notably so-called *National Contact Points*

---

[331] Equator principles (2019) The Equator principles, https://equator-principles.com/about/ (last accessed 14 May 2021).

[332] Equator principles (2013), p. 2.

[333] OECD (2011). On the 2011 amendments of the OECDG, Liberti (2012).

[334] OECD (2011), p. 13.

[335] Cf. OECD (2011), p. 3.

[336] All of the above, OECD (2011), pp. 19–20.

[337] OECD (2011), p. 31.

[338] OECD (2011), p. 44.

(NCPs). Countries adhering to the OECDG are obliged to establish these NCPs, which shall 'operate in accordance with core criteria of visibility, accessibility, transparency and accountability.'[339] Moreover, NCPs are supposed to operate in an impartial manner, yet to still maintain an 'adequate level of accountability to the adhering government.'[340]

The UN Global Compact (UN GC) provides further general guidance on responsible business conduct in line with accepted international standards.[341] It constitutes 'both a policy platform and a practical framework for companies that are committed to sustainability and responsible business practices.'[342] The latter is composed of i.a. *ten principles* stemming from *four* different *issue areas*: HR; labour; environment; and anti-corruption.[343] Accordingly, companies should for instance support and respect the protection of HR (principle #1); make sure not to become complicit in HR abuses (principle #2); uphold the freedom of association as well as the right to collective bargaining (principle #3), the elimination of all forms of forced or compulsory labour (principle #4), the effective abolition of child labour (principle #5), and the elimination of employment- or occupation-related discrimination (principle #6); and promote greater environmental sustainability (principle #8).[344] The UN GC i.a. aims to mainstream its ten principles into business operations worldwide, as well as catalyse actions, particularly through public-private partnerships in support of broader UN targets, especially the SDGs.[345] In this context, it is also providing elaborate guidance on how to effectively embed SDGs into Corporate Reporting, thus seeking to further 'operationalise' SDGs in business contexts.[346] The same holds true for the so-called action platforms the UN GC has created, which expressly relate to specific SDGs.[347]

---

[339] OECD (2011), p. 71. On the normative, potentially binding, effects of the OECDG Procedural Guidance, Ochoa Sanchez (2015), pp. 94–95 with reference to ICJ (1996) *Legality of the Threat or Use of Nuclear Weapons*, Advisory Opinion of 8 July 1996, para. 70.

[340] OECD (2011), p. 71; on the requirement of *functional equivalence*, Ochoa Sanchez (2015), pp. 94–95, 114–115.

[341] At the time of writing, 9946 companies from 162 countries had committed to the UN GC and issued 65,808 (sustainability) reports on their progress to implement the ten principles, UN GC (2019) https://www.unglobalcompact.org/ (last accessed 14 May 2021).

[342] UN GC (2008), p. 2.

[343] UN GC (2014), p. 6.

[344] All of the above, UN GC (2014), p. 6.

[345] UN GC (2008), p. 2. On the SDGs and their relevance in the commodity sector, see already Sect. 2.2.5 above.

[346] UN GC (2018).

[347] UN GC (2017a), p. 21. Regarding the relationship between the UN GC and the UN GP, it shall be noted that the latter provide 'conceptual and operational clarity for the two human rights principles championed by the [UN GC]' and thus reinforce the UN GC (2011a), p. 2. However, the UN GC also goes beyond the HR respect required by the UN GP in that its participants 'have committed to support the promotion of human rights, that is, to make a positive contribution to the realization of human rights especially in ways that are relevant for their business. Such efforts can be through core business activities, social investment and philanthropy, public policy engagement and advocacy, and partnerships and collective action', UN GC (2011a), p. 2.

A variety of standards elaborated i.a. by chambers of commerce, NGOs, and standard-setting organisations provide further 'indirect' guidance on corporate best practices. They include the ICC Business Charter for Sustainable Development, which provides further guidelines seeking to streamline sustainability in global business conduct;[348] the CERES roadmap for sustainability, which formulates 20 expectations for companies 'in order to transform into truly sustainable enterprises';[349] the Business Principles for Countering Bribery, which are meant 'to assist companies in the design and implementation of effective anti-bribery policies';[350] the ICC Rules of Conduct and Recommendations on Combating Extortion and Bribery, which 'are intended as a method of self-regulation by business against the background of applicable national laws';[351] and the OECD Transfer Pricing Guidelines for Multinational Corporations and Tax Administration, which provide specific guidance on how to avoid transfer-pricing disputes and i.a. guide the implementation of the *arm's length principle*.[352]

4.2.2.2.2.2 Private, Direct TCL

Incidents of private, direct TCL are mostly embedded in this general system of corporate responsibility.

One field, which poses a particular issue for companies operating in the commodity sector, is the one of *security*. Mines, refineries or farms generally need to be protected from trespassers. Where commodity operations have elicited opposition from local communities or indigenous peoples, violent clashes between security personnel acting on behalf of the private corporation and protesters may cause serious HR violations—the situation being even more intricate when public security forces or military intervenes on behalf of the private company.[353]

The latter for instance were the facts that gave rise to the proceedings in the notorious *Kiobel* case, which even reached the US Supreme Court in 2013.[354] In *Kiobel*, the petitioners alleged that Royal Dutch Petroleum aided and abetted the Nigerian government in stopping protests against its oil operations in the Ogoni delta.[355] They claimed that Nigerian military forces committed a series of HR violations against the Ogoni people, including rape, torture, and extrajudicial killings and that Royal Dutch Petroleum provided them 'with food, transportation, and

---

[348] Cf. ICC (2015), p. 5.

[349] CERES (2010), p. 1. The CERES roadmap defines natural resources as one of three 'priority areas', CERES (2010), p. 3.

[350] Transparency International (2013), p. 2.

[351] ICC (2005), p. 5.

[352] OECD (2017b).

[353] UN OHCHR (2015), p. 23.

[354] US Supreme Court (2013) *Kiobel v. Royal Dutch Petroleum*, Judgment of 17 April 2013.

[355] US Supreme Court (2013) *Kiobel v. Royal Dutch Petroleum*, Judgment of 17 April 2013, p. 2.

compensation, as well as [. . .] allowing the Nigerian military to use respondents' property as a staging ground for attacks.'[356]

'Direct' guidelines on how to handle these situations for corporations are provided particularly by the Voluntary Principles on Security and Human Rights for the Extractive and Energy Sectors (VPSHR), which allegedly constitute 'the only human rights guidelines designed specifically for extractive sector companies.'[357] Having been elaborated based on a multi-stakeholder approach involving i.a. governments and commodity companies, some of the largest commodity TNCs number among its participants.[358] The VPSHR are divided up into *three categories*: risk assessment, as well as relations with public security and relations with private security.[359]

Not least in order to prevent violent clashes in tense environments, the Conflict–Sensitive Business Practice: Guidance for Extractive Industries provides comprehensive guidance and best practices on how to adopt 'conflict-sensitive' approaches in commodity operations.[360] For that purpose, the publication provides operational guidance charts, as well as screening tools for both macro- and project level conflict risk and impact assessment.[361]

Regarding *transparency*, we have seen that the EITI constitutes a standard, which is primarily aimed at governments. The latter are the ones signing up to the EITI and consequently charged with implementing it.[362] As a consequence, corporations are concerned by the EITI standard rather indirectly—for instance whenever a state, in which a company is active or domiciled, decides to incorporate disclosure requirements under the EITI in its domestic legal system. However, companies can acquire

---

[356]US Supreme Court (2013) *Kiobel v. Royal Dutch Petroleum*, Judgment of 17 April 2013, p. 2. Apart from Kiobel, commodity TNCs were confronted with allegations of HR breaches in several different proceedings before domestic courts. In the US, many of these proceedings were—like Kiobel—based on the Alien Tort Statute (ATS), see the list of cases provided by Dederer (2012), p. 45, n 47. However, in its 2013 judgment, the US Supreme Court interpreted the ATS restrictively, introducing the so-called 'touch and concern' test and ultimately denying jurisdiction to hear the claim brought by Esther Kiobel, US Supreme Court (2013) *Kiobel v. Royal Dutch Petroleum*, Judgment of 17 April 2013, p. 14; see also Sanger (2014). As a consequence, the likelihood that ATS cases are going to lead to the redress sought by claimants has decreased substantially, as argued by Sanger (2014), p. e-24: 'The lower courts have already relied on the Kiobel decision to quickly dismiss pending cases, suggesting that, even if the Supreme Court did not close the door to transnational tort litigation, the decision may well prove to be the end of transnational ATS litigation.' Cf. in this respect also Grosswald Curran and Sloss (2013), pp. 858–863 who are proposing legislative action in order to preserve the benefits of ATS litigation.

[357]VPSHR (2019) Pillars, http://www.voluntaryprinciples.org/ (last accessed 14 May 2021).

[358]This is the case for instance with regard to BP, ExxonMobil, Glencore, Rio Tinto and Shell, VPSHR (2019) For companies, http://www.voluntaryprinciples.org/ (last accessed 14 May 2021).

[359]VPSHR (2000), pp. 2–7.

[360]International Alert (2005), foreword, p. 1.

[361]International Alert (2005), section 2.

[362]Cf. Sect. 4.2.2.2.1.1 above.

the status of so-called EITI supporting companies,[363] which requires corporations to officially sign up to the EITI, issue a public statement of their support for the EITI, including its *ten principles*.[364] In addition, the status also entails disclosure obligations regarding payments to EITI implementing countries, taxes, and beneficial ownership.[365] Also, supporting companies are held to support the disclosure of commodity contracts, including licenses, by governments and to 'deliver natural resources in a manner that benefits societies and communities.'[366] Today, various commodity TNCs are listed as EITI supporting companies.[367]

Moreover, private, direct TCL often approaches commodity activities from a *'shared value'* perspective. Employing the latter, the UN GC for instance compiled the SDG Natural Resource industry matrix, which sets forth 'industry specific ideas for action and industry specific practical examples for each relevant SDG.'[368] As such, it for instance spells out detailed measures on how to foster 'sustainable production' through the elimination of routine flaring during oil production, the reduction of methane emissions in the gas value chain, waste minimisation, and the developing and sharing of scalable sustainability systems.[369] An OECD Framework for Extractive Projects titled Collaborative Strategies for In-Country Shared Value Creation provides guidance on how extractive corporations can work together with other stakeholders of GCG to foster shared value creation.[370]

Also for *investors* seeking to become active in the commodity sector, specific guidelines have been elaborated, i.a. by the UN Principles for Responsible

---

[363] EITI (2019) Company support of the EITI, https://eiti.org/company-support-of-eiti (last accessed 14 May 2021).

[364] EITI (2019) Company support of the EITI, https://eiti.org/company-support-of-eiti (last accessed 14 May 2021).

[365] EITI (2019) Company support of the EITI, https://eiti.org/company-support-of-eiti; on the beneficial ownership requirement, requirement 2.5 of the 2019 EITI standard, EITI (2019) Beneficial ownership, https://eiti.org/beneficial-ownership (both last accessed 14 May 2021).

[366] EITI (2019) Company support of the EITI, https://eiti.org/company-support-of-eiti; cf. also principle #1, EITI (2019) EITI principles, https://eiti.org/document/eiti-principles (both last accessed 14 May 2021); further guidance on how corporations can support EITI has been produced in a corresponding business guide, EITI (2013). Generally, commodity companies can shape process of EITI implementation by participating in the respective EITI multi-stakeholder group, EITI (2013), pp. 9–10.

[367] This includes e.g. BP, ExxonMobil and Glencore, EITI (2019) Companies, https://eiti.org/supporters/companies (last accessed 14 May 2021).

[368] UN GC (2017b), p. 5.

[369] UN GC (2017b), p. 9.

[370] OECD (2016a), p. 4. Notably, the OECD authors somewhat *en passant* provide a list of what may be identified as *stakeholders of commodity governance*: 'central government agencies, regions, municipalities, upstream, midstream and downstream industry, chambers of commerce and industry associations, workers (including local and migrant workers) and trade unions, entities related through a business relationship (suppliers, contractors, shareholders), research institutes and universities, centres of excellence, training institutions, trade unions, local and affected communities (e.g. communities living downstream from a river near the site, or along a transport route), civil society, and vulnerable groups, such as indigenous peoples and women', OECD (2016a), p. 12.

Investment (UN PRI) initiative as well as the UN GC.[371] In its publication 'Human Rights and the Extractive Industry', the UN PRI identified six 'areas of engagement' for investors in the extractive sector to engage their investee companies regarding their HR performance.[372] Moreover, the UN GC, in collaboration with the Swiss government, the UN PRI, and an NGO, has developed 'The Responsible Investor's Guide to Commodities'.[373]

4.2.2.2.3   Interim Conclusion

In view of the rather sparse hard law instruments in direct TCL, it is not surprising that most of those policy responses, which are specifically designed to address issues in the commodity sector, are often the result of initiatives driven by NGOs, international organisations or the private sector. These policies frequently correspond with soft standards that have been elaborated by multi-stakeholder institutions or fora. Where, for instance, systemic mapping of licenses, concessions, and customary land rights in protected areas constitutes a specific response to corruption that has occurred due to opaque land tenure systems, such policies are on the transnational level rarely accompanied by a binding legal framework—but rather left to voluntary commitments on the part of IOs, private actors and host governments.

The interaction of binding hard law frameworks and voluntary, e.g. certification schemes is displayed by FAO for aquaculture products as follows:[374]

> There is an extensive national and international legal framework in place for various aspects of aquaculture and its value chain, covering such issues as aquatic animal disease control, food safety and conservation of biodiversity. Legislation is particularly strong for processing, export and import of aquatic products. Recognized competent authorities are normally empowered to verify compliance with mandatory national and international legislation. Other issues such as environmental sustainability and socio-economic aspects may not be covered in such a binding manner and open the opportunity for voluntary certification as a means to demonstrate that a particular aquaculture system is managed responsibly.[375]

While FAO puts this status quo in a positive light and speaks of an 'opportunity for voluntary' standards that it may leave behind, one risk that corresponds with this

---

[371] UN PRI (2019) About the PRI, https://www.unpri.org/pri/what-are-the-principles-for-responsible-investment (last accessed 14 May 2021).

[372] UN GC (2015), p. 4.

[373] UN GC (2011b), p. 6.

[374] While *aquaculture* does not constitute commodity activity *per se*, given its similarities to especially fishing and farming—in view of the cultivation of sea—and freshwater, the handling of living species, as well as the particular form of 'removal', which occurs, when aquatic organisms are being farmed, cf. the definition provided by FAO (2019) Global aquaculture production, http://www.fao.org/fishery/statistics/global-aquaculture-production/en (last accessed 14 May 2021)—it constitutes a 'normative commodity' for the purposes of this book, see on this definitional basis Sect. 2.1.1.4 above.

[375] FAO (2011) Technical guidelines for aquaculture certification, http://www.fao.org/3/a-i2296t.pdf (last accessed 14 May 2021), para. 9.

kind of guidance, particularly those instruments that have been elaborated under the stewardship of businesses and their associations, is that they may be driven by corporate self-interest rather than a sense for the common good.[376] Indeed, CSR measures—which frequently include pursuit of or adherence to standard-setting initiatives—may in the most extreme case be used as a means to mitigate the 'threat' of government regulation.[377]

Another observation insofar is noteworthy. During those times of regulatory action in the commodity sector, which were dominated by the doctrine of state intervention—that sought to obtain regulatory control over commodity subsectors, which were deemed to play key roles in the development of especially CDDCs— direct TCL in the form of hard law was a lot more proliferate, especially in the form of ICAs.[378] Evidently, with the advent of the neoliberal doctrine in global trade law certain regulatory endeavours were cut back or even entirely abandoned. Insofar, the emergence of more and more standard-setting initiatives led by private sector organizations could be seen as not simply the filling of a regulatory gap through alternative means, but rather as a somewhat causal effect: In a domain where the public institutions have decided to abandon their regulatory task, the influence of well-resourced private actors increased. As a consequence, a large share of direct TCL today consists of private standards that have been elaborated by corporates and their associations.

4.2.2.3 Specific, Direct TCL Is Largely Private

This is also reflected in our analysis when we are approaching TCL from yet another angle: the one of specificity. Whereas we have already discussed the distinction between direct and indirect TCL, specificity here refers to the nature of individual norms regulating commodity activities—whether they provide guidance of a rather abstract, general nature or spell out detailed, concrete imperatives, which the addressee must follow. Direct TCL, which reflects a conscious consideration of commodity activities and related stakeholder interests, can be both: rather abstract or rather specific in nature. The same holds true for indirect TCL. As will become clear subsequently, most of direct, specific TCL addresses private actors.

An example for an abstract rule of direct TCL is the one of sustainable use. The norm requires states to balance socio-economic development and environmental protection when exploiting natural resources yet does not provide strict guidance on *how* this balancing exercise should be performed.

---

[376] Cf. Bloom and Rhodes (2018b).

[377] Bloom and Rhodes (2018b). [a]gain, here we see how corporations engage in seemingly responsible practices in order to increase their own political power, and to diminish the power of nation states over their own operations.' [. . .] Not 'being good', but 'looking good' is the objective', ibid. Cf. also the book by the same authors, Bloom and Rhodes (2018a).

[378] See Sect. 2.2 above. ICAs will be discussed in greater detail in Sect. 5.2 below.

A specific example of direct TCL, to the contrary, is clause 4.6.4.4.b of the Initiative for Responsible Mining Assurance (IRMA) Standard for Responsible Mining IRMA-STD-001, which obliges the operating company of a mine site when implementing and developing a biodiversity management plan to outline i.a. measurable conservation outcomes, timelines and locations.

Further examples are provided i.a. by the ISO Standards 73, which address specific technical issues of mining activity, such as the method of determining coalbed methane content (ISO 18871:2015) or creating structures for mine shafts (ISO 19426-5:2018).[379] They also provide specific guidance regarding different ores, such as iron, manganese, chromium or aluminium,[380] and e.g. set the standard for determining the total iron content of iron ore (ISO 2597-1:2006) or for sampling and sample preparation procedures (ISO 3082:2017).[381] The same holds true for other commodity sectors, such as farming and forestry,[382] as well as fisheries.[383]

With regard to the oil and gas sector, the standards maintained by the International Association of Oil and Gas Producers (IOGP) and the International Petroleum Industry Environmental Conservation Association (IPIECA) exhibit a comparable degree of specificity.[384] In fact, many examples of specific, direct TCL are provided by standards addressing technical matters of commodity operations carried out by corporations. The 'direct' norms, which presumably are most specific, target either individual commodities or commodity-subsectors, such as mining, oil and gas, forestry, farming, or fisheries. While it lies beyond the scope of this book to portray these subsector- and commodity-specific standards in greater detail, the TCL outline contained in the annex provides a respective overview.

These observations demonstrate that while *inter*national commodity law will typically be of quite abstract nature, the more specific rules addressing commodity activities usually feature in those standards and guidelines of *trans*national commodity law, which have been elaborated by multi-stakeholder or private sector organisations.[385]

---

[379]ISO (2019) Standards catalogue: mining and minerals, https://www.iso.org/ics/73/x/ (last accessed 14 May 2021).

[380]ISO (2019) Standards catalogue: metalliferous minerals and their concentrates, https://www.iso.org/ics/73.060/x/ (last accessed 14 May 2021).

[381]ISO (2019) Standards catalogue: iron ores, https://www.iso.org/ics/73.060.10/x/ (last accessed 14 May 2021).

[382]ISO (2019) Standards catalogue: agriculture, https://www.iso.org/ics/65/x/ (last accessed 14 May 2021).

[383]ISO (2019) Standards catalogue: fishing and fish breeding, https://www.iso.org/ics/65.150/x/; ISO (2019) Standards catalogue: fish and fishery products, https://www.iso.org/ics/67.120.30/x/ (both last accessed 14 May 2021).

[384]IOGP (2017); IPIECA (2019) Resources, http://www.ipieca.org/resources/ (last accessed 14 May 2021).

[385]Cf. Sect. 4.2.2.2 as well as the TCL outline in the annex, especially with regard to the (sub)-sector- as well as commodity-specific standards, which tend to exhibit a particularly specific nature.

Evidently, it lies in the nature of international law that it will often provide rather broad legal concepts, which will then have to be interpreted and concretised by states and/or courts and tribunals implementing them. This generally ensures that sufficient policy space remains with states—and respective discretion for the courts and tribunals whose jurisdiction they have subjected themselves to—in translating the content of the rather general concept into concrete rules for the case at hand. Whereas the imperative of generally respecting this policy space of national legislators is clear,[386] the question arises to what degree *inter*national rules can serve to provide more concrete guidelines on *how* states—and potentially other stakeholders—should apply and interpret the principle of sustainable use, i.a. in their domestic legal acts. Chapter 5 is going to reflect on this question and will, moreover, discuss other potential avenues for rendering TCL more effective.

4.2.2.4   Interim Conclusion

Our analysis has brought about that direct TCL is limited in its effectiveness. This is due, first, to the fact that where it constitutes 'hard' law, it mostly serves to balance a maximum of two commodity interests with one another; to address issues of interstate balance alone; or to ultimately be 'declaratory' rather than requiring concrete actions.

Second, direct TCL is largely of 'soft' normative character and therefore already exhibits no formal binding force for states. Moreover, these incidents of soft, direct TCL rarely exhibit balancing elements. By way of example, the Extractive Industries Transparency Initiative (EITI) is focused on transparency, the FAO Voluntary Guidelines on the Responsible Governance on Tenure of Land Fisheries and Forests (VGGT) cover land tenure, and the base erosion and profit shifting (BEPS) initiative as well as the fiscal transparency handbook both tackle specific fiscal challenges. Where soft, direct TCL is more comprehensive and seeks to address commodity policy trade-offs, it does so mostly in sector-specific contexts, as reflected for instance in the Berlin II Guidelines, the Intergovernmental Forum on Mining, Minerals, Metals and Sustainable Development (IGF), or the regional Africa Mining Vision (AMV). These standards and fora, however, constitute rather minor fora compared to the central global governance mechanisms maintained by e.g., the UN or WTO. Insofar, it is quite paradigmatic that the most comprehensive, coherent guidance for states in their decision to extract appears to the Natural Resource

---

[386] This obligation originates from the sovereign equality of states, as well as the principle of PSNR as its commodity-related concretisation. Accordingly, all (commodity-related) competences generally lie with the state, cf. however Sect. 4.1 on how these competences have been qualified by PSNR. Wherever self-imposed qualifications under international law exist, cf. Sect. 3.3.2 above, the state thus also bears the competence to concretise and implement these limitations. Regardless of whether states act accordingly, however, transnational regulation through e.g., multi-stakeholder processes may wear on, therefore potentially 'hardening' voluntary commitments into generally accepted standards.

Charter, which notably constitutes an NGO publication. Thus, despite its wide recognition among the stakeholders of GCG its reach is likewise very limited when it comes to disciplining states' actions.

Third, apart from the incidents of hard as well as soft direct TCL addressing states, the probably greatest volume of commodity-directed standards is intended to provide guidance for corporations operating in the commodity sector. Examples include a diverse range of instruments, such as the Voluntary Principles on Security and Human Rights for the Extractive and Energy Sectors (VPSHR), the International Responsible Mining Assurance (IRMA) Standard for Responsible Mining, various ISO standards, as well as the guidance elaborated by the International Association of Oil and Gas Producers (IOGP) and the International Petroleum Industry Environmental Conservation Association (IPIECA) for the oil and gas sector. An overview of further private commodity standards can be found in the TCL outline in the annex. These instruments addressing private actors at times provide highly detailed, specific guidance.

To conclude, under the current framework states, to the contrary, are largely left without specific guidance on how to take a decision to extract, i.e. how to balance commodity interests and what governance scheme to establish for that purpose. The most obvious obligation they are faced with in this context as of now is to make *sustainable use* of their commodity deposits.[387]

4.2.3   The Standards of TCL Are Hardly Integrated

Achieving equilibrium between the interests associated with commodity activity requires not only commodity-directed, specific norms, but also an overall *coherent* framework. What prevents TCL from being more coherent—and thus effective—is the limited degree of integration it displays.

Throughout the substance of TCL, one can witness international agreements, standards and other guidance documents *cross-referencing* one another. For instance, the OECD Guidelines for MNEs (OECDG) refer to several international standards, which can roughly be grouped according to their issuing organisations as UN, OECD and private instruments.[388] The OECD recognizes that '[m]any international instruments provide useful guidance for evaluating risks and identifying appropriate business conduct', and in this connection for instance in their OECD Risk Awareness Tool for MNEs in Weak Governance Zones allude to the example that the Convention on Combating Bribery requires states to 'mak[e] bribery a criminal offence for companies and individuals.'[389]

---

[387] Therefore, a potential pathway towards a coherent commodity policy, which we shall discuss in Chap. 5 below, lies in detailing what sustainable use requires.

[388] OECD (2006), pp. 39–40.

[389] OECD (2006), p. 39.

Also the International Responsible Mining Assurance (IRMA) explicitly acknowledges the existence of a 'number of standards and schemes' that address specific materials, processes, product sectors, or supply chains.[390] As reflected in the glossary of terms annexed to the IRMA Standard, it has been developed based on many different transnational guidelines and international conventions, including the UN Guiding Principles on Business and Human Rights (UN GP), OECD Due Diligence Guidance for Responsible Supply Chains (DDG), IFC Performance Standards, Convention on Biological Diversity (CBD) and others.[391]

When it comes to the *integration* of one regulatory instrument with another, one can distinguish between two techniques: Either the integrated standard is merely referred to in the integrating instrument in the sense that its addressees are held to *also* comply with it (formal integration); or the integrated standard is being *fully integrated* in the sense that it is defined as a *benchmark*, (non-)compliance with which will entail concrete legal consequences within the integrating instrument (full integration).

4.2.3.1 Formal Integration

The OECD Guidelines for Multinational Enterprises (OECDG) largely integrate a variety of international standards and best practices. While some of these standards were already originally intended to govern corporate behaviour, such as the UN GP, other standards like the International Bill of HR or the Rio Principles are being translated from an intergovernmental into a private sector context.[392] The latter is also reflected in the environmental chapter of the OECDG, which i.a. draws on the Rio Principles and the Aarhus convention. For instance, it particularly emphasises the precautionary principle and translates it into a corporate context.[393] This corresponds to the express nature of the OECDG as 'recommendations addressed by governments to [MNEs]', which consist of 'voluntary principles and standards for responsible business conduct consistent with applicable laws and internationally recognised standards.'[394]

The OECDG therefore represent an example of *formal integration* in international standard-setting: by reconciling norms from different 'branches' of

---

[390]IRMA (2018), p. 15. Some of these standards will feature below. On product sector initiatives, cf. e.g. the Responsible Minerals Assurance Process (RMAP), formerly Conflict-Free Smelter Program, RMI (2019) RMAP, http://www.responsiblemineralsinitiative.org/responsible-minerals-assurance-process/ (last accessed 14 May 2021), developed by the Responsible Business Alliance, formerly Electronic Industry Citizenship Coalition (EICC), and Global e-Sustainability Initiative (GeSI).

[391]IRMA (2018), pp. 180–203; see also pp. 10–11.

[392]Cf. OECD (2011), p. 32, para. 39.

[393]Cf. OECD (2011), p. 44, para. 60.

[394]OECD (2011), p. 3.

international law in one instrument, they contribute to cohering the (voluntary) norms that corporations should respect during their business activities.

Another example for this type of integrative function is provided by the Voluntary Principles on Security and Human Rights for the Extractive and Energy Sectors (VPSHR). Accordingly, companies are held to promote several principles regarding public security, including the principle that

> (c) the rights of individuals should not be violated while exercising the right to exercise freedom of association and peaceful assembly, the right to engage in collective bargaining, or other related rights of Company employees as recognized by the Universal Declaration of Human Rights and the ILO Declaration on Fundamental Principles and Rights at Work.[395]

In addition, they spell out that companies should promote 'applicable international law enforcement principles', especially the ones provided for in the UN Code of Conduct for Law Enforcement Officials as well as the UN Basic Principles on the Use of Force and Firearms.[396] The VPSHR for their part are being integrated by the OECD Due Diligence Guidance for Responsible Supply Chains (DDG). According to their model supply chain policy, the respective corporation needs to commit neither to benefit from nor to get involved in any way in serious abuses of HR.[397] In that connection, companies should i.a. commit to engagement of public or private security forces exclusively in accordance with the VPSHR.[398]

Further formal integration can be observed in the environmental protection clauses of recent joint development agreements already touched upon above.[399]

4.2.3.2   The Normative Deficits of Formal Integration

What makes the regulatory picture so complex, however, is the fact that several instruments of TCL have been designed based on the same principle. They choose from the 'menu'—presented in those international agreements and standards that are most established—what appears suitable for the given context, potentially modifying the norms in a way that they fit the concrete scenarios and addressees for which they are henceforth being employed. Consequently, several standards have emerged that each present a different, yet similar 'order of courses'. What is more, also the 'restaurants', i.e. the regulatory environment in which these courses are offered, likewise greatly resemble one another, often simply diverging in terms of the regulatory angle that the instrument at hand employs—e.g. from a corporate responsibility, anti-corruption, sustainable development, transparency, or security and Human Rights (HR) angle.

---

[395] VPSHR (2000), p. 4.

[396] VPSHR (2000), p. 4; cf. UN OHCHR (2015), p. 24.

[397] OECD (2013), p. 20.

[398] All of the above, OECD (2013), pp. 20–24.

[399] Ong (2003), p. 140; also, Ong (2011), para. 17.

This paints a regulatory picture, in which several 'neighbouring' international instruments contain similar provisions for a similar purpose. Typically, they are being drafted and administered by different organisations and are accompanied by separate implementation mechanisms. From the perspective of a stakeholder, particularly from the private sector, trying to navigate through this regulatory field is quite challenging to say the least. From a dogmatic point of view, identifying overlaps between the different instruments frequently only leads back to the original, usually highly authoritative, established text—such as the International Bill of HR or the Rio Principles. This raises the question what the benefit is of drafting such instruments then in the first place? Instead of merely translating existing established international agreements into domestic law, which is also binding for private actors?

Evidently, the objective here is to *specify* the (voluntary) principles that addressees should observe for a concrete factual scenario, which again can differ in terms of the degree of its specificity—e.g. Multinational Enterprises (MNEs) operating in weak governance zones, or sustainability reporting of oil and gas producers. Against that backdrop, it appears natural that only instruments, which successfully deduce from rather abstract, general rules originating from internationally accepted instruments *sufficiently specific* guidance for the respective scenario, contribute to the development of the legal framework. Those instruments, to the contrary, which simply repeat already existing norms and portray them in a (slightly) different setting and context, may serve to further underline how coherent a field of law has already become.

Yet, if they fail to emerge to a proper field of law, they will simply 'co-exist' in a relationship that resembles a form of 'splendid isolation'. As such, the references in various instruments to those agreements and standards, which had been utilised during the elaboration of the instrument often appears as the expression of a 'struggle' to understand what exactly one should do with these similar texts. Simply citing or referring to these 'other' standards has no real integrative or cohering effect.[400] In that connection, the ICC's Commission on Anti-Corruption for instance is held to urge international organisations responsible for individual anti-corruption conventions, such as the OECD convention prohibiting bribery of foreign public officials and the UNCAC,[401] to coordinate their anti-corruption efforts.[402] It stresses that from a 'business standpoint' the proliferation of such conventions raises concerns about inconsistencies and overall about an incoherent approach to battling corruption.[403]

---

[400] Instead, if one intends to leverage the regulatory potential of standards, which relate to similar topics and which in the end are pursuing the same objective—raising the contribution of commodity activity to SD—one needs to perceive these standards as belonging to one field of law and create dogmatic interlinkages between them. Cf. Chap. 3 above.

[401] See Sect. 4.2.2.2.1.1 above.

[402] ICC (2005), p. 11.

[403] ICC (2005), p. 11. The ICC even spells out concrete aspects that individual conventions should focus on: 1) 'The OECD Convention should remain the principal instrument focusing on the supply side of international corruption'; 2) 'Regional conventions – the instruments adopted by OAS,

4.2.3.3   Full Integration

One example to the contrary, where *full integration* between two legal instruments occurs, is for instance provided by section 10.2 of the Model Mine Development Agreement (MMDA), which reads as follows:

> Where Applicable Law and regulations on environmental and social impact assessment and management, and pollution prevention *are less stringent* than the IFC Performance Standards, the Company shall undertake its activities in a manner consistent with the IFC Performance Standards.[404]

In this case, the IFC Performance Standards serve as the minimum benchmark for environmental and social impact assessment (ESIA) and pollution prevention under the MMDA. The MMDA here fully integrates the standard set by the IFC Performance Standard. Similarly, section 19.1 MMDA integrates the 'arm's length principle' contained in the OECD Transfer Pricing Guidelines for MNEs and Tax Administrations. Instead of merely referring to e.g. companies' duty to respect HR as in chapter IV, para. 1 of the OECDG, sections 10.2 and 19.1 MMDA explicitly integrate the specific standard contained in the IFC Performance Standards and OECD Transfer Pricing Guidelines respectively. Consequently, the instrument from which the norm/benchmark is 'borrowed' does not serve as simply one of the means of *interpreting* the clause *under the newly created standard*, but instead when applying the said provision, the user is *referred to the original standard*. In other words, the instrument from which the norm/benchmark has been seized, instead of serving as a mere tool in interpreting the respective provision, becomes an integral part of the application of the norm.[405]

Council of Europe, African Union – should give priority to issues on which progress can be made by cooperation among their participating parties – such as technical assistance, preventive measures, criminalization and law enforcement, including combating extortion by public officials;' 3) 'UNCAC should give priority to issues requiring worldwide cooperation, particularly strengthening mutual legal assistance procedures for investigating and prosecuting foreign bribery cases and improving arrangements for repatriating the proceeds of corruption. UNCAC should also serve as the principal source for anti-corruption rules in areas which are not covered by regional conventions;' 4) 'Monitoring programs at OECD and at regional and UNCAC levels should be coordinated to avoid duplication, to share information and to utilize limited resources to best advantage.' Apart from OECD and UN, the ICC aims to cooperate with IFIs, the World Bank, the WTO, as well as UN GC. It also seeks to encourage national governments to implement specific policies in the fight against bribery and extortion, including capacity building, the strengthening of enforcement efforts, minimizing the issuance of individual permits, as well as transparent public procurement standards, ICC (2005), p. 12.

[404] Emphasis added.

[405] According to German legal dogmatics, such an approach is referred to as 'Rechtsgrundverweisung', which describes the technique of integrating the application of an external norm, including its normative requirements ('Tatbestandsmerkmale'), into the application of the rule at hand, cf. e.g. Wörlen and Leinhas (2006). Another example of full integration, which has already featured in Sect. 4.2.2.1.5 above, is provided by the UN HRC (2018), para. 62. Accordingly, states in order to fulfil their duties under Article 6(1) ICCPR need to act in conformity with applicable IEL.

Full integration has also been suggested with a view to filling the *lacunae* of the law applicable to commodities in situations of armed conflict by interpreting the terms 'destruction' in Article 23(g) Hague Regulations and Article 8 Rome Statute as well as 'widespread, long-term and severe damage' in Articles 35(3) and 55 AP-I, in a manner that 'take[s] into account definitions from international environmental law as well as the obligations of states under relevant treaties, such as those under the CBD.'[406]

The technique of full integration can be observed in the current framework of TCL less frequently than those numerous incidents of *cross-references* and *formal* integration. The so-called 'Rechtsgrundverweisungen' can be interpreted as an indicator of a higher degree of sophistication of the legal field at hand. Simply restating existing obligations, yet in a different setting, to the contrary can be seen as a sign for a less developed, incoherent framework. In such frameworks, the drafters of new instruments may be aware of other 'relevant' standards in the field yet feel unable to more intensively intertwine their work with already existing instruments. Perceiving these co-existing instruments as one field of law pursuing the same overall regulatory objective may help to induce drafters to create legal instruments with a greater degree of integration—thus contributing to gradually cohering the field.[407]

4.2.4 Interim Conclusion

Our analysis of the current TCL framework has revealed that it provides little to no guidance on how commodity interests should be balanced with one another.

This is due first to the largely indirect nature of the norms it is composed of. Whereas norm subsets addressing for instance Human Rights, environmental protection or armed conflict are creating 'regulatory islands' within the field of GCG, there is no coherent system, which addresses the central issues of commodity governance—namely remedying its trade-offs.

Second, where direct TCL exists, it is rarely of 'hard' legal character, but rather consists of soft law or private standards. Where hard, direct TCL exists, it mostly only serves either to balance two commodity interests with one another, to address issues of inter-state balance alone, or to ultimately be 'declaratory' rather than requiring concrete actions. Those incidents of direct, soft TCL that exhibit a coherent approach are mostly confined to individual commodity sectors and establish rather minor fora. Most of direct, *specific* TCL addresses private actors and is concerned with technical aspects of commodity activities in particular subsectors or industries. As a result, in their task of balancing commodity interests, states are, apart from notably the sustainable use principle, largely left without authoritative guidance.

---

[406] Dam-de Jong (2010), p. 56.

[407] See Chap. 5.

Third, what despite these deficits further impedes TCL from being more effective is the lack of *full integration* between its respective rules and standards—and thus coherence—it exhibits. As a result, GCG stakeholders are faced with a broad net of guidance documents, which creates lacunae, may be difficult to comprehend, and thus complicates implementation.

4.3 The Imbalance of TCL in Favour of Economic Objectives

These configurations are both illustrated and intensified by the imbalance in favour of economic objectives, which the current TCL framework exhibits. The rules of international investment law (Sect. 4.3.1) as well as the law of trade liberalisation (Sect. 4.3.2) currently feature the most clear-cut, 'hard' obligations. In addition, they display the most vigorous implementation mechanisms. As a consequence, other rules of TCL, including environmental protection norms and Human Rights can be marginalised—thus fostering the resolution of commodity policy trade-offs in favour of the interest of economic gain.

4.3.1 System, Shifting Paradigms and Unbalancing Effects of International Investment Law

Many states have entered into binding obligations to accord transnational transactions specific protections, which are contained primarily in Bilateral Investment Treaties (BITs) as well as investment chapters of Free Trade Agreements (FTAs). These international investment agreements (IIAs) spell out various requirements that need to be met in order for a transaction to be protected.[408] Moreover, also investor-state contracts can provide such protections.[409] First and foremost, a transaction needs to constitute an 'investment'. Absent a generally accepted definition in international investment law (IIL), most BITs introduce their own definition of an 'investment'.[410] These definitions typically exhibit a broad perception of the term.[411] While natural resource exploitation has been described as the 'paradigmatic

---

[408] On the foundations of international investment law, see comprehensively Bungenberg et al. (2015); Dolzer and Schreuer (2012), pp. 1–27; Pauwelyn (2014).

[409] Cf. Schreuer (2013), paras. 24–30.

[410] Schreuer (2013), paras. 37–40.

[411] Schreuer (2013), paras. 37, 39. On the definition of an investment according to Article 25(1) ICSID, e.g. the debate whether or not an 'investment' needs to contribute to the host state's development in order to qualify as such, see extensively de Figueiredo (2012); Muchlinski (2016), p. 44.

example' of foreign direct investment,[412] other activities include e.g. large infrastructure projects.[413] Moreover, the investment needs to be 'made' by a 'foreign investor'—additional terms that are typically equally spelled out in the applicable IIA.[414]

What makes the investment regime particularly efficacious is the fact that it gives investors the possibility to directly institute arbitral proceedings against the host state before an international *ad hoc* tribunal.[415] Ever since the award in *AAPL v. Sri Lanka*, this possibility does not necessarily have to arise from a contractual relationship between investor and host state—the type of claims ICSID had originally been established for –,[416] but can also be based on arbitration clauses contained in an IIA.[417] Since the 1990s the number of investment arbitration claims rose exponentially from six ICSID proceedings initiated in 1996 to 16 in 2001, 42 in 2009 and finally the record number of 80 in 2015.[418]

4.3.1.1   Expansion of Investment Protection

From a public interest perspective, the rationale behind the investment protection regime lies in the expected development benefits that foreign investment entails. It has historically been intended to be reserved for *exceptional* scenarios, in which granting particular protections may be necessary in order to attract the inflow of foreign assets, which in turn foster development.[419] It is in such scenarios that states

---

[412] Viñuales (2016), p. 30.

[413] Schreuer (2013), para. 37; Viñuales (2016), p. 30. However, also the mere purchase of shares in a company by a foreign investor or the granting of loans has been qualified as an (portfolio) investment, Viñuales (2016), p. 30.

[414] Cf. Viñuales (2016), p. 27.

[415] Cf. Viñuales (2016), p. 44. Some arbitral clauses may however require the investor to first exhaust local remedies, cf. Viñuales (2016), p. 44.

[416] Cf. Bottini (2008), p. 565.

[417] ICSID (1990) *Asian Agricultural Products LTD (AAPL) v. Republic of Sri Lanka*, Final Award, 27 June 1990; Viñuales (2016), p. 29. As such, filing for arbitration is said to sufficiently reflect the implicit acceptance of the arbitration clause by the investor, Viñuales (2016), p. 29; Asiedu-Akrofi (1992).

[418] UNCTAD (2019) Investment dispute settlement navigator, http://investmentpolicyhub.unctad.org/ISDS/FilterByYear (last accessed 14 May 2021).

[419] Viñuales (2016), p. 30; UN GA (1962) Resolution 1803 (XVII) of 14 December 1962, https://www.un.org/ga/search/view_doc.asp?symbol=A/RES/1803%28XVII%29 (last accessed 14 May 2021), paras. 1–3, 6, and 8; whether or not IIAs foster development depends on two factors: for one, whether IIAs have a positive effect on FDI inflows, and, for the other, whether FDI actually fosters development. As Pohl (2018), pp. 28–30 summarises, there is little empirical evidence with regard to both questions. While the most sound studies seem to suggest slightly positive effects of IIAs on FDI inflows, Pohl (2018), p. 31 with reference to Egger and Merlo (2012), p. 1240 as well as Kerner and Lawrence (2012), p. 107, positive development effects of FDI according to 'a growing consensus [...] are contingent on multiple parameters in the host country – e.g. varying levels of indigenous human resources, private-sector sophistication, competition, and host-country policies

were willing to accept the qualifications of their permanent sovereignty over natural resources (PSNR) that follow from their obligations under the investment regime.

However, as the numbers of arbitral proceedings above indicate, over time investment protection evolved to be more than just an exceptional safeguard.[420] Viñuales claims that this has been due largely to two processes: for one, states continuously expanded the definitions of 'investment' and 'foreign investor' that they included in IIAs; for the other, investment tribunals gradually extended their interpretations of the term, increasingly also including portfolio investments, such as commercial loans or other financial instruments.[421] The same phenomenon of expansive interpretation can be observed with regard to many of the core obligations that states typically confer upon investors under international investment law.[422] These primarily include protection against expropriation; fair and equitable treatment; full protection and security; and most-favoured nation as well as national treatment.[423]

Originally, international investment law was intended to particularly protect investors against hardships resulting from expropriation or nationalisation.[424] While direct, i.e. formal, expropriations occurred primarily in the direct aftermath of decolonisation,[425] particularly the interpretation of what constitutes an indirect, i.e. non-targeted, expropriation was subject to much discussion especially during the first decade of the new millennium.[426] Yet, ever since expansive tendencies in the interpretation of the term 'indirect' have been contained, other standards, especially the fair and equitable treatment (FET) standard, have inherited the central role in the protection of foreign investments.[427]

The FET standard is generally not shaped by domestic laws, but constitutes a standard of international law.[428] It represents a very flexible principle, which needs to be concretised by the respective tribunal for the case at hand.[429] While there is no

---

including trade- and investment policies', Pohl (2018), p. 15. Bringing new conceptual clarity to the issue, see Bonnitcha et al. (2017).

[420] Viñuales (2016), p. 30.

[421] Viñuales (2016), pp. 30–31.

[422] Cf. Viñuales (2016), pp. 31–32.

[423] Schreuer (2013), paras. 49–75; 85–90; Viñuales (2016), p. 29; extensively Bungenberg et al. (2015), pp. 700–1030.

[424] Viñuales (2016), p. 31.

[425] Cf. e.g. how investment law is mentioned explicitly in the context of nationalisations in UN GA (1962) Resolution 1803, 14 December 1962, paras. 1, 4 and 8; Viñuales (2016), p. 31.

[426] Schreuer (2013), paras. 85–88; with a profound discussion of i.a. the relevant case law Kriebaum (2015), pp. 971–981.

[427] Schreuer (2013), para. 90.

[428] Angelet (2011), para. 3; extensively on FET, and particularly the distinction between 'autonomous' FET clauses and 'MST-FET' clauses, which define FET by reference to customary international law, Gaukrodger (2017).

[429] Angelet (2011), para. 4; in the case of autonomous FET clauses, the room for interpretation for arbitral tribunals is naturally greater, Gaukrodger (2017), p. 13.

general definition of what constitutes FET or a breach thereof, the principle is typically described as a reflection of the good faith principle.[430] It thus is concerned particularly with upholding the rule of law with regard to every aspect of the investment process and therefore has brought about several related principles, such as transparency, consistency, stability or due process.[431] Moreover, arbitral tribunals have tended to describe FET by referring to the *legitimate expectations* of the investor.[432]

Further trends in investment arbitration that led to a significant expansion of the regime and therefore the surge in the number of proceedings included the

> expansive interpretation of the MFN clause for jurisdictional purposes or the dismissal of the rule – widely acknowledged in inter-State dispute settlement – that consent to jurisdiction cannot be presumed and is to be interpreted restrictively.[433]

These expansive tendencies in state as well as arbitral practice have led to investment protection constituting a particularly dominant paradigm in global governance. Apart from the broad scope of investment safeguards, especially the possibility for investors to depart from conventional judicial avenues and institute arbitral proceedings against the host state creates what has been perceived as an 'imbalance' between investment protection and states' duty to protect the environment as well as Human Rights (HR).[434] For instance, the right to freely dispose over natural resources (RFD) 'has been largely forgotten in the development of areas of international law that have had a direct impact on the issue of control over natural resources.'[435] This observation is being alluded to also in the 'warnings' e.g. included in principle #9 of the UN Guiding Principles on Business and Human Rights (UN GP), which calls upon states to reserve sufficient domestic

---

[430] Angelet (2011), para. 5.

[431] Angelet (2011), para. 5; Schreuer (2013), para. 52; on the interpretation of e.g. the NAFTA governments of these principles originating from FET, Gaukrodger (2017), pp. 40–51.

[432] Angelet (2011), para. 6. However, several tribunals have pointed out that FET cannot be understood as solely protecting investors' interests. Rather, also this standard needs to be interpreted against the backdrop of the object and purpose of the individual IIA, which lies not exclusively in the protection of investments, but rather in the promotion of foreign direct investment and (sustainable) development. Consequently, also the FET standard needs to be subjected to a 'balanced approach' in its interpretation, which takes the public interest dimension into account, PCA (2006) *Saluka Investments BV v. Czech Republic*, Partial Award, 17 March 2006, paras. 300, 305; Angelet (2011), para. 6.

[433] Viñuales (2016), p. 32; moreover, also *umbrella clauses* have contributed their bit to this trend. These clauses have the effect of 'elevating' contractual obligations to the international level, i.e. breaches of contract automatically constitute a breach also of the international obligation of the host state. In Schreuer's words, '[c]ontracts and other obligations are put under the treaty's protective umbrella', Schreuer (2013), para. 80. Viñuales (2016), p. 31.

[434] UN HRC (2008) Report of the Special Representative of the Secretary-General on the Issue of Human Rights and Transnational Corporations and Other Business Enterprises, John Ruggie, 7 April 2008, UN Doc. A/HRC/8/55, available at http://www.reports-and-materials.org/Ruggie-report-7-Apr-2008.pdf (last accessed 14 May 2021), paras 34–35; Lindsay et al. (2013), p. 49.

[435] Gilbert (2013), p. 333.

policy space for the implementation of HR in spite of IIAs or investment contracts. Ruggie has described this trend as being 'particularly problematic' for developing countries—given their limited resources and development needs.[436] Especially these states run the risk of allocating too much attention and resources to according safeguards to foreign investors at the expense of other policy fields.

4.3.1.2   Turn to SD

As a consequence, several important stakeholders of international investment governance have initiated steps to strengthen states' right to regulate in the public interest in spite of their obligations under IIL. This 'alliance' for the 'recalibration' of the investor-state dispute settlement system includes i.a. the EU and UNCTAD, as well as NGOs such as the World Economic Forum or the International Institute for Sustainable Development.[437] These 'shifting paradigms' in IIL in many ways describe a turn of the international investment regime towards SD.[438] This is reflected i.a. in the UNCTAD's Investment Policy Framework for SD, which provides guidance on how to better integrate investment protection and SD policies.[439]

Moreover, international legal scholarship in the recent years has produced both comprehensive analysis and guidance regarding innovative legal instruments that foster SD effects of foreign investment.[440] Sacerdoti in this respect however first alludes to the fact that BITs should not be misunderstood as 'development cooperation instruments'.[441] Their ultimate object and purpose is to protect investments. Nevertheless, investment protection provisions should be interpreted in light of SD and corresponding international standards, which are being respected by both parties, including HR, environmental and health agreements.[442] This may also open avenues towards an evolutionary interpretation of older treaties and guide the reconciliation of investment protection with other objectives of economic

---

[436]UN HRC (2008) Report of the Special Representative, John Ruggie, para. 36; Lindsay et al. (2013), p. 49.

[437]Viñuales (2016), p. 43; Muchlinski (2016), p. 41.

[438]Krajewski and Hindelang (2016); see also Cordonier Segger et al. (2011).

[439]UNCTAD (2015). See also VanDuzer et al. (2012); Muchlinski (2016), p. 41.

[440]The fact that—generally speaking—investments can constitute important drivers of development has been acknowledged repeatedly, cf. then-UN SG Ban Ki-Moon, UNCTAD (2014), p. iii; Sacerdoti (2016), p. 20; Muchlinski (2016), p. 43. For more critical accounts of the matter, Center for International Environmental Law et al (2018) Reform options for ISDS, http://www.uncitral. org/pdf/english/workinggroups/wg_3/UNCITRAL_recs_and_justification_final.pdf (last accessed 14 May 2021), p. 1 i.a. referring to the summary by Pohl (2018), pp. 14–36; Johnson et al. (2018). See also fundamentally De Schutter et al. (2013); Bonnitcha et al. (2017).

[441]Sacerdoti (2016), p. 39.

[442]Sacerdoti (2016), p. 39; on this effect of SD, which operates as a regulatory objective, see Chap. 5 below.

regulation.[443] In general, BITs and investment chapters in FTAs should make use of innovative drafting in order to make

> BITs more respectful of the policy space of host States in the pursuit of legitimate general interest, balancing these values while maintaining the essential protection from arbitrary, discriminatory conduct and outright expropriation without compensation of foreign investors by host countries.[444]

Concrete provisions fostering this objective are provided i.a. by UNCTAD in its Investment Policy Framework as well as by the Commonwealth Secretariat. For instance, BITs could set out a general exception modelled on Article XX GATT,[445] which could also apply to measures 'designed and applied' to protect e.g. HR or labour rights.[446] Moreover, Bilateral Investment Treaties (BITs) could include investor responsibilities and obligations. Investment protection could be made dependent upon an investor fulfilling these duties, including respecting HR and domestic host state law.[447]

Also, parties to an IIA could agree not to lower especially social and environmental standards in order to attract investment.[448] The home state could be required to assist its less-developed contracting partner with the implementation of its obligations under the IIA.[449] In addition, the parties could establish an institutional mechanism to discuss the interpretation of investment provisions on a regular basis with a view to ensuring more consistency in arbitral awards and fostering the contributions of investments to the SDGs.[450] Further suggestions include special treatment provisions for Least Developed Countries (LDCs), such as replacing binding obligations with 'best-endeavour' clauses, or requiring sustainability assessments from the investor.[451] In addition, also changes to investor-state dispute settlement (ISDS) are being advised. For instance, certain claims could be excluded from ISDS, such as ones that relate to measures, which have been taken in the pursuit of key objectives of SD.[452] Also, investors could be required to first exhaust

---

[443] Sacerdoti (2016), p. 39.

[444] Sacerdoti (2016), p. 39; in the same vein, Chi (2017), chapter 8 on '[f]illing the compatibility gap between IIAs and sustainable development'.

[445] Cf. e.g. Article 10 2004 Canadian model agreement, Italaw (2019) Canada model FIPA, https://www.italaw.com/documents/Canadian2004-FIPA-model-en.pdf (last accessed 14 May 2021); VanDuzer et al. (2012), p. 225; Muchlinski (2016), p. 56.

[446] Cf. COMESA Investment Agreement; VanDuzer et al. (2012), pp. 249–250; Muchlinski (2016), p. 57.

[447] Muchlinski (2016), p. 57; the UN GP, cf. Sect. 4.2.2.2.2.1, as well as commodity-directed guidance as discussed in Sect. 4.2.2.2.2.2 above, could serve as benchmarks in this respect.

[448] Muchlinski (2016), p. 59.

[449] Cf. Muchlinski (2016), p. 59.

[450] Cf. Moreira (2018); see also the 2015 Norwegian draft model BIT; Muchlinski (2016), p. 59.

[451] Muchlinski (2016), pp. 60–61; with more suggestions, see also Gehring et al. (2018). On the design of *future innovative tools* that are rebalancing investment protection as well as the overall framework of TCL in favour of SD, cf. in more detail Chap. 5 below.

[452] Muchlinski (2016), p. 62.

domestic remedies.[453] Moreover, alternative dispute resolution mechanisms, as well as an appellate instance could be introduced.[454]

The recalibration of international investment law is now increasingly reflected also in state practice.[455] Examples include the COMESA Investment Agreement, which for instance according to its Article 14.3 requires tribunals to consider the state's level of development when examining a breach of fair and equitable treatment (FET), or the SADC Model Bilateral Investment Treaty Template, which requires investors to maintain an environmental management system according to its Article 14.1.[456] Recent EU FTAs explicitly promote trade and sustainable development. For instance, according to Article 13.10 EU-Vietnam FTA,

> [e]ach [p]arty affirms its commitment to enhance the contribution of trade and investment to the goal of sustainable development in its economic, social and environmental dimensions.[457]

As such, they i.a. seek to promote investment in environmental goods and services (EGS), as provided for e.g. in Articles 12.11 EU-Singapore FTA and 13.10.2(b) EU-Vietnam FTA.[458] Also, according to Article 3(4) of the 2018 Netherlands model BIT (NLBIT) parties shall promote sustainable investments. In general, according to Article 6(1) NLBIT parties commit to promote international investment in a way conducive to SD. Moreover, recent EU FTAs generally call for 'full implementation of MEAs as well as multilateral labour agreements.'[459] Article 7(1) NLBIT explicitly requires

---

[453] Muchlinski (2016), p. 62.

[454] Muchlinski (2016), p. 62. Instructively on the general dynamic debate about the future of ISDS, Bungenberg and Reinisch (2018). On the ongoing discussions within working group III of UNCITRAL tasked with ISDS reform, see UNCITRAL (2018) Possible reform of ISDS, 5 September 2018, UN Doc. A/CN.9/WG.III/WP.149, http://www.uncitral.org/pdf/english/workinggroups/wg_3/WGIII-36th-session/149_main_paper_7_September_DRAFT.pdf (last accessed 14 May 2021).

[455] Gehring et al. (2018); sceptical however as regards the development of IIL into a global standard, which fails to adequately consider the specific characteristics of domestic law, Stoll and Holterhus (2016), who instead advocate for strengthening the human rights approach to property protection.

[456] Gehring et al. (2018) with numerous further examples. With regard to ICAs de lege ferenda, see Sect. 5.2 below in more detail.

[457] Chapter 13 of the EU-Vietnam FTA is dedicated to Trade and SD and i.a. emphasises the need to uphold environmental and labour protection levels (Article 13.3), multilateral labour standards and agreements (Article 13.4), and MEAs (Article 13.5). It moreover explicitly recognises the importance of the CBD (Article 13.7), sustainable forest management (Article 13.8), as well as of sustainable management of living marine resources and aquaculture products (Article 13.9). In order to review the implementation of this chapter, it establishes a specific Committee on Trade and SD, according to Articles 13.5, 17.2 EU-Vietnam FTA. Likewise, Article 16.13 EU-Japan FTA; Articles 22.4, 26.2.1(g) CETA. See also—the trade and SD—chapter 12 of the EU-Singapore FTA.

[458] Gehring et al. (2018), p. 21.

[459] Gehring et al. (2018), p. 21; cf. also Article 6(2) NLBIT.

[i]nvestors and their investments [to] comply with domestic laws and regulations of the host state, including laws and regulations on human rights, environmental protection and labor laws.[460]

The Brazilian Cooperation and Facilitation Investment Agreements (CFIA) arguably stand for the most far-reaching departure from the 'old' investment protection system, i.a. exclusively protecting direct expropriations, introducing clauses on CSR, and particularly entirely abandoning ISDS.[461]

4.3.1.3 Economic Imbalance: Investment Protection as a Matter of Conflict Between Host States and Foreign Investors

As mentioned above, commodity activities have been described as 'paradigmatic example' of an investment. Often, TNCs domiciled in industrialised states are conducting commodity operations in less developed, yet resource-rich countries.[462] The investment case law is rich in precedents, which originated from conflicts over state measures affecting investors' control or title over commodity investments or their profitability.[463] In fact, more than 28 % of all arbitral proceedings under the ICSID Convention to date concerned commodity operations, which is by far the largest overall share by sector.[464]

Correspondingly, some signature cases of international investment law, such as the arbitrations between BP, TEXACO, LIAMCO and Libya,[465] the *Kuwait*

---

[460]The CSR provision contained in Article 7 NLBIT moreover makes express mention of due diligence (Article 7(3)); liability of investors in home state jurisdiction where their 'acts or decisions lead to significant damage, personal injuries or loss of life in the host state' (Article 7(4)); and parties' commitment to the UN GP as well as the OECDG (Article 7(5)).

[461]Articles 17–24 Brazil-Ethiopia CFIA, UNCTAD (2019) https://investmentpolicyhub.unctad.org/Download/TreatyFile/5717; Articles 18–25 Brazil-Suriname CFIA, UNCTAD (2019) https://investmentpolicyhub.unctad.org/Download/TreatyFile/5715; Moreira (2018).

[462]See already Sect. 2.1.2 above.

[463]Eljuri and Trevino (2015), p. 313; Childs (2011). On inter-state disputes over the commercial terms of commodity extraction see also already the early case law of both the PCIJ and the ICJ as summarised by Higgins (1999): PCIJ (1924–1927) *Mavrommatis Concessions Case*, Judgments of 30 August 1924, 26 March 1925, 10 October 1927, available at https://www.icj-cij.org/en/pcij-series-a; PCIJ (1928) *Phosphates in Morocco Case*, Judgment of 14 June 1938, https://www.icj-cij.org/files/permanent-court-of-international-justice/serie_AB/AB_74/01_Phosphates_du_Maroc_Arret.pdf; ICJ (1952) *Anglo-Iranian Oil Company Case*, Judgment of 22 July 1952, https://www.icj-cij.org/files/case-related/16/016-19520722-JUD-01-00-EN.pdf (all last accessed 14 May 2021).

[464]ICSID (2018) Caseload statistics, issue 2018-2, https://icsid.worldbank.org/en/Documents/resources/ICSID%20Web%20Stats%202018-2%20(English).pdf (last accessed 14 May 2021), p. 12. Disputes arising from oil, gas and mining accounted for 24%, agriculture, fishing and forestry for an additional 4% of all disputes. Out of the 17% of cases concerning electric power and other energy disputes, it is quite likely that a considerable part likewise more or less directly concerns commodity operations, such as the sourcing or trade of energy commodities.

[465]Sole arbitrator (1973) *BP Exploration v. Libya*, Award of 10 October 1973, 53 ILR 297, available at https://kupdf.net/download/bp-exploration-v-libyan-arab-republic-53-ilr-297-1973_

v. Aminoil,[466] or the *Occidental v. Ecuador* proceedings, arose in connection with commodity activities.[467] These cases share that they typically represent conflicts between host state and investor over the economic benefits of a commodity operation.[468] Paradigmatically, many of the historic commodity investment arbitrations originated from the termination of concessions or PSAs, direct as well as indirect expropriations, and nationalisations.[469]

While direct expropriations and nationalisations concerned international arbitrators especially during the NIEO era in the 1970s and 80s, they still constitute a current topic. This is particularly due to measures taken by Venezuela in 2007, which sought to nationalise oil production in the so-called Orinoco belt.[470] This step impacted projects maintained by large transnational oil companies, such as Chevron, ExxonMobil and ConocoPhillips; several affected corporations initiated arbitral proceedings.[471] Further specific state measures that gave rise to commodity investment arbitrations and were raised as especially forms of indirect expropriations or breach of the FET standard respectively, included windfall profit taxes, export taxes, denial of the right to reimbursement of VAT, export restrictions, price regulations, and domestic market obligations (DMOs).[472]

The subject at issue in several proceedings involving Ecuador for instance was a tax that the state introduced in order to capture a share of 'extraordinary incomes'

5a1aec14e2b6f5f95564e0e1_pdf; sole arbitrator (1977) *TEXACO v. Libya*, Award of 19 January 1977, available at https://www.trans-lex.org/261700; sole arbitrator (1977) *Liamco v. Libya*, Award of 12 April 1977, available at https://www.trans-lex.org/261400 (all last accessed 14 May 2021).

[466] AMINOIL tribunal (1982) *Kuwait v. AMINOIL*, Award of 24 March 1982, 21 ILM 976, available at https://www.trans-lex.org/261900 (last accessed 14 May 2021).

[467] LCIA (2004) *Occidental v. Republic of Ecuador*, LCIA Case No UN 3467, Final Award, 1 July 2004; see also the 'Vivendi saga', Italaw (2019) *Vivendi v. Argentina*, https://www.italaw.com/cases/309, Italaw (2019) *Suez, Vivendi v. Argentina* https://www.italaw.com/cases/1057 (both last accessed 14 May 2021), which concerned water, a product, which is explicitly not classified as a commodity for the purposes of this book. The dispute, however, arose over the privatisation of water supply in an Argentinian province—and is thus paradigmatic for the 'commoditisation of nature', cf. Chap. 1 above. For more lead cases, see i.a. Bernasconi-Osterwalder and Johnson (2011); Weiler (2005).

[468] Cf. Viñuales (2016), p. 33.

[469] Ruzza (2017), paras. 7, 12–14; for a recent example of nationalisation, ICSID (2010) *Mobil Corporation v. Bolivarian Republic of Venezuela*, Decision on Jurisdiction, 10 June 2010, paras. 16–25, 30–36, 145–146; Childs (2011), pp. 251–252.

[470] Eljuri and Trevino (2015), pp. 314–315.

[471] ICSID (2013) *ConocoPhillips v. Venezuela*, Decision on Jurisdiction and the Merits, 3 September 2013; Italaw (2019) *Mobil Corp., Venezuela Holdings et al. [ExxonMobil] v. Venezuela*, https://www.italaw.com/cases/713; ICSID (2013) *OPIC Karimum Corporation v. Venezuela*, Award, 22 May 2013; Eljuri and Trevino (2015), pp. 314–315 with further references. See too the proceedings between Repsol and Argentina, which ended in settlement, Italaw (2019) *Repsol. v. Argentina*, https://www.italaw.com/cases/2046 (both last accessed 14 May 2021); Eljuri and Trevino (2015), p. 315.

[472] For cases concerning DMOs, see e.g. PCA (2010) *Chevron Corporation v. Republic of Ecuador*, Partial Award on the Merits, 30 March 2010; Childs (2011), pp. 241–243 with further references.

generated by oil corporations.[473] The tax was set first at 50 %, later at 99 %.[474] Both the *Burlington* and *Perenco* tribunals, which had to assess the identical operative facts, held that the windfall profits tax did *not* constitute an indirect expropriation.[475] The *Perenco* tribunal noted that

> . . .it would be unsurprising to an experienced oil company that given its access to the State's exhaustible natural resources, with the substantial increase in world oil prices, there was a chance that the State would wish to revisit the economic bargain underlying the contracts.[476]

In 2002, 2004 and 2007 respectively, Argentina introduced export taxes on hydrocarbons, which had been 'designed to prevent producers from receiving more than forty-two U.S. dollars per barrel of oil produced.'[477] In reaction to these taxes, at least five corporations initiated arbitral proceedings against Argentina, including the French TNC Total.[478] Total claimed that the export tax would constitute a breach of the FET standard. The tribunal, however, considered that the tax constituted an ordinary fiscal measure as part of the general fiscal framework therefore dismissing Total's claim.[479]

Another measure taken by Ecuador involved changes in the right to be reimbursed of the value-added tax (VAT) paid when purchasing goods and services that were needed for commodity activities.[480] This gave rise to two arbitrations, one involving the US corporation Occidental Exploration and Production Company (Occidental).[481] The tribunal in *Occidental* held that the changes in the VAT reimbursement scheme constituted a breach of the FET standard given that it

---

[473] 'Extraordinary income' constituted 'the difference between the market price of Ecuadorian oil actually sold and the average market price of oil at the time the contracts were executed, multiplied by the number of barrels produced', Eljuri and Trevino (2015), p. 321; Italaw (2019) *City Oriente v. Ecuador*, ICSID Case No ARB/06/21, https://www.italaw.com/cases/3432; Italaw (2019) *Perenco v. Ecuador*, ICSID Case No ARB/08/6, https://www.italaw.com/cases/819; Italaw (2019) *Burlington v. Ecuador*, ICSID Case No ARB/08/5, https://www.italaw.com/cases/181; Italaw (2019) *Murphy Exploration v. Ecuador*, ICSID Case No ARB/08/4, https://www.italaw.com/cases/723 (all last accessed 14 May 2021); Childs (2011), p. 233; Eljuri and Trevino (2015), pp. 321–3.

[474] Eljuri and Trevino (2015), p. 321.

[475] Eljuri and Trevino (2015), p. 322.

[476] ICSID (2014) *Perenco v. Ecuador*, Decision on Remaining Issues of Jurisdiction and on Liability, 12 September 2014, para. 588; the tribunal held, however, that the introduction of the windfall profit tax i.a. constituted a breach of contract, Eljuri and Trevino (2015), p. 322.

[477] Eljuri and Trevino (2015), p. 323; Childs (2011), pp. 235–237.

[478] ICSID (2011) *El Paso v. Argentina*, Award of 31 October 2011; ICSID (2006) *Pan Am. v. Argentina*, Decision on Preliminary Objections, 27 July 2006; ICSID (2008) *Wintershall v. Argentina*, Award of 8 December 2008; ICSID (2010) *Total v. Argentina*, Decision on Liability, 27 December 2010; Eljuri and Trevino (2015), p. 323; Childs (2011), p. 235.

[479] Eljuri and Trevino (2015), p. 324.

[480] Eljuri and Trevino (2015), p. 324.

[481] LCIA (2004) *Occidental v. Ecuador*, Final Award of 1 July 2004; and LCIA (2006) *EnCana v. Ecuador*, Award, 3 February 2006; Eljuri and Trevino (2015), p. 325.

'significantly changed the framework under which its investment had been made.'[482]

4.3.1.4   Societal and Environmental Imbalance

Things become even more intricate when activities associated with investments are causing negative externalities, e.g. for local populations or the environment. Recalling the organisational framework of TCL, corresponding interests are the one of development, preservation, and participation.[483] Viñuales describes this situation, which is paradigmatic for GCG, as the 'State–Investor–Population (SIP) triangle'.[484]

Within this triangle, separate bodies of international law are regulating the relationships between the different stakeholders: HR and IEL apply between host state and the population; between the latter and investors only domestic law is applicable; and the relation between host state and investors is covered by international investment law.[485] This isolation of the different relationships and norm subsets that are applicable to them is particularly problematic:

> Understanding international investment law as a mere "protective" framework has a particularly significant *unbalancing effect* if its operation is "detached" from the broader body of domestic and international law governing negative externalities, such as the adverse impact on human rights and the environment.[486]

Perceiving international investment law in this isolated manner has led to a situation in which—out of all the different policy fields that a state needs to cover in order to pursue and maintain good commodity governance—investment protection has been put centre stage, not least in view of the financial ramifications that may ensue from infringements upon the investment law framework. The severe consequences of this imbalanced legal framework are prominently portrayed in the arbitral proceedings that arose after the Argentinian economic depression at the beginning of the new millennium.[487] Moreover, this imbalance can be particularly

---

[482]Eljuri and Trevino (2015), p. 325. Moreover, the tribunal also held that the measures also violated the national treatment clause under the BIT, Eljuri and Trevino (2015), p. 325.

[483]Cf. Sect. 2.1.3 above.

[484]Viñuales (2016), pp. 32–34.

[485]Viñuales (2016), p. 34.

[486]Viñuales (2016), p. 36. Emphasis added.

[487]Viñuales (2016), p. 38 alludes to the fact that the respective awards in *CMS v. Argentina* as well as *LG&E v. Argentina* 'wrongly concluded [...] that the customary requirement for necessity governed the application of a treaty-based emergency clause.' As a result, Argentina—although in an economic emergency—was faced with significant impending compensation duties; ICSID (2005) *CMS v. Argentina*, Award of 12 May 2005; see also ICSID (2007) *Enron and Ponderosa v. Argentina*, Award of 22 May 2007; ICSID (2007) *Sempra Energy v. Argentina*, Award of 28 September 2007; ICSID (2006) *LG&E v. Argentina*, Decision on Liability, 3 October 2006; ICSID (2008) *Continental Casualty v. Argentina*, Award of 5 September 2008; Viñuales (2016),

problematic where the interests of investors and local populations collide.[488] For instance, in the *Ominayak v. Canada* case before the Human Rights Committee, the UN HRC considered that Canada's authorisations of oil and gas exploration on ancestral lands could potentially constitute a breach of the community's right to enjoy one's culture according to Article 27 ICCPR.[489] Even though no foreign investor was involved in this case, it illustrates how differently facts that from one angle may be determined to constitute a breach of investment protection provisions, may represent a violation of HR norms from the 'prism' of communities affected by commodity activities.[490] Similarly, in the *Länsman* cases, mining and logging activities respectively were raised as potential violations of Article 27 ICCPR.[491]

In the case before the IACtHR between the *Sawhoyamaxa* community and Paraguay, the applicants claimed that the state had breached their right to property due to failure to guarantee the community their rights over ancestral lands.[492] When the state claimed that the owner of the respective lands—a German investor—was protected under an IIA, the 'different legal frameworks applicable to different sides of the SIP triangle were thus laid bare.'[493] Moreover, it exhibits how the (economic) interests of host states and investors may often coincide.[494]

How detrimental the current configuration of investment protection may be in these situations where public and governmental interests diverge, is furthermore reflected in the *Ogoni* case before the African Commission on Human and Peoples'

---

pp. 37–39. With a contrasting view on the 'paradoxical' Argentina cases Alvarez and Topalian (2012).

[488] Viñuales (2016), p. 40.

[489] UN HRC (1990) *Bernard Ominayak and the Lubicon Band v. Canada*, Views of the committee, 26 March 1990, HRC Communication No. 167/1984, http://juris.ohchr.org/Search/Details/665 (last accessed 14 May 2021), paras. 13.4, 14; Viñuales (2016), p. 40.

[490] Viñuales (2016), p. 40.

[491] Both complaints were ultimately rejected, UN HRC (1994) *Ilmari Länsman and others v. Finland*, Views of the committee, 26 October 1994, HRC Communication No. 511/1992, https://www.escr-net.org/sites/default/files/HR%27s_Committee_Decision_0.html; UN HRC (1996) *Jouni E. Länsman et al v. Finland*, Views of the committee, 30 October 1996, HRC Communication No. 671/1995, available at http://hrlibrary.umn.edu/undocs/html/VWS67158.htm (both last accessed 14 May 2021); Viñuales (2015), p. 9.

[492] IACtHR (2006) *Sawhoyamaxa Indigenous Community v. Paraguay*, Judgment, 29 March 2006, ICtHR Series C No 146, http://www.cidh.org/ninez/sawhoyamaxa%20(80)/sentencia%20fondo,%20reparaciones%20marzo%2029%202006eng.doc (last accessed 14 May 2021), paras. 113–115; Viñuales (2016), p. 40.

[493] Viñuales (2016), p. 41.

[494] Viñuales (2016), p. 42. 'Moreover, the Court considers that the enforcement of bilateral commercial treaties negates vindication of non-compliance with state obligations under the American Convention; on the contrary, their enforcement should always be compatible with the American Convention, which is a multilateral treaty on human rights that stands in a class of its own and that generates rights for individual human beings and does not depend entirely on reciprocity among States', IACtHR (2006) *Sawhoyamaxa Indigenous Community v. Paraguay*, Judgment, 29 March 2006, para. 140; Viñuales (2016), p. 41.

Rights, in which the commission i.a. held that Nigeria had violated the Ogoni people's right to freely dispose over natural resources (RFD) according to Article 21:

> The Commission notes that in the present case, despite its obligation to protect persons against interferences in the enjoyment of their rights, the Government of Nigeria facilitated the destruction of the Ogoniland. Contrary to its Charter obligations and despite such internationally established principles, the Nigerian Government has given the green light to private actors, and the oil Companies in particular, to devastatingly affect the well-being of the Ogonis. By any measure of standards, its practice falls short of the minimum conduct expected of governments, and therefore, is in violation of Article 21 of the African Charter.[495]

These cases illustrate how substantially other legal positions than investments may be concerned by commodity activity. Once one changes the perspective on these activities—and for instance assumes the one of the affected communities or local populations—the transnational legal framework appears to be imbalanced in favour not only of investors, but in general of economic over other public interests, including HR and environmental protection.[496]

4.3.1.5   Integrating Investment Protection into the TCL Framework

The structure of TCL demonstrates that the norm subset addressing investment protection constitutes *but one* qualification of a state's PSNR. This one objective, however, is being pursued with the most vigorous normative as well as implementation means. What can remedy this situation is a more integrated understanding of the entire field covering commodity activities. As such, investment protection could be made exclusively available to investors that comply with HR, environmental protection and other domestic laws.[497] Moreover, ISDS could be turned into a reciprocal mechanism, which allows especially developing states to initiate claims against commodity corporations.[498]

Apart from the reform discussions within UNCITRAL as well as international legal scholarship, also investment case law exhibits signs for a greater integration of

---

[495] ACHPR (2002) *Social and Economic Rights Action Center and the Center for Economic and Social Rights v. Nigeria*, Communication No. 155/96, 27 May 2002, ACHPR/COMM/A044/1, https://www.escr-net.org/sites/default/files/serac.pdf (last accessed 14 May 2021), para. 58; Viñuales (2016), p. 42.

[496] Viñuales (2016), p. 42.

[497] See already Sect. 4.3.1.2 above; Center for International Environmental Law et al (2018) Reform options for ISDS, http://www.uncitral.org/pdf/english/workinggroups/wg_3/UNCITRAL_recs_and_justification_final.pdf, pp. 7–8 on the so-called 'clean hands clause'. In the same vein, Hauert (2016), pp. 136–144; on carve-outs, legality clauses or standing commissions, see also Viñuales (2016), p. 45.

[498] Cf. Viñuales (2016), p. 45; counterclaims are an 'additional concern' still being deliberated as part of the UNCITRAL reform process, UNCITRAL (2019) Possible reform of investor-State dispute settlement, 30 July 2019, UN Doc. A/CN.9/WG.III/WP.166, https://undocs.org/A/CN.9/WG.III/WP.166 (last accessed 14 May 2021).

the investment discipline with other fields of international law. For instance, in the *Al-Warraq* case, the tribunal largely relied on international HR law to determine the scope of the FET standard, which describes 'a major departure in the conceptualisation of the relationship between [international investment law] and [international Human Rights law].'[499] Moreover, the tribunal applied the 'clean hands' approach and ultimately dismissed the investor's claim on these grounds.[500] However, as Cotula rightly points out, greater integration of investment law and HR as displayed in *Al-Warraq* may also bring about risks by e.g. opening up the opportunity for investors to claim breaches of HR law in front of arbitral tribunals—thus bypassing the domestic remedies requirements, which apply in HR law.[501]

4.3.2   The Law of Liberalised Trade

As this book has already briefly touched upon, states' PSNR is qualified by extensive obligations to liberalise trade.[502] Commodity trade is largely covered by WTO discipline.[503] Whereas the GATT unlike the Havana Charter does not entail a separate chapter on commodities, it still contains some commodity-directed provisions, particularly in the trade and development context. While these provisions address many issues that appear crucial to the sustainable development of CDDCs, such as market access, price stabilisation and stable growth in export earnings, their effect has proven to be limited in the past due to their rather 'declaratory' nature as well as to a lack of enforcement mechanisms.[504]

As a result, the most contentious aspects in commodity trade, e.g. export restrictions and subsidies, were decided not on the basis of these commodity-directed, but rather based on the general rules of WTO law. Therefore, commodity-directed provisions seeking to protect the interests of commodity-dependent states can be said to have remained largely dead letters in the past. While thus the general liberalisation scheme of world trade is quite clearly spelled out in international law, many issues that arise with regard to the at times opposed interests of

---

[499]Cotula (2016), p. 154, commenting on Warraq tribunal (2014) *Hesham Talaat M. Al-Warraq v. The Republic of Indonesia*, UNCITRAL Arbitration, Final Award of 15 December 2014, https://www.italaw.com/sites/default/files/case-documents/italaw4164.pdf (last accessed 14 May 2021).

[500]Cotula (2016), p. 149. The respective provision was contained in Article 9 of the applicable OIC Agreement: 'The investor shall be bound by the laws and regulations in force in the host state and shall refrain from all acts that may disturb public order or morals or that may be prejudicial to the public interest. He is also to refrain from exercising restrictive practices and from trying to achieve gains through unlawful means', Cotula (2016), p. 151.

[501]Cotula (2016), p. 156.

[502]Cf. Sects. 3.3.2, 3.3.3 and 4.2.2.1.4.2 above.

[503]Cf. Pitschas (2011), p. 60.

[504]Lee (2011), p. 114; cf. Sect. 3.3.3 above.

producers—typically seeking to raise their export earnings and maintain price stability—and consumers—generally longing for market access and corresponding supply security—are being left largely unacknowledged. This lack of effective norms addressing the balance between these interests, is what describes the *internal* imbalance, which the trade regime brings about.

In addition, the law of liberalised trade also contributes to an *external* imbalance, that is—similarly to the effects of international investment law—in relation to the other components of TCL. The dominance that WTO disciplines may unfold within the commodity sector, is displayed in the cases involving China.[505] *Export tariffs* are only peripherally covered by the MFN rule of Article I:1 GATT.[506] Article II GATT exclusively applies to *import* tariffs.[507] The general prohibition envisaged in Article XI:1 GATT is limited to quantitative measures. Consequently, the China cases were based significantly on the Chinese Accession Protocol.

The dispute in *China – Raw Materials* concerned measures that China had imposed on different forms of bauxite, coke, fluorspar, magnesium, manganese, silicon metal, yellow phosphorous and zinc.[508] In *China – Rare Earths* export restrictions had been introduced with regard to rare earth elements, tungsten and molybdenum.[509] The currently pending third dispute *China – Raw Materials II* challenges the Chinese export duties imposed on different forms of antimony, chromium, cobalt, copper, ferro-nickel, graphite, lead, magnesia, talc, tantalum and tin, as well as the export quotas applied to antimony, indium, magnesia, talc and tin.[510]

---

[505] WTO DSB (2014a) *China – Rare Earths*, Panel Reports, 26 March 2014; modified by WTO DSB (2014b) *China – Rare Earths*, Appellate Body Reports, 7 August 2014; WTO DSB (2011) *China – Raw Materials*, Panel Reports, 5 July 2011; modified by WTO DSB (2012) *China – Raw Materials*, Appellate Body Reports, 30 January 2012; cf. also the pending dispute *China – Raw Materials II*, WTO. China – Export Duties on Certain Raw Materials, WT/DS508, https://www.wto.org/english/tratop_e/dispu_e/cases_e/ds508_e.htm and WTO. China – Duties and other Measures concerning the Exportation of Certain Raw Materials, WT/DS509, https://www.wto.org/english/tratop_e/dispu_e/cases_e/ds509_e.htm (both last accessed 14 May 2021). On the entire topic, cf. expertly Espa (2015); succinctly Espa and Oehl (2018), pp. 9–10; cf. also Pitschas (2011), p. 79.

[506] Pitschas (2011), p. 79.

[507] Cf. Pitschas (2011), p. 62.

[508] WTO DSB (2011) *China – Raw Materials*, Panel Reports, 5 July 2011; modified by WTO DSB (2012) *China – Raw Materials*, Appellate Body Reports, 30 January 2012; cf. Espa and Oehl (2018), p. 9, n 45.

[509] WTO DSB (2014a) *China – Rare Earths*, Panel Reports, 26 March 2014; modified by WTO DSB (2014b) *China – Rare Earths*, Appellate Body Reports, 7 August 2014; cf. Espa and Oehl (2018), p. 9, n 45.

[510] See WTO (2019) China – Export Duties on Certain Raw Materials, WT/DS508, https://www.wto.org/english/tratop_e/dispu_e/cases_e/ds508_e.htm and WTO (2019) China – Duties and other Measures concerning the Exportation of Certain Raw Materials, WT/DS509, https://www.wto.org/english/tratop_e/dispu_e/cases_e/ds509_e.htm (both last accessed 14 May 2021); cf. Espa and Oehl (2018), p. 9.

The export *duties* that China had applied were deemed to be a breach of paragraph 11.3 of China's Accession Protocol.[511] According to the Appellate Body's decision, paragraph 11.3 sets forth a standalone provision, which does not exhibit an 'objective link' to the GATT.[512] As a consequence, it held that Article XX GATT exceptions were not applicable.[513] The export *quotas* China had introduced constituted a violation of Article XI:1 GATT.[514] The Appellate Body (AB) held that they could not be justified according to the exception of Article XI:2:a GATT.[515] Such an exception essentially requires that two conditions are met: for one, there needs to be a 'critical shortage' of the commodity in question; for the other, the respective commodity needs to constitute a 'product essential to the exporting party'.[516] A critical shortage needs to be ascertained based on objective parameters, i.e. the actual current need of the exporting country. The AB held that only such commodities, which are absolutely indispensable or necessary commodities could constitute 'essential products'.[517] However, Article XI:2:a GATT applies exclusively to *tem-*

---

[511] The provision reads: 'China shall eliminate all taxes and charges applied to exports unless specifically provided for in Annex 6 of this Protocol or applied in conformity with the provisions of Article VIII of the GATT 1994.'

[512] WTO DSB (2012) *China – Raw Materials*, Appellate Body Reports, 30 January 2012, para. 293; WTO DSB (2014b) *China – Rare Earths*, Appellate Body Reports, 7 August 2014, para. 5.65. Cf. also Espa (2015), pp. 145–163.

[513] WTO DSB (2012) *China – Raw Materials*, Appellate Body Reports, 30 January 2012, para. 293; WTO DSB (2014b) *China – Rare Earths*, Appellate Body Reports, 7 August 2014, para. 5.65. Cf. also Espa (2015), pp. 145–163; this decision elicited strong criticism given that Articles XX (b) and (g) GATT are typically considered to be the only 'gateways' for SD considerations within the GATT framework, cf. also Birnie et al. (2009), pp. 759–761. Due to its obligations under the Accession Protocol, China is now permanently impeded from introducing export tariffs as an instrument of environmental conservation, cf. Espa and Oehl (2018), p. 10.

[514] WTO DSB (2011) *China – Raw Materials*, Panel Reports, 5 July 2011, paras. 7.218–24; cf. WTO DSB (2014b) *China – Rare Earths*, Appellate Body Reports, 7 August 2014, para. 5.76; cf. Pitschas (2011), pp. 65–66.

[515] WTO DSB (2012) *China – Raw Materials*, Appellate Body Reports, 30 January 2012, paras. 329–344; cf. WTO DSB (2011) *China – Raw Materials*, Panel Reports, 5 July 2011, paras. 7.238–355; the export quotas discussed here concerned refractory-grade bauxite; cf. Pitschas (2011), pp. 69–73.

[516] Cf. Pitschas (2011), pp. 69–72.

[517] WTO DSB (2012) *China – Raw Materials*, Appellate Body Reports, 30 January 2012, para. 326; Pitschas (2011), p. 72. Beforehand, the panel, WTO DSB (2011) *China – Raw Materials*, Panel Reports, 5 July 2011, para. 7.276, had clarified that the concrete circumstances, which the exporting country is facing at the time of introduction of the restrictive measures are the decisive parameters in determining whether or not a product can be held to be 'essential'. Pitschas (2011), pp. 71–72 criticises that against this backdrop it would not be understandable, why the developmental stage of an exporting country shall, according to the panel's opinion, not be taken into account when making this determination. This can be relevant in particular with regard to the situation of CDDCs.

porary restrictions.[518] For *permanent* restrictions that seek to protect exhaustible natural resources, Article XX:g GATT is applicable.[519]

With regard to China's Article XX GATT defences, the AB pointed to the fact that typically environmental risks do not arise from exportation, but from production—which is naturally domestic.[520] It thus warned not to use SD and PSNR as 'pretexts' to justify export restrictions.[521] According to the WTO adjudicators, export restrictions cannot be justified as environmental conservation measures in the sense that they 'allow a WTO Member to allocate the available stock of a product between foreign and domestic consumers because, once extracted and in commerce, natural resources are subject to WTO law.'[522] While states remain free to design environmental conservation measures according to their own policy considerations, the notion of 'conservation' cannot be unduly expanded so as to include objectives of supply chain management or other industrial policy goals.[523] As Espa and I have put it elsewhere with regard to mineral commodities,

> under WTO law Members are free to decide to which extent they want to authorize mineral exploitation (e.g. through the granting of mining concessions) within their territories but, once reserves are mined, mineral commodities (i.e. tradable mine output) are treated just like any other goods for the purpose of WTO law application.[524]

As a consequence, the Appellate Body held the Chinese measures to be illegal in both cases.

Primarily commodity exporting developing countries have criticised the AB's decision. They consider the stance taken by the AB an undue restriction of their PSNR and of corresponding policy space when it comes to implementing resource conservation measures.[525] Yet, the panel in *China–Rare Earths* emphasised that,

---

[518] WTO DSB (2011) *China – Raw Materials*, Panel Reports, 5 July 2011, paras. 7.255, 7.257–8; WTO DSB (2012) *China – Raw Materials*, Appellate Body Reports, 30 January 2012, para. 323; Pitschas (2011), p. 72.

[519] Still the AB held that the two provisions are *not* mutually exclusive, WTO DSB (2012) *China – Raw Materials*, Appellate Body Reports, 30 January 2012, para. 337; cf. Pitschas (2011), p. 71.

[520] Cf. Espa and Oehl (2018), p. 10.

[521] Cf. Espa and Oehl (2018), p. 10.

[522] Espa and Oehl (2018), p. 10; cf. WTO DSB (2014a) *China – Rare Earths*, Panel Reports, 26 March 2014, para. 7.462. Cf. already above.

[523] WTO DSB (2014a) *China – Rare Earths*, Panel Reports, 26 March 2014, paras. 7.451–2 and 7.459–60; cf. Espa and Oehl (2018), p. 10.

[524] Espa and Oehl (2018), p. 10. As such, the panel did not address issues of ownership more generally, thus apparently reflecting a 'general consensus' that WTO disciplines are not applicable to natural resources in their natural state, Yanovich (2011), p. 3. Consequently, 'internationally traded natural resources are treated as any other goods in WTO law', Espa and Oehl (2018), p. 10, n 51. Nevertheless, as reflected in WTO DSB (2004) *US – Softwood Lumber IV*, Report of the Appellate Body, 19 January 2004, para. 67, governmental decisions to subject resources in their natural state to contractual arrangements may have the effect to expose them also to WTO discipline; Yanovich (2011), p. 3.

[525] See Espa (2016). http://worldtradelaw.typepad.com/ielpblog/2016/09/guest-post-new-raw-materials-dispute-revives-trade-tensions-between-china-and-the-useu.html (last accessed 14 May 2021);

like any other trade restriction, export quotas could well be justified as conservation measures under Article XX:g GATT. GATT conformity of export quotas for such purposes thus needs to be assessed on a case-by-case basis.[526]

From the systemic perspective approaching the overall legal framework of GCG, the decisions raise questions regarding the scope of PSNR and the policy space that should remain with states when implementing objectives of SD. If the dispute settlement mechanism of an organisation aiming to liberalise global trade is competent to adjudicate whether or not an export restriction or other limitations on domestic production actually constitutes a conservation measure or not, it at least seems questionable whether this mechanism will bring about results that appear well-founded also from the perspective of SD as the overall global agenda. Put differently, what mechanism ensures the SD of the global economy? Is it sufficient to have several mechanisms in place, which each on their own seek to implement the primary objectives that they have been implemented for? Or is it time to seek more clarity regarding *how* states need to balance their various obligations with regard to socio-economic development and environmental protection? Without such clarity, the imbalance between the three—economic, social and environmental—pillars of SD may persist and could in fact thwart the entire SD agenda. In order to avoid SD to become a mere scheme of 'Mickey Mouse sustainability'[527]—and thus a 'pretext' for ever more economic growth—socio-environmental objectives need to be effectively integrated into the functioning of the economy.[528]

What further complicates things and what so far does not seem to have been addressed by any tribunal, court or—be it international or national—legislator, is the relationship between domestic and global dimensions of SD. What if, for instance, national SD policies, such as limitations on the extraction of Rare Earths, conflict

---

the panel in *China–Rare Earths* seems to have somewhat anticipated this critique and points to the line of argument already put forward by the panel in *China–Raw Materials* that 'a State's sovereignty is also expressed in its decision to ratify an international treaty and accept the benefits and obligations that such ratification entails. In becoming a WTO Member, China has of course not forfeited permanent sovereignty over its natural resources, which it enjoys as a natural corollary of its statehood. Nor, (...) has China or any other WTO Member "given up" its right to adopt export quotas or any other measure in pursuit of conservation. China has, however, agreed to exercise its rights in conformity with WTO rules, and to respect WTO provisions when developing and implementing policies to conserve exhaustible natural resources...', WTO DSB (2014a) *China – Rare Earths*, Panel Reports, 26 March 2014, para. 7.270; cf. Espa and Oehl (2018), p. 10.

[526] WTO DSB (2014a) *China – Rare Earths*, Panel Reports, 26 March 2014, para. 7.293; Espa and Oehl (2018), p. 10. The debate points to pertinent systemic questions regarding the scope of PSNR and the policy space, which objectives of SD allow for—an aspect, which we shall revisit in our discussion of ICAs *de lege ferenda* in Sect. 5.2.2 below.

[527] The notion relates to the usual way to illustrate the three pillars of SD as three overlapping circles, which turn into what looks like a 'Mickey Mouse' when the economic pillar is being enlarged as the mouse's 'face' and the social as well as environmental pillars are being reduced to depict the small 'ears' of the mouse no longer overlapping with its 'face', thus depicting the imbalance of the concept in favour of economic objectives, cf. Mulia et al. (2016).

[528] Mastering this challenge will require concrete legal guidelines—which could be established for the commodity sector through ICAs *de lege ferenda*, cf. Sect. 5.2.2 below.

with global initiatives that push for the production of more renewable energies, which require these commodities? As Espa has elaborated elsewhere, export restrictions and other limitations on commodity production can indeed constitute effective instruments in mitigating resource exhaustion.[529] However, the answer that one gives regarding their legality may very well depend on the perspective that one employs—of liberalising trade, protecting the environment, or perhaps fostering SD. This raises questions regarding the relationship between national and global SD objectives: Does international law give any sort of preference to one to the disadvantage of the other? Should there be scenarios, in which a state may be mandated by international law to extract and market specific resources globally?

4.3.3   Interim Conclusion

The structure of TCL provides a clear display of the qualifications of states' PSNR. While one could assume that each of these qualifications is held of at least equal value,[530] the degree to which it actually succeeds in disciplining a state's action depends on the design of the specific subset of norms pursuing that purpose. The layout of TCL thus neatly illustrates the incongruences in effectiveness between the separate sets of norms fostering the various objectives of GCG. The picture that this layout creates is one of a regulatory landscape of GCG, which is imbalanced in favour of economic objectives.

  Without balancing mechanisms that remedy this status quo, states may continue what many of them have done in the past: demonstrate the greatest respect for those disciplines, which 'bite' the most—which dispose of the most clear-cut, compulsory rules as well as the most rigorous, effective implementation mechanisms. Such is the case for the obligation to protect investments in view of the 'threat' of binding arbitral awards, and for WTO proceedings due to the 'threat' of economic backlashes in the case of non-compliance with decisions rendered by the WTO DSB. What fights for respecting their HR obligations, in contrast, is largely a 'naming and shaming' mechanism based on the decisions issued by Human Rights bodies.[531]

---

[529] Espa and Oehl (2018), p. 9; extensively Espa (2015).

[530] In a Humanitarian tradition, and in view of the origins of the current international legal order in the aftermath of WWII, safeguarding HR should clearly constitute the primary objective of international law. Given that human beings require an environment to live in, the objective of environmental protection likewise constitutes a fundamental objective of global governance. Economic development, to the contrary, substantially relates to issues of wealth redistribution between different groups—as long as no one disputes that it in general also constitutes an integral part of sustaining human life, the question to *what degree* an economy should develop and what instruments need to be put in place, cf. e.g. the 'degrowth' movement and its relationship to 'post-extractivism' as summarised by Brand (2015), is a rather *relative* one in comparison to the more *absolute* imperatives of protecting Human dignity, life and the Human habitat, i.e. our planet.

[531] The situation is similar regarding environmental obligations as illustrated for instance by the system of 'nationally determined contributions' according to Article 4(2) Paris Agreement.

Even where HR court systems have been established, non-compliance with such judgments typically comes without greater—at least economic—repercussions.[532]

Overcoming this imbalance in favour of economic objectives—for instance by implementing a sophisticated regime aiming to ensure sustainable commodity use— therefore is a key challenge in fostering the effectiveness of TCL.

4.4   Regulatory Gaps Within the TCL Framework

Apart from the normative patterns of TCL discussed above, the effectiveness of TCL is also limited in view of the regulatory gaps it exhibits. In this connection, we shall distinguish between two kinds of regulatory gaps. For one, we can ascertain the fact that to date there has been no multilateral undertaking to comprehensively regulate the commodity sector on the global level.[533] This could *per se* be seen as a regulatory gap, especially given the great economic and developmental significance of the sector. However, as this book has demonstrated, the international community has already elaborated several sets of norms, which regulate the sector—despite the fact that many of them do not reflect a conscious consideration of commodity activities. This thus brings us back to the distinction between direct and indirect TCL. These rules that are already in existence fill the gap, which originates from the inactivity of global legislators in this respect.

They do so more or less effectively. One of the underlying hypotheses of this book relates to direct TCL being the more effective tool in regulating the commodity sector as opposed to indirect norms that are somewhat 'accidentally' *also* applicable to commodity activities. What seems to confirm this hypothesis are the recent developments in the field of GCG, which exhibit intensified activities by states, IOs, NGOs, and the private sector that consciously reflect the specifics of commodity governance and introduce corresponding initiatives, such as the EITI, the Kimberley process, the EU Raw Materials Initiative or the like. All these initiatives appear to bear within them the conviction that this particular topic requires to be dealt with specifically and not simply as a subcategory to already existing transparency or development frameworks and policies. The 'drive' towards specifically dealing with commodity activities can therefore already be witnessed in various instances. Against this backdrop, the conceptualisation of TCL shall pave the way for a gradual evolution of the existing framework towards a more sophisticated, commodity-directed legal regime.

Based on the conceptualisation of TCL, which we have provided in Chap. 3 above, we can now turn to the second kind of regulatory gaps—those subject-matters, which are neither being addressed by rules of direct nor indirect TCL.

---

[532] However, as the example of the ECtHR demonstrates, HR court systems can lead to a remarkable degree of compliance of member states. On respective challenges, however, Voeten (2017), p. 121.
[533] On respective attempts through ICAs, see Sect. 5.2.1 below.

Evidently, given the complex nature of the sets of norms that the legal framework of GCG is made up of, it would go beyond the scope of this book to claim that there would be an *absolute* regulatory gap, i.e. that the subject-matter is not being addressed by any rule or standard *anywhere*. For instance, domestic rules *somewhere* may very well govern a certain subject-matter, yet without this rule thus far having evolved to be of transnational scope.[534] The claim to a regulatory gap here is thus meant to be a *relative* one in the sense that transnational instruments so far do not appear to cover the very subject matter. Also, the scope of this book allows covering only a selection of regulatory issues that thus far are not addressed by TCL.

Given the finding that much of TCL qualifies as indirect TCL, it is little surprising that many regulatory gaps occur where commodity activity is distinct from other activities. For instance, there is no rule in Human Rights (HR) law, which provides guidance on how responsibility chains in commodity-related HR violations should be dealt with, i.e. which of the actors involved can and should be held accountable.[535] Given the MNE structures behind many commodity operations, as well as complex supply/value chains, it can be particularly intricate to identify what actor is accountable for what action. Commodity-directed HR law could impose specific duties in this respect onto specific actors. Likewise, TCL so far does not provide concrete guidance on how typical power asymmetries with regard to land tenure between e.g. indigenous peoples, small- and large-scale landowners or also between ethnic groups should be remedied.[536]

Generally speaking, the transnational legal framework appears to lack effective remedies against harmful conduct of *transnational corporations* (TNCs).[537] Given the corporate structure especially of commodity companies, which often spans considerable parts of the entire globe,[538] holding corporations accountable for violations of HR or environmental laws through national enforcement mechanisms has proved difficult in the past.[539] Especially 'lifting the *corporate veil*', can constitute a significant legal obstacle in holding corporate parents accountable for rights violations committed by or attributable to their subsidiary entities.[540] One

---

[534] On what domestic rules have been considered to constitute significant transnational norms and thus feature in our conceptualisation of TCL, see Sect. 3.3 above.

[535] Bürgi Bonanomi et al. (2015), p. 31.

[536] Bürgi Bonanomi et al. (2015), p. 35.

[537] Skinner (2014), pp. 171–173.

[538] The highly capital-intensive extractive industries are particularly subject to domination by MNEs, Neelankavil and Rai (2015), p. 135.

[539] Skinner (2014), p. 171.

[540] Lindsay et al. (2013), p. 58; Skinner (2014) in this respect has identified *eight barriers*, mostly in a US context, which impede plaintiffs from successfully litigating against TNCs. They include i.a. lack of access to judicial remedies for extraterritorial harms in general; the *forum non conveniens* doctrine; limited liability and limited personal jurisdiction; the unsettled standard for proving vicarious liability; as well as practical hurdles, such as costs of litigation and evidentiary matters, Skinner (2014), pp. 196–247. She moreover alludes to the fact that the ICJ (1970) *Barcelona Traction*, Judgment of 5 February 1970, paras. 56–58 has not only recognised the limited liability of

prominent example of this difficulty in international case law is the *Kiobel* case, which involved a Nigerian applicant, who sought remedy for HR violations, and Royal Dutch Petroleum as respondent.[541]

It appears evident that in scenarios, in which a commodity TNC headquartered in the economic 'centre' of the globe commits or contributes to HR violations in a host state, which is unable or unwilling to offer the respective victims effective access to justice, the home state courts of this corporation will have a role to play.[542] In this connection, it is worthy to note various incidents of case law in the EU, in which courts have assumed jurisdiction over extraterritorial claims, therefore providing victims with effective remedies.[543]

Moreover, the question may arise whether SD requires states to refrain from granting companies aiming to pursue 'high-input agro-industrial agriculture' respective licenses given their potential effects on agrobiodiversity.[544] Again, TCL currently here may simply require the state to conduct an EIA and to balance the three pillars of SD, yet does not provide any guidance on how this balancing exercise should be carried out. The same holds true regarding best practices for government support of local SD impacts—and the overall regulation of global commodity markets for that purpose.[545] Another topic may be clashes between global, national, and local SD interests.[546]

Furthermore, TCL provides little to no guidance on how foreign investments as well as trade need to be designed in order to foster a sustainable commodity sector.[547] The UNCTAD Sustainable Investment Framework for instance, while

---

a parent company for rights violations of its subsidiaries, but also the concept of 'lifting the corporate veil', Skinner (2014), pp. 215–216.

[541] US Supreme Court (2013) *Kiobel v. Royal Dutch Petroleum*, Judgment of 17 April 2013; cf. Skinner (2014), pp. 159–162.

[542] See Skinner (2014), p. 183, who, based on the 'respect, protect, remedy' framework of the UN GP, recognises a duty for states 'to ensure that there are no barriers preventing victims from seeking remedies against transnational businesses, especially where victims cannot access legal remedies in their host countries.'

[543] Holly (2017); the facts of the *Vedanta* case concern alleged harmful releases from a Zambian copper mine into local waterways, ibid. The UK Supreme Court (2019) in its Judgment of 10 April 2019, UKSC 2017/0185, https://www.supremecourt.uk/cases/uksc-2017-0185.html (both last accessed 14 May 2021) confirmed the jurisdiction of English courts. Holly, ibid, also points to the decision in Arrondissementsrechtbank Den Haag (2013) *Akpan v. Royal Dutch Shell*, Case No C/09/337050/HA ZA 09-1580, Judgment of 30 January 2013, in which a Dutch district court awarded damages to a Nigerian farmer due to harm suffered in connection with an oil spill caused by negligence of one of Shell's subsidiary companies. Especially in light of the restrictive interpretation of the ATS by the US Supreme Court in *Kiobel*, Sanders (2014), p. 4 contends that henceforth UK courts may represent the more promising forum for enforcing HR obligations of TNCs.

[544] Bürgi Bonanomi et al. (2015), p. 35, who claim that even scientific studies on the effects of such undertakings are still 'largely lacking'.

[545] Bürgi Bonanomi et al. (2015), p. 35.

[546] Bürgi Bonanomi et al. (2015), p. 37; cf. already Sect. 4.3.2 above.

[547] Bürgi Bonanomi et al. (2015), p. 50.

somewhat consciously reflecting a consideration for commodity activities and thus constituting direct TCL, provides rather abstract guidance. Direct TCL could define those areas, in which respecting domestic policy space is particularly important and simultaneously spell out how such policy space should be used. It could moreover define parameters for commodity investments fostering SD—and as a result confine investment protection exclusively to those investments that meet these criteria.[548]

When it comes to commodity trade, similar questions ensue, such as adequate policy space for SD measures, integrating market incentives that foster sustainability in trade disciplines, or how to support states in achieving an 'optimal degree of commodity export dependence'.[549] Current trade rules largely consist of indirect TCL and therefore do not exhibit an adequate balance of trade liberalisation with the imperatives of SD, which is based on commodity trade. Given that these imperatives may differ according to the type of commodity that is being traded, a sector-specific approach to rebalancing these rules might have to be sought.[550]

In terms of the fight against corruption, drafting a comprehensive, multilateral civil law convention dealing with corporate liability in the commodity sector could help further narrow down loopholes in the existing transnational framework.[551] Moreover, a duty to cooperate exists in environmental law as an international obligation between states; however, there is no transnational norm that regulates how the stakeholders involved in commodity activities should collaborate.

In situations of armed conflict, commodity deposits can be protected as part of the environment, civilian objects or property,[552] yet there is no commodity-directed provision in place. The existing framework insofar creates several *lacunae*: there is no prohibition to damage the environment in a non-international armed conflict (NIAC); the prohibition to damage indispensable civilian objects only applies to natural resources, which are needed for the survival of the population; the 'prohibition against pillage only applies to the plundering of natural resources for personal gain, thereby excluding the exploitation of natural resources by or under the authority of the government for the purpose of financing the armed conflict';[553] and the prohibition to cause widespread, long-term, and severe damage sets such a high threshold that it excludes most forms of damage to the environment from its scope.[554]

---

[548] Bürgi Bonanomi et al. (2015), p. 50; cf. already Sect. 4.3.1.5 above.

[549] Bürgi Bonanomi et al. (2015), p. 51.

[550] Bürgi Bonanomi et al. (2015), p. 52.

[551] Cf. the CoE Civil Law Convention on Corruption (ECLC) as mentioned in Sect. 4.2.1.5 above as well as the TCL outline in the annex below.

[552] Cf. Sect. 4.2.1.4 above.

[553] Dam-de Jong (2010), p. 54; with a summary of all the lacunae mentioned above, pp. 53–54.

[554] For instance, the setting on fire of Iraqi oil fields as well as NATO bombardments in Yugoslavia were *not* considered to reach that threshold, Dam-de Jong (2010), p. 54; with a similar result: Vöneky and Wolfrum (2016), para. 49.

4.5   Interim Conclusion

As we have seen, TCL is effective where it fosters sustainable use. This requires specific, commodity-directed rules, which form a coherent framework and detail how equilibrium between the interests associated with commodity activity can be achieved. Our analysis has brought about that the effectiveness of TCL is limited in view of the following normative patterns:

Most of TCL is 'indirect', i.e. it has not been created for the purpose of regulating commodity activity. As such, it is not designed to balance commodity interests, but rather pursues distinct regulatory objectives.

The rather scarce incidents of hard, direct TCL are neither balancing commodity interests comprehensively. Instead, they typically balance a maximum of two commodity interests with one another; at times three where for instance environmental protection norms are being integrated with those protecting Human Rights. Besides, as the examples of the law applicable to shared resources as well as the norms covering trade and development within the GATT have demonstrated, those hard rules of direct TCL that address states tend to contribute little to remedying commodity policy trade-offs. They will either be aimed at achieving a mere inter-state balance or, where they could remedy for instance a trade-off between economic and development interests, are 'declaratory' rather than of substantial legal effect.

Moreover, direct TCL is largely of soft or private legal nature, thus unfolding little legal effect on states' actions. The latter, however, are naturally the central actors regarding decisions to extract. Also, we noted that rules addressing private actors, especially those that are intended to cover particular commodity sectors, tend to be more specific than the rather abstract rules addressing states. Another pattern, which hinders coherence and thus limits balancing effects of TCL, are the few incidents of full integration between its rules and standards.

Apart from that, what both contributes to the limited effectiveness of TCL and illustrates this status quo, is the imbalance of the current framework in favour of economic objectives—primarily investment protection and trade liberalisation. Overcoming this imbalance constitutes a major challenge in rendering TCL more effective.

Lastly, the TCL framework exhibits regulatory gaps especially with regard to aspects of commodity activity that are distinct from other activities. It particularly lacks effective remedies against harmful conduct of transnational corporations. Also, it does not address potential clashes between global, national, and local SD objectives; provides little to no guidance on how foreign investments as well as trade need to be designed in order to foster a functional commodity sector; and does not spell out what constitutes adequate policy space for SD measures.

All in all, the current TCL framework barely contours what sustainable commodity use legally requires. It is thus little effective in ensuring a functional commodity sector.

References

Literature and IO/NGO Publications

Aagaard TS (2010) Environmental law as a legal field: an inquiry into legal taxonomy. Cornell Law Rev 95:221–282

Abbott KW (2009) Corruption, fight against. In: Wolfrum R (ed) Max Planck encyclopaedia of public international law. Oxford University Press, Oxford

Almeida LM, Toledano P (2018) Understanding how the various definitions of permanent establishment can limit the taxation ability of resource – rich source countries. CCSI Briefing Note, March 2018. https://ccsi.columbia.edu/sites/default/files/content/docs/our%20focus/extractive%20industries/Optimizing-the-PE-clausefor-resource-riche-source-state-CCSI-2018-2.pdf

Alston P (1984) International law and the human right to food. In: Alston P, Tomasevski K (eds) The right to food. Martinus Nijhoff, Dordrecht, pp 9–68

Alvarez JE, Topalian G (2012) The paradoxical Argentina cases. World Arbitr Mediation Rev 6(3):491–544

AMDC (2014) A country mining vision guidebook: domesticating the Africa Mining Vision. https://www.uneca.org/sites/default/files/PublicationFiles/country_mining_vision_guidebook.pdf

Angelet N (2011) Fair and equitable treatment. In: Wolfrum R (ed) Max Planck encyclopaedia of public international law. Oxford University Press, Oxford

Asiedu-Akrofi D (1992) ICSID arbitral decision: *AAPL v. Sri Lanka*. AJIL 86(2):371–376

AU (2009) Africa mining vision. February 2009. http://www.africaminingvision.org/amv_resources/AMV/Africa_Mining_Vision_English.pdf

AU (2011) Building a sustainable future for Africa's extractive industry: from vision to action. Draft action plan for implementing the AMV, December 2011. https://www.uneca.org/sites/default/files/PublicationFiles/draft_action_plan_for_implementing_the_amv_2011.pdf

AU (2015) Agenda 2063: The Africa we want. First ten year implementation plan 2014–2023, https://au.int/sites/default/files/documents/33126-doc-ten_year_implementation_book.pdf

Baker B, Share A (2013) Regional seas, environmental protection. In: Wolfrum R (ed) Max Planck encyclopaedia of public international law. Oxford University Press, Oxford

Barral V (2012) Sustainable development in international law: nature and operation of an evolutive legal norm. EJIL 23(2) http://www.ejil.org/pdfs/23/2/2292.pdf

Bastida E, Wälde TW, Warden-Fernández J (2005) International and comparative mineral law and policy: trends and prospects. Kluwer Law International, The Hague

Bernasconi-Osterwalder N, Johnson L (2011) International investment law and sustainable development: key cases from 2000–2010. IISD. https://www.iisd.org/pdf/2011/int_investment_law_and_sd_key_cases_2010.pdf

Besson S (2011) Sovereignty. In: Wolfrum R (ed) Max Planck encyclopaedia of public international law. Oxford University Press, Oxford

Beyerlin U (2013) Sustainable development. In: Wolfrum R (ed) Max Planck encyclopaedia of public international law. Oxford University Press, Oxford

Beyerlin U, Grote Stoutenberg J (2013) Environment, international protection. In: Wolfrum R (ed) Max Planck encyclopaedia of public international law. Oxford University Press, Oxford

Birnie P, Boyle A, Redgwell C (2009) International trade and environmental protection. In: Birnie P, Boyle A, Redgwell C (eds) International law and the environment, 3rd edn. Oxford University Press, Oxford, pp 754–810

Bloom P, Rhodes C (2018a) CEO society: the corporate takeover of everyday life. Zed Books, London

Bloom P and Rhodes C (2018b) The trouble with charitable billionaires. The Guardian, 24 May 2018. https://www.theguardian.com/news/2018/may/24/the-trouble-with-charitable-billionaires-philanthrocapitalism (last accessed 14 May 2021)

Bonnitcha J, Poulsen LNS, Waibel M (2017) The political economy of the investment treaty regime. Oxford University Press, Oxford

Bottini G (2008) Indirect claims under the ICSID convention. Univ Pa J Int Law 29(3):563–639

Boyle A (2009) Environment and human rights. In: Wolfrum R (ed) Max Planck encyclopaedia of public international law. Oxford University Press, Oxford

Bradbrook AJ, Gardam JG (2006) Placing the access to energy services within a human rights framework. Hum Rights Q 28(2):389–415

Brand U (2015) Degrowth und Post-Extraktivismus: Zwei Seiten einer Medaille? Working Paper 5/2015, DFG-Kolleg Postwachstumsgesellschaften. http://www.kolleg-postwachstum.de/sozwgmedia/dokumente/WorkingPaper/wp5_2015.pdf

Bungenberg M, Reinisch A (2018) From bilateral arbitral tribunals and investment courts to a Multilateral Investment Court: options regarding the institutionalization of investor-state dispute settlement. Springer, Cham

Bungenberg M, Griebel J, Hobe S, Reinisch A (2015) International investment law: a handbook. Beck/Hart/Nomos, Baden-Baden

Bürgi Bonanomi E et al (2015) The commodity sector and related governance challenges from a sustainable development perspective: the example of Switzerland. CDE WTI IWE Joint Working Paper No. 1, 14 July 2015. https://boris.unibe.ch/71327/1/WTI_CDE_IWE%20Working%20paper%20July%202015_The%20Commodity%20Sector%20and%20Related%20Gov....pdf

Cançado Trindade AA (2010) International law for humankind: towards a new jus gentium, 2nd revised edn. Brill Nijhoff, Leiden

Cançado Trindade AA (2015) Principle 15. In: Viñuales JE (ed) The Rio declaration on environment and development: a commentary. Oxford University Press, Oxford, pp 403–428

Carbonnier G, Zweynert de Cadena A (2015) Commodity trading and illicit financial flows. International development policy, Policy Briefs/Working Papers, June 2015. https://journals.openedition.org/poldev/2054

CERES (2010) The Ceres roadmap for sustainability. https://www.ceres.org/sites/default/files/2018-02/ceres-rfs-8.5x11-rd7-v1-1-sm_updated.pdf

Chen L (2016) Realizing the precautionary principle in due diligence. Dalhousie J Leg Stud 25:1–23

Chêne M (2016) Linkages between corruption and commodity trading. U4 Expert Answer 2016:1, 5 April 2016. https://www.transparency.org/files/content/corruptionqas/Corruption_and_commodity_trading_2016.pdf

Chi M (2017) Integrating sustainable development in international investment law. Routledge, New York

Childs T (2011) Update on lex petrolea: the continuing development of customary law relating to international oil and gas exploration and production. J World Energy Law Bus 4(3):214–259

Cordonier Segger MC, Gehring MW, Newcombe AP (2011) Sustainable development in world investment law. Kluwer Law International, Alphen aan den Rijn

Cotula L (2016) Human rights and investor obligations in investor-state arbitration. J World Invest Trade (JWIT) 17:148–157

Dam-de Jong D (2010) International law and resource plunder: the protection of natural resources during armed conflict. In: Fauchald OK, Hunter D, Xi W (eds) Yearbook of international environmental law 2008, vol 19(1). Oxford University Press, Oxford, pp 27–57. https://ssrn.com/abstract=1601782

de Figueiredo RC (2012) The contribution of foreign investments to the economic development of host states as a jurisdictional requirement under the ICSID convention. PhD thesis, submitted June 2012, London. https://qmro.qmul.ac.uk/xmlui/bitstream/handle/123456789/8376/Castro%20de%20Figueiredo_R_PhD_fina.pdf?sequence=1&isAllowed=y

De Schutter O, Swinnen J, Wouters J (2013) Foreign direct investment and human development. Routledge, New York

Dederer HG (2012) Rohstoffausbeutung, -bewirtschaftung und -verteilung aus Sicht des allgemeinen Völkerrechts. In: Ehlers D, Herrmann C, Wolffgang HM, Schröder UJ (eds)

Rechtsfragen des internationalen Rohstoffhandels. Deutscher Fachverlag GmbH, Fachmedien Recht und Wirtschaft, Frankfurt am Main, pp 37–56

del Castillo-Laborde L (2010) Equitable utilization of shared resources. In: Wolfrum R (ed) Max Planck encyclopaedia of public international law. Oxford University Press, Oxford

Desta MG (2010) Commodities, international regulation of production and trade. In: Wolfrum R (ed) Max Planck encyclopaedia of public international law. Oxford University Press, Oxford

Desta MG, Hirsch M (2012) African countries in the world trading system: international trade, domestic institutions and the role of international law. Int Comp Law Q 61:127–170

Diallo Y, Etienne A, Mehran F (2013) Global child labour trends 2008 to 2012. Governance and Tripartism Department, IPEC, International Labour Office, Geneva

Dolzer R, Schreuer C (2012) Principles of international investment law. Oxford University Press, Oxford

Ebbesson J (2009a) Access to information on environmental matters. In: Wolfrum R (ed) Max Planck encyclopaedia of public international law. Oxford University Press, Oxford

Ebbesson J (2009b) Public participation in environmental matters. In: Wolfrum R (ed) Max Planck encyclopaedia of public international law. Oxford University Press, Oxford

Egger P, Merlo V (2012) BITs bite: an anatomy of the impact of bilateral investment treaties on multinational firms. Scandinavian J Econ 114(4):1240–1266

EITI (2013) Business guide: how companies can support EITI implementation. Oslo, May 2013. https://eiti.org/sites/default/files/documents/business-guide-may-2013.pdf

EITI (2018) Progress report. EITI International Secretariat, 12 February 2018. https://eiti.org/sites/default/files/documents/2018_eiti_progress_report_en.pdf

EITI (2019) The EITI Standard 2019. EITI International Secretariat, 15 October 2019. https://eiti.org/sites/default/files/documents/eiti_standard_2019_en_a4_web.pdf

Eljuri E, Trevino C (2015) Energy investment disputes in Latin America: the pursuit of stability. Berkeley J Int Law 33:306–347. http://scholarship.law.berkeley.edu/bjil/vol33/iss2/4

Equator Principles (2013) The Equator Principles: a financial industry benchmark for determining, assessing and managing environmental and social risk in projects. June 2013. http://equator-principles.com/wp-content/uploads/2017/03/equator_principles_III.pdf

Espa I (2015) Export restrictions on critical minerals and metals. Cambridge University Press, Cambridge

Espa I (2016) New raw materials dispute revives trade tensions between China and the US/EU. Guest post, International Economic Law and Policy Blog, 1 September 2016. http://worldtradelaw.typepad.com/ielpblog/2016/09/guest-post-new-raw-materials-dispute-revives-trade-tensions-between-china-and-the-useu.html (last accessed 14 May 2021)

Espa I, Oehl M (2018) Rules and practices of international law for the sustainable management of mineral commodities, including nickel, copper, bauxite and a special focus on rare earths. In: ILA Sydney conference report of the committee on the role of international law in sustainable natural resource management for development, second report of the committee, 2016–2018, pp 5–11. https://ila.vettoreweb.com/Storage/Download.aspx?DbStorageId=11926&StorageFileGuid=dc356ab0-e751-4f8b-a3c5-a41d362cb732

European Commission (2011) Tackling the challenges in commodity markets and on raw materials: communication from the commission to the European parliament, the council, the European economic and social committee and the committee of the regions. COM(2011) 25 final. http://www.europarl.europa.eu/meetdocs/2009_2014/documents/com/com_com(2011)0025_/com_com(2011)0025_en.pdf

FAO (2002) Land tenure studies, land tenure and rural development. Rome. http://www.fao.org/docrep/005/y4307e/y4307e00.htm#Contents

FAO (2012) Voluntary Guidelines on the Responsible Governance on Tenure of Land, Fisheries and Forests in the Context of National Food Security. Rome. http://www.fao.org/docrep/016/i2801e/i2801e.pdf

Gaukrodger D (2017) Addressing the balance of interests in investment treaties: the limitation of fair and equitable treatment provisions to the minimum standard of treatment under customary international law. OECD Working Papers on International Investment, 2017/03, OECD Publishing, Paris. https://doi.org/10.1787/0a62034b-en

Gehring M, Andrade Correa F, Barra M (2018) The principle of sustainable resource use in innovative economic law instruments. In: ILA Sydney conference report of the committee on the role of international law in sustainable natural resource management for development, second report of the committee, 2016–2018, pp 20–26. https://ila.vettoreweb.com/Storage/Download.aspx?DbStorageId=11926&StorageFileGuid=dc356ab0-e751-4f8b-a3c5-a41d362cb732

Gilbert J (2013) The right to freely dispose of natural resources: utopia or forgotten right? Netherlands Q Hum Rights 31(3):314–341

Grondona V (2018) Transfer pricing: concepts and practices of the 'Sixth Method' in transfer pricing. Tax cooperation policy brief, no. 2, May 2018. https://www.southcentre.int/wp-content/uploads/2018/05/TCPB2_Transfer-Pricing-Concepts-and-Practices-of-the-%E2%80%98Sixth-Method%E2%80%99-in-Transfer-Pricing_EN.pdf

Grosswald Curran V, Sloss D (2013) Reviving human rights litigation after Kiobel. AJIL 107(4):858–863

Hansson M (2006) Ending child labour in mining – field experience and analysis of interventions from Mongolia. IPEC, International Labour Office, Geneva. http://www.ilo.org/ipecinfo/product/download.do?type=document&id=5365

Hauert J (2016) Die Stärkung von "in accordance with the law"- Klauseln: eine Alternative zu Investorenpflichten? Kölner Schrift zum Wirtschaftsrecht (KSzW) 7(2):136–144

Hey E (2011) Common but differentiated responsibilities. In: Wolfrum R (ed) Max Planck encyclopaedia of public international law. Oxford University Press, Oxford

Higgins R (1999) Natural resources in the case law of the International Court. In: Boyle A, Freestone D (eds) International law and sustainable development: past achievements and future challenges. Oxford University Press, Oxford

Hinton JJ, Veiga MM, Beinhoff C (2003) Women, mercury and artisanal gold mining: risk communication and mitigation. Journal de Physique 107(4):617–620

Hobe S (2015) Evolution of the principle on permanent sovereignty over natural resources: from soft law to a customary law principle? In: Bungenberg M, Hobe S (eds) Permanent sovereignty over natural resources. Springer, Cham, pp 1–13

Holly G (2017) Access to remedy under the UNGPs: Vedanta and the expansion of parent company liability. EJIL: Talk!, 30 October 2017. https://www.ejiltalk.org/if-the-pleading-represents-the-actuality-vedanta-access-to-remedy-and-the-prospect-of-a-duty-of-care-owed-by-a-parent-company-to-those-affected-by-acts-of-subsidiaries/

ICC (2005) Combating extortion and bribery: ICC Rules of Conduct and Recommendations. https://cdn.iccwbo.org/content/uploads/sites/3/2005/10/Combating-Extortion-and-Bribery-ICC-Rules-of-Conduct-and-Recommendations.pdf

ICC (2015) Business Charter for Sustainable Development. https://cdn.iccwbo.org/content/uploads/sites/3/2015/01/ICC-Business-Charter-for-Sustainable-Development.pdf

IFC (2012) Performance standards on environmental and social sustainability. January 2012. https://www.ifc.org/wps/wcm/connect/115482804a0255db96fbffd1a5d13d27/PS_English_2012_Full-Document.pdf?MOD=AJPERES

IGF (2013) Mining Policy Framework: mining and sustainable development. October 2013. https://www.igfmining.org/wp-content/uploads/2018/08/MPF-EN.pdf

IGF (2017) IGF-OECD Program on tax base erosion and profit shifting in the mining sector: tax base erosion workplan. https://www.igfmining.org/wp-content/uploads/2018/08/tax-base-erosion-workplan.pdf

ILA (2002) New Delhi Declaration of Principles of International Law Relating to Sustainable Development. 2 April 2002, UN Doc. A/CONF.199/8, 9 August 2002. http://www.un.org/ga/search/view_doc.asp?symbol=A/CONF.199/8&Lang=E

ILA (2012) Sofia Conference, Committee on International Law on Sustainable Development, Final Report. https://ila.vettoreweb.com/Storage/Download.aspx?DbStorageId=1177&StorageFileGuid=7dcf2ffb-6010-48cf-ad92-32453d8ee2b9

ILO (2009) Indigenous and tribal peoples' rights in practice: a guide to ILO Convention no. 169. International Labour Office, Geneva. https://www.ilo.org/wcmsp5/groups/public/@ed_norm/@normes/documents/publication/wcms_106474.pdf

IMF (2016) Draft Natural Resources Fiscal Transparency Code (NRFTC). Draft as of 9 May 2016. https://www.imf.org/external/np/exr/consult/2016/ftc/pdf/050916.pdf

IMF (2019) Fiscal transparency initiative: integration of natural resource management issues. IMF policy paper, January 2019. https://www.imf.org/~/media/Files/Publications/PP/2019/pp122818fiscal-transparency-initiative-integration-of-natural-resource-management-issues.ashx

International Alert (2005) Conflict-sensitive business practice: guidance for extractive industries. March 2005. https://www.international-alert.org/sites/default/files/Economy_2005_CSBPGuidanceForExtractives_All_EN_v2013.pdf

Ioannides NA (2019) The China-Japan and Venezuela-Guyana Maritime Disputes: how the law on undelimited maritime areas addresses unilateral hydrocarbon activities. EJIL:Talk!, 25 January 2019. https://www.ejiltalk.org/the-china-japan-and-venezuela-guyana-maritime-disputes-how-the-law-on-undelimited-maritime-areas-addresses-unilateral-hydrocarbon-activities/ (last accessed 14 May 2021)

IOGP (2017) Standards bulletin. November 2017. https://www.iogp.org/bookstore/product/iogp-standards-bulletin-2017/

IRMA (2018) Standard for Responsible Mining IRMA-STD-001. June 2018. https://responsiblemining.net/wp-content/uploads/2018/07/IRMA_STANDARD_v.1.0_FINAL_2018.pdf

Johnson L, Sachs L, Güven B, Coleman J (2018) Costs and benefits of investment treaties: practical considerations for states. CCSI, policy paper, March 2018. http://ccsi.columbia.edu/files/2018/04/Cost-and-Benefits-of-Investment-Treaties-Practical-Considerations-for-States-ENG-mr.pdf

Kaufmann D (2002) Public governance and finance matter for each other: toward transparency and empirics for a virtuous cycle. 4th Annual Financial Markets and Development Conference, New York

Kerner A, Lawrence J (2012) What's the risk? Bilateral investment treaties, political risk and fixed capital accumulation. Br J Polit Sci 44:107–121

Krajewski M (2016) Menschenrechte als Antwort auf Verteilungsfragen im transnationalen Rohstoffrecht, Völkerrechtsblog, 11 May 2016. https://voelkerrechtsblog.org/menschenrechte-als-antwort-auf-verteilungsfragen-im-transnationalen-rohstoffrecht/ (last accessed 14 May 2021)

Krajewski M, Hindelang S (2016) Shifting paradigms in international investment law. Oxford University Press, Oxford

Kriebaum U (2015) Expropriation. In: Bungenberg M, Griebel J, Hobe S, Reinisch A (eds) International investment law: a handbook. Beck/Hart/Nomos, pp 959–1030

Landry D (2018) The risks and rewards of resource-for-infrastructure deals: lessons from the Congo's Sicomines agreement. Resour Policy 58:165–174

Le Billion P (2005) Fuelling war: natural resources and armed conflict. Adelphi Paper, vol 45, issue 373. Oxford University Press, Oxford

Le Billion P, Kishen Gamu J, Condé M (2016) Volatile commodities: a review of conflicts and security issues related to extractive sectors. Knowledge Synthesis Report submitted to the Social Sciences and Humanities Research Council of Canada, May 2016. http://blogs.ubc.ca/lebillon/files/2017/01/KSG-FINAL-REPORT-12-MAY-PLB-1.pdf

Lee YS (2011) World trade organization and developing countries. In: Lee YS, Horlick G, Choi WM, Broude T (eds) Law and development perspective on international trade law. Cambridge University Press, Cambridge, pp 105–129

Lehmann V (2015) Natural resources, the Extractive Industries Transparency Initiative, and global governance. Commission on Global Security, Justice & Governance, Background Paper. https://www.stimson.org/sites/default/files/Commission_BP_Lehmann.pdf

Liberti L (2012) OECD 50th anniversary: the updated OECD Guidelines for Multinational Enterprises and the new OECD Recommendation on Due Diligence Guidance for Conflict-Free Mineral Supply Chains. Bus Law Int 13(1):35–50

Lindsay R et al (2013) Human rights responsibilities in the oil and gas sector: applying the UN guiding principles. J World Energy Law Bus 6(1):2–66

Margalioth Y (2011a) Double taxation. In: Wolfrum R (ed) Max Planck encyclopaedia of public international law. Oxford University Press, Oxford

Margalioth Y (2011b) International taxation. In: Wolfrum R (ed) Max Planck encyclopaedia of public international law. Oxford University Press, Oxford

Marks S (2004) The human right to development: between rhetoric and reality. Harv Hum Rights J 17:137–168

Marong A (2010) Development, right to, international protection. In: Wolfrum R (ed) Max Planck encyclopaedia of public international law. Oxford University Press, Oxford

Marshall IE (2001) A survey of corruption issues in the mining and mineral sector. MMSD, November 2001, No. 15. http://pubs.iied.org/pdfs/G00949.pdf

Meessen KM (2001) Zu einer Neuaufteilung des Fächerkanons: Wirtschaftsrecht im Zeichen internationaler und vergleichender Rechtstheorie. Zeitschrift für vergleichende Rechtswissenschaft (ZVglRWiss) 100:41–47

Mooslechner P, Schürz M, Weber B (2004) Transparency as a mechanism of governance in financial systems. In: Puntscher Riekmann S, Mokre M, Latzer M (eds) The State of Europe: transformations of statehood from a European perspective. Campus, Frankfurt

Moreira NC (2018) Cooperation and facilitation investment agreements in Brazil: the path for host state development. Kluwer Arbitration Blog, 13 September 2018. http://arbitrationblog.kluwerarbitration.com/2018/09/13/cooperation-and-facilitation-investment-agreements-in-brazil-the-path-for-host-state-development/ (last accessed 14 May 2021)

Muchlinski PT (2016) Negotiating new generation international investment agreements: new sustainable development oriented initiatives. In: Hindelang S, Krajewski M (eds) Shifting paradigms in international investment law. Oxford University Press, Oxford

Mulia P, Behura A, Kar S (2016) Categorical imperative in defense of strong sustainability (August 24, 2016). Problemy ekorozwoju: Probl Sustain Dev 11(2):29–36. https://ssrn.com/abstract=2858188

Neelankavil J, Rai A (2015) Basics of international business. Routledge, London

NRGI (2014) Natural Resource Charter, 2nd edition. https://resourcegovernance.org/sites/default/files/documents/nrcj1193_natural_resource_charter_19.6.14.pdf

NRGI (2015–2019) Organizational strategy: a living document. https://resourcegovernance.org/sites/default/files/documents/nrgi-strategy.pdf

NRGI (2015) Publish what you pay. NRGI reader, March 2015. https://resourcegovernance.org/sites/default/files/nrgi_PWYP.pdf

NRGI (2016) Commodities trading transparency: game-changing opportunity for U.K. leadership at the London Anti-Corruption Summit. Briefing May 2016. https://resourcegovernance.org/sites/default/files/documents/commodities-trading-trans.pdf

Ochoa Sanchez JC (2015) The roles and powers of the OECD national contact points regarding complaints on an alleged breach of the OECD guidelines for multinational enterprises by a transnational corporation. Nordic J Int Law 84:89–126

OECD (2006) Risk awareness tool for multinational enterprises in weak governance zones. OECD Publications, Paris. https://www.oecd.org/daf/inv/corporateresponsibility/36885821.pdf

OECD (2008) Corruption: a glossary of international standards in criminal law. OECD Publishing, Paris. http://www.oecd.org/daf/anti-bribery/41194428.pdf

OECD (2011) OECD guidelines for multinational enterprises. OECD Publishing. https://doi.org/10.1787/9789264115415-en

OECD (2013) OECD due diligence guidance for responsible supply chains of minerals from conflict-affected and high-risk areas, 2nd edn. OECD Publishing. https://doi.org/10.1787/9789264185050-en

OECD (2015) Aligning transfer pricing outcomes with value creation: actions 8-10 – 2015 final reports. OECD/G20 Base Erosion and Profit Shifting Project, OECD Publishing, Paris. https://doi.org/10.1787/9789264241244-en

OECD (2016a) Collaborative strategies for in-country shared value creation: framework for extractive projects. OECD Development Policy Tools, 12 August 2016, OECD Publishing, Paris. https://doi.org/10.1787/9789264257702-en

OECD (2016b) Corruption in the extractive value chain: typology of risks, mitigation measures and incentives. 18 August 2016, OECD Development Policy Tools. https://doi.org/10.1787/9789264256569-en

OECD (2017a) Tax transparency: report on progress. Global Forum on Transparency and Exchange of Information for Tax Purposes. http://www.oecd.org/tax/transparency/global-forum-annual-report-2017.pdf

OECD (2017b) Transfer Pricing Guidelines for Multinational Enterprises and Tax Administrations. July 2017. https://doi.org/10.1787/tpg-2017-en

Oehl M (2019) The role of sustainable development in natural resources law. In: Bungenberg M, Krajewski M, Tams C, Terhechte JP, Ziegler AR (eds) European yearbook of international economic law 2018. Springer, pp 3–38

Ong DM (1999) Joint development of common offshore oil and gas deposits: 'mere' state practice or customary international law? AJIL 93:788–792

Ong DM (2003) The progressive integration of environmental protection within offshore joint development agreements. In: Fitzmaurice M, Szuniewicz M (eds) Exploitation of natural resources in the 21st century: the challenge of sustainable development. Kluwer, The Hague, pp 113–141

Ong DM (2011) Joint exploitation areas. In: Wolfrum R (ed) Max Planck encyclopaedia of public international law. Oxford University Press, Oxford

Ottinger RL (2014) Adrian J Bradbrook's contributions to the laws governing energy, climate change and poverty alleviation. In: Babie P, Leadbeter P (eds) Engaging with the Life and Scholarship of Adrian Bradbrook. University of Adelaide Press, South Australia, pp 201–222

Oxfam (2017) From aspiration to reality: unpacking the Africa Mining Vision. Oxfam briefing paper, March 2017. https://www.oxfam.org/sites/www.oxfam.org/files/bp-africa-mining-vision-090317-en.pdf

Pauwelyn J (2014) Rational design or accidental evolution? The emergence of international investment law. In: Douglas Z, Pauwelyn J, Viñuales JE (eds) The foundations of international investment law. Oxford University Press, Oxford, pp 11–43

Pereira R, Gough O (2013) Permanent sovereignty over natural resources in the 21st century: natural resource governance and the right to self-determination of indigenous peoples under international law. Melbourne J Int Law 14(2):451–495

Pitschas C (2011) Internationaler Rohstoffhandel aus der Sicht des WTO-Rechts. In: Ehlers D, Herrmann C, Wolffgang HM, Schröder UJ (eds) Rechtsfragen des internationalen Rohstoffhandels. Deutscher Fachverlag GmbH, Fachmedien Recht und Wirtschaft, Frankfurt am Main, pp 57–79

Pohl J (2018) Societal benefits and costs of International Investment Agreements: a critical review of aspects and available empirical evidence. OECD Working Papers on International Investment, 2018/01, OECD Publishing, Paris. https://doi.org/10.1787/e5f85c3d-en

Pring GR, Noé SY (2002) The emerging international law of public participation affecting mining, energy and resources development. In: Zillman DM, Lucas A, Pring GR (eds) Human rights in natural resource development: public participation in the sustainable development of mining and energy resources. Oxford University Press, Oxford, pp 11–76

Reeh G (2019) Human rights and the environment: the UN Human Rights Committee affirms the duty to protect, EJIL:Talk!, 9 September 2019. http://www.ejiltalk.org/human-rights-and-the-environment-the-un-human-rights-committee-affirms-the-duty-to-protect/ (last accessed 14 May 2021)

Rummel-Bulska I (2008) Experiences in negotiating transboundary agreements. In: Hart S (ed) Shared resources: issues of governance. IUCN, Gland. https://portals.iucn.org/library/sites/library/files/documents/EPLP-072.pdf

Ruzza A (2017) Expropriation and nationalization. In: Wolfrum R (ed) Max Planck encyclopaedia of public international law. Oxford University Press, Oxford

Sacerdoti G (2016) Investment protection and sustainable development: key issues. In: Hindelang S, Krajewski M (eds) Shifting paradigms in international investment law. Oxford University Press, Oxford

Sanders A (2014) The impact of the 'Ruggie framework' and the United Nations Guiding Principles on Business and Human Rights on transnational human rights litigation. LSE Law, Society and Economy Working Papers 18/2014. http://eprints.lse.ac.uk/63675/1/SSRN-id2457983_final.pdf

Sands P, Peel J (2018) Principles of international environmental law, 4th edn. Cambridge University Press, Cambridge

Sanger A (2014) Corporations and transnational litigation: comparing Kiobel with the jurisprudence of English courts. AJIL Unbound, pp e-23–30

Scanteam (2011) Achievements and strategic options: evaluation of the Extractive Industries Transparency Initiative. Final report, Oslo, May 2011. https://eiti.org/sites/default/files/documents/2011-EITI-evaluation-report.pdf

Schreuer C (2013) Investments, international protection. In: Wolfrum R (ed) Max Planck encyclopaedia of public international law. Oxford University Press, Oxford

Schrijver N (1997) Sovereignty over natural resources: balancing rights and duties. Cambridge University Press, Cambridge

Schrijver N (2008) Natural resources, permanent sovereignty over. In: Wolfrum R (ed) Max Planck encyclopaedia of public international law. Oxford University Press, Oxford

Schrijver N (2015) Fifty years permanent sovereignty over natural resources: the 1962 UN Declaration as the opinio iuris communis. In: Bungenberg M, Hobe S (eds) Permanent sovereignty over natural resources. Springer, Cham, pp 15–28

Secretariat of the CBD (2004) Akwé: Kon Voluntary Guidelines for the Conduct of Cultural, Environmental and Social Impact Assessment regarding Developments Proposed to Take Place on, or which are Likely to Impact on, Sacred Sites and on Lands and Waters Traditionally Occupied or Used by Indigenous and Local Communities. Montreal. https://www.cbd.int/doc/publications/akwe-brochure-en.pdf

Shattuck A, Holt-Giménez E (2010) Moving from food crisis to food sovereignty. Yale Hum Rights Dev J 13(2):421–434

Shelton D (2006) Human rights, remedies. In: Wolfrum R (ed) Max Planck encyclopaedia of public international law. Oxford University Press, Oxford

Shelton D (2008) International cooperation on shared natural resources. In: Hart S (ed) Shared resources: issues of governance. IUCN, Gland. https://portals.iucn.org/library/sites/library/files/documents/EPLP-072.pdf

Skinner GL (2014) Beyond Kiobel: providing access to judicial remedies for violations of international human rights norms by transnational business in a new (post-Kiobel) world. Columbia Hum Rights Law Rev 46:158–265

Spohr M (2016) Human rights risk in mining: a baseline study. German Federal Institute for Geosciences and Natural Resources (BGR), Max-Planck-Foundation for International Peace and the Rule of Law (MPFPR). https://www.bmz.de/rue/includes/downloads/BGR_MPFPR__2016__Human_Rights_Risks_in_Mining.pdf

Stoll PT (2014) World Trade Organisation. In: Wolfrum R (ed) Max Planck encyclopaedia of public international law. Oxford University Press, Oxford

Stoll PT, Holterhus TP (2016) The 'generalization' of international investment law in constitutional perspective. In: Hindelang S, Krajewski M (eds) Shifting paradigms in international investment law. Oxford University Press, Oxford

Strydom (2013) Environment and indigenous peoples. In: Wolfrum R (ed) Max Planck encyclopaedia of public international law. Oxford University Press, Oxford

Tian GY (2018) Cloud computing and cross-border transfer pricing: implications of recent OECD and Australian transferpricing laws on cloud related multinational enterprises and possible solutions. Rutgers Comput Technol Law J 44(1):33–91

Ticehurst R (1997) The Martens Clause and the laws of armed conflict. Int Rev Red Cross 37:125–134

Transparency International (2013) Business principles for countering bribery, 3rd edn. October 2013. http://files.transparency.org/content/download/707/3036/file/2013_Business%20Principles_EN.pdf

UN (2002) Berlin II Guidelines for Mining and Sustainable Development. https://commdev.org/userfiles/files/903_file_Berlin_II_Guidelines.pdf

UN (2011) Guiding Principles on Business and Human Rights: implementing the United Nations 'Protect, Respect and Remedy' Framework. New York and Geneva, HR/PUB/11/04. https://www.ohchr.org/Documents/Publications/GuidingPrinciplesBusinessHR_EN.pdf

UN (2017a) Handbook on extractive industries taxation by developing countries. United Nations, New York. https://www.un.org/esa/ffd/wp-content/uploads/2018/05/Extractives-Handbook_2017.pdf

UN (2017b) Model Double Taxation Convention between developed and developing countries. 2017 Update, New York. https://www.un.org/esa/ffd/wp-content/uploads/2018/05/MDT_2017.pdf

UN CESCR (2000) General Comment No 14: the right to the highest attainable standards of health (Art. 12). https://digitallibrary.un.org/record/425041/files/E_C.12_2000_4-EN.pdf

UN CESCR (2003) General Comment No 15: The Right to Water (Arts 11 and 12). 20 January 2003. https://www.refworld.org/docid/4538838d11.html

UN ECA (2011) Minerals and Africa's development: the International Study Group report on Africa's mineral regimes. Addis Ababa, November 2011. http://www.africaminingvision.org/amv_resources/AMV/ISG%20Report_eng.pdf

UN ECA (2017) Africa Mining Vision: African Minerals Governance Framework. https://repository.uneca.org/bitstream/handle/10855/24172/b11875884.pdf?sequence=5

UN GA (2015) Transforming our world: the 2030 agenda for sustainable development. Resolution A/RES/70/1, 25 September 2015. http://www.un.org/ga/search/view_doc.asp?symbol=A/RES/70/1&Lang=E

UN GC (2008) Corporate citizenship in the world economy. October 2008. https://www.unido.org/sites/default/files/2010-11/GC_brochure_English_0.PDF

UN GC (2011a) The UN Guiding Principles on Business and Human Rights: relationship to UN Global Compact commitments. July 2011, updated June 2014. https://www.unglobalcompact.org/docs/issues_doc/human_rights/Resources/GPs_GC%20note.pdf

UN GC (2011b) The responsible investor's guide to commodities: an overview of best practices across commodity-exposed asset classes. September 2011. https://www.unglobalcompact.org/docs/issues_doc/Financial_markets/Commodities_Guide.pdf

UN GC (2014) Corporate sustainability in the world economy. January 2014. https://www.unglobalcompact.org/docs/news_events/8.1/GC_brochure_FINAL.pdf

UN GC (2015) Human rights and the extractive industry. https://www.unglobalcompact.org/docs/issues_doc/Financial_markets/PRI_Human_rights_extractive_industry.pdf

UN GC (2017a) Making global goals local business. September 2017. https://www.unglobalcompact.org/docs/publications/MGGLB-2017-UNGA.pdf

UN GC (2017b) SDG industry matrix: energy, natural resources & chemicals. January 2017. https://www.unglobalcompact.org/docs/issues_doc/development/SDG-industry-matrix-enrc.pdf

UN GC (2018) Integrating the SDGs into corporate reporting: a practical guide. August 2018. https://www.unglobalcompact.org/docs/publications/Practical_Guide_SDG_Reporting.pdf
UN HRC (2018) General comment no. 36 on article 6 of the International Covenant on Civil and Political Rights, on the right to life. CCPR/C/GC/36. https://tbinternet.ohchr.org/Treaties/CCPR/Shared%20Documents/1_Global/CCPR_C_GC_36_8785_E.pdf
UN OHCHR (2013) Free, prior and informed consent of indigenous peoples. September 2013. https://www.ohchr.org/Documents/Issues/IPeoples/FreePriorandInformedConsent.pdf
UN OHCHR (2015) Principles for responsible contracts: integrating the management of human rights risks into state—investor contract negotiations. Guidance for negotiators, HR/PUB/15/1. https://www.ohchr.org/Documents/Publications/Principles_ResponsibleContracts_HR_PUB_15_1_EN.pdf
UNCTAD (2014) World Investment Report 2014: investing in the SDGs: an action plan. United Nations. https://unctad.org/en/PublicationsLibrary/wir2014_en.pdf
UNCTAD (2015) Investment Policy Framework for Sustainable Development, UNCTAD/DIAE/PCB/2015/5. https://unctad.org/en/PublicationsLibrary/diaepcb2015d5_en.pdf
UNCTAD (2016) Trade misinvoicing in primary commodities in developing countries: the cases of Chile, Côte d'Ivoire, Nigeria, South Africa and Zambia. https://unctad.org/en/PublicationsLibrary/suc2016d2_en.pdf
UNCTAD (2019) Trade and development report 2019: financing a global green new deal. UN, Geneva. https://unctad.org/en/PublicationsLibrary/tdr2019_en.pdf
VanDuzer JA, Simons P, Mayeda G (2012) Integrating sustainable development into international investment agreements: a guide for developing country negotiators. Commonwealth Secretariat. https://www.iisd.org/pdf/2012/6th_annual_forum_commonwealth_guide.pdf
Viñuales JE (2012) Legal techniques for dealing with scientific uncertainty in environmental law. Vanderbilt J Transnatl Law 43:437–503
Viñuales JE (2015) International investment law and natural resource governance. E15 Expert Group on Trade and Investment in Extractive Industries. Think piece, September 2015. http://e15initiative.org/wp-content/uploads/2015/07/Extractive-Vinuales-FINAL1.pdf
Viñuales JE (2016) Foreign direct investment: international investment law and natural resource governance. In: Kulovesi K, Morgera E (eds) Research handbook on international law and natural resources. Edward Elgar, Cheltenham, pp 26–45
Vishwanath T, Kaufmann D (1999) Towards transparency in finance and governance. https://doi.org/10.2139/ssrn.258978
Voeten E (2017) Competition and complementarity between global and regional human rights institutions. Glob Policy 8(1):119–123. https://onlinelibrary.wiley.com/doi/epdf/10.1111/1758-5899.12395
Vöneky S, Wolfrum R (2016) Environment, protection in armed conflict. In: Wolfrum R (ed) Max Planck encyclopaedia of public international law. Oxford University Press, Oxford
VPSHR (2000) Voluntary principles on security and human rights for the extractive and energy sectors. http://docs.wixstatic.com/ugd/f623ce_60604aa96d1c4bdcbb633916da951f25.pdf
Walter C (2007) Subjects of international law. In: Wolfrum R (ed) Max Planck encyclopaedia of public international law. Oxford University Press, Oxford
Weiler T (2005) International investment law and arbitration: leading cases from the ICSID, NAFTA, Bilateral Treaties and Customary International Law. Cameron May, London
Weiss F, Scherzer B (2015) Existence of common or universal principles for resource management? In: Bungenberg M, Hobe S (eds) Permanent sovereignty over natural resources. Springer, Cham, pp 29–59

Wolfrum R (2010) International law of cooperation. In: Wolfrum R (ed) Max Planck encyclopaedia of public international law. Oxford University Press, Oxford

Wörlen R, Leinhas S (2006) Rechtsfolgen- und Rechtsgrundverweisungen im BGB. Juristische Ausbildung (JA) 1:22–27

Yanovich A (2011) WTO rules and the energy sector. In: Selivanova Y (ed) Regulation of energy in international trade law. Kluwer Law International, Alphen aan den Rijn

Yotova R (2016) The principles of due diligence and prevention in international environmental law. Camb Law J 75(3):445–448

Cases

ACHPR (2001) *The Social and Economic Rights Action Center and the Center for Economic and Social Rights v. Nigeria* (*Ogoniland* case), 155/96, decision of 27 October 2001, http://www.achpr.org/files/sessions/30th/comunications/155.96/achpr30_155_96_eng.pdf

ACHPR (2002) *Social and Economic Rights Action Center and the Center for Economic and Social Rights v. Nigeria,* communication no. 155/96, 27 May 2002, ACHPR/COMM/A044/1, https://www.escr-net.org/sites/default/files/serac.pdf

AMINOIL Tribunal (1982) *Kuwait v. AMINOIL,* award of 24 March 1982, 21 ILM 976, https://www.trans-lex.org/261900

Arrondissementsrechtbank Den Haag (2013) *Akpan v. Royal Dutch Shell,* Case no. C/09/337050/HA ZA 09-1580, judgment of 30 January 2013

ECtHR (2005) *Taşkin and others v. Turkey,* application no. 46117/99, judgment of 30 March 2005, https://hudoc.echr.coe.int/webservices/content/pdf/001-67401?TID=soudeazyxk

IACtHR (2001) *Mayagna (Sumo) Awas Tingni Community v. Nicaragua,* IACtHR Series C no. 79, judgment of 31 August 2001

ICJ (1952) *Anglo-Iranian Oil Company Case,* judgment of 22 July 1952, https://www.icj-cij.org/files/case-related/16/016-19520722-JUD-01-00-EN.pdf

ICJ (1970) *Case Concerning the Barcelona Traction, Light and Power Company,* judgment of 5 February 1970, https://www.icj-cij.org/files/case-related/50/050-19700205-JUD-01-00-EN.pdf

ICJ (1996) *Legality of the Threat or Use of Nuclear Weapons,* advisory opinion of 8 July 1996, ICJ Reports 1996, https://www.icj-cij.org/files/case-related/95/095-19960708-ADV-01-00-EN.pdf

ICJ (2005) *Armed Activities on the Territory of the Congo* (Democratic Republic of the Congo v. Uganda), judgment of 19 December 2005, ICJ Reports 2005, https://www.icj-cij.org/files/case-related/116/116-20051219-JUD-01-00-EN.pdf

ICJ (2010a) *Pulp Mills on the River Uruguay* (Argentina v. Uruguay), judgment of 20 April 2010, ICJ Reports 2010, https://www.icj-cij.org/files/case-related/135/135-20100420-JUD-01-00-EN.pdf

ICJ (2010b) *Pulp Mills on the River Uruguay* (Argentina v. Uruguay), separate opinion, judge Cançado Trindade, ICJ Reports 2010, https://www.icj-cij.org/files/case-related/135/135-20100420-JUD-01-04-EN.pdf

ICJ (2015b) *Certain Activities Carried out by Nicaragua* (Costa Rica v. Nicaragua), separate opinion, judge ad hoc Dugard, https://www.icj-cij.org/files/case-related/150/18868.pdf

ICSID (1990) *Asian Agricultural Products LTD (AAPL) v. Republic of Sri Lanka,* ICSID Case No. ARB/87/3, final award of 27 June 1990

ICSID (2005) *CMS Gas Transmission Company v. Argentina,* ICSID case no. ARB/01/08, award of 12 May 2005

ICSID (2011) *El Paso Energy Int'l Co. v. Argentine Republic,* ICSID case no. ARB/03/15, award of 31 October 2011, http://www.italaw.com/documents/El_Paso_v._Argentina_Award_ENG.pdf

ICSID (2014) *Perenco Ecuador Limited v. Republic of Ecuador*, ICSID case no. ARB/08/6, decision on remaining issues of jurisdiction and on liability of 12 September 2014, http://www.italaw.com/sites/default/files/case-documents/italaw4003.pdf

ITLOS (2001) *MOX Plant* (Ireland v. United Kingdom), order of 3 December 2011, provisional measures, https://www.itlos.org/fileadmin/itlos/documents/cases/case_no_10/published/C10-O-3_dec_01.pdf

ITLOS (2011) *Responsibilities and obligations of states sponsoring persons and entities with respect to activities in the area*, Seabed Disputes Chamber, advisory opinion of 1 February 2011, case no. 17. https://www.itlos.org/fileadmin/itlos/documents/cases/case_no_17/adv_op_010211.pdf

LCIA (2004) *Occidental Exploration and Production Company v. Republic of Ecuador*, LCIA case no. UN3467, final award of 1 July 2004

LCIA (2006) *EnCana Corporation v. Republic of Ecuador*, LCIA case no. UN3481, award of 3 February 2006

PCA (2006) *Saluka Investments BV v. Czech Republic*, UNCITRAL, partial award of 17 March 2006

PCA (2010) *Chevron Corporation v. Republic of Ecuador*, UNCITRAL, PCA case no. 2007-2, partial award on the merits of 30 March 2010

PCA (2016) *The South China Sea Arbitration* (Philippines v. China), case no. 2013-19, award of 12 July 2016, https://pca-cpa.org/wp-content/uploads/sites/175/2016/07/PH-CN-20160712-Award.pdf

PCIJ (1924–1927) *Mavrommatis Concessions Case*, judgments of 30 August 1924, 26 March 1925, 10 October 1927, https://www.icj-cij.org/en/pcij-series-a

PCIJ (1928) *Phosphates in Morocco Case*, judgment of 14 June 1938, https://www.icj-cij.org/files/permanent-court-of-international-justice/serie_AB/AB_74/01_Phosphates_du_Maroc_Arret.pdf

Sole Arbitrator (1973) *BP Exploration v. Libya*, award of 10 October 1973, 53 ILR 297, https://kupdf.net/download/bp-exploration-v-libyan-arab-republic-53-ilr-297-1973_5a1aec14e2b6f5f95564e0e1_pdf

Texaco Arbitral Tribunal (1977) *Texaco v. Libya*, award on the merits in dispute between Texaco Overseas Petroleum Company/California Asiatic Oil Company and the Government of the Libyan Arab Republic of 19 January 1977. International Legal Materials, vol. 17, no. 1, January 1978, https://www.jstor.org/stable/20691828, pp 1–37

UK Supreme Court (2019) *Vedanta Resources v. Lungowe and others*, judgment of 10 April 2019, UKSC 2017/0185, https://www.supremecourt.uk/cases/uksc-2017-0185.html

UN HRC (1990) *Bernard Ominayak and the Lubicon Band v. Canada*, views of the committee of 26 March 1990, HRC communication no. 167/1984, http://juris.ohchr.org/Search/Details/665

UN HRC (1996) *Jouni E. Länsman et al v. Finland*, views of the committee of 30 October 1996, HRC communication no. 671/1995, http://hrlibrary.umn.edu/undocs/html/VWS67158.htm

UN HRC (2019) *Portillo Caceres v. Paraguay*, decision of 25 July 2019, https://tbinternet.ohchr.org/_layouts/15/treatybodyexternal/Download.aspx?symbolno=CCPR%2FC%2F126%2FD%2F2751%2F2016&Lang=en

US Supreme Court (2013) *Kiobel v. Royal Dutch Petroleum*, judgment of 17 April 2013, 569 US 108, https://www.supremecourt.gov/opinions/12pdf/10-1491_l6gn.pdf

Warraq Tribunal (2014) *Hesham Talaat M. Al-Warraq v. The Republic of Indonesia*, final award of 15 December 2014

WTO DSB (1998) *United States – Import Prohibition of Certain Shrimp and Shrimp Products*, report of the Appellate Body, adopted 12 October 1998, WT/DS58/AB/R, https://docs.wto.org/dol2fe/Pages/FE_Search/FE_S_S009-DP.aspx?language=E&CatalogueIdList=58544&CurrentCatalogueIndex=0&FullTextHash=&HasEnglishRecord=True&HasFrenchRecord=True&HasSpanishRecord=True

WTO DSB (2004) *United States – Final Countervailing Duty Determination with Respect to Certain Softwood Lumber from Canada ('Softwood Lumber IV')*, report of the Appellate

Body, adopted 19 January 2004, WT/DS257/AB/R, https://www.wto.org/english/tratop_e/dispu_e/257abr_e.doc

WTO DSB (2011) *China – Measures Related to the Exportation of Various Raw Materials*, Panel reports, adopted 5 July 2011, WT/DS394/R, WT/DS395/R, WT/DS398/R

WTO DSB (2012) *China – Measures Related to the Exportation of Various Raw Materials*, Appellate Body reports, adopted 30 January 2012, WT/DS394/AB/R, WT/DS395/AB/R WT/DS398/AB/R

WTO DSB (2014a) *China – Measures Related to the Exportation of Rare Earths, Tungsten and Molybdenum*, Panel reports, adopted 26 March 2014, WT/DS431/R/, WT/DS432/R/, WT/DS433/R/Add.1

WTO DSB (2014b) *China – Measures Related to the Exportation of Rare Earths, Tungsten and Molybdenum*, Appellate Body reports, adopted 7 August 2014 WT/DS431/AB/R, WT/DS432/AB/R, WT/DS433/AB/R

Chapter 5
Fostering the Effectiveness of TCL

What fosters the effectiveness of Transnational Commodity Law (TCL) is to render the sustainable use principle as effective as possible. For that purpose, we shall first turn to some reflections on how the normative potential of sustainable development (SD) as a legal concept can be unfolded (Sect. 5.1). Secondly, we will turn to International Commodity Agreements (ICAs) as potential instruments codifying what sustainable commodity use requires (Sect. 5.2).

5.1 Unfolding the Normative Potential of SD

To my mind, there are two ways to unfold the normative potential of SD: By defining it as the object and purpose of TCL (Sect. 5.1.1) and by employing the technique of full integration in order to more concretely delineate what 'sustainable use' means (Sect. 5.1.2). Both will lead to a more coherent—and thus more effective—TCL framework.

5.1.1 Defining SD as the Object and Purpose of TCL

This section is ultimately dedicated to displaying the ramifications of defining sustainable development (SD) as the object and purpose of TCL (Sect. 5.1.1.3). In order to arrive at these observations, I, shall first, however, exhibit the origins, core conceptual contents, and general legal effects of SD (Sect. 5.1.1.1). Moreover, I will provide an *aperçu* of the discussion on the legal nature of SD as well as a series of

M. E. Oehl, *Sustainable Commodity Use*, EYIEL Monographs - Studies in European and International Economic Law 21, https://doi.org/10.1007/978-3-030-89496-2_5

arguments to support my claim that it constitutes a regulatory objective (Sect. 5.1.1.2).[1]

5.1.1.1 Conceptual and Normative Characteristics of SD

Subsequently, we shall revisit the origins (Sect. 5.1.1.1.1), core conceptual contents (Sect. 5.1.1.1.2) as well as general legal effects (Sect. 5.1.1.1.3) of SD.

5.1.1.1.1 The Origins of SD as a Political Objective

The concept of SD has evolved remarkably over the past decades. While the origins of the notion of sustainability lie in theories on sustainable forest management from the eighteenth century, it had increasingly been referenced in the context of wholesome economic growth since the 1970s.[2]

SD as a concept made its appearance on the stage of international politics in 1980 through the publication of the International Union for Conservation of Nature (IUCN) World Conservation Strategy, which carried the subtitle Living Resource Conservation for Sustainable Development.[3] When the Brundtland report was released in 1987, the SD gained significant popularity. According to the report, SD was defined as a 'development that meets the needs of the present without compromising the ability of future generations to meet their own needs.'[4]

In the following, 'SD featured prominently in the 1992 Rio Declaration on Environment and Development, which in its Principle #1 puts human beings at the centre of concerns for SD.'[5] As another result of the Rio conference, a far-reaching process regarding a 'new global partnership for sustainable development' was set in

---

[1] The following section essentially summarises the core arguments I have put forward in Oehl (2019).

[2] Proelß (2017), para. 50; Gehne (2011), pp. 11, 21 with reference to the UN GA (1970) International development strategy for the second United Nations development decade, 24 October 1970, UN Doc. A/RES/2626(XXV), http://www.un-documents.net/a25r2626.htm (last accessed 14 May 2021); cf. Oehl (2019), p. 7.

[3] Cf. Oehl (2019), p. 7 pointing also to the prior UN GA International Development Strategy for the Third United Nations Development Decade, 5 December 1980, UN Doc. A/RES/35/56; cf. Beyerlin (2013), para. 3.

[4] World Commission on Environment and Development (1987) Report: our common future, 4 August 1987, UN Doc. A/42/427, http://www.un-documents.net/our-common-future.pdf (last accessed 14 May 2021), chapter 1, para. 49; Oehl (2019), p. 7.

[5] Oehl (2019), p. 7. Moreover, it is expressly referred to in principles 4, 5, 7, 8, 9, 12, 20, 21, 22, 24 and 27 of the 1992 Rio Declaration on Environment and Development, 12 August 1992, UN Doc. A/CONF.151/26 (Vol. I), http://www.un.org/documents/ga/conf151/aconf15126-1annex1.htm (last accessed 14 May 2021); cf. ibid.

motion by the so-called Agenda 21[6]—a process, which eventually led to the central status of SD within international relations today.

The 2000 Millennium Development Goals featured environmental sustainability as Goal #7. In 2002, the Johannesburg World Summit was dedicated entirely to SD. The World Summit on Sustainable Development (WSSD) Plan of Implementation, which resulted from it, 'explicitly built on the achievements since the 1992 Rio conference and covered a broad range of SD-related issues from poverty eradication, consumption and production patterns, natural resource management as base of economic and social development, health and SD to the institutional framework for SD.'[7] In 2005, the UN General Assembly in its World Summit Outcome Resolution reaffirmed SD as a 'key element of the overarching framework of United Nations activities.'[8]

The international community reiterated its commitment to SD at the so-called Rio + 20 conference in 2012. Henceforth, SD was particularly being summarised by referring to 'three constituent elements': economic as well as social development and environmental protection.[9] As a means to concentrate the common efforts on concrete objectives, the outcome document demanded the compilation of sustainable development goals (SDGs).[10]

The 2030 Agenda for Sustainable Development, which carries the title Transforming Our World, spells out these SDGs. The UN General Assembly, in its 2015 Resolution, describes the introduction of this agenda as an 'historic decision on a comprehensive, far-reaching and people-centred set of universal and transformative Goals and targets.'[11] As I have put it elsewhere,

> [t]he *SD Agenda* marks the end point of the evolution of SD from a notion originating in forest management and later gaining relevance in environmental protection policy to *the* universal political agenda of our time. Mindful of the great weight this agenda carries, the UN General Assembly describes it as: "...an Agenda of unprecedented scope and significance. It is accepted by all countries and is applicable to all, taking into account different national realities, capacities and levels of development and respecting national policies and

---

[6]Cf. Beyerlin (2013), para. 5; Oehl (2019), p. 8.

[7]Oehl (2019), p. 8 referring to the Plan of implementation of the world summit on sustainable development, 4 September 2002, UN Doc. A/CONF.199/20, http://www.un.org/esa/sustdev/documents/WSSD_POI_PD/English/WSSD_PlanImpl.pdf (last accessed 14 May 2021).

[8]UN GA (2005) World summit outcome, 24 October 2015, UN Doc. A/RES60/1, http://www.un.org/en/ga/search/view_doc.asp?symbol=A/RES/60/1 (last accessed 14 May 2021), para. 10; cf. Oehl (2019), p. 8.

[9]UN GA (2012) The future we want, 11 September 2012, UN Doc. A/RES/66/288, http://www.un.org/ga/search/view_doc.asp?symbol=A/RES/66/288&Lang=E (last accessed 14 May 2021), para. 1; Oehl (2019), p. 8.

[10]UN GA (2012) The future we want, 11 September 2012, UN Doc. A/RES/66/288, http://www.un.org/ga/search/view_doc.asp?symbol=A/RES/66/288&Lang=E (last accessed 14 May 2021), para. 246; Oehl (2019), p. 8.

[11]UN GA (2015) Transforming our world: the 2030 Agenda for Sustainable Development, Resolution A/RES/70/1, 25 September 2015, http://www.un.org/ga/search/view_doc.asp?symbol=A/RES/70/1&Lang=E (last accessed 14 May 2021), para. 2; Oehl (2019), p. 8.

priorities. These are universal goals and targets which involve the entire world, developed and developing countries alike. They are integrated and indivisible and balance the three dimensions of sustainable development."[12]

5.1.1.1.2 The Core Conceptual Contents of SD

Over the past decade, the core conceptual contents of SD have emerged quite clearly. While the Brundtland report was initially based on especially an *inter*generational understanding of SD, thus emphasising planetary conservation for the sake of future generations, SD gradually evolved 'to a concept that puts human beings and their need for sufficient socio-economic development at the centre', therefore integrating *intra*generational elements, 'yet without fully abandoning the intergenerational perspective.'[13]

When it comes to legal terms, principle 4 of the non-binding 1992 Rio Declaration first put the concept of SD into the operational language of what resembles a legal norm by stating that

[i]n order to achieve sustainable development, environmental protection shall constitute an integral part of the development process and cannot be considered in isolation from it.[14]

As Barral points out, the synthesis of the various international documents featuring SD exhibits a remarkable degree of consistency with regard to the core concept of SD.[15] Since the adoption of the 1997 Programme for the Further Implementation of Agenda 21, SD is generally being referred to as requiring 'the integration of its economic, environmental and social components.'[16] The 2002 WSSD Plan of Implementation describes SD as consisting of the 'interdependent and mutually reinforcing pillars' of 'economic development, social development and environmental protection.'[17] This definition of SD has, worded only slightly differently, been used repetitively in numerous international documents, including the 2005 World

---

[12]UN GA (2015) Transforming our world: the 2030 Agenda for Sustainable Development, Resolution A/RES/70/1, 25 September 2015, http://www.un.org/ga/search/view_doc.asp?symbol=A/RES/70/1&Lang=E (last accessed 14 May 2021), para. 5; Oehl (2019), pp. 8–9.

[13]Oehl (2019), pp. 9–10, referring to Barral (2012), pp. 380–381 who 'defines the element of socio-economic growth as a matter of the *intra*generational, the element of environmental protection as the *inter*generational equity that SD postulates'.

[14]Oehl (2019), p. 10.

[15]Barral (2012), p. 380; cf. Oehl (2019), pp. 10–11 with an overview of relevant documents.

[16]UN GA (1997) Programme for the further implementation of agenda 21, 28 June 1997, UN Doc. A/RES/S-19/2, https://digitallibrary.un.org/record/244113 (last accessed 14 May 2021), annex, para. 3; Oehl (2019), p. 12.

[17]UN (2002) Plan of implementation of the world summit on sustainable development, 4 September 2002, UN Doc. A/CONF.199/20, http://www.un.org/esa/sustdev/documents/WSSD_POI_PD/English/WSSD_PlanImpl.pdf (last accessed 14 May 2021), para. 2; Oehl (2019), p. 12.

Summit Outcome,[18] the Rio+20 outcome document 'The Future We Want'[19] or the SD Agenda.[20]

These definitions of SD, as well as the ones employed by international legal scholars,[21] convey the 'three constituent elements of SD: environmental protection, social and economic development.'[22] Consequently, the core conceptual content of SD 'can be defined as the consolidation of socio-economic development and environmental protection.'[23]

Around these conceptual contents of SD, international legal scholarship has conceptualised what it defines as International SD Law—the corpus of international law, which addresses the relevant intersections of international environmental, economic and social law, towards SD.[24] This body of law has been further characterised by the 2002 New Delhi Principles *Relating to* SD, which have been elaborated by the International Law Association. The non-exhaustive seven principles include the duty of States to ensure sustainable use of natural resources; the principle of equity and the eradication of poverty; the principle of common but differentiated responsibilities; the principle of the precautionary approach to human health, natural resources and ecosystems; the principle of public participation and access to information and justice; the principle of good governance; and the principle of integration and interrelationship, in particular in relation to human rights and social, economic and environmental objectives.[25]

5.1.1.1.3 The General Legal Effects of SD

Apart from these characterisations of SD, naturally its legal effects are particularly pertinent to our further discussion. They can generally be said to be twofold.

---

[18] UN GA (2005) World summit outcome, 24 October 2015, UN Doc. A/RES60/1, http://www.un.org/en/ga/search/view_doc.asp?symbol=A/RES/60/1 (last accessed 14 May 2021), para. 10.

[19] UN GA (2012) The future we want, 11 September 2012, UN Doc. A/RES/66/288, http://www.un.org/ga/search/view_doc.asp?symbol=A/RES/66/288&Lang=E (last accessed 14 May 2021), para. 3.

[20] UN GA (2015) Transforming our world: the 2030 Agenda for Sustainable Development, Resolution A/RES/70/1, 25 September 2015, http://www.un.org/ga/search/view_doc.asp?symbol=A/RES/70/1&Lang=E (last accessed 14 May 2021), para. 2; cf. Oehl (2019), p. 12.

[21] Oehl (2019), p. 12 pointing to the characterisation of 'SD as the "conceptual bridge" between right to social and economic development and the imperative to protect the environment' by Cordonier Segger and Weeramantry (2017), p. 6.

[22] Oehl (2019), p. 12.

[23] Oehl (2019), p. 12.

[24] CISDL (2005) What is sustainable development law, CISDL concept paper, Montreal, 2005, http://cisdl.org/public/docs/What%20is%20Sustainable%20Development.pdf (last accessed 14 May 2021), p. 1; Oehl (2019), p. 13.

[25] ILA (2002); Oehl (2019), p. 13.

For one, it constitutes a *primary norm* that obliges states to 'act sustainably', i.e. to carry out a balancing exercise between the social, economic and environmental pillars of SD before taking (regulatory, e.g. legislative, or other) action. This effect is for instance reflected in the cases *Gabcikovo-Nagymaros* and *Pulp Mills*.[26] Barral insofar describes an 'obligation of means', which states need to abide by. They only need to make the necessary efforts of carrying out the balancing exercise and are not required to arrive at a specific result.[27]

For the other, SD also exhibits a *methodical dimension* in that it serves as a guideline how legal obligations shall be interpreted.[28] This is naturally the effect, where SD forms part of a specific treaty, such as the WTO agreement that was subject to the WTO Appellate Body's decision in *US-Shrimp*.[29] Accordingly, SD has been said to add 'colour, texture and shading' to the challenge of interpreting the term 'exhaustible natural resources' according to Article XX(g) GATT, thus being employed as an interpretation guideline.[30]

5.1.1.2   The Legal Nature of SD

To date, there has been much debate regarding the legal status of SD as for instance, a principle of international law, an 'interstitial' norm or a primary rule (Sect. 5.1.1.2.1). To my mind, it can best be classified as regulatory objective (Sect. 5.1.1.2.2).

5.1.1.2.1   The General Debate

There has generally for long been a wide spectrum of opinions on the legal nature of SD. While some authors have argued that SD merely constitutes a political ideal that is void of any normative force,[31] others have categorised SD as a 'meta principle' or

---

[26] ICJ (1997) *Gabcikovo-Nagymaros Project*, Judgment of 25 September 1997; ICJ (2010a) *Pulp Mills on the River Uruguay*, Judgment of 20 April 2010.

[27] Barral (2012), p. 388; Oehl (2019), p. 14. However, as we will discuss in detail in Sect. 5.1.2 below, not only the SDGs and their targets and sub-targets respectively are specifying what exactly is required from states, but potentially all norms that are being *fully integrated* into the 'sustainable use' rule.

[28] Oehl (2019), pp. 14–15; the operation of SD as a primary norm can be observed e.g. in ICJ (1997) *Gabcikovo-Nagymaros Project*, Judgment of 25 September 1997; ICJ (2010a) *Pulp Mills on the River Uruguay*, Judgment of 20 April 2010; as well as PCA (2005) *Iron Rhine arbitration*, Award of 24 May 2005. Its application as a methodical norm is demonstrated e.g. in WTO DSB (1998) *US – Shrimps*, Report of the Appellate Body, 12 October 1998, para. 153; Gehne (2011), p. 294.

[29] WTO DSB (1998) *US – Shrimps*, Report of the Appellate Body, 12 October 1998, para. 153; cf. Gehne (2011), p. 294.

[30] Cf. Barral (2012), p. 392; Oehl (2019), p. 15.

[31] Beyerlin (2007), pp. 444–445; cf. Proelß (2017) para. 53; also Beyerlin (2013), para. 19; cf. Oehl (2019), p. 16.

'constitutional guiding concept'.[32] These meta principles have been said to 'set the bounds for the types of proposals and arguments that can be made' during international negotiations. They thus 'establish the context' for codifications of concrete norms, for instance in international treaties.[33] Insofar, Lowe described SD as forming part of the category of 'modifying' or 'interstitial' norms that 'are pushing and pulling the boundaries of true primary norms' where they interfere.[34] These norms do 'not seek to regulate the conduct of legal persons directly.'[35] Instead, they particularly apply when it comes to interpreting the law.[36]

Whereas this viewpoint was quite dominant within international legal scholarship for some time, authors appear to have increasingly abandoned it in the more recent past.[37] For instance, Proelß argues that categorizing SD as a 'modifying'—and therefore *secondary*—norm of international law allows moving beyond discussions about its customary status as a *primary norm*.[38] Also other authors identify a clear rule, which SD is setting forth—one that obliges states to 'act sustainably' or, more precisely, 'to balance social, economic and ecological interests.'[39]

Still, what classical international law would now require from legal scholarship, would be a categorisation of SD according to the types of sources spelled out in Article 38 ICJ Statute. In fact, there has been quite some debate whether SD could be qualified as a principle of international law.[40] Koskenniemi in this context points to the *constructivist exercise*, which needs to be performed for a new principle to emerge. Yet, according to Virally '. . .the existence or non-existence of common principles is a question of fact to be solved by examination rather than *a priori* opinion.'[41] This view may perhaps be the one of most international lawyers today, who perceive principles as 'generalizing descriptions of certain regularities in State behaviour'[42]—a view that may have been responsible for the 'continued and genuine reluctance to formalise a distinctive legal status' of SD that the ILA scholars witnessed.[43]

---

[32] Scheyli (2008), pp. 296–298, 352–353; cf. Proelß (2017), para. 53; cf. Oehl (2019), p. 16.

[33] Bodansky (2009), p. 203; cf. Proelß (2017), para. 53; cf. Oehl (2019), p. 16.

[34] Lowe (1999), pp. 31, 33; cf. Proelß (2017), para. 53; Beyerlin (2013), para. 17.

[35] Lowe (1999), p. 33; cf. Barral (2012), p. 387; cf. Oehl (2019), p. 16.

[36] Gehne (2011), pp. 32–322; Lowe (1999), p. 34; cf. Barral (2012), p. 387; cf. Oehl (2019), p. 16.

[37] Oehl (2019), p. 16.

[38] Proelß (2017), para. 54; cf. Oehl (2019), p. 17.

[39] Cf. Oehl (2019), p. 17 pointing to Barral (2012), p. 378, who 'refers to SD as a primary norm of international law, which "purports to directly regulate conduct and has properly material and direct legal implications"'; also Barral (2012), p. 388; Gehne (2011), p. 314; Proelß (2017), paras. 54–55. Proelß (2017), para. 56 views this rule as part of customary international law.

[40] Oehl (2019), pp. 17–19.

[41] Virally (1968), p. 147; cf. Koskenniemi (2000), p. 385; cf. Oehl (2019), p. 19.

[42] Koskenniemi (2000), p. 385; cf. Oehl (2019), p. 19.

[43] ILA (2012), p. 36; Oehl (2019), p. 19.

Proceeding further down this path, we would now have to examine the large volume of international treaties, guidance documents and jurisprudence in order to assess whether SD can be said to constitute a principle of international law. This approach essentially limits legal analysis with regard to an emerging principle or rule to a 'matter of relative numbers'.[44] While some would deem the results it would bring about to be sufficient for ascertaining the existence of a legal principle or rule of SD, others would presumably disagree.[45]

In this context, allow me to point to the problems that rigid approaches to identifying emerging norms of international law can create for the international legal order.[46] As Jennings, referring to customary international law, wrote in 1981, the international community needs to

> face squarely the fact that the orthodox tests of custom – practice and opinio juris – are often not only inadequate but even irrelevant for the identification of much new law today. And the reason is not far to seek: much of this new law is not custom at all, and does not even resemble custom. It is recent, it is innovatory, it involves topical policy decisions and it is often the focus of contention.[47]

According to Jennings, we need to apply Article 38 ICJ Statute as well as the respective methodologies applicable to identifying sources of international law in a way that is mindful of the fact that they originate from the 1920s—and could thus be somewhat out-dated. He argues that 'mould[ing]' the more recent phenomena of emerging new law 'into one or the other compartments [of Article 38 ICJ Statute]' would constitute a mistake.[48] In his view, new modes of how rules of international law emerge, necessitate more flexible methodological approaches to examining them.[49] This relates to his additional observation that jurisprudence as well as international legal scholarship may be of greater significance than ever before with regard

> to bring[ing] certainty and clarity in the places where the mass of material evidences is so large and confused, as to obscure the basic distinction between law and proposal.[50]

---

[44]ICJ (2012) *Jurisdictional Immunities*, dissenting opinion of Judge Yusuf, p. 297; cf. Oehl (2019), p. 21.

[45]Oehl (2019), p. 20 i.a. pointing to the separate opinion of Vice-President Weeramantry to ICJ (1997) *Gabcikovo-Nagymaros Project*, Judgment of 25 September 1997, p. 104 'who already in 1997 saw "plentiful indications", which justify giving "the principle of sustainable development the nature of customary law".' In favour also Proelß (2017), para. 56; Barral (2012), p. 386; arguably Sands (2012), p. 217 as well. Cautious Cordonier Segger (2017), p. 92. Against Beyerlin (2013), para. 18; Lowe (1999), p. 33.

[46]In lieu of many Jennings (1998), p. 737 indicating the challenges in elaborating or modifying customary international law during the interwar period; cf. Oehl (2019), p. 20.

[47]Jennings (1998), p. 738; cf. Oehl (2019), p. 20.

[48]Jennings (1998), p. 742; cf. Oehl (2019), p. 20.

[49]Cf. ILA (2012), p. 6; Oehl (2019), p. 20.

[50]Jennings (1998), p. 749; Oehl (2019), p. 21.

Also with regard to SD, a substantial volume of international documents and proof of state practice exists, yet hitherto these materials have brought about rather confusion than clarity. This may well be perceived as a call for international legal scholars to contribute more clarity, be it through their respective functions as international judges or publicists.[51]

However, it appears unlikely that judges and publicists will be able to provide the former President of the ICJ with satisfying responses—that is if they continue to adhere to an analysis of the law that resembles a 'matter of relative numbers.' Koskenniemi pointed out that the idea that a judge would be *finding* a principle— or, for that matter, any other emerging rule—by carrying out some sort of empirical exercise describes an ideal, but generally not reality.[52] Rather, judges are *constructing* principles or rules based on their perceptions of what are the fundamental goals and values of the international legal order.[53]

Yet, what the empirical approach may entail, is the benefit of providing international law making with some sort of reliable, objective parameters, which may thus help convince many of the legitimacy and objectivity of the law itself. In contrast, the constructivist approach,

decreases the reliability of the law making exercise since the constructions of the fundamental goals and values that serve as the testing ground for new rules may differ from, particularly, judge to judge that is performing the task.[54]

When it comes to SD, however, the constructivist approach does not appear to face these kinds of challenges. In view of the international community's acceptance of SD as its universal agenda—which is even specified by respective goals, targets and sub-targets—the 'normative testing ground' is exposed quite concretely and unambiguously. This scenario constitutes an opportunity for international jurisprudence and international publicists respectively to elaborate norms that find vast support within the international community. Naturally, balancing the diverging interests and understandings between (state) actors becomes more intricate the more concrete the rules that are being elaborated are required to be. Yet, given the widely anticipated need to establish more specific legal guidance for SD, there may well be still sufficient room for ascertaining new norms even before one enters these challenging realms.[55]

To conclude, however, I would like to point out that whether or not SD has acquired the status of a principle of international to my mind is of rather secondary importance—if not even a 'sterile' question as the ILA scholars expressed in 2008.[56] Whereas also the judges at the ICJ—as reflected in their decision in the *Gabcikovo-*

---

[51] Oehl (2019), p. 21.

[52] Koskenniemi (2000), p. 389; Oehl (2019), p. 21.

[53] Cf. also Shaw (2017), p. 52. On the 'myth of (in)determinacy' in international law, Bianchi (2010); Oehl (2019), p. 21.

[54] Oehl (2019), p. 21; cf. Koskenniemi (2000), p. 396.

[55] Oehl (2019), p. 22.

[56] ILA (2008), p. 7; cf. ILA (2012), p. 6; Oehl (2019), p. 22.

Nagymaros case and Judge Weeramantry's separate opinion respectively—were divided on this issue, we should rather bear in mind the guidance received from President Jennings. SD indeed appears to be a 'perfect example for a legal concept that deserves to "be released from the shackles of legal formalism in order to be given operational meaning", because in the end, what really counts are the practical, legal effects it elicits.'[57] The subsequent section will display how abandoning the classical 'boxes' of the sources of international law allows to not only fittingly categorize SD, but also 'to conflate its legal effects as a *primary rule* and a *methodical norm*.'[58]

5.1.1.2.2   SD as Regulatory Objective

To my mind, SD constitutes a fundamental regulatory objective of the international legal order. In the following, I shall provide a series of arguments to support this claim.

5.1.1.2.2.1   *Political Objectives Typically Evolve to Regulatory Objectives*

The first argument relates to the observation that political objectives typically sooner or later evolve to become regulatory objectives. They are normally being formulated as the outcome of corresponding decision-making processes within governments. As soon as a political objective has been established, the government generally moves to the *implementation phase*. Presumably all states, yet certainly their majority, take *legal* measures whenever they are pursuing an objective.[59] Therefore, on the national level, an openly articulated political objective typically evolves to a regulatory objective of those legal instruments, which are being introduced to attain it.

The situation on the international level is quite similar. Once the respective decision-making process within for instance a UN institution, such as the UN General Assembly or the Security Council, has brought about a shared political objective, members typically adopt a resolution in its pursuit. Routinely, the *political* objective is being included in a preambulatory paragraph—thus henceforth constituting the *regulatory* objective of the respective resolution, which its operative paragraphs are intended to fulfil.[60] Even in incidents, in which the international community first articulates the objective exclusively in a declaratory, non-legal manner, this is typically followed by the introduction of international or national

---

[57] Oehl (2019), p. 22, i.a. pointing to Sands (2012), p. 217 'who states in a *nonchalant* manner that SD "is recognized as principle (or concept) of international law"'; ILA (2012), p. 6.

[58] Oehl (2019), p. 22.

[59] Oehl (2019), p. 23 pointing to the fact that even repressive regimes and dictatorships 'tend to carry out their actions in legal form. cf. only the disastrous example of Nazi Germany, which exhibited a rule of law that served the most unlawful purposes, including war crimes and the Holocaust.'

[60] Oehl (2019), p. 23.

legal instruments later on.[61] In this context, the 'aspirational' nature of the SDGs referenced in e.g. the Rio+20 outcome document or the SD agenda does not rebut the claim that SD is a regulatory objective: Whereas its specific *goals and targets* may be aspirational, the *measures* introduced by governments, as actors tasked with driving the implementation of the SD agenda,[62] will generally be of a legal nature—and thus pursue SD as regulatory objective.[63]

Furthermore, while it can naturally not be ruled out that in some exceptional cases, a political objective is never being included in any legal instrument and therefore never evolves to a regulatory objective, there are no indications that SD is one of these rare exceptions. While we have seen above that there had been substantial debate among international legal scholars about the normative nature of SD, the discussants did not examine the quality of SD as a regulatory objective and consequently also did not provide a statement to the contrary.[64] Instead, the ICJ referred to it as a 'concept' of international law, thereby avoiding any more explicit remark about its legal nature. In fact, the WTO Appellate Body stated in its decision in *US-Shrimps* that the WTO Agreement 'explicitly acknowledges "the objective of sustainable development".'[65] Therefore, by interpreting individual provisions in its light, i.e. employing the technique of *teleological interpretation*, the Appellate Body essentially applied SD as a regulatory objective.[66] As we will see subsequently, there are several further examples of international agreements, including the United Nations Framework Convention on Climate Change (UNFCCC) or the Convention on Biological Diversity (CBD), which feature SD as a regulatory objective.[67]

5.1.1.2.2.2 Law Fosters the Development of Society

What moreover supports the claim that SD constitutes a regulatory objective, is its conceptual content. This argument relates to the observation that in general,

---

[61] Oehl (2019), p. 23 referring to the example of the 2002 WSSD Plan of Implementation, UN Doc. A/CONF.199/20, http://www.un.org/esa/sustdev/documents/WSSD_POI_PD/English/WSSD_PlanImpl.pdf (last accessed 14 May 2021), para. 162(a).

[62] UN GA (2015) Resolution A/RES/70/1, 25 September 2015, Transforming our world: the 2030 Agenda for Sustainable Development. http://www.un.org/ga/search/view_doc.asp?symbol=A/RES/70/1&Lang=E (last accessed 14 May 2021), paras. 39–47; Oehl (2019), p. 24.

[63] Oehl (2019), p. 23 pointing to 'the catalogue of measures that states shall implement in order to foster SD in UN GA (2015), para. 41: "We recognize that these will include the mobilization of financial resources as well as capacity building and the transfer of environmentally sound technologies to developing countries on favourable terms, including on concessional and preferential terms, as mutually agreed. Public finance, both domestic and international, will play a vital role in providing essential services and public goods and in catalysing other sources of finance." Naturally the implementation of such measures requires legal instruments.'

[64] Oehl (2019), p. 24; Cordonier Segger (2017), p. 72 refers to a 'search in the wrong direction'.

[65] Oehl (2019), p. 24; WTO DSB (1998) *US – Shrimps,* Report of the Appellate Body, 12 October 1998, WT/DS58/AB/R, para. 129.

[66] On the 'teleological school of thought' briefly Shaw (2017), p. 707; cf. Oehl (2019), p. 25.

[67] Cf. Sect. 5.1.1.2.2.3 below.

law is conceptually meant to ultimately foster the development of the respective society it applies for. Every individual instrument, in fact every rule, contributes its modest or greater part to the functioning of a greater whole, which is at least *intended to* or *portrayed as* advancing the development of its constituents.[68]

With regard to the international legal order, in this connection even rather 'remote' fields, such as the law of consular relations can be interpreted as *ultimately* serving the objective of development: By disciplining international relations, it adds to stable diplomacy and therefore ideally peace—which constitutes a major precondition for a society's development.[69] We can make the same claim in regard to any rule of international law, however with naturally varying lengths of the 'causal chain' between the norm's individual command and the ultimate objective of development.[70]

Therefore, one can quite easily argue that law, as a general concept, *ultimately* serves the objective of development of society; in spite of naturally remaining debates on the right approaches in pursuing development between the various stakeholders, the law is generally 'at least *intended to*' or, in states ruled by a rogue government, '*portrayed as*' promoting development.[71]

5.1.1.2.2.3   SD as Regulatory Objective in International Treaties

The various international agreements, which reference SD, typically include it as regulatory objective.[72] This holds true i.a. with regard to Articles 2 and 3-(4) UNFCCC; Articles 1 and 8(e) CBD; Articles 2 and 4(2)(b) of the 1994 UN Convention to Combat Desertification and Drought; Article 1(c) of the 1994 International Tropical Timber Agreement; Article 1(3) of the 2007 International Coffee Agreement; Article 1(2) of the 2015 International Agreement on Olive Oil and Table Olives; Article 1 of the 2010 International Cocoa Agreement;[73] Article 2 of the 1995 Straddling Stocks Convention; the preamble of the 1994 WTO agreement; as well as Article 2(1) of the 2015 Paris Agreement.[74]

Moreover, SD also features in the preamble of the 1991 (Espoo) Convention on Environmental Impact Assessment in a Transboundary Context; the preamble of the

---

[68] Oehl (2019), p. 25.

[69] Oehl (2019), p. 25; ibid., n 131 more extensively on how the international legal order regulates war as well as its characterisation by Sen (1999), pp. 3–4 as an 'unfreedom', which needs to be removed for societies to prosper.

[70] Oehl (2019), p. 25; ibid., n 132 discussing further examples, including International Humanitarian Law and procedural rules of international courts and tribunals.

[71] Oehl (2019), p. 26; ibid., n 133 referring to the relationship between this observation and the important contributions of the TWAIL movement, as i.a. expressed by Mutua and Anghie (2000); cf. also Oehl (2019), pp. 26–28 on the evolution of the development objective from a purely economic understanding to the integrated model of SD.

[72] Oehl (2019), p. 29; UN GA (2015), para. 5.

[73] More extensively on International Commodity Agreements, see Sect. 5.2 below.

[74] Oehl (2019), p. 29.

1992 (Ospar) Convention for the Protection of the Marine Environment of the North-East Atlantic; Articles 2, 10 and 12 of the 1998 UNFCCC Kyoto Protocol; Article 4(3) of the 2004 Barcelona Convention for the Protection of the Mediterranean; Article 2(3) of the 1998 Danube River Protection Convention; Articles 1.1 and 6.2 lit. f) of the 2009 FAO International Treaty on Plant Genetic Resources for Food and Agriculture ('Seed Treaty');[75] Article 1(2)(a) of the Energy Charter Treaty; the preamble as well as Article 915(c) of the NAFTA; Article 1(2) of the 2001 EU-ACP Cotonou Agreement; Article 1(a) of the 2008 EU-CARIFORUM Economic Partnership Agreement (EPA); Article 1(a) of the 2016 EU-SADC-EPA; the preamble, Articles 22.1 and 24.2 of the Comprehensive Economic and Trade Agreement (CETA); Article 3 of the 2014 EU-Ukraine Association Agreement; as well as Articles 3(3) and (5), 21(2)(d) and (f) of the EU-treaty and Article 11 of the Treaty on the Functioning of the EU.[76] Likewise, the German commodity partnership agreements with Kazakhstan, Mongolia and Peru feature the objective of SD.[77]

These provisions attest that SD in numerous instances has been codified as a regulatory objective within international agreements. As we shall learn subsequently, SD can also operate as a regulatory objective outside of these treaty regimes.[78]

5.1.1.2.2.4 SD as Regulatory Objective Beyond Treaty Regimes

As the ILA scholars have emphasised in their 2012 Guiding Statement #2,

> treaties and rules of customary international law should, as far as possible, be interpreted in the light of principles of sustainable development and interpretations which might seem to undermine the goal of sustainable development should only take precedence where to do otherwise would be to undermine territorial boundaries and other fundamental aspects of the global legal order, would otherwise infringe the express wording of a treaty or would breach a rule of jus cogens[.][79]

The ILA scholars here are essentially advocating to apply SD in a way, which 'is tantamount to the *teleological interpretation* of *all* treaties and custom in the light of SD and its related principles respectively.'[80] Within domestic legal systems, these effects are typically caused by constitutional objectives—all law generally needs to be interpreted in their light. Only where they interfere with other norms or

---

[75] Cf. Cordonier Segger (2017), p. 81; Oehl (2019), p. 30.

[76] Oehl (2019), p. 29–30; cf. also the catalogues provided by Schrijver (2017), p. 100 and Barral (2012), p. 388, Fn. 59. On the EU-CARIFORUM-EPA and SD as an objective Grosse Ruse-Kahn (2010).

[77] Oehl (2019), p. 30; on the German commodity partnership agreements, cf. also Sect. 5.2.1.2.3.1 below.

[78] Oehl (2019), p. 29.

[79] ILA (2012), p. 36; Oehl (2019), p. 31.

[80] Oehl (2019), p. 31.

objectives, which are equally of constitutional value, a balance needs to be struck between them and the latter.

Moreover, as expressed by the ICJ in its *Gabcikovo-Nagymaros* and *Pulp Mills* decisions, the award in *Iron Rhine*, and the ILA scholars in their Guiding Statement #3 states are held to 'act sustainably', that is to perform the necessary balancing exercise whenever they take action. Therefore, 'not only existing law needs to be interpreted in light of SD, but also new law that is being created—or any measures that are being taken—needs to be designed mindful of the objectives of SD.'[81]

These twofold effects of SD, as a *methodical norm* on the one hand and a *primary norm* on the other, are characteristic for the operation of an object and purpose of, for instance, a field of law or constitution.[82]

Turning to deliberations on legal doctrine, the question arises how such effects of SD within the international legal order can be explicated and legitimised.[83] One approach would lie in classifying the primary rule of SD as a rule of customary international law.[84] In that context, the methodical norm, which SD entails, could be perceived as a principle of international law, which is likewise derived from custom. Yet, as a consequence, the typical challenges related to the identification of new custom would occur. Paradigmatically, while some authors ascertained a customary status of SD—others have not.[85]

An alternative approach would consist of categorising SD as a general principle, which is derived from domestic law and applies to international relations. However, such endeavour would confront similar challenges as the ones of identifying custom. A sort of comparative exercise between different legal orders would need be carried out, which would presumably bring about equally ambiguous results.[86]

Therefore, it appears to be purposive as well as simpler 'to leave the classical "boxes" of Article 38 of the ICJ Statute and recognize the fact that SD may constitute a source of international law in its own right—as a fundamental *object and purpose* of international law.'[87]

What can be said to follow from this categorization regarding the normative force of SD beyond the treaties in which it features? One initial step could lie in examining whether SD can be qualified as a sort of 'customary object and purpose'. In order to

---

[81] Oehl (2019), p. 31.

[82] Oehl (2019), p. 31.

[83] Barral (2012), p. 391 appears to see such effects of SD as an "extraneous conventional rule" and thus regardless of its status as international custom; cf. Oehl (2019), p. 31.

[84] Proelß (2017), para. 56; Barral (2012), p. 386; cf. Oehl (2019), p. 31.

[85] Cf. already above, Sect. 5.1.1.2.1; Oehl (2019), p. 32.

[86] Oehl (2019), p. 32.

[87] Oehl (2019), p. 32, pointing to Cordonier Segger (2017), p. 93 as well as Schrijver (2017), p. 101; referencing SD as an 'objective' also ICJ (2010a) *Pulp Mills on the River Uruguay*, Judgment of 20 April 2010, p. 74, para. 177; on the need to leave the 'boxes' of Article 38 ICJ Statute cf. Sect. 5.1.1.2.1 above on the remarks by Jennings (1998).

do so, 'one would have to conduct the usual "two factor test" and analyse relevant state practice as well as corresponding opinio juris.'[88]

Yet, in view of the special nature of SD, this approach does not appear to be appropriate, as it does not adequately capture the legal value, which states have assigned to SD:

> While the element of state practice can be held to maintain its relevance also when examining the normative force of a regulatory objective, the subjective element of opinio juris needs to be modified given that we are dealing with a different type of norm. Instead of asking whether states considered SD to entail a legal obligation, we shall ask – more precisely – whether they wanted to set SD as a regulatory objective, thus expressing their consent to the typical legal effects it brings about. Given the natural "kinship" between political and regulatory objectives, the proliferation of SD as a regulatory objective in international treaty law, the fact that law generally seeks to foster development and the universal nature of the SD Agenda I believe that there are good reasons to answer this question in the positive.[89]

Therefore, SD can unfold its normative effects beyond the treaty regimes, in which it expressly features.[90]

5.1.1.3 The Legal Impact of SD as the Object and Purpose of TCL

As I have demonstrated, there are good reasons to qualify SD as the regulatory objective of fields of international law.

When it comes to Natural Resources Law (NRL), as 'the field of law, which regulates all [natural resources]-related activities, especially exploration, exploitation or other commercial usage, and preservation',[91] I arrived at this conclusion, after having observed the manifold factual interrelations between the SD agenda and natural resources, as well as particularly after having studied the applicable jurisprudence and legal instruments. When it comes to international jurisprudence, 'nearly all prominent cases dealing with SD as a legal concept [. . .] relate to natural resources.'[92] Moreover, most international agreements that refer to SD are part of

---

[88] Oehl (2019), p. 32. In addition, one could examine the 'fundamental norm creating character' of SD, cf. Cordonier Segger (2017), pp. 69–72.

[89] Oehl (2019), p. 32.

[90] Oehl (2019), p. 33; ibid., n 156 pointing to the line of argument by Barral (2012), p. 394 with reference to the *Iron Rhine* decision. Accordingly, 'this *external* normative force can be of such intensity as to even "revise" an individual treaty norm. According to Article XII of the 1839 Treaty, Belgium would have had to bear the costs for the construction of the railway, while in the end the tribunal, interpreting the provision i.a. in light of SD, ruled that costs would have to be shared between the Parties, i.a. in order to factor in the obligation carried by the Netherlands to construct the railway in conformity with contemporary environmental standards' (original emphasis); cf. PCA (2005) *Iron Rhine arbitration*, award of 24 May 2005, pp. 115–121.

[91] Oehl (2019), p. 6.

[92] Oehl (2019), p. 33.

NRL; also international legal scholarship on NRL is vocal in relying on SD as a 'foundational reference.'[93]

Furthermore, the principles of international law relating to SD are of great importance in NRL:[94]

Such is evident regarding the duty of States to ensure sustainable use of natural resources (principle #1) and the precautionary approach to human health, natural resources and ecosystems (principle #4). The principle of common but differentiated responsibilities (principle #3) must be borne in mind in NR protection efforts, particularly with regard to shared resources. Evidently, good governance (principle #6) is key when it comes to sustainably managing NR (and thus fulfilling the duty of principle #1), including the need to ensure adequate public participation and access to information and justice (principle #5) for all stakeholders concerned by a particular NR activity and pursuing integrated approaches in particular in relation to human rights and social, economic and environmental objectives (principle #7). Correctly managed, NR activities contribute to both inter- and intragenerational equity and to the eradication of poverty (principle #2).[95]

Now what follows from these observations regarding NRL for our appraisal of TCL? Both fields significantly overlap, with TCL exhibiting the narrower scope. Recalling our statement from above, the focus on commodities, instead of natural resources alludes to the 'stronger economic connotation' of TCL.[96] It

focuses exclusively on those items originating from natural resources [...] that are typically being traded and/or refined/processed for specific end uses as e.g. foodstuffs or industrial goods.[97]

TCL provides the more suitable framework and terminology

whenever one is seeking to address this specific economic use of natural resources—or, for that matter more precisely, commodities. In this sense, the broader field of NRL appears to be the more favourable concept whenever, beyond their use as commodities also other economic usages of natural resources, such as navigation, or energy generation and their related governance challenges are concerned.[98]

Given that TCL thus constitutes a subcategory of NRL, we can infer that SD also constitutes the regulatory objective of this field of law focusing on *commodities*. This is all the more so, in view of the interrelations between commodity operations and SD objectives, which may be even greater—at least in terms of the economic

---

[93] Wälde (2004), p. 119; Oehl (2019), p. 34.

[94] The ILA principles consist of the following seven principles: (1) The duty of States to ensure sustainable use of natural resources; (2) The principle of equity and the eradication of poverty; (3) The principle of common but differentiated responsibilities; (4) The principle of the precautionary approach to human health, natural resources and ecosystems, (5) The principle of public participation and access to information and justice; (6) The principle of good governance; (7) The principle of integration and interrelationship, in particular in relation to human rights and social, economic and environmental objectives, ILA (2002).

[95] Oehl (2019), pp. 34–35.

[96] Oehl (2019), p. 6.

[97] Oehl (2019), p. 6, n 20.

[98] Oehl (2019), p. 6, n 20.

significance of commodity trade as compared to other uses of natural resources.[99] The *sustainable use* principle constitutes the concretisation of the broader principle of SD in a natural resource or commodity context[100]—fostering SD in connection with commodity activity means using resources sustainably.

Consequently, SD guides the elaboration, application and interpretation of all norms of TCL. Sustainable use not only constitutes a balancing norm of TCL. Through TCL, all stakeholders are held to 'act sustainably';[101] the norms of TCL need to be interpreted in a way so as to give the greatest possible effect to SD.

Through this mode of operation, SD constitutes the pattern cohering the fragmented body of TCL. By defining SD as the object and purpose of TCL, it provides a guideline for balancing conflicts between individual rules, interests and respective norms, as well as entire norm subsets (or 'branches'). As a consequence, over time those norms, which appear to rather impede respective aspects of SD will either—within the boundaries set by the wording of the rule—be (re-)interpreted so as to reinforce its effect in the interest of SD or be replaced by more conducive rules. These developments will gradually cohere TCL—towards the sub-branch of Sustainable Development Law (SDL), which regulates commodity activity.[102]

The fact that SD has this effect, is most instructively illustrated by the example of permanent sovereignty over natural resources (PSNR). As we have seen above, the principle of PSNR has evolved gradually from a mere competence norm to a principle, which requires states to use natural resources sustainably.[103] In light of our observations above, it seems natural that this is the consequence of SD having become accepted not only as the universal political agenda of the current era, but also as the fundamental object and purpose of TCL.[104]

---

[99] In view of the great economic interrelations of the globalised economy and the fact that commodities constitute a major precondition for *any* industrial value creation, it relates intensively to matters of international economic equity, cf. Sect. 2.1.2 above.

[100] Oehl (2019), p. 35.

[101] Cf. Gehne (2011), p. 314.

[102] See already Oehl (2019), p. 35: NRL as a sub-branch of SDL. SDL has been defined as the 'intersection of social, ecological and economic subject-matters of international law', Oehl (2019), p. 13; Gehne (2011), p. 54; CISDL (2005), p. 1. Yet, as I have already indicated elsewhere, in view of the universal nature of SD and against the backdrop of its dogmatic understanding as a fundamental regulatory objective of international law, it would not seem to be entirely abstruse to classify SD as the ultimate object and purpose of all of international law—which would therefore in its aggregate become SDL, Oehl (2019), p. 35.

[103] Beyond that, Cabrera Medaglia and Perron-Welch (2018a, b) see the PSNR principle as increasingly intertwined with an obligation to share the benefits from commodity operations equitably.

[104] See already Oehl (2019), pp. 8–9, 36 with regard to NRL.

5.1.2 Operationalising SD Through Full Integration

Yet, evidently the normative content of SD is still rather broad. While it may require norm addressees to carry out a balancing exercise between its three pillars, there have for long existed little to no guidelines on *how* this balancing exercise should be performed.[105] The same holds true with regard to the sustainable use principle as its commodity-directed emanation. What currently prevents the sustainable use principle from more regulatory vigour, are its broad terms. If we are to take sustainability seriously, we need to be more specific. The *full integration* technique to my mind is a promising way to proceed.

The terms, which define the sustainable use principle, such as 'rational', 'development', 'rights of indigenous peoples', or the 'needs of future generations', need to gradually be determined by using concrete benchmarks. As has become clear throughout our analysis of the substance of TCL, this body of law provides a vast volume of material in this respect. As a consequence, 'sustainable use' could require states not only to comply with the principle themselves, but also to take legislative and regulatory measures, which ensure that commodity activities performed by their state-owned enterprises (SOEs), corporate, and natural citizens, or on their territory respectively be carried out in accordance with these benchmarks.[106] In addition to legislators, this finding is also addressed to the judiciary, which appears to be quite well suited to develop more specific guidelines, which detail the legal obligations that 'flow' from SD in a commodity context.[107]

However, given the complexity of the task, the enterprise of elaborating such a sophisticated TCL framework will be challenging. It will require to identify the 'best rules', which shall serve as benchmarks. In this regard, the new possibilities provided by computational text analysis may be part of the solution.[108] Moreover, the interaction of the instruments used needs to be properly coordinated and especially integrated in a quest for coherence.

One of the challenges in detailing the obligations that stem from SD quite naturally lies in the imperative to confer sufficient regulatory space to actors operating below the global, i.e. on regional, but especially national and local levels. Evidently, what constitutes sustainable practice needs to be determined to a significant degree on a case-by-case basis. However, there also is a certain *grey area* between the individual case-level on the one hand and the guidance currently provided by—in this ascending order in terms of level of detail—SD, the SDGs, and corresponding publications on the other.

---

[105] Oehl (2019), p. 17, n 90 pointing to Proelß (2017), para. 56.

[106] On the potential to codify this obligation in International Commodity Agreements (ICAs) *de lege ferenda*, see Sect. 5.2.2.1.4 below.

[107] Cf. Cordonier Segger and Weeramantry (2017), pp. 5–6.

[108] It is hoped that the TCL outline provided in the annex in that respect may be a useful starting point.

The 17 goals, as well as their targets and sub-targets considerably specify what exactly SD means. However, they do so—in accordance with their name—primarily by laying out benchmarks that need to be met by a certain date. When it comes to the *measures* that might lead the global community to reach these benchmarks, the SDGs generally do not specify what practices are in effect sustainable and which ones are not. Such, however, could of course still rather easily be done through programmes or initiatives complementing the respective SDGs, targets and sub-targets.[109] In this grey area, what needs to be done more intensively on the global level is to establish a selection of *best practices*, from which national and local regulators as well as other stakeholders could then choose.[110] This is arguably also the intention of the substantial volume of so-called SDG maps, atlases and matrices issued by international organisations, NGOs and research institutes.[111]

The UN Global Compact's SDG Industry Matrix on Energy, Natural Resources and Chemicals provides one example in this connection. With regard to SDG 12, for instance, it i.a. recommends to '[w]henever possible, collect previously used materials and repurpose them instead of extracting new raw materials.'[112] Specifying in what scenarios such repurposing is in fact 'possible'—e.g. by providing a list of circumstances or previous uses that typically require repurposing—could further sharpen this best practice. International standard setting bodies that dispose of sophisticated technical expertise, such as ISO, could play an important role in further breaking down what sustainable practices mean in the commodity sector and its various subsectors respectively.

Apart from these 'legal design' challenges, also corresponding implementation mechanisms need to be elaborated, which would effectively be tasked with ensuring the SD of the global commodity sector. It appears natural that parts of the answer in that respect will lie in decentralised multistakeholder formats, which are being combined with legally binding enforcement mechanisms.

---

[109] See e.g. High Level Political Forum on SD (2014) 10-Year Framework of Programmes on Sustainable Consumption and Production Patterns, https://sustainabledevelopment.un.org/content/documents/1444HLPF_10YFP2.pdf (last accessed 14 May 2021), which was launched formally before the introduction of the SDGs and appears to be little specific itself.

[110] For instance, through binding ICAs *de lege ferenda*, see Sect. 5.2.2 below.

[111] UNDP (2016); UN GC (2017); IPIECA (2017). What SD means with regard to investment policy, has been detailed e.g. by UNCTAD (2015). Cf. also the ICC Business Charter for Sustainable Development as well as the CERES roadmap, which both seek to enhance sustainability in business operations; for more examples cf. the TCL outline in the annex.

[112] UN GC (2017), p. 42.

5.1.3 Learning from International Labour Law

When analysing the substance of TCL, one area—or norm subset—exhibits a remarkable degree of coherence: the one of international labour law. Core International Labour Organisation (ILO) conventions not only apply to states, but also feature in many standards addressing private actors, particularly enterprises. Not surprisingly, a study on the state of sustainability initiatives found that 'virtually all initiatives requir[e] compliance with core ILO conventions. . .'.[113]

While the International Bill of Human Rights (HR) likewise constitutes a widely accepted set of norms, TCL standards addressing private actors refer to it less frequently than to transnational labour norms. This may be due not least to the very nature of labour law. Employers can generally organise work according to their will. Thus, they are assuming a pivotal role in protecting the labour rights of their 'subordinate' employees.[114] Consequently, labour norms quite naturally need to address businesses as private actors directly.

As we have seen above, business respect for HR is ensured by the UN Guiding Principles for Business and Human Rights (UN GP), which then in turn are pointing to the International Bill of HR, according to UN GP #12. Through this latter 'technique', obligations designed primarily for state-citizen relationships are being translated into voluntary commitments for business actors to do their part to respect these obligations.

ILO conventions, to the contrary, are from the outset being drafted based on a tripartite approach, which involves states, as well as employer and employee representatives. As research has found, the involvement of the so-called Governance Triangle consisting of states, businesses, and NGOs in regulatory endeavours is a key factor for building sufficient regulatory capacity in tackling transnational challenges.[115] The wide proliferation and acceptance of labour norms in both classical international law as well as private standards appears to confirm the research on the importance of the Governance Triangle being involved in transnational regulation.

This wide acceptance has also led to the relatively higher degree of coherence that one can observe with regard to these norms as opposed to other norms of TCL: The more accepted a certain norm set is, the more readily drafters of new agreements and standards may include it in their works—therefore contributing to a coherent overall framework as regards this particular field of labour regulation. As a result, these tripartite approaches involving the Governance Triangle in creating transnational regulatory frameworks may be another ingredient towards producing a coherent, effective legal field.

Yet, apart from the tripartite approach, another element of international labour regulation may be relevant in the 'quest for coherence'.[116] Instead of relying on

---

[113] IISD (2010), p. vii.

[114] Cf. Preis and Temming (2020), pp. 1, 30; in this connection speaking of an 'imbalance of power', Bercusson (2009), p. 336.

[115] Abbott and Snidal (2009); Beinisch (2017), p. 3.

[116] Aagaard (2010), p. 229; cf. Sect. 3.1 above.

purely voluntary standards, ILO conventions are legally binding upon member states. As a consequence, states are held to implement the labour rules in their domestic legal systems. When doing so, the tripartite, multi-stakeholder origins of these rules may foster compliance by businesses and therefore lead to a further consolidation of these norms. A lesson learned from transnational labour regulation for cohering legal fields may therefore be to combine tripartite approaches with binding international agreements.

This lesson relates to the more abstract question on what level of multilevel governance duties of corporations should be regulated to what extent. Currently, on the global level typically merely some voluntary benchmarks are being set, whereas the actual legally binding regulation occurs primarily on the national level. This i.a. corresponds to the discussion within the international legal community whether or not to introduce a legally binding convention on corporate accountability.[117] As for instance the International Finance Corporation (IFC) Standards and the Equator Principles, which are said to be 'key driver[s] for improvements' regarding the environmental and social impact of commodity companies,[118] show, *global* standard-setting may prove to be particularly useful when it comes to creating a *coherent* regulatory environment conducive to SD. If corporate accountability, as well as other issues of SD for that matter, continue to be specified largely on the national level, there is a high risk that national approaches will conflict with one another,[119] thus leaving behind an incoherent regulatory framework, which does not effectively foster a functional commodity sector.

5.1.4 Interim Conclusion

The aim of fostering the effectiveness of TCL corresponds with the objective of creating a coherent field of law—and *vice versa*. 'Taxonomy inevitably and inherently is a quest for coherence'.[120] As such, 'legal taxonomy may advocate for particular norms to draw aspects of the field together, as well as create paradigms

---

[117]UN (2003) Norms on the responsibilities of transnational corporations and other business enterprises with regard to human rights, UN Sub-Commission on the Promotion and Protection of HR, UN Doc. E/CN.4/Sub.2/2003/12/Rev.2, https://undocs.org/en/E/CN.4/Sub.2/2003/12/Rev.2; UN HRC (2014) Elaboration of an international legally binding instrument on transnational corporations and other business enterprises with respect to human rights, Resolution 26/9 of 26 June 2014, https://documents-dds-ny.un.org/doc/UNDOC/GEN/G14/082/52/PDF/G1408252.pdf?OpenElement; OHCHR (2019) Revised draft of 16 July 2019, https://www.ohchr.org/Documents/HRBodies/HRCouncil/WGTransCorp/OEIGWG_RevisedDraft_LBI.pdf (all last accessed 14 May 2021).

[118]Lindsay et al. (2013), p. 46.

[119]On potential conflicts between global, regional and national SD objectives and measures, cf. already Sects. 4.3.2 and 4.4 above.

[120]Aagaard (2010), p. 229.

under which a particular field is understood.'[121] Coherence is 'the strength, simplicity, and predominance of the field's patterns'.[122]

This chapter illustrated how SD can serve as the 'cohering pattern' of TCL. In accordance with the methodological foundations we have cast in Chap. 3 above, coherence here is understood as the 'flexible' concept advocated for by Ruger.[123] Yet, even from the perspective of more narrow understandings of the concept, which i.a. require 'linear historical development' and 'a high level of institutional specification and centralization',[124] TCL can claim to exhibit at least *indications* of coherence in view of its historical normative bases of i.a. the Havana Charter and International Commodity Agreements (ICAs), as well as the institutionalisation which ensued in the form of international commodity organisations (ICOs), the Common Fund for Commodities (CFC) and—to a certain degree—UNCTAD overall. Thus, our understanding—in line with Ruger—is more 'flexible' especially with regard to the remaining two requirements of 'internal logic' and 'essential legal form', which ultimately corresponds with the concepts of 'governance' and 'transnationalism', as introduced and discussed in Chaps. 2 and 3 respectively that this treatise is based on.

SD constitutes the object and purpose of this field of law. It draws the various objectives and norm subsets together, constitutes the paradigm under which the field of TCL is understood,[125] and therefore opens avenues towards cohering the legal framework of GCG. By fully integrating benchmarks from the vast body of TCL into the terms, which define the sustainable use principle, the entire field gains simplicity, and therefore regulatory vigour. Involving the governance triangle in this process may serve to enhance its acceptance as a legal concept, thus further reinforcing the field's coherence and effectiveness.

5.2   ICAs as Instruments Specifying Sustainable Commodity Use

Beyond this challenge of coherence, our analysis of the current TCL framework has revealed several parameters, which limit its effectiveness. We have seen that it consists of too many indirect, soft, and private norms, many of which lack sufficient specificity, particularly where they address states. Therefore, what would remedy

---

[121] Tai (2015), p. 120. She moreover points out that '[c]oherence [. . .] comes with a number of benefits', which include 'ease of learning, practicing, and theorising within that defined field. They also include more pragmatic concerns, such as more legitimacy within the legal academy, where coherence is regarded as important for academic legitimacy', Tai (2015), p. 120.

[122] Aagaard (2010), p. 231; cf. Sect. 3.1 above.

[123] Ruger (2008), p. 648, cf. Sect. 3.1 above.

[124] Ruger (2008), p. 629, cf. Sect. 3.1 above.

[125] Cf. Tai (2015), p. 120.

these deficits would be instruments codifying direct, hard, specific, state-oriented law, which balances all five commodity interest comprehensively. Instruments that appear suitable in this respect are international agreements regulating commodity activity—International Commodity Agreements. They can foster the effectiveness of TCL where they codify balancing norms—and thus spell out more precisely what sustainable use means.

Subsequently, we shall first analyse current types of ICAs, whereby we will focus particularly on whether they provide balancing norms, or at least guidance that addresses some of the commodity policy trade-offs (Sect. 5.2.1). Second, we will, based on these findings, reflect on how ICAs *de lege ferenda* could be designed to foster the effectiveness of TCL (Sect. 5.2.2).

5.2.1   Analysis of Current ICAs

This section assesses the relevance of current International Commodity Agreements (ICAs) for GCG.[126] The chapter first outlines and categorises the types of ICAs, which currently feature in the international legal order (Sect. 5.2.1.1). Second, it analyses ICAs *sensu originali* and a selection of central ICAs *sensu stricto*, particularly their object and purpose, substantive provisions and dispute settlement mechanisms (Sect. 5.2.1.2). Third, some reflections on the role of ICAs *sensu lato* in GCG will be shared (Sect. 5.2.1.3). Lastly, an interim conclusion will be drawn regarding the current relevance of the different types of ICAs in GCG (Sect. 5.2.1.4).

5.2.1.1   Types of ICAs

We shall distinguish between ICAs *sensu originali* (Sect. 5.2.1.1.1), *sensu stricto* (Sect. 5.2.1.1.2) and *sensu lato* (Sect. 5.2.1.1.3).

5.2.1.1.1   ICAs *sensu originali*

The category of ICAs *sensu originali* stands for those commodity agreements that were paradigmatic for the market-interventionist approach of the 1970s and 80s.[127] ICAs 'in the original sense' were instruments seeking to rebalance the economic

---

[126]This chapter is exclusively confined to 'international agreements' in the sense of 'treaties' according to Article 2(1)(a) VCLT, which are concluded between states, can dispose of any possible designation and be of bi-, pluri-, or multilateral nature. Private standards, working groups and other initiatives, which are not of inter-state or treaty character, are thus being excluded here. See however Sect. 5.2.2 on how ICAs *de lege ferenda* and these non-inter-state and/or non-treaty instruments may intertwine in the future.

[127]Cf. Sect. 2.2.3 above on the NIEO-UNCTAD phase of global commodity policy.

equilibrium between consumers and producers by maintaining stable commodity prices. The Havana Charter explicitly addressed ICAs (using the term 'Inter-Governmental Commodity Agreements') and established a series of principles applicable to them, but refrained from giving an abstract definition.[128] The term 'ICA' has become most commonly known in connection with the agreements negotiated under the auspices of UNCTAD as an element of establishing the New International Economic Order (NIEO). Article 1(2) of the Agreement Establishing the Common Fund for Commodities (CFC), which builds on Articles 60(d) and 63(b) Havana Charter,[129] provides the authoritative definition of this type of ICAs. Accordingly, ICAs *sensu originali* were defined as

> [a]ny intergovernmental agreement or arrangement to promote international cooperation in a commodity, the parties to which include producers and consumers covering the bulk of world trade in the commodity concerned.[130]

The definition's qualification 'covering the bulk of world trade in the commodity concerned' demonstrates that UNCTAD's approach was explicitly targeting multilateral commodity agreements (since bilateral relations will generally not cover the 'bulk of world trade' in a specific commodity). Likewise excluded are development, free trade, partnership, environmental, and diplomatic agreements, which are generally not intended 'to promote international cooperation in a commodity'. Also, these agreements will ordinarily not cover the bulk of world trade in a specific commodity.

'Original' ICAs therefore constitute commodity-specific instruments and thus belong to the category of 'direct TCL' delineated above. Their scope, legal nature and effectiveness were subject to several comprehensive studies within international legal scholarship between the 1960s and mid-1990s.[131]

However, as has been outlined above, all of the market-interventionist devices of these ICAs had been abandoned by the mid-1990s in view of the emerging doctrine of liberalised markets, which has been prevailing since. While some agreements were vacated entirely,[132] many others have been transformed into cooperation

---

[128] Cf. Articles 55–70 HC.

[129] Desta (2010), paras. 17–19.

[130] Article 1(2) CFC Agreement, UN treaty collection (2019) Agreement establishing the CFC, https://treaties.un.org/doc/Treaties/1989/06/19890619%2004-23%20AM/Ch_XIX_21p.pdf (last accessed 14 May 2021); Chimni (1987), p. 33.

[131] The most pertinent treatises were elaborated by Johnston (1976); Khan (1982); Chimni (1987); Weberpals (1989); and Pelikahn (1990), summary of the monograph available at Pelikahn (1988). Other works, in chronological order, are the ones provided by Wenzel (1961); Greve (1961); Knote (1964); Bohrisch (1965); Thees (1967); Krappel (1975); Rudolph (1983); Habermayer (1984); Hoffmeyer et al. (1988); Michaelowa and Naini (1994); Raffaelli (1995); see also the comprehensive study—the only one of its kind thus far—on international commodity law in general by Jaenicke et al. (1977–1986), summarised by Mertens and Spindler (1989).

[132] Historical treaties that have been abandoned e.g. include the International Wheat Agreement (replaced by the International Grains Agreement in 1995); the International Natural Rubber Agreement (terminated on 30 September 1999, effective 13 October 1999, Resolution

agreements, such as the International Coffee Agreement, the International Tropical Timber Agreement, or the International Cocoa Agreement. A full list of these transformed ICAs *sensu originali* as well as an analysis of their objectives and substantive provisions will be provided in Sect. 5.2.1.2.2 below.

5.2.1.1.2   ICAs *sensu stricto*

The second category of ICAs consists of those agreements that do not constitute ICAs in the original sense, i.e. do not fit the definition of Article 1(2) of the CFC Agreement, yet still are explicitly directed at the regulation of commodity activities. *Explicitness* here implies that these agreements exhibit an express, 'conscious consideration for the specificities of commodity activities.'[133] Like ICAs *sensu originali*, these ICAs *sensu stricto* therefore form part of direct TCL. This is what distinguishes them from indirect TCL and ICAs *sensu lato*. ICAs *sensu stricto* shall be defined as

> international agreements, which, in whole or in part, are explicitly directed at the regulation of commodity activity or particular aspects of the latter.

Thus, examples of ICAs *sensu stricto* include diverse forms of treaties, such as the OPEC statute, the Convention on the Regulation of Antarctic Mineral Resource Activities (CRAMRA), Part XI of the United Nations Convention on the Law of the Sea (UNCLOS), Bilateral Commodity Agreements (BCAs), including German commodity partnerships, as well as the ASEAN Agreement on the Conservation of Nature and Natural Resources and ILO Convention 176 concerning Safety and Health in Mines. As reflected for instance in the case of Part XI of UNCLOS, agreements, which are not themselves commodity-directed, may nevertheless contain entire chapters dedicated to commodity activities.[134]

---

212 (XXXXI) International Rubber Council); in reaction to the termination of the agreement, Malaysia, Indonesia and Thailand initiated the International Rubber Consortium in 2001, https://ircorubber.com/about-us/ (last accessed 14 May 2021); the International Tin Agreement (terminated on 31 June 1989); the International Agreement on Jute and Jute Products (terminated on 11 April 2000); the International Bovine Meat Agreement (terminated on 30 September 1997, effective 31 December 1997); cf. Desta (2010), paras. 26–27; Gilbert (2011), pp. 21–22; on the geopolitical backdrop see already Sect. 1.2.3 above. On erstwhile commodity cartels—which do *not* constitute ICAs *sensu originali*–, cf. e.g. the 1935 World Copper Agreement or the 1972 International Uranium Cartel, Desta (2010), para. 15.

[133] Aagaard (2010), p. 262 as well as already Chap. 4 above.

[134] Given that these norms constitute a commodity-directed normative subsystem, regardless of their inclusion in an agreement of broader or a different overall scope, the UNCLOS for our purposes shall be studied as part of our analysis of ICA *sensu stricto*. Those international agreements, which—from the perspective of GCG—operate in even more remote spheres, could therefore be described as ICAs *sensu latissimo*. These agreements may have some sort of impact on commodity activities, but one that will only be discernible when one closely analyses the corresponding normative 'causal chain'. Evidently, there is little to gain from an analysis of these 'remote' legal instruments for the purposes of our investigation, which seeks to identify those international

5.2.1.1.3 ICAs *sensu lato*

The third and last category of ICAs consists of those agreements, which significantly impact commodity activities, yet without explicitly pursuing a commodity-directed object and purpose or exhibiting a 'conscious consideration' of commodity activities. These ICAs *sensu lato* therefore fall under the category of indirect TCL. In the broadest sense, this type of ICA could be defined as

> any international agreement that exhibits a substantial regulatory impact on commodity activity, yet without having been explicitly directed at or designed for that purpose.

Consequently, ICAs *sensu lato* can stem from any original background and be aimed at any purpose that factually corresponds to GCG. As such, for instance Free Trade Agreements (FTAs), Preferential Trade Agreements (PTAs), the General Agreement on Tariffs and Trade (GATT), the International Bill of Human Rights, as well as international environmental agreements can constitute ICAs *sensu lato*. This category will thus largely coincide with the (self-imposed) qualifications of a state's permanent sovereignty over natural resources (PSNR) under international law that have been briefly touched upon in Chap. 3 above.

5.2.1.2 Analysis of ICAs *sensu originali* and *sensu stricto*

This section aims to provide an account of the central normative contents of current ICAs. For that purpose, it analyses objectives, substantive provisions and institutional arrangements of both ICAs *sensu originali* (Sect. 5.2.1.2.2) and *sensu stricto* (Sect. 5.2.1.2.3). In order to better understand the role and status of ICAs *sensu originali*, we shall first, however, turn to so-called International Commodity Bodies (ICBs) as a category, which somewhat 'frames' ICAs *sensu originali* and elucidates their current role and functioning (Sect. 5.2.1.2.1).

5.2.1.2.1 International Commodity Bodies

ICBs are organisations or institutions, which have been recognised by the Common Fund for Commodities (CFC) in accordance with Schedule C 'Eligibility Criteria for ICBs' of the CFC Agreement.[135] Accordingly, ICBs are intergovernmental bodies that all member states of the UN, its specialised agencies or the International Atomic Energy Agency (IAEA) can join. Regarding its objectives and activities, the CFC

---

agreements that actually have a bearing on commodity activities today. This category thus rather serves the purpose of theoretical completeness than to contribute substantially to the knowledge we are seeking to gain from this analysis. It appears to be appropriate to limit an analysis of ICAs—as well as a conceptualisation of TCL—to the boundaries, which are represented by ICAs *sensu lato*. Beyond these boundaries, assuming a 'commodity perspective' on the normative landscape of, for instance, the law of consular and diplomatic relations, appears more and more absurd.

[135] UNCTAD (2016), p. 1.

Agreement sets forth that '[i]t shall be concerned on a continuing basis with trade, production and consumption of the commodity in question.' Moreover, '[i]ts membership shall comprise producers and consumers which shall represent an adequate share of exports and of imports of the commodity concerned.' Also, it needs to dispose of 'an effective decision making process that reflects the interests of its participants.' ICBs are eligible for projects financed by the CFC.[136]

Given that they meet all criteria under Schedule C of the CFC Agreement, UNCTAD has designated all international commodity organisations (ICOs) corresponding with an International Commodity Agreement (ICA) as ICBs.[137] ICAs *sensu originali* thus need to be perceived in the context of other arrangements, which likewise qualify as ICBs. Apart from ICOs, several so-called *International Study Groups* (ISGs) qualify as ICBs and perform similar duties. These ISGs include the International Rubber Study Group (established 1934); the International Lead and Zinc Study Group (ILZSG; established 1959); the International Nickel Study Group (INSG; established 1990); the International Copper Study Group (ICSG; established 1992); the International Network for Bamboo and Rattan (INBAR; established in 1997); as well as the International Jute Study Group (IJSG; established in 2002).[138]

Similar to the international commodity organisations (ICOs), the international study groups are intergovernmental organisations, which are being governed and financed primarily by states. They usually function based on an intergovernmental agreement, typically either termed 'constitution' or 'terms of reference' and accompanied by some sort of procedural rules.[139] The various study groups tend to be quite similar regarding their organisational design and objectives.[140] Their main goals generally lie in ensuring transparency of the respective sector and correspondingly providing accurate production, trade, and consumption data, e.g. through monthly

---

[136]UNCTAD (2016), p. 1. In these projects, study groups typically 'prioritize[], formulate[] and[/ or] supervise[] CFC-financed projects', ICSG (2019) Current work and activities, https://www.icsg. org/index.php/who-we-are/current-work-and-activities (last accessed 14 May 2021). While the CFC agreement provides the definition of ICAs *sensu originali*, it does not fall under this category itself. Instead, it constitutes an ICA *sensu stricto*, yet without significant balancing norms.

[137]UNCTAD (2016), p. 1. This appears to include the International Cotton Advisory Committee (ICAC), UNCTAD (2016), p. 2; UNCTAD (2019) ICBs, https://unctad.org/en/Pages/SUC/ Commodities/International-Commodity-Bodies.aspx (last accessed 14 May 2021).

[138]IJSG (2003) About, http://www.jute.org/index1.htm; cf. UNCTAD (2016), p. 1; UNCTAD (2019) ICBs, https://unctad.org/en/Pages/SUC/Commodities/International-Commodity-Bodies. aspx (both last accessed 14 May 2021); cf. Espa and Oehl (2018), p. 8, n 34.

[139]Not all appear to have been published. IRSG (2011) Constitution, http://www.rubberstudy.com/ documents/IRSG%20Constitution%20-Effective%201%20July%202011.pdf; IRSG (2011) Rules of procedure, http://www.rubberstudy.com/documents/IRSG%20ROP%20-Effective%201% 20July%202011%20Rvsd%201%20Jul%2012.pdf; INSG (2015) Terms of reference, http://insg. org/wp-content/uploads/2019/01/doc_INSG_TERMS_OF_REFERENCE_Jan2015.pdf;   INSG (2015) Rules of procedure, http://insg.org/wp-content/uploads/2019/01/doc_INSG_RULES_OF_ PROCEDURE_May2015.pdf (all last accessed 14 May 2021).

[140]The INSG and the ICSG for instance have been explicitly modelled after the ILZSG (2019) Who we are, http://www.ilzsg.org/static/howwebegan.aspx?from=1 (last accessed 14 May 2021).

newsletters, annual reports and market forecasts.[141] Moreover, they usually implement a forum for exchange, often on an annual basis, such as the World Rubber Summit. While study groups are typically being controlled through member state delegates and respective standing or executive committees, they also dispose of so-called industry advisory panels and allow NGOs or other international organisations to participate in their meetings as observers. This opens their exchange fora for multi-stakeholder debates. Consequently, the respective study group is frequently described as the premier forum for sector-specific exchange.[142]

While study groups are typically comparatively small organisations, the most recent study group, INBAR, not only disposes of a Secretariat with over 35 employees, but also seeks to 'promote[] environmentally sustainable development using bamboo and rattan.'[143] Thus going beyond the objectives of the other study groups, INBAR aligns its activities with the SDGs[144] and according to its own 'Strategic Plan 2015–2030' engages in i.a. lobbying, advocacy, knowledge sharing, and country-level capacity building.[145]

Further entities that have been recognised as ICBs are various institutions at FAO.[146] This includes so-called *FAO Intergovernmental Groups* (IGGs) on individual agricultural commodities, including Bananas and Tropical Fruits;[147] Citrus Fruit;[148] Grains;[149] Hard Fibres;[150] Meat and Dairy Products;[151] Oilseeds, Oils and

---

[141] See already Espa and Oehl (2018), p. 8, n 34.

[142] See e.g. IRSG (2019) Mission statement, http://www.rubberstudy.com/mission-statement.aspx (last accessed 14 May 2021): 'The IRSG shall be THE FORUM for the discussion of matters affecting the supply and demand for natural as well as synthetic rubber.'

[143] INBAR (2019) Promoting the use of bamboo and rattan for SD, https://www.inbar.int/about-inbar/#2 (last accessed 14 May 2021).

[144] Notably SDGs #1, #7, #11, #12, #13 and #15, INBAR (2019) Mission & strategy, https://www.inbar.int/about-inbar/mission-strategy/#1 (last accessed 14 May 2021).

[145] INBAR (2019) Mission & strategy, https://www.inbar.int/about-inbar/mission-strategy/#1 (last accessed 14 May 2021).

[146] UNCTAD (2019) ICBs, https://unctad.org/en/Pages/SUC/Commodities/International-Commodity-Bodies.aspx (last accessed 14 May 2021).

[147] 'Established by the Committee on Commodity Problems (CCP) at is Sixty-second Session (1999). It replaced the former Intergovernmental Group on Bananas', FAO (2019) Governing and statutory bodies, http://www.fao.org/unfao/govbodies/gsb-subject-matter/statutory-bodies-details/en/c/162/?no_cache=1 (last accessed 14 May 2021); FAO (2019) IGG on bananas and tropical fruits, http://www.fao.org/economic/est/est-commodities/bananas/meetings-on-bananas-and-tropical-fruits/en/ (last accessed 14 May 2021).

[148] 'Established by the Committee on Commodity Problems (CCP) at its Thirty-second Session (1959)', FAO (2019) Governing and statutory bodies, http://www.fao.org/unfao/govbodies/gsb-subject-matter/statutory-bodies-details/en/c/140/ (last accessed 14 May 2021); FAO (2019) IGG on citrus fruit, http://www.fao.org/economic/est/est-commodities/citrus-fruit/citrus-fruit-meetings/en/ (last accessed 14 May 2021).

[149] FAO (2019) IGG on grains, http://www.fao.org/unfao/govbodies/gsb-subject-matter/statutory-bodies-details/en/c/135/ (last accessed 14 May 2021).

[150] FAO (2019) IGG on hard fibres, http://www.fao.org/unfao/govbodies/gsb-subject-matter/statutory-bodies-details/en/c/173/ (last accessed 14 May 2021).

[151] FAO (2019) IGG on meat and dairy products, http://www.fao.org/unfao/govbodies/gsb-subject-matter/statutory-bodies-details/en/c/210/ (last accessed 14 May 2021).

Fats;[152] Rice;[153] and Tea.[154] These IGGs were established as subsidiary entities to the FAO Committee on Commodity Problems and are focussing on trade issues regarding individual commodities.[155] While their coverage is constantly shifting depending on current challenges in the respective sector at hand, they are—quite similarly to the ISGs—seeking to provide forums

> for intergovernmental consultation and exchange on trends in production, consumption, trade and prices of key commodities, including regular appraisal of the global market situation and short-term outlook. The IGGs consider changes in policies and examine their effects relating to the current and prospective market situation.[156]

In addition, 'technical side events' are intended to engage other stakeholders in the conversation on the individual sectors at hand.[157] Further recognised ICBs include the FAO Sub-Group on Hides and Skins, which operates as a subsidiary of the IGG on Meat and Dairy Products, as well as the FAO Intergovernmental Sub-Committee on Fish Trade.[158] The latter constitutes a sub-entity of the FAO Committee on Fisheries (COFI).[159]

5.2.1.2.2 ICAs *sensu originali*

Given that we aim to sketch the normative contents of International Commodity Agreements (ICAs) as they are applicable to commodity activities *today*, our analysis is focused on ICAs that are still in existence. With regard to ICAs *sensu originali*, our evaluation is thus exclusively concerned with those *transformed*, post-market-interventionist ICAs that have not been eliminated entirely.[160] ICAs that

---

[152]FAO (2019) IGG on oilseeds, oils and fats, http://www.fao.org/unfao/govbodies/gsb-subject-matter/statutory-bodies-details/en/c/158/ (last accessed 14 May 2021).

[153]FAO (2019) IGG on rice, http://www.fao.org/unfao/govbodies/gsb-subject-matter/statutory-bodies-details/en/c/127/ (last accessed 14 May 2021).

[154]FAO (2019) IGG on tea, http://www.fao.org/unfao/govbodies/gsb-subject-matter/statutory-bodies-details/en/c/205/ (last accessed 14 May 2021); FAO (2019) IGGs, http://www.fao.org/ccp/igg/en/ (last accessed 14 May 2021).

[155]FAO (2019) IGGs, http://www.fao.org/ccp/igg/en/ (last accessed 14 May 2021).

[156]FAO (2019) IGGs, http://www.fao.org/ccp/igg/en/ (last accessed 14 May 2021).

[157]FAO (2019) IGGs, http://www.fao.org/ccp/igg/en/ (last accessed 14 May 2021).

[158]UNCTAD (2019) ICBs, https://unctad.org/en/Pages/SUC/Commodities/International-Commodity-Bodies.aspx (last accessed 14 May 2021).

[159]UNCTAD (2019) ICBs, https://unctad.org/en/Pages/SUC/Commodities/International-Commodity-Bodies.aspx; 'Established by the Committee on Fisheries (COFI) at its Sixteenth Session (1985) in accordance with Rule XXX-10 of the General Rules of the Organization and Rule VII of the COFI Rules of Procedure', FAO (2019) Sub-committee on fish trade, http://www.fao.org/fishery/about/cofi/trade/en (both last accessed 14 May 2021).

[160]On historical ICAs—especially *sensu originali*—that have been vacated or terminated, see Sect. 5.2.1.1.1 above. See also for instance Article 22 GTC, which still—perhaps somewhat hopeful—refers to potentially adopting a new agreement that includes 'economic provisions' in the future.

qualify as such, include the International Grains Agreement, more precisely the Grains Trade Convention (GTC);[161] the International Sugar Agreement (ISA);[162] the International Tropical Timber Agreement (ITTA);[163] the International Cocoa Agreement (ICocA);[164] the International Coffee Agreement (ICofA);[165] as well as the International Agreement on Olive Oil and Table Olives (IAO).[166] These ICAs generally correspond with respective international commodity organisations (ICOs) administering the individual agreement, such as the International Olive Council (IOC), International Cocoa Organisation (ICCO), or the International Coffee Organisation (ICofO).[167]

In the following, we will analyse the provisions of these ICAs *sensu originali* in more detail. For that purpose, we are comparing and clustering their respective objectives (Sect. 5.2.1.2.2.1), substantive obligations (Sect. 5.2.1.2.2.2), institutional arrangements (Sect. 5.2.1.2.2.3) and dispute settlement mechanisms (Sect. 5.2.1.2.2.4).

5.2.1.2.2.1 Objectives

Arguably *the* central objective of ICAs *sensu originali* is fostering *international cooperation* with regard to the respective commodity sectors, as reflected in Articles 1(a) ICocA, 1(a) ITTA, 1(a) ISA, 1(1) ICofA,1(a) GTC, as well as Article 1 (c) ICACRR. In some cases, the mode of international cooperation is further specified so as to include particularly technology and technical cooperation, for instance according to Articles 1(2) IAO and 1(p) ITTA. This may involve training

---

[161] IGC (1995) International Grains Agreement, http://igc.int/en/downloads/brochure/iga1995.pdf (last accessed 14 May 2021).

[162] ISO (1992) International Sugar Agreement, https://www.isosugar.org/membership/isa-agreement (last accessed 14 May 2021).

[163] ITTO (2006) International Tropical Timber Agreement, https://www.itto.int/direct/topics/topics_pdf_download/topics_id=3363&no=1&disp=inline (last accessed 14 May 2021); entered into force on 7 December 2011, superseding the 1994 ITTA.

[164] ICCO (2010) International Cocoa Agreement, https://www.icco.org/about-us/international-cocoa-agreements/doc_download/6-english-2010-international-cocoa-agreement.html   (last accessed 14 May 2021).

[165] ICO (2007) International Coffee Agreement, http://www.ico.org/ica2007.asp (last accessed 14 May 2021).

[166] UN treaty collection (2015) International Agreement on Olive Oil and Table Olives, https://treaties.un.org/doc/Treaties/2015/10/20151009%2010-35%20AM/Ch_XIX-49.pdf (last accessed 14 May 2021).

[167] While the International Cotton Advisory Committee (ICAC) has been founded already in 1939, and designated as a public international organisation by means of the US presidential executive order no. 9911 of 19 December 1947, what is more pertinent for its operation *today*, are its Rules and Regulations (ICACRR), ICAC (2015) ICACRR, https://icac.org/Content/Pdf%20Files910ff222_e6a9_4d39_939b_7cf3663d6b52/E_Rules-Regs_dec2015_FINAL.pdf.pdf (last accessed 14 May 2021), which consequently also feature in our analysis below. In line with UNCTAD, it thus appears fair to speak of *seven* ICAs *sensu originali*, which are in existence today, UNCTAD (2016), p. 2.

programmes to promote technology transfer according to Articles 1(f) ICocA and 1(11) ICofA; capacity building for poverty alleviation as set forth in Articles 1 (j) ICocA and 1(12) ICofA; capacity building for sustainable forest management, as provided for in Article 1(d) ITTA; encouraging members to develop food safety standards according to Articles 1(i) ICocA and 1(10) ICofA; as well as generally the objective to promote the quality of the commodity at hand, such as coffee according to Article 1(9) ICofA.

Another central objective of ICAs *sensu originali* lies in providing an intergovernmental discussion *forum*, as reflected in Articles 1(b) ITTA, 1(d) GTC, 1(b) ISA, as well as Article 1(d) ICACRR. In some cases, also exchanges with the private sector or other non-governmental stakeholders are already mentioned explicitly as an objective of the respective agreement, for instance according to Articles 1(b) ICocA and 1(2) ICofA.[168] These fora are not least intended to foster the *exchange of* all sorts of commodity-relevant *information*. In this respect, one can largely distinguish two types of information dissemination. The first type relates to the objective of achieving the greatest possible degree of market transparency between members and thus involves the dissemination of statistics, studies, reports, and other trade-related data, as e.g. provided for according to Articles 1(g) ICocA, 1(h) and 1(l) ITTA, as well as Article 1(6) ICofA. The second type concerns the dissemination and exchange of information, which serves to promote the consumption of the respective commodity or corresponding secondary products, such as scientific information on nutritional, health or other properties of the commodity in question, as set forth in i.a. Articles 1(3) IAO, 1(h) ICocA, 1(d) ISA, and 1(7) ICofA.[169]

Exchange of information is one of the instruments raised when it comes to the objective of facilitating, expanding or promoting *trade* in the respective commodity, as provided for in e.g. Articles 1(c) ISA and 1(5) ICofA. For this purpose, also the elimination of trade barriers and discriminatory practices is being aimed for, as reflected e.g. in Article 1(b) GTC. Besides, what constitutes an objective of various ICAs *sensu originali* is specifically strengthening the respective *national commodity sectors*, as for instance set forth in Article 1 ICocA. More precisely, objectives include the seeking of finance for projects strengthening the respective sector, according to Articles 1(c) ICocA as well as 1(8) ICofA; improving marketing and distribution of timber, according to Article 1(k) ITTA; and fostering the availability of information on financial tools for coffee producers, according to Article 1(13) ICofA.

Apart from purely economic objectives, remarkably most ICAs *sensu originali*— and all which have been adopted in the past decade—also explicitly refer to SD. Fostering the SD of the respective sector is the objective of various agreements according to Articles 1, 1(e) ICocA, 1, 1(c) ITTA, 1(3) ICofA, and 1(2) IAO. Some agreements specify this commitment by including the objectives of promoting sustainable utilisation, according to Article 1(m) ITTA; encouraging members to

---

[168] On the institutional arrangements for involving non-state actors, see Sect. 5.2.1.2.2.3 below.

[169] On respective substantive obligations of members, see Sect. 5.2.1.2.2.2 below.

recognise the role of indigenous and local communities for sustainable forest management, according to Article 1(r) ITTA; encouraging information sharing on certification mechanisms in order to foster sustainable forest management, Article 1 (o) ITTA; or particularly calling upon members to develop a sustainable coffee sector, according to Article 1(3) ICofA. Article 2 of the ICocA even provides a detailed definition of what constitutes a 'sustainable cocoa economy'. Accordingly, the latter

> implies an integrated value chain in which all stakeholders develop and promote appropriate policies to achieve levels of production, processing and consumption that are economically viable, environmentally sound and socially responsible for the benefit of present and future generations, with the aim of improving productivity and profitability in the cocoa value chain for all stakeholders concerned, in particular for the smallholder producers[.][170]

Four out of seven ICAs analysed also refer to objectives that relate to creating a long-term *economic equilibrium* between producers and consumers and ultimately a balanced world trade system with regard to the commodity at hand. Respective provisions include Articles 1(d) ICocA, 1(4) ICofA, 1(i) ITTA, and 1(c) GTC.

5.2.1.2.2.2   Substantive Obligations

Member states are generally held to *cooperate* and take measures, which foster the objectives of the agreement, as set forth in Articles 28 ISA and 3(1) ICofA. In some agreements, this obligation is formulated in the negative, i.e. as an obligation not to take measures that conflict with the objectives of the agreement, for instance according to Articles 22 IAO, 29(1) ITTA.

Again remarkably, members have widely obliged themselves to *foster the SD* of the respective sectors. According to Article 24 IAO, members commit to promote the 'development of sustainable olive growing', which relates 'to the improvement of practices at all stages of olive and olive oil production'. The ICocA even dedicates a separate chapter to SD. According to Article 42 ICocA, members 'shall give consideration' to improving living and working conditions of people engaged in cocoa production in line with ILO standards and internationally recognised principles. Moreover, according to Article 43(1) ICocA,

> Members shall make all necessary efforts to accomplish a sustainable cocoa economy, taking into account the sustainable development principles and objectives contained, inter alia, in the Rio Declaration on Environment and Development and in Agenda 21 adopted in Rio de Janeiro in 1992, the United Nations Millennium Declaration adopted in New York in 2000, the Report of the World Summit on Sustainable Development held in Johannesburg in 2002, the 2002 Monterrey Consensus on Financing for Development, and the 2001 Ministerial Declaration on the Doha Development Agenda.

The ICCO shall support members in the pursuit of this objective, and as such provide a forum for 'permanent dialogue', encourage cooperation between

---

[170]Likewise, the ITTA touches upon the definition of sustainable forest management, for this purposes however refers to the ITTO's internal guidelines, Article 2(2) ITTA.

members, adopt and periodically review work programmes and projects fostering a sustainable cocoa economy, and seek corresponding finance from multi—and bilateral donors, according to Article 43(2)–(6) ICocA.

Also, according to Article 36 ICofA, '[m]embers shall give due consideration to sustainable management of coffee resources and processing', again in line with the principles contained in Agenda 21 and formulated at the World Summit on Sustainable Development (WSSD) in 2002. Individual 'pillars' of SD are furthermore being addressed i.a. in Articles 29 ISA and 37 ICofA, according to which members shall ensure that fair labour standards are being maintained in the respective industries and be committed to improving living conditions for farmers and workers. According to Article 30 ISA, '[m]embers shall give due consideration to environmental aspects in all stages of sugar production.' Further specifications of what the duty to foster the SD of the respective sector entails, is generally not included in the agreements.

Furthermore, members commit to *promoting* markets and *consumption* of the respective commodity, according to Articles 37(1) ICocA and 25(1) ICofA. For this purpose, they i.a. oblige themselves to 'remove or reduce substantially domestic obstacles to the expansion of cocoa consumption' according to Article 37(2) ICocA; task the respective ICOs to conduct thorough market analyses along the entire commodity value chain, according to Articles 36(1), 38(1) ICocA; or to improve product quality according to Article 25(1) ICofA. According to Article 25(2) ICofA, such market promotion may furthermore be pursued for example through information campaigns, research, and capacity building.

Perhaps the most far-reaching, 'biting' obligations provided for in ICAs *sensu originali* concern the *collection and dissemination of data*. Not least for the purpose of ensuring the greatest possible degree of market transparency, members are tasking the respective ICOs to act as 'global information centres' for the commodity in question, as reflected in Articles 30(1) ICocA, 32, 33 ISA, 32 ICofA, as well as 1 (b) ICACRR. This entails the duty, for one, to collect relevant data from members and other international organisations, according to Articles 25 IAO, 27 ITTA, 30(2), (3) ICocA. Data to be made available includes information on commodity stocks (Article 31(1) ICocA), supply, demand and market conditions (Article 3(a) GTC), trade statistics and national commodity policies (Article 25 IAO, 3(b) GTC), accurate data on re-exports by importers (Article 3(3) ICofA), geographical indications and their legal protections (Article 20(6) IAO), as well as annual reports on all commercial and special transactions in the commodity at hand (Article 7(1) GTC).[171] However, where a member does not comply with this obligation, the agreements typically do not provide the option of introducing specific sanctions beyond the offering of assistance in compiling and transmitting the data as well as asking for an explanation for non-compliance, as set forth e.g. in Article 30(4) ICocA. Yet, Article 32(5) ICofA goes further in this respect, allowing the

---

[171] Article IX(1) ICACRR in this respect refers to 'available information as may be required to carry out the work program'.

Council to 'take initiatives likely to lead such a Member to furnish the required information.'

For the other, ICOs are required to publish their own studies, surveys and reports on the respective commodity sectors (Articles 34 ICofA, 32(1) ISA, 7(1)(d) IAO, 1 (b) ICACRR), promote scientific research (Article 35 ICocA) or calculate commodity indicator prices (Articles 33(1) ICocA, 32(3) ICofA).[172] This naturally requires a continuous review of the market (Articles 4(1), 16 GTC, 33(2) ISA, 7(2) (c) ICACRR, 36(3) ICocA, 28 ITTA).

Apart from that, members may be required to remove obstacles from trade and to commit to non-discrimination. According to Article 34 ITTA for instance,

> [n]othing in this Agreement authorizes the use of measures to restrict or ban international trade in, and in particular as they concern imports of, and utilization of, timber and timber products.

According to Article 24(1) ICofA, members 'recognize' the importance of removing obstacles to trade, yet at the same time recognise their right to regulate, particularly mentioning 'national health and environmental policy objectives' and respective commitments under international agreements, including ones addressing trade.

While thus generally ICAs *sensu originali* exhibit quite similar, at times identical, provisions, they also entail some *specific obligations*, which typically correspond with specific traits of the commodity in question. For instance, the IAO especially emphasises its definition of olive products according to Articles 19, 20 IAO as well as annexes B, C. According to Article 20(1) IAO, members 'undertake to apply' these designations in international trade. Moreover, according to Article 27(1) ICofA members commit to prohibit the sale of products as coffee that 'contain less than the equivalent of 95% green coffee as the basic raw material', a term equally defined by the agreement in its Article 2(1)(a). According to Article 32(1) ICocA, members recognise that it may be generally advisable to renounce substitutes and observe corresponding recommendations of competent international bodies as well as the provisions of the Codex Alimentarius. Article 21 IAO refers to the international guarantee label of the IOC,[173] the ICofA according to its Articles 3(2), 33 ICofA establishes a scheme for certificates of origin, and Article 21 ITTA establishes the Bali Partnership Fund for sustainable tropical timber management.

Lastly, one should note that *obligations* that relate to the 'big picture' of commodity governance, such as the challenge of balancing the global trading system

---

[172] In addition, ICOs typically publish annual reports on their activities (Articles 18 ICocA, 28(1) ITTA), policy works or action plans (Article 24 ITTA) as well as draft forward work programs (Article 33(4) ISA, IV(3)(a)(3) ICACRR), which usually besides issues of market transparency also touch upon a variety of other topics, see for instance ITTO (2018) Annual report 2017, https://www.itto.int/direct/topics/topics_pdf_download/topics_id=5734&no=1 (last accessed 14 May 2021).

[173] On the standard- and certification-related work of the IOC (2019) Standards, http://www.internationaloliveoil.org/estaticos/view/222-standards (last accessed 14 May 2021).

between consumer and producer interests, are only reflected in one provision. According to Article 26 ICofA,

[m]embers recognize the need of developing countries to broaden the base of their economies through, inter alia, industrialization and the export of manufactured products, including the processing of coffee and the export of processed coffee...[174]

To summarise, 'big picture' perspectives on commodity governance still played a considerably greater role in the *objectives* of the various agreements. The fact that the operative section of only one ICA *sensu originali* features a clause addressing this perspective, and notably a clause, which merely 'recognize[s]' the needs of developing countries, is quite paradigmatic. It demonstrates how these agreements have largely lost their 'bite'. While they primarily implement fora for exchange and cooperation and task ICOs as well as member states with compiling and disseminating data, *tools* to effectively address challenges of development, participation, or environmental protection, are missing almost entirely.[175] As such, ICAs *sensu originali* are not suited to remedy imbalances in the current design of the TCL framework.

5.2.1.2.2.3 Institutional Arrangements

When it comes to institutional arrangements, ICAs *sensu originali* exhibit quite a straightforward, typical design for international treaties. All of them explicitly establish or confirm their corresponding international organisations, which are responsible for implementing the provisions of the agreement. They include the International Olive Council (IOC), according to Article 3 IAO; the International Cocoa Organisation (ICCO), according to Article 3(1) ICocA; the International Tropical Timber Organisation (ITTO), according to Article 3(1) ITTA; the International Sugar Organisation (ISugO), according to Article 3(1) ISA; the International Coffee Organisation (ICofO), according to Article 6(1) ICofA; and the International Grains Council (IGC), according to Article 9(1) GTC.[176]

---

[174] Article 6(1) GTC merely states that '[m]embers undertake to conduct any concessional transactions in grains in such a way as to avoid harmful interference with normal patterns of production and international commercial trade.'

[175] This is especially reflected in the ICocA, which in Article 1(d) states that it is one of the objectives of the agreement to 'strive towards obtaining fair prices leading to equitable economic returns to both producers and consumers in the cocoa value chain, and to contribute to a balanced development of the world cocoa economy in the interest of all Members', cf. Sect. 5.2.1.2.2.1 above. Yet, in terms of concrete measures it merely refers to an option for the Council, which 'may also promote studies likely to contribute to greater market transparency and facilitate the development of a balanced and sustainable world cocoa economy', according to Article 38(2) ICocA. Articles 42 and 43 ICocA, which have been discussed above, do not appear to refer to matters of *global* equity, but to instead be concerned primarily with efforts to implement sustainable cocoa industries on the *national* level. In any case, they do not mention the need for a 'balanced' economy or other matters of ISI as referred to in Article 26 ICofA.

[176] On the special case of ICAC, see already n 167 above. The organisations are typically being granted legal personality under the individual agreement.

In terms of the organs that are competent to carry out respective tasks and duties of the international commodity organisations (ICOs), one can discern a typical governing structure of an international organisation consisting of an executive council or standing committee, in which representatives from member states decide on strategy and work programme of the organisation; potentially topic-specific sub-committees to the council; as well as a secretariat tasked with daily operations of the ICO.[177] Moreover, all ICOs are explicitly encouraged to enter co-operations with other IOs, particularly UNCTAD or FAO, according to the respective provisions (Articles 12 IAO, 13 ICocA, 15 ITTA, 14 ISA, 15 ICofA, 19 GTC, XII ICACRR). Often, non-member states as well as IOs are invited to join annual meetings as observes, as for instance provided for in Articles 13, 14 ICocA, 15, 16 ITTA, 16(2) ISA.

Additional institutional arrangements can turn the ICOs into full-fledged multi-stakeholder fora,[178] for instance through advisory committees, or consultative boards, which comprise experts especially from the private sector.[179] Some clauses in this respect are very wide, such as Article 14(3) ISA, which allows the ISugO to enter into 'whatever arrangements' for effective contacts with sugar producers, traders and manufacturers. Likewise, Article 16 ICofA generally opens the ICofO for co-operations with NGOs and other experts.

5.2.1.2.2.4   Dispute Settlement

Five out of the seven agreements analysed contain dispute settlement clauses.[180] These clauses exclusively apply to cases of disputes between members regarding the functioning of the respective ICA. Typically, the council is declared competent to decide disputes. Arguably the most comprehensive dispute settlement clause is provided in Article 26 IAO, which i.a. grants a member that is to be excluded from the agreement the right to recourse to the ICJ, according to Article 26(4) IAO. Article 32 ITTA provides a special provision for remedies in favour of developing countries and LDCs respectively that have been affected adversely by measures taken under the agreement.

---

[177] See the respective provisions: Article 7 IAO; Article 3(4) ICocA; Articles 3(2), 26 ITTA; Articles 7, 18, 23 ISA; Article 6(3) ICofA; Articles 9, 15–17 GTC; Articles IV, VII ICACRR.

[178] For example, the ICofA explicitly mentions the World Coffee Conference, according to Article 30 ICofA, as well as the Consultative Forum on Coffee Sector Finance, according to Article 31 ICofA, both of which are designed as multi-stakeholder fora.

[179] See for instance Article 44 ICocA as well as the Private Sector Consultative Board, according to Article 29 ICofA. On the advisory board of the IOC, which serves scientific purposes, see IOC (2019) Scientific research, http://www.internationaloliveoil.org/estaticos/view/239-scientific-research (last accessed 14 May 2021). According to Article XII ICACRR, non-members, including private organisations may also be invited to meetings of the Advisory Committee.

[180] See Article 26 IAO; Article 50 ICocA; Article 31 ITTA; Article 39 ICofA, which merely states that dispute settlement procedures shall be determined by the Council as well as Article 8 GTC.

5.2.1.2.2.5   *Interim Conclusion*

To conclude, International Commodity Agreements (ICAs) *sensu originali* primarily serve commodity-specific cooperative purposes. While most agreements refer to SD, it is typically defined as a mere objective, yet does not translate into significant commitments or measures in the operative parts of the agreements.[181] Also when it comes to the challenge of creating a balance in world commodity trade between consumer and producer interests, particularly with regard to the producers' need to diversify their often commodity-dependent economies, ICAs *sensu originali* do not provide for any specific commitments. Instead, they have been said to be 'similar to existing [International Study Groups]' in many respects.[182]

Moreover, it shall be noted that ICAs *sensu originali* currently only exist for seven commodities—namely cocoa, coffee, cotton, grains, olives and olive oil, sugar, and tropical timber. They are thus not only limited regarding their substantive obligations, but also in their number. Naturally, this status quo needs to be perceived against the backdrop of the 'ideological shift' away from market-interventionist agreements to the current form of agreements in the 1980s and 1990s.[183] This is not likely to change, as UNCTAD notes:

> At present, Governments do not appear to be prepared for discussions concerning the producer-consumer schemes for price stabilization through market intervention in the framework of existing ICAs.[184]

However, regardless of these little promising prospects for market-interventionist tools and the limited number of ICAs *sensu originali*, the design especially of the more recent agreements alludes to what constitutes Global Commodity Governance (GCG) today. For one, their multi-stakeholder, open, and transparent fora illustrate the mode of collaboration in this respect. For the other, they demonstrate how distinct and complex governance challenges are already with regard to individual commodity sectors, and how important it is to build and exchange specific expertise between all stakeholders.[185] What is more, however, by definition these ICAs are designed to address both consumer as well as producer interests.[186] While focusing primarily on cooperation and information exchange, they thus still are intended to employ a comprehensive perspective on an entire commodity sector as well as to foster a thorough understanding of its functioning. As such, some agreements at least

---

[181] This is, to some degree, with the exception of Article 43 ICocA.

[182] UNCTAD (2016), p. 2.

[183] See Sect. 2.2.4 above. However, also during the 'high time' of market-interventionist ICAs, only a comparatively small number of commodities was covered by such instruments; cf. on the slow progress in the conclusion of the treaties in the 1980s, Kirthisingha (1983).

[184] UNCTAD (2016), p. 2.

[185] Cf. UNCTAD (2016), p. 2. In this respect see also the IGF, which is convened in the framework of UNCTAD, cf. already Sect. 4.2.2.2.1.1 above.

[186] Cf. Sect. 5.2.1.1.1 above.

refer to the challenge of diversifying commodity-dependent economies, and building an equitable, sustainable world trade system.

5.2.1.2.3 ICAs *sensu stricto*

With regard to ICAs *sensu stricto*—the object of examination in this section—, this comprehensive perspective constitutes the exception rather than the general rule.

5.2.1.2.3.1 Agreements with a Narrow Scope

Most ICAs *sensu stricto* exhibit a rather *narrow* scope in the sense that they are regulating specific, clearly delimited factual scenarios. They are frequently intended to serve a clear-cut, somewhat 'singular' purpose—as opposed to other 'comprehensive' instruments, which are seeking to reconcile and balance multiple competing interests.[187] Instead of addressing a sector in aggregate, many ICAs *sensu stricto* are regulating a specific element of commodity activity, often exclusively in a particular geographic *location*, or particular uses or effects of a specific commodity. In other words, they typically cover some *aspects* of GCG, but are not intended to remedy its various policy trade-offs.

For instance, the OPEC statute essentially serves to establish a producer cartel for petroleum. According to its Article 2(a), its 'principle aim' lies in

> the coordination and unification of the petroleum policies of Member Countries and the determination of the best means for safeguarding their interests, individually and collectively.

While it also mentions the interest of consuming nations to obtain 'an efficient, economic and regular supply of petroleum', according to Article 2(c) OPEC statute, membership is generally only open to countries 'with a substantial net export of crude petroleum, which ha[ve] fundamentally similar interests to those of [the other members]', according to Article 7(c) OPEC statute. The OPEC statute does not dispose of mechanisms for balancing competing consumer and producer interests or promoting international cooperation beyond the membership of the cartel and thus exhibits a rather narrow focus.

Another field, which has already been discussed in our account of the substance of TCL above and is dominated by ICAs *sensu stricto*, is the one of *joint development* of commodity deposits, particularly hydrocarbon fields.[188] Corresponding joint development agreements seek to regulate the conditions under which the exploitation of the respective areas takes place. They generally serve the purpose of balancing the interests of two producers, which both dispose of sovereign rights

---

[187] Often, one will perceive the latter kind of instruments as assuming somewhat more of a '*big picture*' perspective, whereas the former kind is occupied with one *detail* of the overall picture—which in our case, of course, is GCG.

[188] See Sect. 4.2.2.1.4.1 above.

over the deposit in question. Their function thus lies in establishing an equitable exploitation scheme between those stakeholders, only rarely and if so, peripherally touching upon other interests at stake, such as environmental protection. However, especially more recent 'model III'-type agreements tend to also address environmental concerns. With increased awareness of the need to balance commodity policy trade-offs, i.e. further proliferation of the objectives and concepts associated with Global Commodity Governance (GCG), the negotiation and conclusion of such agreements will provide opportunities to include commodity-directed standards and therefore develop the TCL framework further.[189]

Furthermore, three ICAs *sensu stricto* are providing the regulatory framework for the civil liability of ship owners in the case of oil pollution.[190] According to Article 3(1) of the International Convention on Civil Liability for Oil Pollution Damage (CPC), as a general rule

> the owner of a ship at the time of an incident [. . .] shall be liable for any pollution damage caused by oil which has escaped or been discharged from the ship as a result of the incident.

The rest of the convention is essentially dedicated to the implementation of this general rule, including i.a. respective exceptions. The 1992 Fund Convention supplements the compensation scheme provided by the CPC.[191] The International Convention on Oil Pollution Preparedness, Response and Cooperation (OPRC) according to its Article 1(1) requires members 'to take all appropriate measures [. . .] to prepare for and respond to an oil pollution incident.' The function of these agreements therefore lies in implementing a compensation mechanism for oil spill incidents.

Moreover, the Minamata Convention on Mercury puts in place a legal framework for the protection of 'human health and the environment from anthropogenic emissions and releases of mercury and mercury compounds', according to its Article 1, and for that purpose addresses i.a. both mining of mercury ores, such as cinnabar, as well as particularly the usage of mercury in artisanal and small-scale gold mining.[192] According to its Article 3(3), the convention implements an effective ban on all new primary mercury mining projects that had not been commenced prior to the date of entry into force of the agreement. Similarly to ICAs *sensu originali*, it therefore addresses several mercury-related aspects. However, it does not touch upon potentially opposing interests of e.g. consumers and producers, but instead gives effect to measures intended to contain harmful consequences of mercury use, thus balancing environmental protection and economic objectives.

---

[189] Cf. Ong (2003), p. 141; Sect. 4.2.2.1.4.1 above.

[190] Given that the conventions apply to shipping, one could also argue that they rather constitute indirect TCL, and thus ICAs *sensu lato* rather than *stricto*. However, since they are particularly addressing *oil* pollution, it appears valid to classify them as ICAs *sensu stricto*.

[191] IOPC Funds (2019) 1992 Fund convention, https://www.iopcfunds.org/about-us/legal-framework/1992-fund-convention-and-supplementary-fund-protocol/ (last accessed 14 May 2021).

[192] Cf. Espa and Oehl (2018), p. 9.

In addition, ICAs *sensu stricto* regulate working conditions in several commodity sectors. While naturally ILO conventions are concerned with regulating labour, some of them are explicitly directed at commodity activities. This is the case i.a. for ILO Convention 110 concerning Conditions of Employment of Plantation Workers; ILO Convention 176 concerning Safety and Health in Mines; ILO Convention 184 concerning Safety and Health in Agriculture; and ILO Convention 188 concerning Work in the Fishing Sector.[193] All of the agreements are addressing specific risks associated with the respective activities, including e.g. preventive and protective measures at mine sites; engagement and recruitment of migrant workers in the plantation sector; machinery safety and ergonomics in agriculture; and minimum requirements for work on board fishing vessels.

Further examples of ICAs *sensu stricto* with a 'narrow' scope include the presumably great number of bilateral commodity agreements (BCAs).[194] BCAs can for instance regulate trade, investment, or other cooperation parameters between two countries with regard to a specific commodity or sector.[195] One particular kind are the commodity partnership agreements, which Germany concluded with Kazakhstan, Mongolia, and Peru.[196] These agreements are intended to foster

---

[193] Also several other ILO Conventions appear to qualify as ICAs *sensu stricto*, e.g. ILO (1965) Convention 124—Medical Examination of Young Persons (Underground Work); ILO (1969) Convention 129—Labour Inspection (Agriculture), ILO (2019) List of instruments, https://www.ilo.org/dyn/normlex/en/f?p=1000:12030:::NO (last accessed 14 May 2021); yet, it would go beyond the scope of this monograph to address all of them in more detail.

[194] Examples for BCAs include so-called voluntary partnership agreements, which the EU concludes with timber exporting developing countries, EUFLEGT (2019) What is a VPA, http://www.euflegt.efi.int/what-is-a-vpa; cf. also e.g. the 2006 Softwood Lumber Agreement between the US and Canada, which expired on 12 October 2015, Global Affairs Canada (2019) Softwood Lumber, https://www.international.gc.ca/controls-controles/softwood-bois_oeuvre/index.aspx?lang=eng.
On the numerous agreements that China has concluded with particularly resource-rich African countries Shi (2016), pp. 271–273; cf. e.g. the 2008 'Convention de Collaboration', which was concluded between China and the DRC in implementation of the 'Sicomines' deal, Landry (2018), p. 10; full text available at http://congomines.org/system/attachments/assets/000/000/276/original/B5bis-Sicomines-Convention-Incl-Anx-2008-Consortium-Entreprises-Chinoises-RDC.pdf?1430928308 (all last accessed 14 May 2021).

[195] Also the joint development agreements mentioned above qualify as such, provided they are being concluded between two state parties.

[196] BMWi (2012) Abkommen zwischen der Regierung der Bundesrepublik Deutschland und der Regierung der Republik Kasachstan über Partnerschaft im Rohstoff-, Industrie- und Technologiebereich https://www.bmwi.de/Redaktion/DE/Downloads/A/abkommen-zwischenbrd-und-kasachstan-partnerschaft-rohstoff-industrie-und-technologiebereich.pdf?__blob=publicationFile&v=1; BMWi (2011) Abkommen zwischen der Regierung der Bundesrepublik Deutschland und der Regierung der Mongolei über Zusammenarbeit im Rohstoff-, Industrie- und Technologiebereich, https://www.bmwi.de/Redaktion/DE/Downloads/A/abkommen-zwischen-brd-und-mongolei-zusammenarbeit-rohstoff-industrie-technologie.pdf?__blob=publicationFile&v=1; BMWi (2014) Abkommen zwischen der Regierung der Bundesrepublik Deutschland und der Regierung der Republik Peru über Zusammenarbeit im Rohstoff-, Industrie- und Technologiebereich, https://www.bmwi.de/Redaktion/DE/Downloads/A/abkommen-zwischen-brd-und-peru-partnerschaft-rohstoff-industrie-und-technologiebereich.

technical cooperation between Germany and its partners and to particularly facilitate investments and the overall conduct of commodity projects, which involve German businesses.[197] While applicable to commodities in general, these German commodity partnership agreements were concluded not least under the impression of Chinese export restrictions on i.a. Rare Earths.[198] Similarly to ICAs *sensu originali*, these agreements are emphasising both consumer interests, i.a. supply security, as well as producer interests, i.a. diversifying the national economy; yet they do entail very broad and 'soft' substantive obligations.[199]

5.2.1.2.3.2 Broader Scope

Naturally, the degree to which ICAs *sensu stricto* exhibit a 'narrow scope' in the sense delineated above differs.

For example, the Convention on the Regulation of Antarctic Mineral Resource Activities (CRAMRA) aims to ensure that mineral resource activities are conducted in a manner that does not significantly harm the environment, according to Article 4(2) CRAMRA.[200] In that interest, and 'to ensure that Antarctica shall continue forever to be used exclusively for peaceful purposes and shall not become the scene or object of international discord', according to Article 2(1) CRAMRA, the convention implements a procedure for adopting so-called Management Schemes, which are applicable to respective 'blocks' in which mineral commodity deposits are detected.[201] With its focus on especially environmental protection, CRAMRA thus exhibits a focus, which is broader than e.g. the one of the OPEC statute or typical joint development agreements. Yet, it still exhibits a narrow scope in the sense that it provides a tailor-made exploitation scheme for specific commodities in a delimited geographic location.[202]

Similarly to CRAMRA, the United Nations Convention on the Law of the Sea (UNCLOS) 'provides a specific regime for the sourcing of mineral commodities that

---

pdf?__blob=publicationFile&v=6. Additional arrangements, i.a. based on memoranda of understanding and mail correspondence, exist with Chile, Australia and Canada, BMWi (2019) Rohstoffe und Ressourcen, https://www.bmwi.de/Redaktion/DE/Dossier/rohstoffe-und-ressourcen.html (all last accessed 14 May 2021).

[197] Nowrot (2013), p. 11.

[198] See Nowrot (2013), pp. 7–8.

[199] Preamble, Germany-Kazakhstan commodity partnership agreement; Nowrot (2013), p. 22. Rüttinger and Scholl (2017), p. 31 suggest that the German commodity partnership agreements could serve as an effective basis to actively promote environmental and social standards in the mining sector.

[200] See already Espa and Oehl (2018), p. 8.

[201] Cf. Espa and Oehl (2018), p. 8. Moreover, see CRAMRA's institutional structure as set forth in Articles 18–36, as well as its norms covering the exploration regime, Articles 39–52.

[202] Yet, since none of the 19 states that signed the CRAMRA eventually ratified the agreement, it has never entered into force. Instead, the states concerned adopted the Protocol on Environmental Protection to the Antarctic Treaty in 1998, Espa and Oehl (2018), p. 8, n 30.

occur on the seabed.'[203] Yet, as reflected in Articles 150 UNCLOS, it differs from CRAMRA in that requires that all activities

> be carried out in such a manner as to foster healthy development of the world economy and balanced growth of international trade, and to promote international cooperation for the over-all development of all countries...

Subsequently, it overtly seeks 'to strike a balance between onshore producers and consumers of the minerals sourced in the Area.'[204] While serving the clear-cut purpose of regulating commodity exploitation in the Area, Part XI thus explicitly addresses potential policy trade-offs not only between different producers, but also between producers and consumers. This perspective resembles the comprehensive one of ICAs *sensu originali*. However, PART XI of the UNCLOS is of rather historical significance for legal analysis today since it has been replaced by Section 6 of the corresponding Implementation Agreement.[205] The latter bases commodity exploitation in the Area on principles of the General Agreement on Tariffs and Trade (GATT) and other WTO disciplines,[206] thus subjecting it mostly to rules stemming from indirect TCL.

5.2.1.2.3.3 Comprehensive Scope

However, some ICAs *sensu stricto* also exhibit a more comprehensive approach to tackling commodity governance. Where they do, they often provide guidance on how to balance at least some of the five major interests associated with commodity activity.[207]

The perhaps most elaborate guidance on what constitutes sustainable use to date has emerged in the context of biodiversity conservation with regard to genetic resources. The Convention on Biological Diversity (CBD) is intended to foster the sustainable use of such resources, as well as 'the fair and equitable sharing of the benefits out of [their] utilization', according to Article 1 CBD. In this connection, the CBD seeks to strike a balance between developing and industrialised states by

---

[203] Espa and Oehl (2018), p. 8.

[204] Espa and Oehl (2018), who also point to Article 151(1)(a) UNCLOS in this context, which reads: 'Without prejudice to the objectives set forth in article 150 and for the purpose of implementing subparagraph (h) of that article, the Authority, acting through existing forums or such new arrangements or agreements as may be appropriate, in which all interested parties, including both producers and consumers, participate, shall take measures necessary to promote the growth, efficiency and stability of markets for those commodities produced from the minerals derived from the Area, at prices remunerative to producers and fair to consumers. All States Parties shall cooperate to this end.'

[205] UN treaty collection (1982) Agreement relating to the implementation of Part XI of the United Nations Convention on the Law of the Sea of 10 December 1982, https://treaties.un.org/doc/Treaties/1994/11/19941116%2006-01%20AM/Ch_XXI_06a_p.pdf (last accessed 14 May 2021).

[206] Espa and Oehl (2018), p. 8; Desta (2010), para. 39.

[207] On the latter, see Sect. 2.1.3 above.

addressing issues of technology transfer; right to access; national conservation; cooperation; and financing.[208]

More detailed guidance on how to enhance sustainable use of biodiversity is provided by the 2004 Addis Ababa Principles and Guidelines for the Sustainable Use of Biodiversity (AAPG). According to its *14 practical principles*, the AAPG i.a. guide states to maintain and link supportive laws, institutions, and policies at all governance levels (principle #1);[209] practice adaptive management based on science as well as traditional and local knowledge (principle #4(a));[210] and that, as a general rule,

> costs of management and conservation of biological diversity should be internalized within the area of management and reflected in the distribution of the benefits from the use (principle #13).[211]

Specific guidance on how benefit sharing shall be implemented, is provided by the Bonn Guidelines as well as the Nagoya Protocol.[212] Regarding plant genetic resources for food and agriculture, the FAO has i.a. put in place a multilateral system of access and benefit sharing, according to Article 10 of its International Treaty on Plant Genetic Resources for Food and Agriculture (ITPGR).[213] According to Article 12.4 ITPGR, 'facilitated access' to resources shall be provided on the basis of a 'standard material transfer agreement'. According to Article 13.2 ITPGR, benefits from the use of plant genetic resources shall be shared through the 'mechanisms' of information exchange, technology transfer, capacity building, and the 'sharing of benefits arising from commercialization'. The latter generally shall be paid to a respective 'Trust Account', according to Articles 13.2(d)(ii), 19.3(f) ITPGR.

Moreover, particularly two regional conventions aimed at the conservation of nature and natural resources are touching upon rules on how to remedy potential use conflicts and corresponding commodity policy trade-offs.

While the ASEAN Agreement on the Conservation of Nature and Natural Resources (ACNR) naturally focuses on conservation, it nevertheless exhibits a comprehensive scope as well as a 'balanced' design in view of the broad scope of measures it addresses.[214] According to its Article 1(1), members shall i.a.

---

[208] Cf. Beyerlin and Grote Stoutenberg (2012), para. 45.

[209] Secretariat of the CBD (2004), p. 8.

[210] Secretariat of the CBD (2004), p. 11.

[211] Secretariat of the CBD (2004), p. 20.

[212] Secretariat of the CBD (2002); Secretariat of the CBD (2011); on the current status of the benefit-sharing principle, cf. Cabrera Medaglia and Perron-Welch (2018a, b).

[213] FAO (2009).

[214] ASEAN (1985) ACNR, http://environment.asean.org/agreement-on-the-conservation-of-nature-and-natural-resources/ (last accessed 14 May 2021). The ACNR i.a. sets forth specific requirements for endangered and endemic species (Article 5 ACNR); vegetation cover and forest resources (Article 6 ACNR); soil (Article 7 ACNR); water (Article 8 ACNR); and air (Article 9 ACNR). According to Article 10 ACNR, states shall 'wherever possible [...] prevent, reduce and control degradation of the natural environment', i.a. by controlling the use of chemicals in agriculture (Article 10(a) ACNR); promoting pollution control (Article 10(b) ACNR); and by considering 'the

ensure the sustainable utilization of harvested natural resources under their jurisdiction in accordance with scientific principles and with a view to attaining the goal of sustainable development.

For this purpose, the parties shall develop and coordinate their national conservation strategies, according to Article 1(2) ACNR. Moreover, according to Article 2(1) ACNR, the conservation and management of NR shall be 'treated as an integral part of development planning', which relates to social, ecological and economic factors, according to Article 2(2) ACNR. According to Article 3(1) ACNR, members are held to 'maintain maximum genetic diversity'.

In addition, members 'shall endeavour to' develop and implement resource management plans fostering the sustainable use of the resources in question, according to Article 4(1) ACNR. This requirement is being spelled out in further detail, i.a. demanding states to prevent decrease of the harvested species below levels, which are required for its 'stable recruitment', according to Article 4(1) (a) ACNR; maintain 'the ecological relationship between harvested, dependent and related populations of living resources of the ecosystem considered', according to Article 4(1)(b) ACNR; and to prevent alterations to the ecosystem, which are 'not reversible over a reasonable period of time', according to Article 4(1)(d) ACNR. Moreover, activities causing 'local distinction' or 'serious disturbance' of species prohibited, according to Article 4(2)(c) ACNR.

Exhibiting several similar provisions to the ACNR, also the African Convention on the Conservation of Nature and Natural Resources (AfCNR; 'Maputo convention') comprehensively tackles the challenges of sustainably developing NR, e.g. expressly according to its Article XIV.[215] Going beyond the scope of the ACNR, the AfCNR also addresses challenges related to commodity activity with regard to military activities (Article XV AfCNR); procedural rights, i.a. with regard to dissemination of and access to environmental information (Article XVI AfCNR); traditional rights of local communities and indigenous knowledge (Article XVII AfCNR); technology transfer (Article XIX AfCNR); and capacity building (Article XX AfCNR).

---

originator of the activity which may lead to environmental degradation responsible for its prevention, reduction and control as well as [...] rehabilitation and remedial measures required' (Article 10(d) ACNR). The Convention also addresses i.a. the prevention of pollution discharges (Article 11 ACNR); land use planning (Article 12 ACNR); protected areas (Article 13 ACNR); shared resources (Article 19 ACNR); and transfrontier environmental effects (Article 20 ACNR). It shall be noted, however, that the ACNR has not yet entered into force, Beyerlin and Grote Stoutenberg (2013), para. 42; Ecolex (2019) ACNR, https://www.ecolex.org/details/asean-agreement-on-the-conservation-of-nature-and-natural-resources-tre-000820/participants/?   (last   accessed 14 May 2021).

[215] AU (2014) Revised AfCNR, https://au.int/en/treaties/african-convention-conservation-nature-and-natural-resources-revised-version (last accessed 14 May 2021). At the time of writing, the convention had been ratified by 17 member states of the AU (2019) List of countries, https://au.int/sites/default/files/treaties/7782-sl-revised_african_convention_on_the_conservation_of_nature_and_natural_resources.pdf (last accessed 14 May 2021).

The Southern African Development Community (SADC) has elaborated further regional guidance on how to balance commodity interests in individual sectors, namely mining and forestry. The SADC Protocol on Mining (SADCPM) seeks to generally foster 'a thriving mining sector' as a means to promote economic development, alleviate poverty and generally raise the living standard in the region, according to Article 2(1).[216] For that purpose, member states i.a. engage in information sharing (Article 3 SADCPM), enhancing their technological capacities (Article 4 SADCPM), developing common standards (Article 5 SADCPM), promoting private sector participation (Article 6 SADCPM), as well as promoting small-scale mining (Article 7 SADCPM) and occupational health and safety (Article 9 SADCPM). Moreover, according to Article 8(1) SADCPM members

> shall promote sustainable development by ensuring that a balance between mineral development and environmental protection is attained.[217]

With regard to the forestry sector, the SADC Protocol on Forestry (SADCPF) shall 'promote the development, conservation, sustainable management and utilisation of all types of forests and trees', according to its Article 3(1)(a). Article 4 SADCPF sets forth various 'guiding principles', which reflect core norms of TCL, i.a. the duty to cooperate, PSNR, the no harm rule, public participation, as well as the benefit sharing principle. Further issues and commodity governance challenges include tenure and ownership (Article 5 SADCPF); the establishment of a regional database (Article 10 SADCPF); community-based forest management (Article 12 SADCPF); participation of women in forest management (Article 13 SADCPF); traditional forest-related knowledge (Article 16 SADCPF); industry, trade and investment (Article 18 SADCPF); and capacity-building as well as public awareness (Article 19 SADCPF).

Moreover, describing a rather recent development, several EU Free Trade Agreements (FTAs) that have been concluded since 2016 provide commodity-directed contents. Besides the fact that these agreements now routinely appear to include so-called 'trade and SD' chapters,[218] especially agreements, which have been concluded or negotiated in 2018 and 2019, moreover address issues of biodiversity, as well as sustainable forest and fisheries management.[219] In addition, these recent agreements seek to promote the integration of various norm subsets of TCL, i.a. by explicitly confirming commitments under multilateral labour as well as

---

[216]The 1997 SADCPM arguably constitutes one of the normative foundations of the 2009 AMV, which has already featured in Sect. 4.2.2.2.1.1 above. See also ZIMCODD (2017), p. 6, which recommends 'SADC countries to fully domesticate the AMV and SADC Mining Protocol through policy and legislative reforms'.

[217]In that connection, member states are also called upon to encourage regional approaches to EIAs, especially when it comes to potential cross-border environmental harm, according to Article 8(2) SADCPM.

[218]Cf. Sect. 4.3.1.2 above, n 457.

[219]See Articles 12.7, 12.8 EU-Singapore FTA; Articles 16.6, 16.7, and 16.8 EU-Japan FTA; Articles 13.7, 13.8, 13.9 EU-Vietnam FTA.

environmental agreements in the context of trade.[220] Furthermore, several recent EU FTAs establish so-called committees on trade and SD, which are i.a. tasked with reviewing the implementation of the agreement's corresponding chapter.[221] The respective reports that these 'sustainability committees' are going to produce, may over time bring about further guidance on how to integrate the three pillars of SD in the context of commodity activity.[222]

5.2.1.2.3.4   Interim Conclusion

As this brief survey has demonstrated, many ICAs *sensu stricto* do *not* address commodity policy trade-offs or questions of how to foster the SD of commodity sectors. Instead, they are frequently designed for clear-cut purposes, such as the joint development of commodity deposits, the civil liability of corporations for oil pollution, or establishing fair and safe working conditions in specific commodity sectors. While some areas exhibit quite a concentrated form of regulation through ICAs *sensu stricto*, other agreements are 'scattered' across a variety of factual scenarios, such as the bilateral German commodity partnerships, or CRAMRA.

However, a number of instruments also seek to address challenges related to commodity governance more comprehensively. Examples include the Convention on Biological Diversity (CBD) and related guidance, the ASEAN Agreement on the Conservation of Nature and Natural Resources (ACNR) and African Convention on the Conservation of Nature and Natural Resources (AfCNR), as well as the Southern African Development Community (SADC) protocols. The ACNR for instance reconciles various aspects of commodity governance in one agreement, including biodiversity, sustainable use, and shared resources. Yet, being especially concerned with *conservation*, it does neither touch upon Human Rights nor aspects of trade or international investment.[223] While the AfCNR expands further, i.a. touching upon traditional and indigenous peoples' as well as procedural rights, it likewise does not integrate said elements of TCL. Nevertheless, these regional examples describe potential avenues towards creating more comprehensive legal instruments regulating commodity activities. In fact, it is this approach that recent EU FTAs, which now increasingly include commodity-directed contents in their respective trade and SD chapters, i.a. touching upon sustainable forest and fisheries management, mirror to a certain degree.

---

[220] See i.a. Articles 12.4, 12.6 EU-Singapore FTA; 16.3, 16.4 EU-Japan FTA; Articles 13.4, 13.5, 13.6 EU-Vietnam FTA; cf. also Gehring et al. (2018), p. 21.

[221] Cf. Sect. 4.3.1.2 above, n 457.

[222] As such, the committees on trade and SD appear to be considerably well-suited to develop parameters for the continuous elaboration of the TCL framework.

[223] The same appears to be true for the current draft of the 'Agreement under the United Nations Convention on the Law of the Sea on the conservation and sustainable use of marine biological diversity of areas beyond national jurisdiction' (BBNJ agreement), UN (2019) Draft text of the agreement, https://undocs.org/a/conf.232/2019/6 (last accessed 14 May 2021).

5.2.1.3   Some Reflections on ICAs *sensu lato*

ICAs *sensu lato* constitute indirect Transnational Commodity Law (TCL), i.e. they are not commodity-directed. This category of commodity agreements includes a wide spectrum of multilateral conventions on the environment, trade, HR, and other subjects. Concrete examples are those, which we have analysed in more detail above, as for instance the International Bill of Human Rights, or the GATT, to name but a few prominent instruments. Also Regional and Bilateral Trade Agreements, such as the Comprehensive and Progressive Agreement for Trans-Pacific Partnership (CPTPP) or the Comprehensive Economic and Trade Agreement (CETA), Preferential Trade Agreements, such as the Cotonou Agreement, Bilateral Investment Treaties, or technical cooperation agreements substantially impact commodity governance and therefore constitute ICAs *sensu lato*.[224] Recalling our broad definition of ICAs *sensu lato* as 'any international agreement that exhibits a substantial regulatory impact on commodity activity, yet without having been explicitly directed at or designed for that purpose', it becomes clear that most of these agreements already featured in our account of TCL in Chaps. 3 and 4 above. Therefore, only a few reflections on the relationship between these agreements and ICAs *sensu originali* and *stricto* respectively shall be shared in brief.

First, ICAs *sensu originali*, *stricto* and *lato* exist largely *in parallel*, meaning that there is typically no or only limited normative interaction between the different instruments. While some agreements may be referring to others, no concrete legal effects usually accompany these references.[225] Despite the fact that many ICAs *sensu lato* are pursuing similar, if not identical objectives, especially fostering the sustainable development (SD) of a specific region, country, or sector,[226] their primary non-commodity-directed purpose is what distinguishes them from ICAs *sensu stricto*. As we have discussed above, this creates an incoherent framework, which, however, may be effectively tied together under SD as the overall regulatory objective of TCL.

Second, while the body of ICAs *sensu lato* is certainly considerably large, one can still identify instruments, which are of greater importance for the framework of TCL than others. First and foremost, one in this connection of course has to refer to

---

[224]Given that some of these agreements contain commodity-directed provisions, such as the Bilateral Dialogue on Raw Materials, which is being established according to Article 25.4 CETA, or the sustainable forest management provisions contained in Articles 13.8 EU-Vietnam FTA and 12.7 EU-Singapore FTA respectively, it is not always evident to qualify them as either ICAs *sensu lato* or *sensu stricto*. In fact, examples of commodity-directed provisions can be found here and there in various ICAs *sensu lato*, which are thus delineating a sort of 'commodity-directed patchwork', as e.g. reflected in the respective GATT provisions, cf. Sects. 4.2.2.1.4.2 and 4.3.2 above as well as shortly below.

[225]On the few incidents in which they do, see already Sect. 4.2.3 above.

[226]In this respect, see especially the EU-ACP agreements, cf. Weiss (2009), para. 25; on SD provisions in recent EU FTAs, see already Sect. 4.3.1.2 above; generally, on EU development cooperation, Oehl (2018a).

the International Bill of HR. One field, however, which exhibits the greatest degree of consistency is international labour law. Particularly the eight 'fundamental conventions' are being referred to in international agreements, standards, and guidelines across the entire field of TCL, be they of intergovernmental or private nature. Naturally also the multilateral environmental conventions and the established principles of international environmental law, which they embody, are playing a key role. The same holds true for the GATT. Integrating these standards with one another under the 'roof' of the regulatory objective of SD certainly remains a central challenge.[227]

Third, apart from the question what instruments currently are of the greatest significance for TCL and the regulation of commodity activity, one can also distinguish between different ICAs *sensu lato* according to how *close* they are to commodity activity. *Closeness* in this connection can arise either from the *factual scenarios* the agreements are designed to govern or their *normative contents*. Naturally, in many cases both will coincide.

For instance, the Convention on the Law of the Non-navigational Uses of International Watercourses (New York Convention) in view of the many commodity-related uses of watercourses as well as potential corresponding damage will regularly be concerned with commodity activity. Non-navigational uses of watercourses are *factually* close to commodity activities. Given that commodities represent a share of roughly 25% of international goods trade,[228] the same holds true for the GATT. Yet, the latter also contains several commodity-directed provisions as we have seen above. Therefore, the GATT is also *normatively* close to commodity activity, albeit not qualifying as an ICA *sensu stricto*.[229] Likewise, also the International Bill of Human Rights in the form of the right to freely dispose over natural resources (RFD) contains a central commodity-directed provision. Given the many forms and dimensions of commodity activity that Human Rights cover, it also appears fair to speak of 'closeness' in this respect.

The Energy Charter Treaty (ECT), and the emerging field of international energy law in general,[230] exhibit significant overlaps with TCL in both respects. This is mostly due to the *fact* that most energy worldwide is still being produced through so-called combustibles, especially oil, gas, coal, or fuel wood, which of course are commodities; also nuclear energy relies on the commodities uranium or plutonium, renewable energy technologies require i.a. Rare Earth Elements and several other minerals, including lithium and cobalt.[231] How closely related these emerging legal

---

[227] On this challenge, see already Sect. 5.1.2 above. See Chi (2017) with regard to international investment law; also, Hilpold (2011) and Bartels (2013) with regard to HR and WTO law; on the related—or perhaps rather preceding—debate on the general *fragmentation* of international law, Koskenniemi and Leino (2002).

[228] WTO (2018), p. 42. According to WTO estimates, fuels and mining products accounted for 15%, agricultural products for 10% of world merchandise exports in 2017, ibid.

[229] On the blurred boundaries between these categories, see already n 224 above.

[230] Viñuales (2013).

[231] Cf. Espa and Oehl (2018), p. 6.

fields are also with regard to their *normative* frameworks, is i.a. reflected in Article 1(4) and the corresponding annex EM of the Energy Charter Treaty (ECT), which define 'Energy Materials and Products'. The list almost exclusively includes commodities, notably except i.a. electrical energy itself. Article 18(1) ECT reaffirms the permanent sovereignty of member states over *energy* resources. According to Article 18(3) ECT, each state shall

> continue[] to hold [...] rights to decide the geographical areas within its Area to be made available for exploration and development of its energy resources, the optimalization of their recovery and the rate at which they may be depleted or otherwise exploited, to specify and enjoy any taxes, royalties or other financial payments payable by virtue of such exploration and exploitation, and to regulate the environmental and safety aspects of such exploration, development and reclamation within its Area, and to participate in such exploration and exploitation, inter alia, through direct participation by the government or through state enterprises.

Furthermore, according to Article 18(4) ECT, the parties

> undertake to facilitate access to energy resources, inter alia, by allocating in a non-discriminatory manner on the basis of published criteria authorizations, licences, concessions and contracts to prospect and explore for or to exploit or extract energy resources.

Both provisions essentially cover issues of commodity governance. For what end uses commodities are being exploited, whether it is used for energy or non-energy purposes, naturally does not impact challenges that are associated with the *removal of an item from earth*.[232] Thus, from the perspective of international legal scholarship, it would make little sense to conceptualise a field of international energy law without doing the same for commodity activity. Whereas the latter should be confined to the 'removal activity' and associated activities along the commodity value chain, international energy law would cover all uses of commodities, which serve the purpose of energy generation.

Nevertheless, according to the parameters we have established above, the ECT does *not* constitute an ICA *sensu stricto*, but an ICA *sensu lato*. This is because—apart from a few provisions—it is not *explicitly* directed at commodities. Instead, commodity activity here is being observed from the prism of energy activity—commodity extraction as the necessary precondition of the generation, trade and sale of electrical energy. While one may read the provisions in Article 18 ECT as reflecting a 'conscious consideration' of the specificities of commodity activity, it more precisely rather appears to be an expression of the great overlap of energy and commodity activity. This distinction is important, since from the 'energy perspective' one may arrive at different normative judgments than from the 'commodity perspective'. The focus on the end use of energy generation could for instance lead to the extraction aspect being seen as rather a 'prefix'. Therefore, one may e.g. overly emphasise the perspective of energy consumers over the one of energy commodity producers. However, naturally the differences here may prove to be nuances. Yet, the example of the ECT and emerging international energy law ultimately

---

[232] Cf. Sect. 3.2.2.1 above.

demonstrates that conceptualising TCL is an obvious step towards elaborating an effective legal framework for GCG.

Examples of agreements exhibiting a lesser degree of closeness to commodity activity are Additional Protocols I and II to the Geneva Convention, despite their commodity-directed provisions. This is due to the fact that—at least ideally—armed conflict constitutes an abnormal situation for commodity activity to occur. Consequently, they also constitute ICAs *sensu lato*. The more 'remotely' agreements operate from commodity activities, the more likely they will constitute ICAs *sensu latissimo*.

5.2.1.4 Interim Conclusion: Relevance of Current ICAs for GCG

To conclude, we can ascertain that the relevance of International Commodity Agreements (ICAs) *sensu originali* for Global Commodity Governance (GCG) today is very limited. Albeit displaying a comprehensive approach, tackling an entire sector and seeking to foster sustainable development (SD), their objectives are not being pursued with significant 'bite' due to a lack of corresponding substantive obligations. ICAs *sensu stricto*, to the contrary, often exhibit a narrow scope, which is focused on a clear-cut, somewhat 'singular' objective. As such, they may quite intensively regulate some specific activities associated with commodity operations in some specific sectors, such as oil spill incidents or timber trade between two parties. While some regional instruments, such as the ASEAN Agreement on the Conservation of Nature and Natural Resources (ACNR), African Convention on the Conservation of Nature and Natural Resources (AfCNR) and the Southern African Development Community (SADC) protocols, address challenges of GCG more comprehensively and recent EU Free Trade Agreements (FTAs) demonstrate a trend to consciously consider specificities of commodity activity, there are only considerably few ICAs *sensu stricto* that provide guidance on how to balance commodity interests. Where they do, these provisions are often rather aspirational or soft and rarely entail concrete obligations.

This status quo basically describes a scenario, in which commodity activities are only in few instances covered by law reflecting a 'conscious consideration' for corresponding regulatory challenges, i.e. by direct Transnational Commodity Law (TCL). Consequently, at present ICAs *sensu lato* clearly are of the greatest significance for GCG. As repeatedly discussed throughout this book, the fact that these agreements have been designed for regulatory objectives, which are not explicitly targeting commodities, leaves behind an incoherent transnational legal framework.[233] As a result, there is close to no guidance with legally binding value, which addresses states' decision to extract and concretises, what sustainable use requires.

---

[233] Cf. i.a. Sects. 4.2.1 and 5.1 above.

5.2.2 ICAs De Lege Ferenda

To the close of this book, the following section shall provide an outlook on potential future ICAs, which could help remedy the current deficits of the legal framework of TCL.[234] Generally speaking, ICAs *de lege ferenda* shall serve to transform the obligations that apply to commodity activities under the various legal instruments into commodity-directed tools. ICAs *de lege ferenda* extract those provisions, which are relevant in a commodity context, from ICAs *sensu lato* and incorporate them in a comprehensive ICA *sensu stricto*. In addition, they include those best practices, which have emerged from transnational standard setting.

This leads to the following central functions of ICAs *de lege ferenda*: First, they codify balancing norms and thus specify what sustainable use means (Sect. 5.2.2.1). Second, they define SD as their object and purpose (Sect. 5.2.2.2). Third, they reinforce the rule of law in the commodity sector and promote international equity (Sect. 5.2.2.3). The section closes with some reflections on formal questions regarding the design of ICAs *de lege ferenda* (Sect. 5.2.2.4), before illustrating how all of these functions ultimately promote a functional, sustainable commodity sector and therefore SD in general (Sect. 5.2.2.5).

5.2.2.1 ICAs as Instruments Codifying Balancing Norms

ICAs *de lege ferenda* can serve to specify what the sustainable use principle, as the central balancing norm of TCL requires. Fundamentally, it obliges states to balance commodity policy trade-offs in the way, which is most conducive to SD.

5.2.2.1.1 General Idea: Qualifying the Policy Space Available to States

In view of their permanent sovereignty over natural resources (PSNR), states generally dispose of the competence to set the parameters on how they balance the five interests that make up the organisational framework of TCL.[235] However, under an ICA *de lege ferenda* states could establish self-imposed qualifications of their PSNR, which require them to prioritise certain interests in specific scenarios. ICAs *de lege ferenda* could introduce legal rules that effectively coordinate the various

---

[234] On this approach of 'updating' existing ICAs, see already Krajewski (2012); also, Nowrot (2013) on the German commodity partnership agreements as 'new regulatory instruments' (my translation). Wilts and Bleischwitz (2012) propose an International Commodity Covenant, which addresses incomplete global material cycles, i.a. by promoting recycling.

[235] However, from the perspective of commodity policy trade-offs, defining commodity deposits as 'common heritage of humankind' in fact appears to be an approach worth considering. Regardless of such enterprise being politically far from realistic, it could help resolve potential conflicts between global, national, and local SD policies. States are of course at all times free to define all or certain types of commodities as 'common heritage'. On the concept cf. Wolfrum (2009).

interests, which characterise commodity activity, in a way that is most conducive to SD. Thus, states would commit themselves to effectively foster a functional commodity sector.

Balancing the five interests associated with commodity activity requires defining in which scenarios which one of them antecedes the other. Proceeding in this way, the global community could, little by little, define concrete parameters for sustainable commodity activity. These parameters would effectively constitute conflict rules, which could either apply to the 'big picture' of sustainable commodity activity or to individual subsectors alone. Moreover, corresponding parameters could serve to identify those commodity subsectors, which are most critical for SD. They could establish different parameters for different sectors. Yet, ultimately, they would all reflect the ultimate objective of SD.

5.2.2.1.2 Principle of Proportionality

Without unduly restricting the policy space of states, ICAs *de lege ferenda* could specify the balancing requirements, which sustainable commodity use entails, by introducing a principle of proportionality. According to its general rule, all five commodity interests would need to be observed in all decisions of a state, which affect commodity activities, thus particularly its decision(s) to extract as well as the overall design of its legal framework applicable to commodity operations.

Contouring its normative content further, the principle of proportionality would require that the degree to which one or more commodity interests are being neglected in a respective state measure needs to be proportionate to the significance of the other interests, which that very measure is intended to foster. For example, where an individual commodity project requires extensive environmental destruction as well as the relocation of several villages, including an indigenous community, it would only be lawful, where these phenomena are proportionate to the economic gain and/or development benefits it promises.

This obligation to carry out a sophisticated balancing exercise between the five interests associated with commodity activity, would go hand in hand with a transparency obligation: the respective state or government would be required to disclose its concrete considerations, balancing method, as well as reasons for its weighting of the different factors.

Moreover, to further specify what constitutes proportionality, ICAs *de lege ferenda* could define that purely economic objectives constitute subordinate aims to the objective of development.[236] As a consequence, they would carry less weight within the balancing exercise to be performed and would generally only be considered where they serve the social advancement of the respective state's society. This

---

[236]Cf. in this respect also Krajewski (2017), pp. 25–26 who is suggesting a clause, which establishes 'supremacy' of human rights over trade and investment treaties.

step would enhance the dogmatic significance of socio-ecological development in relation to the economic pillar of SD.[237]

5.2.2.1.3 Prevention of Irreversible Effects

The principle of proportionality could be further qualified by a rule, according to which irreversible effects caused by commodity activity—e.g. for the natural environment or human livelihoods—should generally be prevented. Weighting results, which violate this rule, would not be proportionate. The rule would thus set a boundary to a state's margin of discretion in weighing the five commodity interests.

For example, this rule could require states to assess whether or not by means of mine closure measures, a certain area can be sufficiently reinstated after commodity extraction has taken place. Where such is unlikely, the objectives of environmental protection and participation would prevail over economic interests. The same principle could also guide decisions to extract with regard to the threat of climate change. Where overall CO_2 emissions already threaten to cause irreversible effects for planet and human species, a decision to extract a large volume of combustibles may be deemed to be a violation of this rule emanating from SD.

However, irreversible effects—in this case particularly for the human species—may of course also impend with regard to the socio-economic pillars of SD. Where for instance economic turmoil or a famine would result from a decision *not* to extract (or plant), commodity activity may in fact be required under such kind of rule.[238]

5.2.2.1.4 Obligation for States to Detail Terms of Sustainable Use in National Regimes

These rules and principles concretise rather abstractly how the balancing exercise required by the sustainable use principle needs to be performed. Another avenue to specifying what is required to achieve commodity equilibrium lies in detailing the terms of the sustainable use principle. An ICA *de lege ferenda* could *fully integrate* concrete sustainability guidelines and best practices, which states would be obligated to implement within commodity-directed legal regimes of their national frameworks.

Generally speaking, the twelve precepts of the Natural Resource Charter can serve as a signpost regarding what aspects the commodity-directed national regime

---

[237] On 'Mickey Mouse' sustainability, cf. already Sect. 4.3.2 above.

[238] Naturally, a significant share of the effects conducive to SD that this kind of provision would bring about will depend on the respective norm addressee's readiness to take their decisions based on *reason* and available *facts*. Wherever they seek to obscure their actual intentions behind pretended reasoning, it will regularly be difficult to 'convict' them of their doing. Nevertheless, what the provision and SD as a regulatory objective generally achieve, is to set SD as *the* point of reference for really any political decision that one may be deliberating to take. See already Oehl (2019), p. 28.

should address, including rights allocation, tax regime, and the offsetting of environmental and social costs of extraction.[239]

Taking up incidents of balancing norms, which can be found in ICAs *sensu stricto*, the national framework could establish the principle of adaptive management, which is based on science as well as traditional and local knowledge (principle #4(a) of the Addis Ababa Principles and Guidelines for the Sustainable Use of Biodiversity (AAPG)).[240] Moreover, it could provide for the internalisation of the social and ecological costs of commodity activity 'within the area of management' and the reflection of these costs in the 'distribution of the benefits from the use' (principle #13 AAPG).[241] Measures to be reflected in this instance could relate to the pricing in of negative externalities caused by commodity activities, including CO_2 emissions.[242] In line with Article 2(1) of the ASEAN Agreement on the Conservation of Nature and Natural Resources (ACNR), states could be required to treat the conservation and management of NR 'as an integral part of development planning'.

Furthermore, the national system could necessitate the elaboration of resource management plans applicable to individual commodities, as provided for in Article 4(1) ACNR. Going beyond the obligation to prevent irreversible effects of commodity activity, the national framework could require the prevention of alterations to the ecosystem, which are 'not reversible over a reasonable period of time' in line with Article 4(1)(d) ACNR. In addition, an ICA *de lege ferenda* could require states to implement within their national regimes a system of community-based resource development, as suggested by Article 12 of the Southern African Development Community Protocol on Forestry (SADCPF); as well as measures fostering the active participation of women in commodity management (Article 13 SADCPF).

Apart from these general principles, ICAs *de lege ferenda* could obligate states to detail the terms of sustainable use also in the context of individual commodity sectors. For example, with regard to the mining sector, states could be required to demonstrate that they are implementing the IGF Mining Policy Framework and to subject themselves to regular review under the World Bank MInGov tool. In addition, they could be obliged to envisage the mandatory use of the Model Mine Development Agreement (MMDA) in all mining-related investor-state contracts. A respective rule could be designed as follows:

> Article x: States shall take all measures necessary to ensure a sustainable mining sector. For that purpose, they shall implement all standards referred to in annex A in their own acts and policies. With regard to stakeholders referred to in annex B, they shall require by law that their commodity activities be conducted in conformity with the following standards: . . .

It shall be noted here that commodity-directed, comprehensive instruments addressing the mining sector, such as the Berlin II Guidelines, the Intergovernmental Forum on Mining, Minerals, Metals and Sustainable Development (IGF) Mining

---

[239]NRGI (2014), pp. 4, 7–35; on the NRC, cf. already Sect. 2.2.5 above.

[240]Secretariat of the CBD (2004), p. 11.

[241]Secretariat of the CBD (2004), p. 20.

[242]Cf. Nordhaus (2007).

Policy Framework, the Initiative for Responsible Mining Assurance (IRMA) Standard for Responsible Mining IRMA-STD-001, or the MMDA exhibit a remarkable degree of *content coherence*, i.e. coherence with regard to what contents need to be covered in order to sufficiently regulate commodity activities.[243] The Berlin II Guidelines as well as the IGF Mining Policy Framework as instruments addressing states for instance both provide guidance on the domestic regulatory framework, including mining and environmental legislation as well as licensing, environmental management, policy coherence, mine closure, and artisanal and small-scale mining. The IRMA standard and the MMDA share contents such as environmental and social impact assessment, local community development and health, labour standards, and mine closure.

With regard to the oil and gas industry, the national framework could require the elimination of routine flaring during oil production, the identification and reduction of methane emissions in the gas value chain, waste minimisation, and the developing and sharing of scalable sustainability systems.[244] Corporations could be obligated to collaborate with the public and non-profit sector in order to foster the socio-economic development of local communities i.a., through building local workforce capacity, sharing health and safety innovations and fostering healthcare provision by means of developing new applications of e.g. renewable energy technologies.[245] Further best practices have been elaborated in the guidance documents issued by the International Association of Oil and Gas Producers (IOGP) as well as the International Petroleum Industry Environmental Conservation Association (IPIECA).[246]

While portraying sector-specific best practices in more detail lies beyond the scope of this book, an overview of relevant standards is provided in the TCL outline in the annex.

As a side benefit of this obligation for states to detail the terms of sustainable use in their national frameworks, ICAs *de lege ferenda* would help aligning regulation on the global, national, and local levels. They would be setting the standards on the global level, which would subsequently be influencing legislation and regulation on national as well as local levels, ideally leading to harmonisation and coherence. As such, the standards set by ICAs *de lege ferenda* would 'trickle down' to the individual commodity activity at hand. Commodity contracts detailing the terms of the respective activity would be embedded in this aligned framework.[247] Thus, potential power asymmetries between corporate and government actors would have less influence on the negotiated terms given the applicable binding national framework.[248]

---

[243] What they are exhibiting to a considerable lesser extent is *norm coherence*—a quality, which SD defined as the object and purpose of TCL would foster.

[244] Cf. UN GC (2017), p. 9.

[245] UN GC (2017), p. 9.

[246] IOGP (2017); IPIECA (2017).

[247] Cf. NRGI (2014), p. 13.

[248] Cf. AU (2009), pp. 17–18.

For example, states could be required to legally oblige companies under national law to fully integrate the Voluntary Principles on Security and Human Rights for the Extractive and Energy Sectors (VPSHR) in their contracts with private security providers.[249] Moreover, states could be held to collect sufficient technical data in order to gain 'a good understanding of the resource base'.[250] Also, the licensing regime applicable to extractive industries should allow for post-exploration reductions of particular licenses in size in order to ensure that not too large of a share of the resource base falls under one license; and that the state can benefit from potential land value increases following respective commodity discoveries.[251] In terms of the procedure of allocating rights to third parties, the Natural Resource Charter advises states to rely on 'well-designed auctions' rather than 'direct negotiations on a license-by-license basis'.[252]

5.2.2.2 ICAs as Instruments Incorporating SD as Their Object and Purpose

ICAs *de lege ferenda* can contribute significantly to the coherence of the framework of TCL. They can do so especially by incorporating SD as their regulatory objective—and therefore confirming its respective status under the TCL framework overall.

As described above, this would have a twofold effect:[253] For one, all rules contained in the ICA would have to be interpreted in light of SD. For the other, SD would guide international, regional, supranational, and national legislators whenever they are designing rules intended to balance commodity policy trade-offs as part of their commitment to give effect to their obligations under the ICA. Reconciling the various standards, which serve as benchmarks specifying the normative contents of the sustainable use principle, under the 'roof' of the ICA and therefore its regulatory objective of SD would over time foster the coherence of all of TCL. In applying the various obligations, addressees, legislators, and international judges would gradually elaborate an arrangement of the applicable norms, which is most conducive to SD—thus balancing its three (social, environmental and economic) pillars in a commodity context.

---

[249] VPSHR (2000), p. 6.

[250] NRGI (2014), p. 13.

[251] NRGI (2014), p. 13.

[252] NRGI (2014), p. 14. Competitive bidding as part of an auction is however only advised whenever there are more than three competitors; otherwise 'a licensing round with strict minimum technical criteria' should be the procedure of choice, NRGI (2014), p. 14. For further guidance on the design of commodity contracts, see Elaw (2013); Cotula (2010); Mandelbaum et al. (2016); Kienzler et al. (2015); Smaller (2014); CCSI (2019) Guides to land contracts, http://ccsi.columbia.edu/work/projects/guides-to-land-contracts/ (last accessed 14 May 2021); Wilson and Kuszewski (2011); and Gathii (2014).

[253] See already Oehl (2019), pp. 14–15.

5.2.2.3 ICAs as Instruments Reinforcing the Rule of Law in the Commodity Sector

ICAs *de lege ferenda* can reinforce the rule of law in the commodity sector by clarifying, expanding, and aligning it. The first function is as simple as essential. ICAs *de lege ferenda* serve to summarise and confirm commitments of states under TCL. As such, they illustrate that the international community is aware of the vital importance of the commodity sector and the need to establish a coherent legal framework for GCG. In view of the many instruments of TCL, ICAs *de lege ferenda* serve as the 'normative scaffolding', which provides clarity regarding the interplay and application of the TCL framework.

Moreover, ICAs *de lege ferenda* can fill gaps in the regulatory framework. Gaps are being created whenever a subset of norms regulates a certain aspect of commodity activity yet fails to provide guidance with regard to a facet of the latter. As we have seen in Chap. 4 above, TCL exhibits several gaps, e.g. when it comes to addressing potential clashes between global, national, and local SD objectives, or protecting natural resources against unsustainable uses during an international armed conflict or non-international armed conflict.[254] ICAs *de lege ferenda* can build on these observations and address gaps in the current framework in a targeted manner.

Besides, ICAs *de lege ferenda* can also serve as instruments for expanding the current framework of TCL by covering additional topics. For instance, concrete guidance could be elaborated with regard to local procurement,[255] antitrust law particularly dealing with commodity TNCs, or licensing and certification of various commodity sub-activities, including exploration, exploitation, and processing. Also, an ICA *de lege ferenda* could set specific parameters for the admission and protection of commodity investments.[256]

In general, ICAs *de lege ferenda* could constitute important tools for fostering *international equity* with regard to the commodity sector. Given the great dominance of TNCs, they could develop rules of a commodity-directed transnational corporate civil liability law.[257] Moreover, with regard to imbalances in the global trade system, they could help specify the rights of Commodity Dependent Developing Countries (CDDCs) under the GATT. They could serve to expand the current infant-industry promotion and trade and development provisions e.g., by requiring more concrete

---

[254]Cf. Sect. 4.4 above.

[255]The guidance could thus detail the requirements set forth in Article 9(1) CAC, cf. Sect. 4.2.1.5 above, for a local context; cf. moreover already the so-called Local Procurement Reporting Mechanism (LPRM), Mining Shared Value (2019) LPRM http://miningsharedvalue.org/mininglprm/ (last accessed 14 May 2021), which could provide a basis for future regulatory approaches in the *mining* sector.

[256]Guidance on how these parameters could serve to foster SD is provided i.a. by UNCTAD (2015). See also VanDuzer et al. (2012); cf. Sect. 4.3.1.2 above.

[257]Cf. Muchlinski (2016), pp. 58–59. As such, for instance, the provision of Article 3(1) ECLC, cf. Sect. 4.2.1.5 above, could be adapted to a commodity context and spell out concrete guidelines of what constitutes an action giving rise to liability as well as regarding the damages to be awarded.

concessions from developed country members as well as allowing more deviations from WTO disciplines for these commodity-dependent countries—thus counteracting detrimental effects arising from the strict liberalisation approach contained therein.[258] In addition, taking up the global multilateral benefit-sharing mechanism mentioned in Article 10 of the Nagoya Protocol, ICAs *de lege ferenda* could consider the elaboration of a benefit-sharing mechanism applicable to non-genetic resources.[259]

Also, with regard to dispute settlement mechanisms, ICAs *de lege ferenda* could implement rules, which are particularly conducive to fostering international equity in the commodity sector. This may for one include implementing those reforms of investor-state dispute settlement (ISDS), which have been suggested by various institutions and scholars, such as: limiting ISDS to particular claims (excluding those against measures that were taken to protect the environment or Human Rights); requiring the exhaustion of local remedies; incorporating a 'u-turn' and 'fork in the road' clause; setting forth strict limitation periods; encouraging alternative dispute resolution mechanisms; or allowing counterclaims for the host state when the investor breaches domestic law or other obligations.[260]

---

[258] Naturally, under the current political reality, this approach would presumably not exactly meet the agreement from WTO members and/or institutions. However, on the long run, it may contribute to a world trade system, which is concerned primarily with contributing to SD and not particularly promoting liberalisation. The latter should always be understood as a subsidiary aim, which is intended to foster SD. Where it is deemed to not have this effect, it should be abandoned. See in this respect, a policy paper i.a. co-authored by former WTO Director General Pascal Lamy, Global Progressive Forum (2018), which reads on p. 6: 'The traditional approach, which argues that "trade is good, but we need to work on the side effects," is out-dated. In today's changing world, "business as usual" does not work. Progressives must guarantee that global trade and investment benefit the many and not the few. Progressives must ensure they promote sustainable development, reduce global poverty, neutralise structural inequalities that exclude certain genders and populations from the global economy, and raise living and welfare standards. Between the faithful and unconditional promoters of free trade and the populist critiques defending protectionist and nationalist visions of the world, there is a critical political space for progressive forces to defend a regulated vision of globalisation. There is political responsibility in safeguarding an even distribution of trade's positive effects both within our societies and between developed and developing countries. It no longer suffices to wait to realise long-promised trickle-down effects or to offer paltry compensation to those disadvantaged by global trade. [. . .] Trade and investment must be embedded in a broader economic development strategy in order to create added value for our economies. At the same time, trade should be complemented by a new social contract, one that ensures equitable distribution of trade's benefits through adequate and extensive social policies and redistribution mechanisms.'

[259] The provision reads: 'Parties shall consider the need for and modalities of a global multilateral benefitsharing mechanism to address the fair and equitable sharing of benefits derived from the utilization of genetic resources and traditional knowledge associated with genetic resources that occur in transboundary situations or for which it is not possible to grant or obtain prior informed consent. The benefits shared by users of genetic resources and traditional knowledge associated with genetic resources through this mechanism shall be used to support the conservation of biological diversity and the sustainable use of its components globally', CBD (2011) Nagoya protocol,   https://www.cbd.int/abs/doc/protocol/nagoya-protocol-en.pdf   (last   accessed 14 May 2021).

[260] All of the above, see also Muchlinski (2016), pp. 61–2; cf. Sect. 4.3.1 above.

Moreover, with regard to procedural and institutional questions, ICAs *de lege ferenda* could incorporate an ISDS appellate mechanism, e.g. as the one envisaged by the EU Investment Court System (ICS),[261] open proceedings to *amicus curiae* and other stakeholders, including potential victims of corporate activity,[262] or joint interpretation mechanisms between the parties to the international investment agreement.[263] In addition, remedies could be limited to monetary compensation, thus henceforth excluding modification or removal of the regulation in question. Also, the calculation of what constitutes an 'equitable' compensation could take into account the host state's level of development.[264]

Apart from that, ICAs *de lege ferenda* could also implement the mechanism suggested above, according to which in general only investors that comply with HR, environmental, and other applicable standards, which are relevant for commodity activity, shall benefit from investment protection.[265] ICAs *de lege ferenda* could step up home state obligations for corporations investing abroad e.g., with regard to transparency standards.[266] As such, they could incorporate for example the benchmarks for responsible commodity investments elaborated by the UN Principles for Responsible Investment (UN PRI).[267]

What would furthermore foster international equity in the commodity sector would be granting victims of corporate activities access to home state courts. This could help remedy situations in which harm caused by corporations remains effectively uncompensated in judicial proceedings as prominently reflected in the *Kiobel* case. ICAs *de lege ferenda* could envisage concrete commitments of states to assume jurisdiction over extraterritorial claims arising from commodity activities.[268] This would allow the claimant to bring her case before the courts of those countries, where typically considerable volumes of the commodities that have been sourced in her country are being consumed and often processed. It would add an important element to the mosaic of a globalised society, which addresses violations across borders and beyond potential capacity boundaries when it comes to the implementation of the rule of law.[269]

---

[261] Muchlinski (2016), p. 62; fundamentally Bungenberg and Reinisch (2018), p. 25.

[262] With a similar suggestion with regard to Bilateral Arbitration Treaties (BATs), Gaffney J (2018) Could BITs and BATs be combined to ensure access to human rights remedies? Columbia FDI Perspectives, 2 July 2018, http://ccsi.columbia.edu/files/2016/10/No-229-Gaffney-FINAL.pdf (last accessed 14 May 2021); Muchlinski (2016), p. 62.

[263] Muchlinski (2016), pp. 62–63.

[264] Muchlinski (2016), pp. 62–63.

[265] Cf. Sect. 4.3.1.5 above.

[266] Bürgi Bonanomi et al. (2015), p. 51.

[267] Bürgi Bonanomi et al. (2015), p. 51; cf. also the Responsible Investor's Guide to Commodities, UN GC (2011).

[268] Cf. Sect. 4.4 above.

[269] See in this respect the excerpt from the Nobel Lecture given by Nobel Peace Prize Laureate 2018 Denis Mukwege, 10 December 2018, Oslo, which features as the prelude to this book above. The full speech is available at The Nobel Prize (2021) Denis Mukwege—Nobel lecture, https://www.

5.2.2.4   Reflections on Formal Questions

Having discussed potential normative contents of ICAs *de lege ferenda*, we shall briefly also touch upon some rather 'formal' questions regarding their design.

As has been suggested by other authors before, one option would lie in introducing a multilateral commodity convention.[270] Such a 'classical' international instrument would typically be of legally binding nature and seek to reconcile the greatest number of member states possible. While such an approach is certainly appealing with regard to the desired outcome of reinforcing the regulation of the commodity sector so as to foster its SD, it appears highly unlikely to be successful in view of the state of play in international relations at the time of writing.

This is especially due to the continued, intense antagonism between Global North and Global South, which significantly coincides with the antagonism between commodity consumers and producers.[271] In view of this pervasive conflict, which appears to stretch across manifold areas of global trade and economic cooperation,[272] also non-binding, voluntary multilateral 'accords' or 'compacts' on commodities appear to stand little chance of finding the support of a majority of states.

An alternative would be an 'open' bilateral approach towards introducing ICAs *de lege ferenda*. Two—or more—states could negotiate and conclude a commodity-directed international agreement and explicitly provide that other states could join the treaty at their will at all times.[273] This would allow for an evolution of commodity-directed regulation, which may over time gradually transcend the current antagonism.

---

nobelprize.org/prizes/peace/2018/mukwege/55721-denis-mukwege-nobel-lecture-2/ (last accessed 14 May 2021).

[270] See especially Wilts and Bleischwitz (2012); arguably, with her call for a Commodity Organisation, also Feichtner (2014), p. 284.

[271] The intensity of this opponency is most prominently reflected in the 'deadlock' of the Doha Development Agenda, which until today has not been successfully adopted. On the reasons why it is in fact far from it, cf. i.a. Sects. 2.2.4 and 2.2.5.

[272] It appears to be ultimately also reflected in the attempts of especially developing countries to push for the introduction of international instruments on corporate liability, UN (2003) Norms on the responsibilities of transnational corporations and other business enterprises with regard to human rights, UN Sub-Commission on the Promotion and Protection of HR, UN Doc. E/CN.4/Sub.2/2003/12/Rev.2, https://undocs.org/en/E/CN.4/Sub.2/2003/12/Rev.2; UN HRC (2014) Elaboration of an international legally binding instrument on transnational corporations and other business enterprises with respect to human rights, Resolution 26/9 of 26 June 2014, https://documents-dds-ny.un.org/doc/UNDOC/GEN/G14/082/52/PDF/G1408252.pdf?OpenElement; the revised draft of 16 July 2019 is provided by OHCHR (2019) Legally binding instrument, https://www.ohchr.org/Documents/HRBodies/HRCouncil/WGTransCorp/OEIGWG_RevisedDraft_LBI.pdf (all last accessed 14 May 2021); cf. Sect. 5.1.3 above.

[273] Cf. on the 'open treaty' approach especially Griebel (2009) as well as Griebel (2010), who advocated for a 'Europe Based Open Investment Treaty'; Bungenberg (2011), p. 237; cf. moreover e.g. the option for non-UNECE states to accede to the Aarhus Convention as provided for in its Article 19(3).

The actor, which would be somewhat 'predestined' to be the driving force behind such an open treaty approach, is the EU. Apart from the fact that it constitutes the largest trading bloc worldwide and therefore disposes of substantial standard setting power in international economic relations,[274] it according to Article 21(2)(f) TEU has also committed to

> help develop international measures to preserve and improve the quality of the environment and the sustainable management of global natural resources, in order to ensure sustainable development[.]

According to Article 207(1) TFEU, this obligation applies particularly also to its Common Commercial Policy. Introducing ICAs *de lege ferenda*, which clarify, reinforce, and cohere the current framework of TCL would allow the EU to live up to these commitments it has made under its own constitutional framework. The fact that the EU according to Article 21(1) TEU has also committed to 'promot[ing] multilateral solutions to common problems, in particular in the framework of the United Nations', does not prevent it from seeking alternative approaches whenever a multilateral solution does not appear to be viable. Given that the 'open treaty' approach is intended to ultimately result in a *de facto* multilateral instrument, pursuing the latter, would explicitly *not* constitute a departure from seeking multilateral solutions, but rather constitute a way of circumventing respective 'roadblocks'.[275]

Instead of introducing ICAs *de lege ferenda* as stand-alone agreements, one option would also be to incorporate their normative contents as a commodity-directed chapter in other agreements, such as Free Trade Agreements (FTAs), Preferential Trade Agreements (PTAs), or Bilateral Investment Treaties (BITs). Particularly PTAs, including the Economic Partnership Agreements with the African, Caribbean and Pacific (ACP) states, appear to be well suited in terms of content and *telos* for the inclusion of a commodity-directed chapter.[276] These chapters could

---

[274] European Commission (2018) Celebrating the Customs Union: the world's largest trading bloc turns 50, 30 June 2018, http://europa.eu/rapid/press-release_IP-18-4265_en.htm (last accessed 14 May 2021); on the competition of economic law systems, fundamentally Meessen (2005); on implications that this power has had on EU policy choices, cf. already Oehl M (2016) The regulatory dimension of TTIP and the global competition of economic systems. Reflections on the on-going dispute over Europe's external trade policy, Völkerrechtsblog, 24 February 2016, https://voelkerrechtsblog.org/the-regulatory-dimension-of-ttip-and-the-global-competition-of-economic-systems/ (last accessed 14 May 2021).

[275] In this respect, see also the current EU practice of concluding various bilateral FTAs, EU (2019) Negotiations and agreements, http://ec.europa.eu/trade/policy/countries-and-regions/negotiations-and-agreements/ (last accessed 14 May 2021).

[276] For a list of the current EU preferential trade arrangements in place, European Commission (2019) Arrangements list, https://ec.europa.eu/taxation_customs/business/calculation-customs-duties/rules-origin/general-aspects-preferential-origin/arrangements-list_en#preferential (last accessed 14 May 2021); on the different types of agreements, cf. Oehl (2018b), p. 325.

build particularly on the trade and SD chapters, which have been provided for in recent EU FTAs.[277]

Lastly, when it comes to the *mode* of how ICAs *de lege ferenda* should be elaborated, it seems natural that such endeavour should be pursued based on a multi-stakeholder approach. Being paradigmatic for the concept of governance,[278] a large share of the commodity standards, which we have analysed in this book, has been developed in this vein. Since, as we have discussed with regard to the ILO tripartite approach above, the involvement of the Governance Triangle, consisting of states, businesses, and civil society, may well constitute an important ingredient for successful transnational regulation,[279] the same procedure appears to be advisable when it comes to the elaboration of ICAs *de lege ferenda*.

5.2.2.5 Interim Conclusion: ICAs as Tools Fostering a Functional Commodity Sector

To conclude, ICAs *de lege ferenda* constitute tools, which foster a functional commodity sector. They do so by specifying what sustainable use means, defining SD as their object and purpose, and reinforcing the rule of law in the global commodity sector. As a result, they clarify, confirm, cohere, and align the TCL framework.

The codification of TCL through a multilateral commodity convention appears to be appealing in an 'academic utopia' yet is currently a little realistic option in view of the *Realpolitik* in times of nationalist rhetoric from powerful political blocs. What appears to be more functional under the current geopolitical conditions, however, is the incorporation of gradually more commodity-directed rules—and eventually chapters—in the FTAs and PTAs particularly of the EU. Moreover, also an 'open treaty' approach to the elaboration of commodity-directed or -specific bi- or plurilateral agreements may be worth considering.

---

[277] See chapter 16 EU-Japan FTA; chapter 12 EU-Singapore FTA; chapter 13 EU-Vietnam FTA; as well as chapter 22 CETA; cf. Sect. 3.3.1.2 above. See also Article 25.4 CETA, which introduces the Bilateral Dialogue on Raw Materials—a discussion forum for 'cooperation in the field of raw materials', for the exchange of respective best practices and regulatory policies.

[278] Cf. Sects. 2.1.4, 2.2.5, and 3.3.1 above.

[279] Cf. Sect. 5.1.3 above. What may moreover bear inspiration in the ILO approach for future regulatory endeavours regarding the commodity sector is the great number of specific instruments, which detail labour rules in the contexts of individual (sub-)sectors or even activities. Starting with a 'commodity framework convention', which clarifies, confirms and amends the fundamental rules and principles of TCL, subsequent instruments could tackle more specific aspects of commodity activity in a more detailed manner.

References

Literature and IO/NGO Publications

Aagaard TS (2010) Environmental law as a legal field: an inquiry into legal taxonomy. Cornell Law Rev 95:221–282

Abbott KW, Snidal D (2009) The governance triangle: regulatory standards institutions and the shadow of the state. In: Mattli W, Woods N (eds) The politics of global regulation. Princeton University Press, Princeton, pp 44–88

AU (2009) Africa mining vision. February 2009. http://www.africaminingvision.org/amv_resources/AMV/Africa_Mining_Vision_English.pdf

Barral V (2012) Sustainable development in international law: nature and operation of an evolutive legal norm. EJIL 23(2) http://www.ejil.org/pdfs/23/2/2292.pdf

Bartels L (2013) Trade and human rights. In: Wolfrum R (ed) Max Planck encyclopaedia of public international law. Oxford University Press, Oxford

Beinisch N (2017) Making it work: the development and evolution of transnational labour regulation. PhD thesis, London School of Economics and Political Science, London. http://etheses.lse.ac.uk/3621/1/Beinisch_making_it_work.pdf

Bercusson B (2009) European labour law, 2nd edn. Cambridge University Press, Cambridge

Beyerlin U (2007) Different types of norms in international environmental law. In: Bodansky D, Brunnée J, Hey E (eds) The Oxford handbook of international environmental law. Oxford University Press, Oxford

Beyerlin U (2013) Sustainable development. In: Wolfrum R (ed) Max Planck encyclopaedia of public international law. Oxford University Press, Oxford

Beyerlin U, Grote Stoutenberg J (2012) Environment, international protection. In: Wolfrum R (ed) Max Planck encyclopaedia of public international law. Oxford University Press, Oxford

Bianchi A (2010) Textual interpretation and (international) law reading: the myth of (in)-determinacy and the genealogy of meaning. In: Bekker P, Dolzer R, Waibel M (eds) Making transnational law work in the global economy: essays in honour of Detlev Vagts. Cambridge University Press, Cambridge, pp 34–56

Bodansky D (2009) The art and craft of international environmental law. Harvard University Press, Cambridge

Bohrisch A (1965) Internationale Rohstoffabkommen auf dem Kaffeemarkt nach dem Zweiten Weltkrieg. Dissertation, Göttingen

Bungenberg M (2011) EU investment treaty-making after Lisbon. In: Hübner K (ed) Europe, Canada and the comprehensive economic partnership agreement. Routledge, London, pp 226–237

Bungenberg M, Reinisch A (2018) From bilateral arbitral tribunals and investment courts to a Multilateral Investment Court: options regarding the institutionalization of investor-state dispute settlement. Springer, Cham

Bürgi Bonanomi E et al (2015) The commodity sector and related governance challenges from a sustainable development perspective: the example of Switzerland. CDE WTI IWE Joint Working Paper No. 1, 14 July 2015. https://boris.unibe.ch/71327/1/WTI_CDE_IWE%20Working%20paper%20July%202015_The%20Commodity%20Sector%20and%20Related%20Gov....pdf

Cabrera Medaglia J, Perron-Welch F (2018a) Current status and future research agenda on benefit-sharing in international sustainable development law. J Korean Law 17:179–216

Cabrera Medaglia J, Perron-Welch F (2018b) The benefit-sharing principle in international law. Gewerblicher Rechtsschutz und Urheberrecht Internationaler Teil (GRUR Int) 67(10):873–884

Chi M (2017) Integrating sustainable development in international investment law. Routledge, New York

Chimni BS (1987) International commodity agreements. Croom Helm, London

CISDL (2005) What is sustainable development law? A CISDL Concept Paper, Montreal. http://cisdl.org/public/docs/What%20is%20Sustainable%20Development.pdf

Cordonier Segger MC (2017) Commitments to sustainable development through international law and policy. In: Cordonier Segger MC, Weeramantry JCG (eds) Sustainable development principles in the decisions of international courts and tribunals 1992–2012. Routledge, New York, pp 31–98

Cordonier Segger MC, Weeramantry JCG (2017) Introduction. In: Cordonier Segger MC, Weeramantry JCG (eds) Sustainable development principles in the decisions of international courts and tribunals 1992–2012. Routledge, New York, pp 1–24

Cotula L (2010) Investment contracts and sustainable development: how to make contracts for fairer and more sustainable natural resource investments. Natural Resource Issues No. 20. IIED, London. http://pubs.iied.org/pdfs/17507IIED.pdf

Desta MG (2010) Commodities, international regulation of production and trade. In: Wolfrum R (ed) Max Planck encyclopaedia of public international law. Oxford University Press, Oxford

Elaw (2013) Natural resource contracts: a practical guide. November 2013. https://www.elaw.org/sites/default/files/images_content/general_page_images/publications/Natural_Resource_Contracts_Guide.pdf

Espa I, Oehl M (2018) Rules and practices of international law for the sustainable management of mineral commodities, including nickel, copper, bauxite and a special focus on rare earths. In: ILA Sydney conference report of the committee on the role of international law in sustainable natural resource management for development, second report of the committee, 2016–2018, pp 5–11. https://ila.vettoreweb.com/Storage/Download.aspx?DbStorageId=11926&StorageFileGuid=dc356ab0-e751-4f8b-a3c5-a41d362cb732

FAO (2009) International Treaty on Plant Genetic Resources for Food and Agriculture. Rome. http://www.fao.org/3/a-i0510e.pdf

Feichtner I (2014) International (investment) law and distribution conflicts over natural resources. In: Hofmann R, Schill SW, Tams CJ (eds) International investment law and sustainable development. Edward Elgar, pp 257–284

Gathii J (2014) Incorporating the third party beneficiary principle in natural resource contracts. Ga J Int Comp Law 43:93–139. https://digitalcommons.law.uga.edu/cgi/viewcontent.cgi?article=2020&context=gjicl

Gehne K (2011) Nachhaltige Entwicklung. Mohr Siebeck, Tübingen

Gehring M, Andrade Correa F, Barra M (2018) The principle of sustainable resource use in innovative economic law instruments. In: ILA Sydney conference report of the committee on the role of international law in sustainable natural resource management for development, second report of the committee, 2016–2018, pp 20–26. https://ila.vettoreweb.com/Storage/Download.aspx?DbStorageId=11926&StorageFileGuid=dc356ab0-e751-4f8b-a3c5-a41d362cb732

Gilbert C (2011) International agreements for commodity price stabilisation: an assessment. OECD Food, Agriculture and Fisheries Papers, No. 53, OECD Publishing. https://doi.org/10.1787/5kg0ps7ds0jl-en

Global Progressive Forum (2018) For the many, not the few: towards a progressive model for international trade and investment. December 2018. https://www.globalprogressiveforum.org/sites/default/files/document/international_trade_and_investment_ok_s.pdf

Greve G (1961) Die Bedeutung der internationalen Rohstoffabkommen für die unterentwickelten Länder. Dissertation, 20 July 1961, Rechts- u. staatswiss. Fakultät, Münster

Griebel J (2009) Überlegungen zur Wahrnehmung der neuen EU-Kompetenz für ausländische Direktinvestitionen nach Inkrafttreten des Vertrags von Lissabon. Recht der Internationalen Wirtschaft, issue 7:469–474

Griebel J (2010) The new great challenge after the entry into force of the Treaty of Lisbon: bringing about a multilateral EU-investment treaty. In: Bungenberg M, Griebel J, Hindelang S (eds) International investment law and EU law – on the eve of a European policy on foreign direct investment. European Yearbook of International Economic Law, Special Issue. Springer, Berlin, pp 139–40

Habermayer W (1984) Internationale Rohstoffabkommen als Beispiel des Nord-Süd-Dialogs. Peter Lang, Frankfurt am Main

Hilpold P (2011) WTO law and Human Rights: bringing together two autopoietic orders. Chinese J Int Law 10(2):323–372

Hoffmeyer M, Schrader JV, Tewes T (1988) Internationale Rohstoffabkommen: Ziele, Ansatzpunkte, Wirkungen. Institut für Weltwittschaft an der Universität Kiel, Kiel

IISD (2010) State of sustainability initiatives review. November 2010. http://citeseerx.ist.psu.edu/viewdoc/download?doi=10.1.1.588.7910&rep=rep1&type=pdf

ILA (2002) New Delhi Declaration of Principles of International Law Relating to Sustainable Development. 2 April 2002, UN Doc. A/CONF.199/8, 9 August 2002. http://www.un.org/ga/search/view_doc.asp?symbol=A/CONF.199/8&Lang=E

ILA (2008) Rio de Janeiro Conference, Committee on International Law on Sustainable Development, Report. https://ila.vettoreweb.com/Storage/Download.aspx?DbStorageId=1179&StorageFileGuid=3d118f92-d796-4ad5-9b78-c22fb3bb3b1c

ILA (2012) Sofia Conference, Committee on International Law on Sustainable Development, Final Report. https://ila.vettoreweb.com/Storage/Download.aspx?DbStorageId=1177&StorageFileGuid=7dcf2ffb-6010-48cf-ad92-32453d8ee2b9

IOGP (2017) Standards bulletin. November 2017. https://www.iogp.org/bookstore/product/iogp-standards-bulletin-2017/

IPIECA (2017) Mapping the oil and gas industry to the Sustainable Development Goals: an atlas. July 2017. http://www.ipieca.org/resources/awareness-briefing/mapping-the-oil-and-gas-industry-to-the-sustainable-development-goals-an-atlas/

Jaenicke G, Mertens HJ, Rehbinder E (1977–1986) Studien zum Internationalen Rohstoffrecht. Alfred Metzner, Frankfurt

Jennings RY (1998) What is international law and how do we tell it when we see it? In: Jennings RY (ed) Collected writings of Sir Robert Jennings, vol 2. Kluwer, The Hague, pp 730–759

Johnston CR (1976) Law & policy of intergovernmental primary commodity agreements. Oceana Publications, Dobbs Ferry

Khan KR (1982) The law and organisation of international commodity agreements. Martinus Nijhoff, The Hague

Kienzler D, Toledano P, Thomashausen S, Szoke-Burke S (2015) Natural resource contracts as a tool for managing the mining sector. Bundesanstalt für Geowissenschaften und Rohstoffe (BGR), June 2015. https://www.bmz.de/g7/includes/Downloadarchiv/Natural_Resource_Contracts.pdf

Kirthisingha PN (1983) International commodity agreements. Int J Soc Econ 10(3):40–65. https://doi.org/10.1108/eb013938

Knote J (1964) Internationale Rohstoffabkommen aus der Nachkriegszeit. Rechts- und Staatswissenschaftliche Fakultät Universität Bonn, Bonn

Koskenniemi M (2000) General principles: reflexions on constructivist thinking in international law. In: Koskenniemi M (ed) Sources of international law. Ashgate Dartmouth, Aldershot, pp 359–402

Koskenniemi M, Leino P (2002) Fragmentation of international law? Postmodern anxieties. Leiden J Int Law 15:553–579

Krajewski M (2012) Entwurf eines Alternativen Rohstoffabkommens der Bundesrepublik Deutschland. October 2012, Greens/EFA, Brussels, FAU, Nuremberg. https://reinhardbuetikofer.eu/wp-content/uploads/2012/10/Alternatives-Rohstoffabkommen-Text-und-Erl%C3%A4uterungen-fin.pdf

Krajewski M (2017) Ensuring the primacy of human rights in trade and investment policies: model clauses for a UN treaty on transnational corporations, other businesses and human rights. CIDSE study, March 2017. https://www.cidse.org/wp-content/uploads/2017/03/CIDSE_Study_Primacy_HR_Trade__Investment_Policies_March_2017.pdf

Krappel F (1975) Die Havanna-Charta und die Entwicklung des Weltrohstoffhandels. Duncker & Humblot, Berlin

Landry D (2018) The risks and rewards of resource-for-infrastructure deals: lessons from the Congo's Sicomines agreement. Resour Policy 58:165–174

Lindsay R et al (2013) Human rights responsibilities in the oil and gas sector: applying the UN guiding principles. J World Energy Law Bus 6(1):2–66

Lowe V (1999) Sustainable development and unsustainable arguments. In: Boyle AE, Freestone D (eds) International law and sustainable development: past achievements and future challenges. Oxford University Press, Oxford, pp 19–37

Mandelbaum J, Swartz SA, Hauert J (2016) Periodic review in natural resource contracts. CCSI, J Sustain Dev Law Policy 7(1):116–136. http://ccsi.columbia.edu/files/2016/07/Periodic-Review-in-Natural-Resource-Contracts.pdf

Meessen KM (2005) Wirtschaftsrecht im Wettbewerb der Systeme. Mohr Siebeck, Tübingen

Mertens HJ, Spindler G (1989) Internationales Rohstoffrecht – Bericht über ein DFG-Forschungsprojekt 1974–1986. Rabels Zeitschrift für ausländisches und internationales Privatrecht (RabelsZ) 53:526–550

Michaelowa K, Naini A (1994) Der gemeinsame Fonds für Rohstoffe und die speziellen Rohstoffabkommen. Nomos, Baden-Baden

Muchlinski PT (2016) Negotiating new generation international investment agreements: new sustainable development oriented initiatives. In: Hindelang S, Krajewski M (eds) Shifting paradigms in international investment law. Oxford University Press, Oxford

Mutua M, Anghie A (2000) What is TWAIL? Proceedings of the Annual Meeting (American Society of International Law), vol 94, 5–8 April 2000, pp 31–40

Nordhaus WD (2007) To tax or not to tax: alternative approaches to slowing global warming. Rev Environ Econ Policy 1(1):26–44. https://doi.org/10.1093/reep/rem008

Nowrot K (2013) Bilaterale Rohstoffpartnerschaften: Betrachtungen zu einem neuen Steuerungsinstrument aus der Perspektive des Europa- und Völkerrechts. Beiträge zum Transnationalen Wirtschaftsrecht, Heft 128, September 2013. http://telc.jura.uni-halle.de/sites/default/files/BeitraegeTWR/Heft%20128.pdf

NRGI (2014) Natural Resource Charter, 2nd edition. https://resourcegovernance.org/sites/default/files/documents/nrcj1193_natural_resource_charter_19.6.14.pdf

Oehl M (2018a) Entwicklungszusammenarbeit. In: Schöbener B (ed) Grundbegriffe des Europarechts. CF Müller, Heidelberg, pp 163–173

Oehl M (2018b) Freihandelsabkommen. In: Schöbener B (ed) Grundbegriffe des Europarechts. CF Müller, Heidelberg, pp 324–334

Oehl M (2019) The role of sustainable development in natural resources law. In: Bungenberg M, Krajewski M, Tams C, Terhechte JP, Ziegler AR (eds) European yearbook of international economic law 2018. Springer, pp 3–38

Ong DM (2003) The progressive integration of environmental protection within offshore joint development agreements. In: Fitzmaurice M, Szuniewicz M (eds) Exploitation of natural resources in the 21ˢᵗ century: the challenge of sustainable development. Kluwer, The Hague, pp 113–141

Pelikahn HM (1988) Internationale Rohstoffabkommen – Neuere Entwicklungen. Archiv des Völkerrechts (AVR) 26:67–88

Pelikahn HM (1990) Internationale Rohstoffabkommen. Nomos, Baden-Baden

Preis U, Temming F (2020) Arbeitsrecht: Individualarbeitsrecht, 6th edn. Otto Schmidt, Köln

Proelß A (2017) Prinzipien des internationalen Umweltrechts. In: Proelß A (ed) Internationales Umweltrecht. De Gruyter, Berlin, pp 71–102

Raffaelli M (1995) Rise and demise of commodity agreements: an investigation into the breakdown of international commodity agreements. Woodhead, Cambridge

Rudolph H (1983) Internationale Rohstoffabkommen und internationaler Rohstofffonds. Staatsverlag der Deutschen Demokratischen Republik, Berlin

Ruger TW (2008) Health law's coherence anxiety. Georgetown Law J 96:625–648

Rüttinger L, Scholl C (2017) Verantwortungsvolle Rohstoffgewinnung? Herausforderungen, Perspektiven, Lösungsansätze. Zusammenfassung der Ergebnisse des Forschungsvorhabens Ansätze zur Reduzierung von Umweltbelastung und negativen sozialen Auswirkungen bei der Gewinnung von Metallrohstoffen (UmSoRess). Umweltbundesamt, Texte 66/2017, https://www.umweltbundesamt.de/sites/default/files/medien/1410/publikationen/2017-08-18_texte_66-2017_umsoress_zusamm.pdf

Sands P (2012) Principles of international environmental law. Cambridge University Press, Cambridge

Scheyli M (2008) Konstitutionelle Gemeinwohlorientierung im Völkerrecht. Duncker & Humblot, Berlin

Schrijver N (2017) Advancements in the principles of international law on sustainable development. In: Cordonier Segger MC, Weeramantry JCG (eds) Sustainable development principles in the decisions of international courts and tribunals 1992–2012. Routledge, London, pp 99–108

Secretariat of the CBD (2002) Bonn guidelines on access to genetic resources and fair and equitable sharing of the benefits arising out of their utilization. Montreal. https://www.cbd.int/doc/publications/cbd-bonn-gdls-en.pdf

Secretariat of the CBD (2004) Addis Ababa principles and guidelines for the sustainable use of biodiversity. Montreal. https://www.cbd.int/doc/publications/addis-gdl-en.pdf

Secretariat of the CBD (2011) Nagoya protocol on access to genetic resources and the fair and equitable sharing of benefits arising from their utilization. Montreal. https://www.cbd.int/abs/doc/protocol/nagoya-protocol-en.pdf

Sen A (1999) Development as freedom. Anchor Books, New York

Shaw MN (2017) International law, 8th edn. Cambridge University Press, Cambridge

Shi C (2016) Rechtliche Rahmenbedingungen für die Entwicklung der Handelsbeziehungen zwischen China und der EU im Rohstoffsektor. LIT, Berlin

Smaller C (2014) The IISD guide to negotiating investment contracts for farmland and water. IISD, Winnipeg, November 2014. https://www.iisd.org/sites/default/files/publications/iisd-guide-negotiating-investment-contracts-farmland-water_1.pdf

Tai S (2015) Food systems law from farm to fork and beyond. Seton Hall Law Rev 45:109–171

Thees (1967) Kapitalistische Rohstoffmärkte – Internationale Rohstoffabkommen. Die Widersprüche auf den kapitalistischen Rohstoffmärkten und die Versuche zu ihrer Lösung mittels internationaler Rohstoffabkommen

UN (2002) Berlin II Guidelines for Mining and Sustainable Development. https://commdev.org/userfiles/files/903_file_Berlin_II_Guidelines.pdf

UN (2003) Norms on the responsibilities of transnational corporations and other business enterprises with regard to human rights. UN Sub-Commission on the Promotion and Protection of HR, UN Doc. E/CN.4/Sub.2/2003/12/Rev.2. https://undocs.org/en/E/CN.4/Sub.2/2003/12/Rev.2

UN GA (2015) Transforming our world: the 2030 agenda for sustainable development. Resolution A/RES/70/1, 25 September 2015. http://www.un.org/ga/search/view_doc.asp?symbol=A/RES/70/1&Lang=E

UN GC (2011) The responsible investor's guide to commodities: an overview of best practices across commodity-exposed asset classes. September 2011. https://www.unglobalcompact.org/docs/issues_doc/Financial_markets/Commodities_Guide.pdf

UN GC (2017) SDG industry matrix: energy, natural resources & chemicals. January 2017. https://www.unglobalcompact.org/docs/issues_doc/development/SDG-industry-matrix-enrc.pdf

UNCTAD (2015) Investment Policy Framework for Sustainable Development, UNCTAD/DIAE/PCB/2015/5. https://unctad.org/en/PublicationsLibrary/diaepcb2015d5_en.pdf

UNCTAD (2016) A brief on international commodity bodies. Updated on 1 February 2016. https://unctad.org/Sections/ditc_commb/docs/suc2016_InternationalCommsBodies_en.pdf

UNCTAD (2019) Trade and development report 2019: financing a global green new deal. UN, Geneva. https://unctad.org/en/PublicationsLibrary/tdr2019_en.pdf

UNDP (2016) Mapping mining to the Sustainable Development Goals: an atlas. White paper, July
    2016. http://www.undp.org/content/dam/undp/library/Sustainable%20Development/Extrac
    tives/Mapping_Mining_SDGs_An_Atlas.pdf
VanDuzer JA, Simons P, Mayeda G (2012) Integrating sustainable development into international
    investment agreements: a guide for developing country negotiators. Commonwealth Secretariat.
    https://www.iisd.org/pdf/2012/6th_annual_forum_commonwealth_guide.pdf
Viñuales JE (2013) Vers un droit international de l'énergie: essai de cartographie. In: Kohen M,
    Bentolila D (eds) Mélanges en l'honneur de Jean-Michel Jacquet. LexisNexis, Paris, pp
    321–344
Virally M (1968) The sources of international law. In: Sorensen M (ed) Manual of international law.
    McMillan, London
VPSHR (2000) Voluntary principles on security and human rights for the extractive and energy
    sectors. http://docs.wixstatic.com/ugd/f623ce_60604aa96d1c4bdcbb633916da951f25.pdf
Wälde T (2004) Natural resources and sustainable development: from 'good intentions' to 'good
    consequences'. In: Schrijver N, Weiss F (eds) International law and sustainable development.
    Martinus Nijhoff, Leiden, pp 119–150
Weberpals T (1989) Internationale Rohstoffabkommen im Völker- und Kartellrecht. VVF,
    München
Weiss F (2009) Internationale Rohstoffmärkte. In: Tietje C (ed) Internationales Wirtschaftsrecht.
    De Gruyter, Berlin, pp 276–286
Wenzel (1961) Das Recht der internationalen Rohstoffabkommen. Institut für Völkerrecht,
    Göttingen
Wilson E, Kuszewski J (2011) Shared value, shared responsibility: a new approach to managing
    contracting chains in the oil and gas sector. IIED, London. http://pubs.iied.org/pdfs/
    16026IIED.pdf
Wilts H, Bleischwitz R (2012) Combating material leakage: a proposal for an International Metal
    Covenant. S.A.P.I.EN.S Online 4(2):1–9. http://sapiens.revues.org/1218
Wolfrum R (2009) Common heritage of mankind. In: Wolfrum R (ed) Max Planck encyclopaedia of
    public international law. Oxford University Press, Oxford
WTO (2018) World Trade Statistical Review. https://www.wto.org/english/res_e/statis_e/
    wts2018_e/wts2018_e.pdf
ZIMCODD (2017) SADC mineral resource management. Policy brief, June 2017. http://www.
    zimcodd.org/sites/default/files/policybriefs/Policy%20Brief%20-%20SADC%20Mineral%
    20Resource%20Management%202017.pdf

Cases

ICJ (1997) *Gabcikovo-Nagymaros Project* (Hungary v. Slovakia), judgment of 25 September 1997,
    ICJ Reports 1997, https://www.icj-cij.org/files/case-related/92/092-19970925-JUD-01-
    00-BI.pdf

ICJ (2010a) *Pulp Mills on the River Uruguay* (Argentina v. Uruguay), judgment of 20 April 2010, ICJ Reports 2010, https://www.icj-cij.org/files/case-related/135/135-20100420-JUD-01-00-EN.pdf

ICJ (2012) *Jurisdictional Immunities of the State* (Germany v. Italy: Greece intervening), judgment of 3 February 2012, dissenting opinion of Judge Yusuf, ICJ Reports 2012, http://www.icj-cij.org/files/case-related/143/143-20120203-JUD-01-05-EN.pdf

PCA (2005) *Award in the Arbitration regarding the Iron Rhine ('Ijzeren Rijn') Railway between the Kingdom of Belgium and the Kingdom of the Netherlands*, award of 24 May 2005, 27 RIAA (2005) 35, http://legal.un.org/riaa/cases/vol_XXVII/35-125.pdf

WTO DSB (1998) *United States – Import Prohibition of Certain Shrimp and Shrimp Products*, report of the Appellate Body, adopted 12 October 1998, WT/DS58/AB/R, https://docs.wto.org/dol2fe/Pages/FE_Search/FE_S_S009-DP.aspx?language=E&CatalogueIdList=58544&CurrentCatalogueIdIndex=0&FullTextHash=&HasEnglishRecord=True&HasFrenchRecord=True&HasSpanishRecord=True

Chapter 6
Conclusions

In this treatise, we set out to answer the following question: How effective is the current legal framework in ensuring a functional commodity sector? In approaching this task, we first provided conceptual clarity regarding its different components before entering a qualitative assessment.

Conceptualising GCG

In a first step, we conceptualised Global Commodity Governance (GCG) as the governing mode of the global commodity sector—which is naturally tasked with ensuring its functionality. Secondly, we clarified the scope of the term 'commodity', which constitutes the historically and dogmatically consistent notion that should be employed for legal purposes. Based on Article 56(1) of the Havana Charter, we defined the term as 'any product of agriculture, forest, fishery or mining and any mineral product in its natural (=raw) form and in such forms that are customarily required for its international trade, especially shipment, in substantial volumes.' Thirdly, we characterised a functional commodity sector as one, in which the *commodity governance matrix* exhibits a balance between the five *commodity interests* it is composed of: economic gain, development, preservation, control, and participation.

As our appraisal of historical approaches to governing the global commodity sector revealed, the disruptive feature of GCG lies in the fact that it perceives commodity activity not exclusively as an economic issue, but as a comprehensive regulatory challenge, which requires the consideration of its social and ecological prerequisites as well as effects. Therefore, it constitutes a commodity-directed emanation of the global sustainable development (SD) agenda and is ultimately faced with the task of achieving and maintaining equilibrium between the interests associated with commodity activity.

Conceptualising TCL as the Legal Framework of GCG

Law can be a catalyst in this quest, where it contributes to the balancing of these interests. It is effective, where it provides guidelines for states—as the central actors of GCG—in their decision to extract.

© The Author(s) 2022
M. E. Oehl, *Sustainable Commodity Use*, EYIEL Monographs - Studies in European and International Economic Law 21, https://doi.org/10.1007/978-3-030-89496-2_6

In order to be able to assess the effectiveness of the current legal framework underpinning GCG, we first conceptualised Transnational Commodity Law (TCL). We started by outlining the methodological foundations of conceptualising fields of law. Accordingly, we elaborated the organisational framework of TCL based on, for one, the definition of commodity law as 'all law that regulates commodity-related human activity and its impacts'; and, for the other, the factual context, in which commodity-related human activity typically occurs: the removal of an item from earth for a specific purpose that relates to the removed item. It is this factual context, which constitutes the pertinent social behaviour that needs to be regulated in order to address the commodity policy trade-offs arising in the commodity matrix. Addressing these trade-offs reflects the 'analytical and instrumental aims' of the conceptualisation of TCL.[1]

The TCL framework has been further qualified by the nature of its *sources*, which can be largely ascribed to the four different categories of the classical inter-national framework; private standards; the domestic legal framework; as well as transnational contract law.

Also, the *structure* of TCL has been sketched pointing to its 'qualified sovereignty' outline. Accordingly, various fields of transnational, especially international law, such as i.a. Human Rights (HR) and environmental protection norms, have qualified how states shall exercise their permanent sovereignty over natural resources (PSNR). Moreover, PSNR comprises the right to transfer commodity rights. Both, the transfers themselves, as well as the responsibilities of rights transferees, are governed by a variety of international standards, most of which are of private nature. Once these transfers have been effectuated, states are under the obligation to protect these rights under international investment law, which is thus further qualifying PSNR. In addition, 'secondary qualifications', which can stem from various norm subsets of TCL, set forth the procedures to regulate externalities, including dispute settlement mechanisms.

Our conceptualisation of TCL has been conducted based on the hypothesis that the effectiveness of a legal framework results at least partly from the degree to which it reflects a conscious consideration of the policy trade-offs it is intended to govern. Therefore, it has been deemed to be effective where it provides '*balancing norms*' that balance the five interests associated with commodity activity and thus answers to questions such as: How much to extract? Where to extract? How to extract? How to process or trade? How to make a decision to extract? How much to trade? How much and what to tax? What resources to protect? What land rights to protect? Where it cannot provide these answers, for instance since the privilege of ultimately answering them falls within the political domain, it has been deemed to be effective where it provides guidelines on how these questions *should* be answered.[2]

---

[1] Feinman (1989), p. 680, cf. Sect. 3.2.2.2 above.

[2] Section 2.3.2 above.

The Limited Effectiveness of TCL

Our assessment revealed that TCL provides only little guidance on how *commodity equilibrium* shall be achieved or maintained.

We ascertained that the sustainable use principle constitutes one of the few balancing norms. Its normative content, as defined by the International Law Association (ILA), reconciles all five commodity interests. Therefore, the sustainable use principle exhibits the *normative contents* needed in order to effectuate a functional sector. Thus, the TCL framework would be effective where it concretises what sustainable use requires. This would involve providing balancing norms, which further detail how the commodity interests need to be balanced in respective commodity scenarios, e.g. depending on the subsector, actors, or individual commodity concerned.

However, the current normative patterns of TCL prevent the field from spelling out more concretely what constitutes sustainable commodity use:

First, most of TCL is 'indirect', i.e. it has not been created for the purpose of regulating commodity activity. As such, it is not designed to balance commodity interests, but pursues distinct regulatory objectives.

Second, the rather scarce incidents of direct TCL are neither balancing commodity interests comprehensively. Instead, they typically balance a maximum of two commodity interests with one another; at times three where for instance environmental protection norms are being integrated with ones protecting Human Rights. Besides, as the examples of the law applicable to shared resources as well as the norms covering trade and development within the GATT have demonstrated, those hard rules of direct TCL that address states tend to contribute little to remedying commodity policy trade-offs. They will either be aimed at achieving a mere interstate balance or, where they could remedy for instance a trade-off between economic and development interests, are 'declaratory' rather than of substantial legal effect. Moreover, direct TCL is largely of soft or private legal nature, thus typically unfolding limited or no legal effects for states. The latter, however, are naturally the central actors when it comes to decisions to extract. Also, direct TCL is generally little specific, i.e. it does not spell out in great detail what is required from the stakeholders of commodity governance. Rules addressing private actors, especially those that are intended to cover particular commodity sectors, tend to be more specific than the abstract norms addressing states.

Third, what, too, hinders coherence and thus limits balancing effects of TCL, are the few incidents of full integration between its rules and standards.

Fourth, what both contributes to the limited effectiveness of TCL and illustrates this status quo, is the imbalance of the current framework in favour of economic objectives—primarily investment protection and trade liberalisation. Overcoming this imbalance constitutes a major challenge in rendering TCL more effective.

Moreover, fifth, the TCL framework exhibits regulatory gaps especially with regard to aspects that are specific to commodity activity. It particularly lacks effective remedies against harmful conduct of transnational commodity corporations. Also, it does not address potential clashes between global, national, and local SD objectives; provides little to no guidance on how foreign investments as well as trade need to be designed in order to foster a functional commodity sector; and does not spell out what constitutes adequate policy space for SD measures.

All in all, the current TCL framework barely contours what sustainable commodity use legally requires. It is thus little effective in ensuring a functional commodity sector.

Fostering the Effectiveness of TCL

To my mind, particularly two approaches can serve to foster the effectiveness of the sustainable use principle and thus of TCL: defining SD as the object and purpose of TCL and specifying the normative content of SD by fully integrating benchmarks from the substance of TCL.

Regarding the former approach, we first noted that the sustainable use principle constitutes the concretisation of SD for the commodity context. We then demonstrated that given the universal nature of the SD agenda, the specific normative quality of SD as a legal concept, and its status within a sizable series of international treaties, *sustainable use* can be defined as a *regulatory objective*. In addition, we pointed to the fact that—as I have argued elsewhere—SD already holds this status with regard to Natural Resources Law (NRL). Subsequently, we illustrated that TCL constitutes a sub-category of NRL, which is more suitable when it comes to this specific economic use of natural resources related to its removal from the natural environment. Consequently, *sustainable use* can be defined as the *object and purpose* also *of Transnational Commodity Law* (TCL). The effects of doing so are generally twofold: For one, it constitutes a primary norm that obliges states to 'act sustainably'; for the other, it constitutes a methodical norm, which serves as a guideline how legal obligations shall be interpreted. As a consequence, it coheres and integrates the field and thus fosters its effectiveness.

The second approach advocated for relates to the full integration of benchmarks from other instruments of TCL into the sustainable use principle, thus rendering it more specific and ultimately effective. Benchmarks in this respect can stem particularly from the many detailed standards regulating technical matters of commodity activity. The SDGs and corresponding industry 'maps' or 'atlases' may be useful in guiding the efforts to identify the most suitable rules and parameters in this respect. Given the complexity of the task and the vast substance of TCL, computational text analysis may constitute a helpful tool.

Apart from these suggestions aimed at the sustainable use principle, developing rules by involving the 'governance triangle', consisting of states, businesses, and NGOs, could foster TCL's acceptance, coherence and ultimately effectiveness. An example insofar is provided by ILO conventions, which are reflected coherently in a large number of TCL instruments. Given their example, what may be particularly effective, could be to combine tripartite approaches with binding international agreements.

ICAs *de lege ferenda* as Instruments Specifying Sustainable Commodity Use

International Commodity Agreements (ICAs) *de lege ferenda* could serve to remedy the current deficits of the TCL framework. They could codify direct, hard, specific, state-oriented law, which balances all five commodity interests comprehensively—and thus spell out more precisely what sustainable commodity use requires.

This would significantly contrast the status quo, in which the legal relevance of ICAs is limited. We insofar distinguished between three *types* of ICAs: ICAs *sensu originali*, albeit pursuing a comprehensive approach tackling an entire sector and seeking to foster SD, remain without 'bite' due to a lack of corresponding substantive obligations. ICAs *sensu stricto*, to the contrary, often exhibit a narrow scope, which is focused on a clear-cut, somewhat 'singular' objective. As such, commodity-directed law may quite intensively regulate some specific activities associated with commodity operations in some specific sectors. While some regional instruments address challenges of GCG more comprehensively and recent EU Free Trade Agreements (FTAs) exhibit a trend to consciously consider specificities of commodity activity, most ICAs *sensu stricto* still provide no guidance on how to balance the five commodity interests. Where they do, these provisions are often rather aspirational or soft and generally do not entail concrete obligations. As a consequence, ICAs *sensu lato* currently clearly are of the greatest significance for GCG—a paradigm which once again underlines the lack of a coherent, targeted legal regime underpinning GCG.

Principle of Proportionality
In order to concretise the sustainable use principle, we have suggested that ICAs *de lege ferenda* could implement a principle of proportionality. Accordingly, the degree to which one or more commodity interests are being emphasised in a concrete balancing decision needs to be proportionate to the degree to which other interests are being neglected. In addition, a rule that requires states to prevent irreversible effects of commodity activities could limit states' scope of discretion when carrying out a balancing exercise. Moreover, the principle could correspond to a transparency obligation for states to disclose their balancing method as well as the line of reasoning that led to the respective weighing of the interests associated with the commodity decision.

Obligation to Detail Terms of Sustainable Use in National Legal Frameworks
Apart from these rather abstract rules, ICAs *de lege ferenda* could obligate states to transform certain best practices into national law. In general, they could be required to elaborate commodity-directed national frameworks, which comprehensively regulate challenges associated with commodity activity, including rights allocation, establishing a robust tax regime, and the offsetting of environmental and social costs of extraction. In line with principle #13 of the Addis Ababa Principles and Guidelines for the Sustainable Use of Biodiversity (AAPG), states could be required to establish the internalisation of the social and ecological costs of commodity activity 'within the area of management' and the reflection of these costs in the 'distribution of the benefits from the use'. Moreover, the conservation and management of NR could be implemented 'as an integral part of development planning', i.a. through resource management plans applicable to individual commodities. Going beyond the obligation to prevent irreversible effects of commodity activity, the national framework could require the prevention of alterations to the ecosystem,

which are 'not reversible over a reasonable period of time' in line with Article 4(1) (d) of the ASEAN Agreement on the Conservation of Nature and Natural Resources (ACNR). In addition to these general principles, ICAs *de lege ferenda* could obligate states to detail the terms of sustainable use also in the context of individual commodity sectors.

As a side benefit of this obligation, ICAs *de lege ferenda* would help aligning regulation on the global, national, and local levels. Public–private contracts should be embedded in this coherent, effective regulatory framework, thus isolating potential power asymmetries between states and transnational corporations.

Further Effects of ICAs *de lege ferenda* Conducive of SD
Furthermore, ICAs can incorporate SD as their regulatory objective, thus contributing to gradually cohering TCL and fostering its effectiveness. Also, ICAs can reinforce the rule of law in the commodity sector by clarifying the applicable legal framework, closing regulatory gaps, and expanding TCL.

Formal Reflections on ICAs *de lege ferenda*
Given the continued, intense antagonism between Global North and Global South, a multilateral ICA—despite being highly desirable—appears to be little realistic. What seems more actionable instead, not least in view of the commitments the EU has made according to Articles 21(2)(f) TEU, 207(1) TFEU, is the incorporation of gradually more commodity-directed rules—and eventually chapters—in the EU FTAs and Preferential Trade Agreements (PTAs). In this respect, an 'open treaty' approach to the elaboration of commodity-directed or -specific bi- or plurilateral agreements appears worthy of consideration.

Outlook: If We Are to Take SD Seriously, We Need To Be More Specific
Commodity activity, i.e. removing (economically) useful items from the natural environment, potentially processing them as required, and then trading, and/or shipping them, constitutes one of the *core economic activities* of our globalised economic system. It is high time for us international lawyers to accord this sector the attention it deserves.

What our examination has brought about in essence comes down to the understanding that the global commodity sector is functional, where it is sustainably managed. The sustainable use principle constitutes the core *balancing norm*—within the vast body of TCL, it is the only concept, which reconciles all five commodity interests. This again points to the extensive regulatory potential, which is associated with SD as a legal concept. It is our task to further operationalise it and to thus deliver guidelines to states and other stakeholders what sustainable commodity activity means. If we are to take SD seriously, we need to be more specific.

Therefore, the international community is now faced with the challenge to create concrete rules on what constitutes sustainable resource use. We shall distinguish between the roles that state governments, academics, and international as well as national jurisprudence should assume in this endeavour.

State governments are now tasked with initiating political processes that lead to the codification of TCL. Elaborating ICAs *de lege ferenda* of the type described above, be they of bi-, pluri- or multilateral character, would be the most direct, clearest way to do so. During their negotiation, it will be crucial to strike the right balance between sufficient specificity of the rules codified and policy space that remains with national governments. This balance can only result from political processes—ideally, they will bring about a robust legal framework ensuring sustainable commodity activity.

Academics worldwide can contribute to this process by perceiving TCL as a proper discipline of international law. The legal rules covering the commodity sector should be researched and discussed in light of their quality to balance the commodity interests at stake. Legal analysis should measure their effectiveness by interrelating the individual rules with TCL's object and purpose of sustainable use. As the normative suggestions made above demonstrate, advancing the legal underpinnings of GCG may require legal scholarship to abandon beaten paths and make innovative propositions—whilst mastering the challenge of adequately tying them to the dogmatic foundations of inter- and transnational law.

Lastly, courts and tribunals worldwide are assuming a key role in the normative evolution necessary for humankind to master the transformation of our economies and societies towards sustainability. They are tasked with interpreting the rules applicable to commodity activities in the light of SD as the object and purpose of TCL—and thus with translating the substantial normative weight of the regulatory objective of sustainable use into specific normative instructions. Particularly where political processes are blocked, judges may be responsible for providing the legal impulses necessary to advance SD.

All in all, we cannot overestimate what bold actions will be needed in order to achieve a functional commodity sector as one of the key requirements of SD.[3] It will depend on lawyers worldwide whether or not this process will be based on a reliable legal framework. In view of the great many challenges and policy trade-offs at stake, we should waste no time to get to work.

The Implementation Challenge Remains
Recalling the words of Dr Denis Mukwege, which have set the tone at the very outset of this treatise, a sentiment of *humility* shall accompany our efforts. The challenge of fostering *good* GCG rather than constituting an issue that could be solved by legal or academic approaches *alone*, to a significant degree is one of *implementation*. As Cotula puts it, '. . .law is only a part of the story.'[4]

---

[3] Paradigmatically, UNCTAD's 2019 Trade and Development Report is dedicated to the financing of 'a global green new deal'—an endeavour, which is said to require investments of 2.5 trillion US-$ in developing countries alone, UNCTAD (2019), pp. iii, 83.

[4] Cotula (2016), p. 13. He goes on to state: 'Policy instruments outside the legal sphere can also influence investment patterns and outcomes [. . .]. Laws are often not properly enforced due to vested interests, power imbalances or resource constraints. Legislation may nominally protect human rights, land rights or labour rights, but often remains a dead letter. Tax laws may be circumvented, and tax payments are not always easy to collect.'

In this story—the great *implementation challenge* for the many stakeholders, public and private, global and local—I hope that my work can contribute to an intensified understanding of the transnational regulatory environment, in which commodity activity is taking place. And perhaps it may be understood as an act of encouragement for the many persons and institutions striving to implement a functional—a *sustainable*—commodity sector. An act, which visualises that their contributions ultimately relate to a greater framework, a shared objective: our universal agenda of sustainable development.

References

Literature and IO/NGO Publications

Cotula L (2016) Foreign investment, law and sustainable development: a handbook on agriculture and extractive industries. Natural Resource Issues no. 31. IIED, London, 2nd edn. http://pubs. iied.org/pdfs/12587IIED.pdf

Feinman JM (1989) The jurisprudence of classification. Stanf Law Rev 41:661–717

UNCTAD (2019) Trade and development report 2019: financing a global green new deal. UN, Geneva. https://unctad.org/en/PublicationsLibrary/tdr2019_en.pdf

Annex: The Substance of TCL: An Outline

© The Author(s) 2022

M. E. Oehl, *Sustainable Commodity Use*, EYIEL Monographs - Studies in European and International Economic Law 21, https://doi.org/10.1007/978-3-030-89496-2

Structure of TCL	Subcategories	Fields	Type of norm/ rule level #1	Rule level #2	Rule level #3/ explanations	Rule level #4/ explanations	Provided for in
Competence to regulate commodity resources			Common heritage of humankind				Article 137 (2) UNCLOS
			Freedom-based approach				Article 87 (1) UNCLOS
			PSNR				UN GA Resolutions 523, 626, 1803, 3201; ERC; Principle 21 Stockholm Declaration; Principle 2 Rio Declaration; Article 56(1)(a) UNCLOS; *Texaco v. Libya* (1977); ICJ (2005) *Armed activities*; Article 1(2) HR Covenants; Article 15(1) CBD
				Sustainable use			Article 2(1) CBD; SDG 12.2
				Benefit sharing			UN GA Resolution 1803; Article 2 (3) Declaration on the Right to Development; Article 1, 15(7) CBD; Bonn Guidelines; Nagoya Protocol

				Producer cartel	PSNR generally entails right to join producer cartels	E.g. OPEC statute, International Tri-partite Rubber Consortium
Qualifications of PSNR	*Human Rights*	RFD				
					Relates to: right to self-determination; operationalized in mainly two contexts: indigenous peoples, right to subsistence	Article 1 (2) ICCPR, ICESCR;
		Right to life		Extractives; toxic substances; mudslides etc.; insufficient labour safety	UN HRC (2018): IEL should inform contents of Article 6 (1) ICCPR	Article 6(1) ICCPR
		Labour rights	Right to work		Comprises general prohibition of discrimination	Article 6 (1) ICESCR; Article 4 ILO Convention 158;
			Prohibition of forced or compulsory labour			ILO Convention 29
			Prohibition of child labour			Article 3 ILO Convention 182; Article 32 CRC; Article 10 (3), 12(2) (a) ICESCR; SDG 8.7

(continued)

(continued)

Structure of TCL	Subcategories	Fields	Type of norm/ rule level #1	Rule level #2	Rule level #3/ explanations	Rule level #4/ explanations	Provided for in
				Protection of vulnerable groups			Ending discrimination of women: SDG 8.5; Indigenous peoples: ILO Convention 169; Convention on Migrant Workers; Article 17(1) of the Convention Relating to the Status of Refugees and the Convention Relating to the Status of Stateless Persons
				Right to just and favourable conditions of work		Includes right to fair wages, to safe and healthy working conditions	Article 7 ICESCR; ILO Convention 155 (Occupational Safety); ILO Convention 174 (Industrial Accidents); ILO Convention 176 (Safety and Health in Mines)
				Collective right to work		Right to form and join trade unions; right to strike;	Article 8 (1) ICESCR; ILO Convention 98; ILO Convention 135

		General freedom of association	Article 20 (1) UDHR; Article 22(1) ICCPR; ILO Convention 87
Land rights	Right to property	Types: use rights, control rights, transfer rights; often informal/customary	Article 17 UDHR; AP I ECHR; Article 21 ACHR; Article 14 AfCHR
	Tenure rights of indigenous peoples	Use rights: Article 15(1) ILO Convention 169; Article 16 (2) ILO Convention: FPIC; Cultural dimension: Article 27 ICCPR, Article 13(1) ILO 169;	Articles 11, 12 ILO Convention 107; Articles 13, 14 ILO Convention 169; Articles 8(b), 25, 26, 29 UNDRIP; FAO Voluntary Guidelines on the Responsible Governance of Land Tenure
Rights to basic needs	Right to an adequate standard of living	Includes right to water, food, and adequate housing	Article 11 (1) ICESCR
	Right to physical and mental health	Frequently employed in context w/ environmental quality	Article 12 (1) ICESCR

(continued)

(continued)

Structure of TCL	Subcategories	Fields	Type of norm/ rule level #1	Rule level #2	Rule level #3/ explanations	Rule level #4/ explanations	Provided for in
				Right to access to basic energy		Relevant for sourcing of energy commodities; sustainably	Articles 11(1), 12 (1) ICESCR; SDG 7
			Participation rights	Right to information			Articles 19, 25 (b) ICCPR
				Right to access to information			Article 19 (2) ICCPR
				Right to transparent administration of public resources			Article 1 (2) ICESCR
				Right to participate in development decisions		For local communities	Article 24 AfCHR
				Right to free, prior and informed consent (FPIC)		Particularly addresses indigenous peoples; Articles 15(2) and 16 (2) ILO 169 address FPIC in relocations induced by commodity activity	Article 6 ILO Convention 169; Article 32 UNDRIP; jurisprudence based on Article 27 ICCPR, Articles 1(2), 15 (1) ICESCR, Article 5(d)(v), (e) (vi) ICERD

HR in situations of commodity-induced violence	Right to life, freedom from torture or cruel, inhuman or degrading treatment or punishment, right to security of the person, freedom of assembly, prohibition of torture			Articles 6, 7, 9(1), 21 ICCPR; Articles 1(1), 2(1) Convention Against Torture
Right to remedy	Access to justice; prevention or redress of rights violations; Article 21(2) AfCHR: right to lawful recovery of property or compensation in case of commodity-induced spoliation			Article 8 UDHR, Article 2 (3) ICCPR, Article 6 CERD, Article 2 (c) CEDAW; Article 13 ECHR, 25 ACHR, Articles 7(1), 21(2), 26 AfCHR; Article 15(2) ILO 69
Right to development				Article 1 Declaration on the Right to Development; Principle 3 Rio Declaration; Article 22 AfCHR
Overall	Clear legal framework, regional efforts, independent monitoring and impact assessment			African Commission on Human and Peoples' Rights (AfCHR) Resolution on a Human Rights-Based Approach to

(continued)

(continued)

Structure of TCL	Subcategories	Fields	Type of norm/ rule level #1	Rule level #2	Rule level #3/ explanations	Rule level #4/ explanations	Provided for in
							Natural Resources Governance
		Environmental protection	Sustainable development			Sustainable use principle constitutes the commodity-directed concretisation of the SD principle	Principle 4 Rio Declaration; Article 3(4) UNFCCC; Article 8 lit. e) CBD; Articles 2,4,5 UN Convention to Combat Desertification and Drought; Article 1 lit. c) ITTA; Article 1 (3) ICofA; Article 1 (2) IAO; Article 1 ICocA; preamble WTO agreement; ICJ (1997) *Gabcikovo-Nagymaros*; ICJ (2010) *Pulp Mills*
			Obligation not to cause transboundary harm				Trail Smelter arbitral tribunal (1941); Principle 21 Stockholm Declaration; ICJ (1996) *Nuclear Weapons*
			Precautionary principle				Principle 15 Rio Declaration

Obligation to carry out EIA				Principle 17 Rio Declaration; Espoo Convention; ICJ (2015) *Certain Activities*; Akwé: Kon Guidelines
Preventive action				ICJ (2010) *Pulp Mills*; Articles 192, 194 UNCLOS
Polluter pays principle				Principle 16 Rio Declaration
Common but differentiated responsibility (CBDR)				Principle 7 Rio Declaration
Duty to cooperate				Principle 7 Rio Declaration; Articles 11.3, 12 Paris Agreement
Public participation			Obligation for states to provide appropriate access to environmental information as well as participation in relevant decision-making processes	Principle 10 Rio Declaration; Aarhus Convention
Special regimes	Conservation		National conservation strategies, integration with development	*Examples:* ASEAN Agreement on the

(continued)

(continued)

Structure of TCL	Subcategories	Fields	Type of norm/ rule level #1	Rule level #2	Rule level #3/ explanations	Rule level #4/ explanations	Provided for in
						planning, maintain maximum genetic diversity, resource management plans, sustainable use	Conservation of Nature and Natural Resources (ACNR); African Convention on the Conservation of Nature and Natural Resources
				Miscellaneous			*Examples:* Oil pollution: International Convention on Oil Pollution Preparedness, Response and Cooperation. Mercury use/waste: Minamata Convention on Mercury. Mineral resource exploitation in Antarctica: CRAMRA. Biodiversity: CBD, AAPG, Bonn guidelines, Nagoya protocol, ITPGR. Special regimes protecting atmosphere; air;

				freshwater; wet-lands; oceans, seas and marine living resources; flora and fauna; forests and soils; Polar regions
Liberalised Trade (focus on goods)	MFN treatment		Note the commodity-directed exceptions with regard to the GATT obligations: Article XI:2 GATT, Article XX:b,g,h,j, Article XXI:b:i GATT	Articles I, II GATT
	National treatment			Article III GATT
	Freedom of transit			Article V GATT
	Prohibition of quantitative restrictions			Article XI:1 GATT
	Trade and development	Infant industry promotion		Article XVIII GATT
		Price stabilisation		Article XXXVI:4 GATT
		Reduction of commodity dependence		Article XXXVI:5 GATT
		Concrete commitments for developed countries		Article XXXVII GATT
		Enabling clause		

(continued)

(continued)

Structure of TCL	Subcategories	Fields	Type of norm/ rule level #1	Rule level #2	Rule level #3/ explanations	Rule level #4/ explanations	Provided for in
		Shared resources	Duty to cooperate				Article 3 Economic Rights Charter; Principle 1 UNEP Draft Principles
			Principle of equitable utilisation				Article 3 Economic Rights Charter; Principle 1 UNEP Draft Principles; Article 4(a) ILC Draft Articles Aquifers
			Joint development				E.g. 1958 Saudi Arabia-Bahrain agreement; 1974 Convention in the Bay of Biscay; 1989 Australia-Indonesia Timor Gap Treaty; ICJ (1969) *North Sea Continental Shelf*
		Good Governance	Overall			12 precepts that offer 'policy options and practical advice for governments, societies and the international community on how best to manage resource wealth.'	Natural Resource Charter

	UN Convention Against Corruption			
Anti-corruption	General obligation: Article 5(1): effective, coordinated anti-corruption policies; Article 7: public sector, civil servants; Article 8: standards/codes of conduct, e.g. International Code of Conduct for Public Officials; Article 9(1): transparent, objective procurement mechanism; Article 10: transparency in public administration; Article 12: prevention of corruption in private sector; Article 13: stakeholder involvement; Articles 14–42: criminalisation and law enforcement regarding corrupt practices, including bribery, embezzlement, misappropriation of property etc.; Articles 43–50:			

(continued)

(continued)

Structure of TCL	Subcategories	Fields	Type of norm/ rule level #1	Rule level #2	Rule level #3/ explanations	Rule level #4/ explanations	Provided for in
						international cooperation, including extraditions, mutual legal assistance, joint investigations	
						Guidance on duties of public officials, such as integrity, effectiveness, fair and impartial performance of functions, no abuse of power, renunciation to carry out potentially conflicting political activities	International Code of Conduct for Public Officials
						Article 1: bribery of foreign officials as criminal offence	Convention on Combating Bribery of Foreign Public Officials in International Business Transactions
						Article III: i.a. creation and strengthening of codes of conduct	1996 Inter-American Convention against Corruption
						Article 5(1): acts of corruption that shall be established as	2003 African Union Convention on Preventing and

		offences; Article 12 (2): enabling environment for civil society to act as a 'watchdog'	Combating Corruption
		Criminal law: establish corrupt practices as offences (Articles 2-14). Civil law: Article 1: effective remedies for persons who suffered damage from corruption; right to initiate action (Article 3(1)); criteria for successful claim (Article 4 (1))	CoE Criminal Law Convention on Corruption; Civil Law Convention on Corruption
	Transparency	Eight EITI requirements, i.a. oversight by national multi-stakeholder groups; focus on contracts and laws, compiling and reconciling company payments and government revenues; as of 2020: including beneficial ownership information	2019 EITI standard

(continued)

(continued)

Structure of TCL	Subcategories	Fields	Type of norm/rule level #1	Rule level #2	Rule level #3/explanations	Rule level #4/explanations	Provided for in
						Campaigning for mandatory disclosure requirements	PWYP coalition, including Revenue Watch, Global Witness, Oxfam, Transparency International
						Promotion of transparency through action plans, elaborated in collaboration with civil society; Independent Reporting Mechanism (IRM)	Open Government Partnership
						Multi-stakeholder forum	G7 Alliance on Resource Efficiency
						One pillar on NR revenue management	IMF Fiscal Transparency Code
			Mining-directed			15 fundamental principles, incl. environmental management, social planning	Berlin II Guidelines
						Mining Policy Framework;	Intergovernmental Forum on Mining,

implementation of sustainable mining sector	Minerals, Metals and Sustainable Development (IGF)
Assessment tool for mining laws, regulations and policies	World Bank Mining Investment and Governance Review (MInGov)
Six 'major intervention areas': i.a. geological data, contract negotiation capacity, infrastructure constraints, elevating ASM	Africa Mining Vision; African Minerals Development Centre; African Minerals Governance Framework
I.a. Protocol against Illegal Exploitation of NR; model law	International Conference on the Great Lakes Region (ICGLR) instruments
Capacity-building, transparency, compliance monitoring	Responsible Minerals Development Initiative (RMDI)
Information sharing, capacity-building, joint standard development, private sector participation, occupational health and safety, small-scale mining	SADC Protocol on Mining

(continued)

(continued)

Structure of TCL	Subcategories	Fields	Type of norm/ rule level #1	Rule level #2	Rule level #3/ explanations	Rule level #4/ explanations	Provided for in
			Other commodity-directed cooperation			Exchange of information; promotion of trade; some: promotion of SD; some: economic equilibrium between consumers and producers; dialogue forum; commodity-specific obligations; some: multistakeholder approach; inter-state dispute settlement	International Commodity Agreements: International Grains Agreement, more precisely Grains Trade Convention (GTC); International Sugar Agreement (ISA); International Tropical Timber Agreement (ITTA); International Cocoa Agreement (ICocA); International Coffee Agreement (ICofA); International Agreement on Olive Oil and Table Olives (IAO)
						Transparency; providing accurate production, trade, and consumption data; forum for exchange, often on an annual basis; INBAR: promote SD	International Study Groups: International Rubber Study Group; International Lead and Zinc Study Group;

International Nickel Study Group; International Copper Study Group; International Network for Bamboo and Rattan; International Jute Study Group	
FAO Intergovernmental Groups: on individual agricultural commodities: Bananas and Tropical Fruits; Citrus Fruit; Grains; Hard Fibres; Meat and Dairy Products; Oilseeds, Oils and Fats; Rice; Tea	Forum for exchange regarding trends in trade, production etc.
SADC Protocol on Forestry	Sustainable forest management, duty to cooperate, PSNR, no harm, public participation, benefit sharing, tenure, regional database, community-based forest management, participation of

(continued)

(continued)

Structure of TCL	Subcategories	Fields	Type of norm/ rule level #1	Rule level #2	Rule level #3/ explanations	Rule level #4/ explanations	Provided for in
						women, capacity-building	
						Examples: German commodity partnership agreements; EU voluntary partnership agreements (timber)	Bilateral Commodity Agreements
		Fiscal framework	Overall/arm's length principle/transfer pricing			Article 7 (corporate residency as basis for taxation); Article 5 (permanent establishment)	Model United Nations Double Taxation Convention between Developed and Developing Nations (UNDTC)
						Article 7 (corporate residency as basis for taxation; arm's length principle); Article 5 (permanent establishment)	OECD Model Tax Convention (OECDMTC) on Income and on Capital
						Guidance on how to apply *arm's length principle*; clarify transfer pricing methods	OECD Transfer Pricing Guidelines for Multinational Corporations and Tax Administration (OECDTPG)

		Description	Instrument
	Fiscal transparency	Identify loopholes in international tax framework; action 10: guidance on analysing transfer pricing in commodity transactions	Base Erosion and Profit Shifting Initiative (BEPS)
			UN Handbook on Extractive Industries Taxation
		Legal framework; company reporting regarding payments and socio-ecological impacts	Draft Natural Resources Fiscal Transparency Code (NRFTC)
		Exchange of information requests (EOIR); automatic exchange of financial account information (AEOI)	OECD Model Agreement on Exchange of Information on Tax Matters
Financial regulation		G20 initiative; 22 principles, incl. i.a. contract design, market surveillance, intervention powers, price discovery	IOSCO Principles for the Regulation and Supervision of Commodity Derivatives Markets
		Position limits and management controls	EU Markets in Financial Instruments Directive II (MiFID II)

(continued)

(continued)

Structure of TCL	Subcategories	Fields	Type of norm/ rule level #1	Rule level #2	Rule level #3/ explanations	Rule level #4/ explanations	Provided for in
						Intervention powers in commodity markets	EU Markets in Financial Instruments Regulation (MiFIR)
						Insider dealing; market manipulation	EU Market Abuse Regulation (MAR)
						Market manipulation commodity spot contracts	EU Market Abuse Directive II (MAD II)
						OTC markets; reporting, risk-management	European Market Infrastructure Regulation (EMIR)
						Accuracy of benchmarks in financial instruments	EU Benchmarks Regulation (BMR)
						Encompass commodity and derivative markets	EU Regulation on Wholesale Energy Market Integrity and Transparency (REMIT)
						Position limits; however, implementation delayed	US Dodd-Frank-Act
							OECD Thematic Dialogue on Commodity Trading Transparency

Armed conflict	PSNR in armed conflict			PSNR
	Protection of commodities	As civilian objects	ICJ (2005) *Armed Activities*: PSNR not generally applicable, but Article 21 AfCHR;	IAC: Art. 52(1); 54 (2) AP-I; NIAC: Art. 14 AP-II
		As part of the environment	Prohibition to cause widespread, long-term, and severe damage	IAC: Art. 35(3), 55 AP-I:
			Article I(1): prohibition of environmental modification techniques, which have widespread, long-lasting or severe effects	Convention on the Prohibition of Military or Any Other Hostile Use of Environmental Modification Techniques (ENMOD Convention)
			Warfare as inherently destructive of SD: states shall respect international law providing environmental protection in times of armed conflict, and cooperate in its further development	Principle 24 Rio Declaration

(continued)

(continued)

Structure of TCL	Subcategories	Fields	Type of norm/ rule level #1	Rule level #2	Rule level #3/ explanations	Rule level #4/ explanations	Provided for in
						Compliance with international law providing environmental protection in times of armed conflict	UN General Assembly Resolution on the Protection of the Environment in Times of Armed Conflict
						'Requirements of public conscience' interpreted as including protection of environment	'Martens Clause', 1899 Hague Convention (II), 1949 Geneva Conventions, 1977 APs
						War crime: damage to environment in excess of military advantage anticipated	Art. 8(2)(b) (iv) Rome Statute
				As property		Prohibition to destroy or seize property	Art. 23(g) 1907 Hague Regulations; Art. 53 Geneva Convention IV
						Prohibition of pillage	Art. 33(2) Geneva Convention IV; during occupation: Art. 47; NIAC: Art. 4(2)(g) AP-II
						War crimes	Unnecessary destruction or seizure of property:

					Art. 8(2)(b)(xiii), (e)(xii) Rome Statute; pillage: Art. 8 (2)(b)(xvi), (e) (v) Rome Statute; Art. 147 Geneva Convention IV w/ Art. 8(2)(a) (iv) Rome Statute
		Situations of occupation	Restitution rights		UN GA Resolution 3336 (XXIX); UN GA Resolution 62/181 ff.
			Occupying state as administrator of immovable public property	Administration in accordance with rules of usufruct	Art. 55 Hague Regulations
				Occupant responsible for plundering of NR by non-state armed groups	ICJ (2005) *Armed Activities*
				HR conventions applicable in armed conflict, thus incl. RFD	ICJ (2004) *Israeli wall*
Norms and standards regulating the transfer of commodity rights	*Best practices in transferring commodity rights*	*General guidance*		Mirror states' obligations under international HR law and translate them into contractual context, i.a. HR risk	UN Principles for Responsible Contracts

(continued)

(continued)

Structure of TCL	Subcategories	Fields	Type of norm/ rule level #1	Rule level #2	Rule level #3/ explanations	Rule level #4/ explanations	Provided for in
						management during negotiation phase; community engagement plan; non-judicial grievance mechanism for third parties; closing gaps in applicable legal framework; careful drafting of stabilisation clauses	
		Commodity-directed guidance				Special consideration of situation of smallholders	FAO Principles for Responsible Investment in Agriculture and Food Systems
						Comprehensive guidance on i.a. tenure, impact assessment, royalties, taxation, HR protection, permits, community development agreements, labour standards, company grievance mechanisms, contract transparency	International Bar Association Model Mine Development Agreement
						Particularly concerned with	Lex petrolea: i.a. AIPN model

| | commercial terms of contract; diverse range of legal principles, touching i.a. on liability, information rights; for an overview cf. Childs (2011) | contracts; international arbitration case law |
| | Transparent, efficient rights allocation mechanism (precept #3): i.a. establish legal framework in advance; gather 'good understanding of resource base'; verify jurisdiction, property rights prior to licensing; not to large share of resource base under one license; 'well-designed auctions' instead of direct negotiation; embed contracts in robust tax regime (precept #4); pursue local benefits (precept #5) | Natural Resource Charter, precept #3 |

(continued)

(continued)

Structure of TCL	Subcategories	Fields	Type of norm/ rule level #1	Rule level #2	Rule level #3/ explanations	Rule level #4/ explanations	Provided for in
						Contract transparency	Open Contracting Partnership's Global Principles; NRGI Open Contracting for Oil, Gas and Mineral Rights
						Support unit for negotiation of large-scale commercial contracts in the extractive sector	G7 CONNEX initiative
	Obligations of transferees	*General responsibilities of corporations*				Principles #11-15: responsibility to respect HR: principle #12: HR = at a minimum International Bill of HR plus ILO Fundamental Principles and Rights at Work; principle #13: required to avoid causing or contributing to HR violations through their own activities as well as to seek to prevent or mitigate adverse HR impacts	UN Guiding Principles on Business and Human Rights (UN GP)

					OECD Guidelines for Multinational
directly linked to them through business relationships; principle #15: policy commitment; due diligence process; remediation process.					
Operationalised through principles #16-24: i.a. principle #16: policy statement to be approved by most senior level management; principle #18: consult potentially affected groups; principle #20: track effectiveness of response to HR risks and violations.					
Remediation: principle #29: ideally through operational-level grievance mechanism; designed according to principle #31					
General policies: i.a. contribute to SD;					

(continued)

(continued)

Structure of TCL	Subcategories	Fields	Type of norm/ rule level #1	Rule level #2	Rule level #3/ explanations	Rule level #4/ explanations	Provided for in
						respect HR; encourage local capacity building; good corporate governance principles; risk-based due diligence; avoid causing or contributing to adverse impacts; abstain from improper involvement in local politics; support multi-stakeholder initiatives on responsible supply chain management.	Enterprises (OECDG)
						Disclosure: timely and accurate information on all material matters regarding activities, structure, financial situation, performance, ownership and governance.	
						HR: [obligations that largely parallel	

	OECD Risk Awareness Tool for MNEs in Weak Governance Zones
those of the UN GP]	
Environmental protection: environmental management system; prevent environmental damage; efficient consumption of NR; precautionary principle	
National Contact Points: make OECDG known; raise awareness of their contents and implementation procedures; respond to enquiries from especially businesses, NGOs, and the public; resolve potential conflicts	Definition of 'weak governance zones'; six particular focus topics, i.a. obeying the law and observing international instruments, heightened managerial

(continued)

(continued)

Structure of TCL	Subcategories	Fields	Type of norm/ rule level #1	Rule level #2	Rule level #3/ explanations	Rule level #4/ explanations	Provided for in
						care, political activities	
						Ten principles, including no HR abuses (principle #2), precautionary approach (principle #3), work against corruption (principle #10). Also, a policy platform/network. Specialised work streams, e.g. CEO Water Mandate; action platforms.	UN Global Compact
						Respect national laws, international bill of HR, UN GP; employment promotion; complement social security mechanisms; eliminate forced, compulsory, and child labour; working conditions; freedom of association, collective bargaining; access to remedies	ILO Tripartite Declaration of Principles concerning Multinational Enterprises and Social Policy

External leverage for commodity corporations	Concept: 'ability to effect change in the wrongful practices of [a third] entity that causes a harm', UN (2011)	Commodity companies on 'receiving end' of external leverage	Where IFC provides direct investment: eight standards, i.a. impact assessments, fair labour, resource efficiency, sustainable NR management, SD benefits for indigenous peoples, equitable sharing of benefits of the use of cultural heritage	IFC Performance Standards on Environmental and Social Sustainability (IFCPS)
			Implemented by 94 financial institutions; general idea: business operations financed/supported by them to be conducted in sound environmental manner. Ten principles, i.a. impact assessment, stakeholder engagement, grievance mechanisms, reporting and transparency	Equator principles
			Required to issue 'non-financial statement' containing information on	Article 19a EU Corporate Social Responsibility Directive

(continued)

(continued)

Structure of TCL	Subcategories	Fields	Type of norm/ rule level #1	Rule level #2	Rule level #3/ explanations	Rule level #4/ explanations	Provided for in
						i.a. impact on environmental, social and employee matters, HR, anti-corruption	
			Additional guidance			Streamline sustainability in global business conduct: i.a. raising awareness, highlighting potential action areas, environmental management, transparency	ICC Business Charter for SD
						Streamlining sustainability governance on all management levels: measuring sustainability performance results; stakeholder dialogue; reporting	CERES roadmap for sustainability
						ISO 14001:2015: environmental management systems. ISO 50001:2018: energy management systems. ISO 26000:2010:	ISO standards

guidance on social responsibility, i.a. HR, labour practices, sustainable resource use, property rights, transparency		
Social accountability requirements regarding nine aspects, i.a. child labour, health and safety, remuneration, management system	Social Accountability standard SA 8000	
Three universal standards: foundations of sustainability reporting (GRI 101); general disclosures (GRI 102); management approach (103). Topic specific standards: economic (GRI 200 series), environmental (GRI 300 series); social (GRI 400 series).	Global Reporting Initiative (GRI) standards	
2010 Conceptual Framework, supplemented by	International Accounting Standards	

(continued)

(continued)

Structure of TCL	Subcategories	Fields	Type of norm/ rule level #1	Rule level #2	Rule level #3/ explanations	Rule level #4/ explanations	Provided for in
						specific standards, e.g. IAS 28 on Investments in Associates and Joint Ventures	
						1: Enterprise shall prohibit bribery; 2: shall commit to implement programme countering bribery, based on multi-stakeholder process, risk assessment; including commitment by board of directors	Business Principles for Countering Bribery
						'Self-regulation of business against the background of applicable national laws'. I.a. Article 1: prohibition of bribery and extortion; Article 3: responsibility towards joint venture partners; Article 5: gifts, hospitality, expenses; Article 6: facilitation payments	ICC Rules of Conduct and Recommendations on Combating Extortion and Bribery

Commodity-directed guidance for corporate responsibility		Cf. already above; also apply to corporations. Guidance how to avoid transfer-pricing disputes	OECD Transfer Pricing Guidelines for Multinational Corporations and Tax Administration
	Shared value perspective	'Coming together of market potential, societal demands and policy action' to foster SD; i.a. multipurpose and multiuser infrastructure	UN GC SDG Natural Resource industry matrix; OECD Framework for Extractive Projects titled Collaborative Strategies for In-Country Shared Value Creation
	Guidance for investors	Specific guidance for different asset classes of commodity investments, i.e. derivatives, physical commodities, real assets, debt/equity investments in companies with 'commodities exposure'	The Responsible Investor's Guide to Commodities
	Security	Mirrors challenge to find adequate judicial redress for HR violations by security personnel acting	*Kiobel* case, i.a. US Supreme Court (2013)

(continued)

(continued)

Structure of TCL	Subcategories	Fields	Type of norm/ rule level #1	Rule level #2	Rule level #3/ explanations	Rule level #4/ explanations	Provided for in
						on behalf of com- modity TNCs	Voluntary Princi- ples on Security and Human Rights for the Extractive and Energy Sectors (VPSHR)
						Risk assessment: collect information; identify security risks, potential for violence, HR records of security personnel; conflict analysis. Interactions with public security forces: consult with host governments and local communi- ties; communicate desire of HR respect; transparency; no personnel with neg- ative HR record; force only when strictly necessary, proportionate; respect for freedom of association, assembly, collective bargaining, ILO fundamental rights at work; report use	

of physical force to authorities; provide medical aid; observe UN Code of Conduct for Law Enforcement Officials and UN Basic Principles on the Use of Force and Firearms; urge investigations	Interactions with private security: observe policies of company on ethical conduct, HR; domestic laws and professional standards; restraint regarding use of force; establish rules of engagement; monitor practices; record, investigate HR abuses; in general: only preventative and defensive services; plus: obligations parallel to the ones applicable				

(continued)

(continued)

Structure of TCL	Subcategories	Fields	Type of norm/ rule level #1	Rule level #2	Rule level #3/ explanations	Rule level #4/ explanations	Provided for in
						to public security forces	Conflict–Sensitive Business Practice: Guidance for Extractive Industries
						Guidance on how to adopt 'conflict-sensitive' approaches in commodity operations: operational guidance charts; screening tools. Eleven 'flashpoints', i.a. stakeholder engagement, armed groups, security arrangements	
			Transparency			Companies that officially sign up to EITI, issue public statement of support for i.a. ten EITI principles. Entails disclosure obligations, including on beneficial ownership, contracts. In general: 'deliver [NR] in a manner that benefits societies and communities'	EITI supporting companies

	US requirements	Disclosure obligations for companies developing oil, natural gas, minerals	I.a. section 1504 Dodd-Frank-Act (however pending repeal)
	EU requirements	Reporting of payments for specific industries, i.a. logging of primary forests; due diligence systems; CMR applies to tin, tantalum, tungsten, gold	Article 44 (1) accounting directive 2013/34/EU; Article 6 EU transparency directive; Articles 4(2), 6 EU timber regulation; EU conflict minerals regulation (CMR)
Subsector-specific guidance	Mining	Overall	Ten best practice principles, i.a. on corporate governance, HR respect, risk management, environmental performance, biodiversity conservation, recycling, stakeholder engagement	ICMM SD Framework
		HR due diligence; FPIC; emergency preparedness; waste, water, air, cyanide, and mercury management	IRMA Standard for Responsible Mining IRMA-STD-001
		Six thematic areas: economic	Responsible Mining Index

(continued)

(continued)

Structure of TCL	Subcategories	Fields	Type of norm/ rule level #1	Rule level #2	Rule level #3/ explanations	Rule level #4/ explanations	Provided for in
						development; business conduct; lifecycle management; community wellbeing; working conditions; environmental responsibility	
						TSM Guiding Principles, including performance indicators; TSM Assessment Protocols	Canadian Towards Sustainable Mining (TSM) initiative
					Supply-chain due diligence	Minerals in general	OECD Due Diligence Guidance for Responsible Supply Chains for Minerals from Conflict-Affected and High-Risk Areas (OECD DDG); Responsible Minerals Assurance Process (RMAP);
						Gold	OECD DDG Supplement on Gold; World Gold Council's Conflict-Free Gold Standard; London Bullion

Market Association's (LBMA) Responsible Gold Guidance (RGG); Alliance for Responsible Mining's Fairmined standard; International Cyanide Management Code (ICMC)						
Diamonds	Kimberley Process Certification Scheme (KPCS); World Diamond Council System of Warranties; Responsible Jewellery Council (RJC) Code of Practices; Diamond Development Initiative					
Tin, tantalum, tungsten	International Tin Association's Tin Supply Chain Initiative (ITSCI); ICGLR Regional Certification Mechanism (RCM) [also applies to gold]					

(continued)

(continued)

Structure of TCL	Subcategories	Fields	Type of norm/ rule level #1	Rule level #2	Rule level #3/ explanations	Rule level #4/ explanations	Provided for in
					Technical standards		ISO standards 73, including i.a. ISO 18871:2015 on coalbed methane and ISO 19426-5:2018 on mine shafts; also, standards on specific ores
					Reporting standards		Global Reporting Initiative's Mining and Metals Sector Disclosures Guideline; IFRS6 standard on Exploration for and Evaluation of Mineral Resources
				Oil and gas		Guidance on technical matters, also on NR resource damage assessment, pollution prevention, e.g. through waste minimisation, environmental design considerations	API standards

	IOGP guidance	List of operators preferred standards		
	IPIECA guidance	Especially IPIECA industry guidance on voluntary sustainability reporting; Global Water Tool for Oil and Gas; Biofuels and Water Nexus; Implementation Guideline for VPSHR etc.		
Further guidance	Global Reporting Initiative's Oil and Gas Sector Disclosures document; EC Oil and Gas Sector Guide on Implementing the UN Guiding Principles on Business and Human Rights			
Overall	FAO Principles for Responsible Investment in Agriculture and Food Systems	Definition of 'food security'; require contribution to sustainable, inclusive development, eradication of poverty; gender equality; land tenure, access to water; respecting cultural heritage,		
Forestry, farming, fisheries				

(continued)

(continued)

Structure of TCL	Subcategories	Fields	Type of norm/ rule level #1	Rule level #2	Rule level #3/ explanations	Rule level #4/ explanations	Provided for in
						traditional knowledge; transparent governance, grievance mechanisms; promoting accountability	
					Forestry	Promotion of Sustainable Forest Management (SFM). PEFC Sustainability Benchmark: criteria for certification systems	Programme for the Endorsement of Forest Certification (PEFC)
						Certification scheme: ten principles: i.a. identifying and upholding indigenous peoples' rights of ownership; conservation of ecosystem services. FSC Normative Framework: mandatory policies, standards, procedures for certificate holders, certification bodies	Forestry Stewardship Council (FSC)

	Sustainable Forestry Initiative	SFI 2015-2019 Forest Management Standard: i.a. conserving biodiversity, protection of cultural sites, respect for indigenous peoples' rights, ensuring efficient use of fibre resources
Farming	OECD-FAO Guidance for Responsible Agricultural Supply Chains	Model enterprise policy; guidance for enterprises on how to implement existing standards; due diligence framework
	UNECE and Codex Alimentarius Standards	More than 100 standards in place, which can be classified according to their reference object as standards applicable to fresh fruit and vegetables; dry and dried produce; seed potatoes; eggs; and meat Provisions on product definition,

(continued)

(continued)

Structure of TCL	Subcategories	Fields	Type of norm/ rule level #1	Rule level #2	Rule level #3/ explanations	Rule level #4/ explanations	Provided for in
						designation, styles, permitted ingredients, quality factors, trade categories, defects, additives, contaminants, hygiene, and labelling	
						Civil society standards & certification schemes	Rainforest Alliance Certified seal; Rainforest Alliance Sustainable Agriculture Standard; Fairtrade Labelling Organisations International; IFOAM Accreditation Program; Common Objectives and Requirements of Organic Standards (COROS); Sustainable Agriculture Framework; GLOBALGAP
						Commodity-specific guidance	Common Code for the Coffee Community (4C); Better Sugarcane Initiative

Fisheries	Conservation of aquatic ecosystem, minimise negative environmental impact	FAO Code of Conduct for Responsible Fisheries (CCRF)
	Good manufacturing practice (GMP) and Hazard Analysis and Critical Control Point (HACCP) for fish and shellfish process management systems; prevention of hazards and defects in fish products	Code of Practice for Fish and Fishery Products

('Bonsucro'); Principles and Criteria of the Roundtable on Sustainable Palm Oil (RSPO); Better Cotton Standard System; Roundtable on Sustainable Biomaterials (RSB) Principles and Criteria

(continued)

(continued)

Structure of TCL	Subcategories	Fields	Type of norm/ rule level #1	Rule level #2	Rule level #3/ explanations	Rule level #4/ explanations	Provided for in
						Complementary to CCRF; i.a. HR, non-discrimination, Rule of law, transparency, gender equality, policy coherence, capacity development	International Guidelines for Securing Sustainable Small-Scale Fisheries
						Requires certification schemes i.a. to be consistent with UNCLOS, Straddling Stocks Convention, CCRF, WTO rules	FAO Guidelines for Ecolabelling of Fish and Fishery Products
						Animal health and welfare, food safety, environmental integrity	FAO Technical Guidance for Aquaculture Certification
						Civil society certification schemes	MSC Fisheries Standard; ASC-MSC Seaweed Standard; Global Aquaculture Alliance's Best Aquaculture Practices (BAP) certification scheme; Responsible

		Other	
			Fishing Scheme Standard; Global Sustainable Seafood Initiative (GSSI)
			ISO standards on fishing and fish breeding
Obligation to protect transferred rights/ investment protection	General system of investment protection	Fair and equitable treatment; protection against expropriation; most-favoured nation (MFN) treatment; national treatment; full protection and security (FPS)	BITs; FTAs; investment contracts
	Turn to SD	Ten core principles: i.a. policy coherence, stakeholder involvement, regular policy review, balanced in setting out rights and obligations for both states and investors, conserving states' right to regulate, investment promotion/ facilitation should be aligned with	UNCTAD Investment Policy Framework for SD

(continued)

(continued)

Structure of TCL	Subcategories	Fields	Type of norm/ rule level #1	Rule level #2	Rule level #3/ explanations	Rule level #4/ explanations	Provided for in
						SDGs, link investment policies to best corporate practices.	
						National investment policy guidelines: strategic level: integrate investment policy in SD road map; normative level: guidance on norms regulating FDI, which foster SDGs; administrative level: guidance on how to ensure effectiveness of investment policies	
						International investment policies: embed international investment policymaking in national development strategies, including reflection on need/function of	

IIAs; integrate SD considerations in investment agreements, including right to regulate, balanced rights and regulations of states and investors, reform of ISDS, further guidance on specific clauses; pursuing multilateral consensus on investment policy to address gaps, overlaps, inconsistencies in current system.

Action menu for the promotion of investment in priority sectors for SD: i.a. partnerships for investment in SDG-related sectors; public private partnerships; guarantee and risk insurance facilities requiring sustainability of | | | | |

(continued)

(continued)

Structure of TCL	Subcategories	Fields	Type of norm/rule level #1	Rule level #2	Rule level #3/explanations	Rule level #4/explanations	Provided for in
						investment; impact investment instruments; vertical, matching funds, crowdfunding; action packages i.a. reorientation of investment incentives, financial markets towards SDGs.	
						General exception to investment protection	Article 10 2004 Canadian model FPIA
						Requires tribunals to consider state's level of development when examining breach of FET	Article 14.3 COMESA investment agreement
						Requires investors to maintain environmental management system	Article 14.1 SADC Model Bilateral Investment Treaty Template
						Promotion of investment in environmental goods and services	Article 13.10.2 (b) EU-Vietnam FTA; Article 12.11 EU-Singapore FTA

Promotion of sustainable investment	Articles 3(4), 6 (1) NLBIT	
Obligation for investors to comply with HR, environmental, and labour laws	Article 7(1) NLBIT	
Promotion of trade and SD	Chapter 13 EU-Vietnam FTA; chapter 12 EU-Singapore FTA